A Physicalist Manifesto

A Physicalist Manifesto is the fullest treatment yet of the comprehensive physicalist view that, in some important sense, everything is physical. Andrew Melnyk argues that the view is best formulated by appeal to a carefully worked-out notion of realization, rather than supervenience; that, so formulated, physicalism must be importantly reductionist; that it need not repudiate causal and explanatory claims framed in nonphysical language; and that it has the a posteriori epistemic status of a broad-scope scientific hypothesis. Two concluding chapters argue in unprecedented detail that contemporary science provides no significant empirical evidence against physicalism and some considerable evidence for it.

Written in a brisk, candid, and exceptionally clear style, this book should appeal to professionals and students in philosophy of mind, metaphysics, and philosophy of science.

Andrew Melnyk is Associate Professor of Philosophy at the University of Missouri, Columbia.

CAMBRIDGE STUDIES IN PHILOSOPHY

General editor   ERNEST SOSA (Brown University)

Advisory Editors

JONATHAN DANCY (University of Reading)
JOHN HALDANE (University of St. Andrews)
GILBERT HARMAN (Princeton University)
FRANK JACKSON (Australian National University)
WILLIAM G. LYCAN (University of North Carolina at Chapel Hill)
SYDNEY SHOEMAKER (Cornell University)
JUDITH J. THOMSON (Massachusetts Institute of Technology)

RECENT TITLES

MICHAEL ZIMMERMAN *The Concept of Moral Obligation*
MICHAEL STOCKER with ELIZABETH HEGEMAN *Valuing Emotions*
SYDNEY SHOEMAKER *The First-Person Perspective and Other Essays*
NORTON NELKIN *Consciousness and the Origins of Thought*
MARK LANCE and JOHN O'LEARY HAWTHORNE *The Grammar of Meaning*
D. M. ARMSTRONG *A World of States of Affairs*
PIERRE JACOB *What Minds Can Do*
ANDRE GALLOIS *The World Without, the Mind Within*
FRED FELDMAN *Utilitarianism, Hedonism, and Desert*
LAURENCE BONJOUR *In Defense of Pure Reason*
DAVID LEWIS *Papers in Philosophical Logic*
WAYNE DAVIS *Implicature*
DAVID COCKBURN *Other Times*
DAVID LEWIS *Papers on Metaphysics and Epistemology*
RAYMOND MARTIN *Self-Concern*
ANNETTE BARNES *Seeing through Self-Deception*
MICHAEL BRATMAN *Faces of Intention*
AMIE THOMASSON *Fiction and Metaphysics*
DAVID LEWIS *Papers on Ethics and Social Philosophy*
FRED DRETSKE *Perception, Knowledge and Belief*
LYNNE RUDDER BAKER *Persons and Bodies*
JOHN GRECO *Putting Skeptics in Their Place*

Series list continued on page after Index.

A Physicalist Manifesto

Thoroughly Modern Materialism

ANDREW MELNYK

University of Missouri, Columbia

CAMBRIDGE UNIVERSITY PRESS
Cambridge, New York, Melbourne, Madrid, Cape Town, Singapore, São Paulo

Cambridge University Press
The Edinburgh Building, Cambridge CB2 8RU, UK

Published in the United States of America by Cambridge University Press, New York

www.cambridge.org
Information on this title: www.cambridge.org/9780521827119

© Andrew Melnyk 2003

This publication is in copyright. Subject to statutory exception
and to the provisions of relevant collective licensing agreements,
no reproduction of any part may take place without the written
permission of Cambridge University Press.

First published 2003
This digitally printed version 2007

A catalogue record for this publication is available from the British Library

Library of Congress Cataloguing in Publication data
Melnyk, Andrew, 1962–
A physicalist manifesto : thoroughly modern materialism / Andrew Melnyk.
p. cm. – (Cambridge studies in philosophy)
Includes bibliographical references (p.) and index.
ISBN 0-521-82711-6
1. Materialism. I. Title. II. Series.
B825.M38   2003
146´.3–dc21   2003041959

ISBN 978-0-521-82711-9 hardback
ISBN 978-0-521-03894-2 paperback

To my mother and in memory of my father

Contents

Preface		page xi
	Introduction	1
1	Realization Physicalism	6
	1. Orientation	6
	2. "Physical"	11
	3. A Canonical Formulation	20
	4. Realization Physicalism and Retentiveness	32
2	But Why Not Supervenience?	49
	1. Realizationism, Supervenience, and Physical Necessitation	49
	2. Can Global Supervenience Provide a Superior Alternative to Realizationism?	57
3	Realizationism and R*d*ct**n*sm	71
	1. Introduction	71
	2. More-or-Less Nonphilosophical Reductionism	72
	3. Two Philosophical Reductionisms	77
	4. Reductionism in the Core Sense	81
	5. Retentive Realizationism's Commitment to Reductionism in the Core Sense	88
	6. How Damaging Is the Commitment?	110

4	Causation and Explanation in a Realizationist World	123
	1. Introduction	123
	2. The Intuitive Roots of the Charge of Epiphenomenalism	129
	3. A Theory of Causation and Causal Relevance	139
	4. The Unobjectionability of Multiple Explanations of the Same Thing	164
5	The Evidence against Realization Physicalism	175
	1. Introduction	175
	2. Direct Evidence against Realization Physicalism: The Mind	176
	3. Direct Evidence against Realization Physicalism: Biology	190
	4. Indirect Evidence against Realization Physicalism	222
6	The Evidence for Realization Physicalism	238
	1. Introduction	238
	2. The Role of Inference to the Best Explanation	240
	3. The Role of Enumerative Induction	256
	4. The Physical Realization of Chemical Phenomena	261
	5. The Physical Realization of Biological Phenomena	266
	6. The Extension of the Argument to Other Scientific Phenomena	278
	7. The Physical Realization of Mental Phenomena	281
	References	311
	Index	323

Preface

I began to think seriously about physicalism in the sense of this book in 1987, when I started work on my doctoral dissertation at Oxford. But by the time the dissertation had been accepted, in 1990, I had entirely lost confidence in the radically eliminativist version of physicalism that it defended. The result of my subsequent efforts to determine what was reasonable and what was not in my earlier views was a series of journal articles on physicalism; and when I began work on the present book, in the fall of 1998, I conceived my task as little more than that of revising those earlier papers, linking them up, and supplementing them here and there.

I conceived wrong. When I reviewed my earlier papers, they somehow seemed to say a lot less than I had remembered; and what they did say was often not quite right. So I decided essentially to start again. I also decided that I had to make an empirical case for physicalism, and in some detail, partly because I was irritated by the charge that adherence to physicalism is entirely unwarranted, but partly also because I had in the meantime grown skeptical about the possibility of a priori philosophical knowledge, and it seemed ludicrous to leave off the project of defending physicalism at exactly the point where, by my own account, it just starts to get interesting. But obviously both decisions made the task of writing this book much harder than I had initially imagined and help to explain why it has taken four years to complete.

I am grateful to the University of Missouri–Columbia Research Council, and to my department, for a sabbatical leave in 1998–9, which enabled me to complete a first draft of most of this book; and to the University of Missouri Research Board for support over the summer of 1999. I am grateful also to several philosophers for their valuable reactions to various parts of the manuscript: to Jonathan Schaffer and his students at the University of Massachusetts for comments on Chapters 1 and 2; to Jennifer McKitrick for comments on Chapter 4; to Barbara Montero, Gene Witmer, and an anonymous reader for the Press for comments on Chapters 1 through 5; and to Carl Gillett and two more anonymous readers for the Press for their comments on the whole thing. Whenever I disregarded their advice, I did so with trepidation.

I am grateful, finally, for kind permission to reuse material (sometimes in revised form) that has appeared in earlier writings of mine: to The Journal of Philosophy, Incorporated, for about thirteen pages from "How to Keep the 'Physical' in Physicalism," *Journal of Philosophy* 94 (1997): 622–37; to the University of Chicago Press for about five pages from "The Testament of a Recovering Eliminativist," *PSA 1996: Proceedings of the 1996 Biennial Meeting of the Philosophy of Science Association: Supplement to Philosophy of Science*, 63 (1996): S185–S193 (© by The Philosophy of Science Association. All rights reserved); to Cambridge University Press for a couple of pages from "Physicalism Unfalsified: Chalmers' Inconclusive Conceivability Argument," in *Physicalism and Its Discontents*, ed. Barry Loewer and Carl Gillett (Cambridge: Cambridge University Press, 2001), 331–49 (reprinted with the permission of Cambridge University Press); and to Kluwer Academic Publishers for a couple of pages from "Being a Physicalist: How and (More Importantly) Why," *Philosophical Studies* 74 (1994): 221–41.

I started my college career as a classicist, and one of the few facts I can remember about classical antiquity is that the Hellenistic poet Callimachus apparently judged that a large book is a large evil. I can only hope that he was wrong – and offer my sincere apologies to those readers who think, at the end of this large book, that he was not.

Introduction

Gilbert Ryle once remarked that "there is no such animal as 'Science'" (1954, 71). His point, of course, was not to deny the obvious existence of science but rather to emphasize the plurality of the sciences. Philosophers have sometimes made it seem as if there were only one science, namely, physics. But even a casual perusal of a university course directory reveals that there are plenty of others. For example, consider meteorology, geology, zoology, biochemistry, neurophysiology, psychology, sociology, ecology, and molecular biology, not to mention honorary sciences such as folk psychology and folk physics. Each of the many sciences has its own characteristic theoretical vocabulary with which, to the extent that it gets things right, it describes a characteristic domain of objects, events, and properties. But the existence of the many sciences presents a problem: how are the many sciences related to one another? And how is the domain of objects, events, and properties proprietary to each science related to the proprietary domains of the others? Do the many sciences somehow speak of different aspects of the same things? Or do they address themselves to distinct segments of reality? If so, do these distinct segments of reality exist quite independently of one another, save perhaps for relations of spatiotemporal contiguity, or do some segments depend in interesting ways upon others? If we follow Wilfrid Sellars in thinking that "The aim of philosophy... is to understand how things in the broadest possible sense of the term hang together in the broadest possible sense of the term," then this problem of the many sciences must rate as the very model of a philosophical problem (1963, 1). Indeed, in view of the proliferation of sciences over the past half century, it must rate as the very model of a *modern* philosophical problem.

Now doctrines of physicalism, as I understand them, can and should be seen as competing responses to the problem of the many sciences: they offer systematic accounts of the relations among the many sciences, and among their many domains. (Hence they are not concerned exclusively or peculiarly with relations between the mental and the physical.) But doctrines of physicalism are distinguished from other possible responses to the problem of the many sciences by the fact that their account of the relations among the many sciences and their domains has the effect of *privileging* physics and its domain, of assigning to physics and the physical some sort of descriptive and metaphysical *primacy*. There are, however, different ways of characterizing the descriptive and metaphysical primacy intended, and the varieties of physicalism usually distinguished differ precisely with regard to how they set about doing so. Perhaps physics is the only science whose ontology we should believe in, with all other sciences awarded the booby prize of an error-theoretic or instrumentalist treatment; that would be a radically eliminativist physicalism. Perhaps every kind of thing spoken of in any science is *identical* with some physical kind of thing; that would be a type-identity physicalism (a view with very few contemporary adherents). Perhaps every *particular* thing spoken of in any science is identical with some *particular* physical thing; that would be a more modest – and more popular – token-identity physicalism. Perhaps every fact expressible in the proprietary vocabulary of any science *supervenes* upon facts expressible in the proprietary vocabulary of physics; that would be a supervenience physicalism, currently the front-runner among philosophers of mind.

Or perhaps a doctrine of physicalism can be formulated in some quite different way. My aim in this book is to persuade philosophers that, by appeal to the relation of *realization*, it can and should be; that, so formulated, physicalism is unavoidably and significantly reductionist; that it does not force us to say anything counterintuitive, still less obviously false, about what causes what and about what explains what; and that the balance of such empirical evidence as we currently possess clearly favors its truth. The book itself falls into two parts and six chapters. The main aim of the first part, which comprises Chapters 1 through 4, is to clear the ground of philosophical debris, so as to open up enough space in the second, which comprises Chapters 5 and 6, for what I take to be the crucial task: the empirical assessment of physicalism.

Chapter 1 aims to get clear on what exactly my thesis of physicalism claims. It provides a full and careful formulation of *realization physicalism*, as I call it, paying much attention, as well it should, to the key notions of *realization* and the *physical*. This chapter should leave no doubt that a substantial and interesting version of physicalism can indeed be formulated; no doubt what physicalism, so formulated, claims; and no doubt that the claims it makes are thoroughly a posteriori. Chapter 2 investigates the relationship between physicalism as formulated by appeal to the relation of realization, on the one hand, and various relations of supervenience, on the other. It concludes, first, that realization physicalism still *entails* a certain claim of global supervenience, even though its canonical formulation does not explicitly include one. More important, however, this chapter also argues that no claim of global supervenience can *by itself* provide a formulation of physicalism that is superior to realization physicalism in the sense that it manages simultaneously to suffice for physicalism and yet also to avoid the distinctive and (some would say) objectionable commitments of realization physicalism.

Chapter 3 addresses the question of whether realization physicalism is committed to reductionism and, if it is, how far this commitment to reductionism is a liability; and it does so by using the obvious but inexplicably neglected strategy of carefully distinguishing between different theses of reductionism and considering each thesis in turn. It argues, first, that realization physicalism is reductionist in more than one good and important sense, though in other, equally legitimate senses, it is not; the crucial thing is to avoid either evasion or mystery mongering in characterizing the autonomy enjoyed by the nonbasic sciences in relation to physics if realization physicalism is true. It argues, second, that the forms of reductionism to which realization physicalism is committed are immune at least to armchair objections. Chapter 4 aims to rebut an important philosophical objection to realization physicalism. The objection is that, if realization physicalism is true, then the only true causes are basic, physical causes, and the only causally relevant properties are basic, physical properties; the objection therefore alleges that realization physicalism cannot solve a suitably generalized version of the much discussed problem of mental causation. The rebuttal proceeds, first, by diagnosing and undermining the intuitive roots of the objection and, second, by developing and defending a general account of both causation and causal relevance according to which realization physicalism is entirely consistent with the truth of causal and causal-explanatory claims framed in the proprietary vocabularies of sciences other than physics. This chapter ends by defending a thesis exploited by the arguments of Chapter 3 but not there defended – that it is unobjectionable for one and the same token to have more than one explanation.

If the conclusions of Chapters 1 through 4 are correct, then the only question that remains about realization physicalism – whether it is true – is an a posteriori one that cannot be answered from the armchair. Instead of the customary physicalist hand waving, Chapters 5 and 6 actually begin the task of evaluating the empirical credentials of realization physicalism. Chapter 5 asks whether there is currently any evidence *against* it. After a critical survey of plausible sources of evidence against realization physicalism, it concludes that there is currently no significant empirical evidence against realization physicalism. Because the survey is inevitably incomplete, any conclusion drawn from it must be tentative; but when a search for counterevidence fails to turn up any in the obvious places, we surely have reason to suspect that none exists. Finally, Chapter 6 asks whether there is currently any evidence *for* realization physicalism. It answers that there is much, although it concedes that the evidence for physicalism about the mental is markedly weaker than that for physicalism about everything else. It argues, moreover, that this evidence is made possible by certain rather uncontroversial scientific findings that are described in textbooks of condensed-matter physics, physical chemistry, molecular biology, physiology, and so on. The fact that these findings are uncontroversial, however, does not entail that it is similarly uncontroversial to claim that they make possible evidence for realization physicalism; so the chapter is largely devoted to exposing the logical sinews of the complex strategy of nondeductive reasoning by which they do. By the chapter's end, it should be clear that physicalism is far from being a scientistic prejudice, as it is sometimes portrayed, but is, rather, a somewhat plausible hypothesis as to the nature of contingent reality. It should also be clear, in some detail, how realization physicalism envisages the relations between the many sciences and their domains.

I anticipate opposition to realization physicalism arising from two distinct quarters: from fellow physicalists (addressed mainly in Chapter 2) who suppose that, by exploiting the concept of supervenience, they can thereby formulate a version of physicalism entirely free from interestingly reductive commitments; and from antiphysicalists (addressed throughout the book) who hold, for any of a variety of reasons, that no interesting doctrine of physicalism is true. Such antiphysicalists, I should stress, need not urge a return to Cartesian dualism, the view that physicalism is very nearly true (since true of everything *except* the mental), though not strictly true (since not true of the mental). The antiphysicalists I am mainly opposing do not even think that physicalism is nearly true; they think it is entirely false. They are best described as *egalitarian pluralists* with regard to the many sciences: they treat folk psychology as no worse off than *any* of the sciences, *none* of which, in their view, especially including physics, merits any sort of metaphysical privilege (see, e.g., Goodman 1978, Putnam 1987, Crane and Mellor 1990, Dupré 1993, Daly 1997).

Although perhaps disproportionately influential, these egalitarian pluralist antiphysicalists still form only a small minority among contemporary philosophers, and today a huge preponderance of current philosophers of mind happily call themselves physicalists (or materialists), as do many other philosophers. Does this mean that in philosophy the question of physicalism has pretty much been settled – and settled in physicalism's favor? It does not. For the appearance of a prophysicalist consensus in current philosophy of mind and elsewhere is in truth quite misleading. For one thing, philosophers content to assume physicalism in their detailed contributions to highly specific issues like phenomenal consciousness or intentionality rarely do so, I suspect, with an entirely easy conscience, often admitting quite candidly that they are simply taking physicalism for granted. Indeed, for all I know, they may even share the occasionally voiced suspicion that the widespread commitment to physicalism among science-minded philosophers reflects no more than an exaggerated regard for physics. A second, and more serious charge is that a consensus about physicalism *at the level of interesting philosophical detail* simply does not exist: how exactly to formulate the physicalism that everyone allegedly espouses, how far this physicalism can and should be nonreductive, what sort of empirical evidence does or even could in principle support it, and how it might overcome the major challenges it apparently faces are questions that, so far from being answered uniformly, are very frequently not answered at all. By confronting the issue of physicalism head on, however, this book will at least provide such questions with clear answers. Naturally I hope that these answers are correct as well as clear; but clarity alone would be ample progress.

1

Realization Physicalism

1. ORIENTATION

The main aim of this first chapter is simply to provide a clear and tolerably precise formulation of realization physicalism, the version of physicalism whose consequences and plausibility the remainder of the book examines.[1] I postpone until Chapters 5 and 6 the question of whether there is actually any evidence for or against it, contenting myself here with getting onto the table a formulation of physicalism definite enough to serve as a rallying point for its friends and a target for its foes. Doing so, however, also yields two desirable by-products: first, it rebuts the charge that physicalism cannot even be formulated adequately (so that any search for evidence in its support is premature);

---

[1] The central insight of realization physicalism is that one can formulate physicalism using the notion of realization. I wish I could claim originality for it, but I cannot: I took it in 1991 from Richard Boyd (1980), with encouragement from William G. Lycan (1987, ch. 4). My development of the insight, however, as presented in Melnyk (1994), (1995a), (1995b), and (1996a), is original, although I cannot say how faithfully it conforms to Boyd's intentions. Recently, however, I have found that many features even of my development of the insight have been arrived at, quite independently, by Jeffrey Poland (1994, ch. 4). Nevertheless, there are still differences between Poland's treatment of physicalism and mine. Most important, he treats physicalism as a *program* for the construction of a certain system of unified scientific knowledge (1, 5) and, though he regards it as one that ought to be pursued (252–3), he seems to hold that we do not now have much in the way of evidence for believing the *theses* of physicalism to be *true*, or even any clear view of what such evidence would look like (232–44); my view, on the other hand, is more sanguine. But even as far as the theses of physicalism are concerned, it is not clear that Poland (ch. 4) and I understand exactly the same thing by "realization," since I make the notion precise in a way Poland might find too restrictive. I have also discovered recently that Hartry Field has devoted a paper (1992) to outlining a version of realization physicalism that for many years he has been mentioning in passing (e.g., 1975, 389; and 1986, 73).

and, second, it reveals realization physicalism's thoroughly a posteriori character.

To get an intuitive grasp of what realizationism claims about the world, consider a humble can opener. Surely there is some good sense in which a can opener is a purely physical object. And yet can openers are in one clear sense *not* physical: fundamental physics does not speak of can openers as such, because "can opener" is not a predicate of any physical theory. So what is the sense in which can openers *are* physical? Well, it is plausible upon reflection to say that all it takes for there to be a can opener is for there to exist some object that meets a certain job description: that of having the capacity to help in the opening of cans (and perhaps of being designed or at least deliberately used for this purpose). And, as long as some object does meet this job description, it does not matter how it meets it: the result is still a can opener. But something that counts as physical by the strictest lights — a suitable system of suitably related fundamental physical objects endowed with fundamental physical properties — might possess the requisite capacity (with the right history of design or use), and hence meet this job description. What makes the humble can opener in your kitchen drawer a purely physical object, then, is that it owes its existence entirely to the existence of some fundamental physical object that, whatever else may be true of it, at least meets the can opener job description. And, to a first approximation, realization physicalism can simply be thought of as a generalization of this idea, the claim that *everything* of a kind that is not mentioned as such in fundamental physics is nevertheless purely physical in the same sense in which the can opener is purely physical: its existence just consists in the existence of something that meets a certain job description, and the something that meets that description, in the world as it actually is, is a fundamental physical system of some sort.

Of course, the can-opener example also has certain features that realizationism need *not* treat as general. First, although a can opener is obviously an artifact, realizationism need not suppose that everything else that is physical without being mentioned as such in fundamental physics is an artifact. Again, although it is obvious upon a moment's reflection what job description to associate with being a can opener, realizationism need not claim that it is always similarly obvious what job description to associate with a given kind of thing. Finally, although being a can opener is associated with a job description of a particular kind, realizationism need not suppose that this kind is the only possible kind of job description.

For philosophers of mind, the best entrée into realizationism is to treat it as a generalization, along more than one dimension, of psychofunctionalism. According to psychofunctionalism, of course, although mental properties cannot be identified with fundamental physical properties, they can be identified with certain *functional* properties, where a functional property is a *higher-order* property, that is, a property that something possesses just in case it possesses some or other *lower-order* property that, in virtue of playing an appropriate causal or computational role, can be said to *realize* the higher-order property. On this view, then, a mental property, M, is identified with the property of having some or other property that plays a certain role, R. But such identifications of mental properties with functional properties need not be determinable a priori, for psychofunctionalism is a view about what mental properties are, not about how mental concepts should be analyzed; and, in fact, such identifications will typically be determinable only a posteriori. But despite their nonidentity with properties that are mentioned as such in fundamental physics, mental properties are nevertheless physical in the following broader sense: the mental properties of all *actual* possessors of mental properties are only ever realized by the appropriate role playing of their possessors' fundamental physical properties. Nothing in the nature of mental properties rules out the possibility that they should have been realized by properties of some utterly different kind, even by ectoplasmic properties (if such there could be); but, in fact, they never are.

Realization physicalism generalizes psychofunctionalism in four respects. First, it claims that not merely mental properties but all (instantiated) properties not mentioned as such in the theories of fundamental physics – presumably including therefore all chemical, biological, sociological, and folk-physical properties – are to be identified a posteriori with functional properties. Second, it claims that all these properties are physically realized in the sense of being realized by properties that are mentioned as such in the theories of fundamental physics. Third, it adds to the notion of a functional *property* analogous notions of a functional *object* and of a functional *event*. For a functional object (e.g., a can opener) to exist is just for some or other object to exist that plays a certain role; and for a functional event to occur is just for some or other event to occur that plays a certain role.[2] With these additional notions, realizationism

---

2   Note that what *has* to play the role in each case is the object's (or the event's) *realizer*, not the object (or the event) itself, and further that it is not assumed that the object (or the event) is *identical* with the object (or event) that is its realizer. However, it is *possible* that the object (or event) itself should *also* play the role. The harmlessness of this possibility will only become clear in Chapter 4, where I defend the possibility and legitimacy of multiple causal explanations of the same effect.

can claim that not only all properties that are not mentioned as such in fundamental physics, but also all objects and all events that are not so mentioned, are functional and, as it happens, always physically realized. Finally, realizationism allows that functional things – whether properties, objects, or events – might need to be characterized in terms of associated roles that are neither causal nor computational, but of other sorts.

So much for intuitive preliminaries. Let me now begin to work toward a fuller and more rigorous formulation of realization physicalism. Realization physicalism can be expressed in slogan form as the universal generalization that everything – every *thing* – is either mentioned as such in fundamental physics or else is realized by things that are. I close this section by explaining two assumptions that I shall be making about these "things" that are the subject of realization physicalism's universal generalization.

First, I assume that they are *actual tokens*, past, present, and future; and, for the sake of definiteness (rather than out of settled metaphysical conviction), I take it that the types of which these things are tokens fall into two or three ontological categories: properties (to include relations), object kinds, and, if events are irreducible to objects and properties, event kinds. The upshot, then, is that realization physicalism claims that all actual property instances, individual objects, and individual events are either mentioned as such in fundamental physics or else realized by things that are. However, if one's ontology also includes such things as states, processes, states of affairs, conditions, and so forth, and if one regards these as irreducible to properties, objects, and events, then one will easily be able to provide a realizationist treatment of them by extending the realizationist treatment of properties, objects, and events.

I have just alluded to one metaphysical issue (that of how many irreducibly distinct ontological categories there are) that I do not discuss in this book. Another metaphysical issue that suffers similar neglect is the nature of *properties* (and, mutatis mutandis, kinds). Not that I will eschew property talk – far from it. But I wish such talk always to be interpreted *modestly*, merely as a way of talking about what it is *in the world* that makes true predications objectively true. Presumably more committed views about the nature of properties, including the view that properties are *universals*, would all be consistent with this modestly construed property talk; but I wish to remain officially neutral as between these metaphysical alternatives. There are three main reasons for this policy. The first is that, for reasons that become progressively clearer as the book proceeds, I regard physicalism as a *scientific hypothesis*, albeit one of exceptionally broad scope and long-standing philosophical interest; and surely there is no *general* obligation for the advocate of a scientific hypothesis to defend a view about the metaphysics of properties before the hypothesis can properly be taken seriously. The second, and an admittedly provocative, reason is that if there were to arise some conflict between realization physicalism, on the one hand, and, on the other, some otherwise plausible metaphysical doctrine about the nature of properties, then I would be inclined to react by rejecting the doctrine about properties, on the grounds that, as we shall see in Chapter 6, realization physicalism is better evidenced than any metaphysical doctrine about properties. (Conversely, if it were to turn out that realization physicalism *required* a certain metaphysical doctrine about the nature of properties, then I would welcome the fact, as providing us with some much-needed traction on a set of issues of which, for all their fascination, I am inclined to despair.)[3] The third reason is that, as a matter of fact, I *think* that nearly all that I have to say in defense of realization physicalism would survive unaltered in substance pretty much however the metaphysical issues were to turn out. (Possible exceptions are discussed in Chapter 1, Section 4, and Chapter 3, Section 2.) At any rate, I hope that this is so.

The second major assumption I make about the things that realization physicalism asserts to be physical is that they exist contingently or they play *some* sort of causal role in the world, possibly just as effects. (Note that the "or" is inclusive.) This assumption constitutes a restriction on the *scope* of realization physicalism, which should therefore be understood as claiming that all actual tokens are physical iff they are contingent or causal. This restriction makes a big difference to what sorts of things would refute realization physicalism were they to exist. Would the existence of God refute realization physicalism, given that God is neither mentioned as such in fundamental physics nor realized by something that is? The answer is yes if God, though a noncontingent existent, causally affected, or were causally affected by, anything else, since in that case he would fall within the scope of realization physicalism. (The answer is no if God were both a noncontingent existent *and* entirely acausal, since then he would not.) Would realization physicalism be refuted by the existence of, say, an epiphenomenal and uncaused instance of some phenomenal

---

3   This possibility may in fact be actual. For realization physicalism requires physical properties, at least, to be sufficiently real to legitimate the quantification over properties involved in specifying higher-order functional properties ("x possesses functional property F iff *there exists* some property P such that x possesses it and it meets condition C"). But I do not know how real would be "sufficiently real."

property that is not physically realized? Yes, for, though entirely acausal, this instance of a phenomenal property would exist contingently, and so on that account would fall within the scope of realization physicalism. By contrast, however, the truth of realization physicalism would *not* be threatened by the existence of items that, like numbers on a traditional platonistic construal of mathematics, are *both* noncontingent *and* acausal; such items simply fall outside the scope of the realization physicalist thesis. Of course, it may turn out that the *rationale* for denying the existence of anything that is neither mentioned as such in fundamental physics nor realized by something that is applies with equal force *both* to things that are contingent or causal *and* to things that are neither contingent nor causal; but it is far from obvious that this is so, and I do not address the question in this book.

2. "PHYSICAL"

What realization physicalism claims about everything (i.e., about every actual token, past, present, and future, that is contingent or causal) is that either it is physical in a narrow sense of "physical" (glossed to this point as "mentioned as such in fundamental physics") or else it is physical in a broader sense of standing in a certain special relation – that of realization – to what is physical in the narrow sense. A full account of physicality in the broader sense – and hence of realization – must await the next section. But what is it for something to be "physical" in the narrow sense? Because the point of answering this question is not to produce a conceptual analysis but merely to give a sufficiently definite meaning to an imprecise thesis, a physicalist's response to it can perfectly well be a *stipulative* definition of "physical," which therefore need not exhibit fidelity to ordinary usage. But even a stipulative definition is subject to some constraints, and any stipulative definition of "physical" must, it seems, at least meet the following three conditions in order to be plausible: when plugged into an otherwise satisfactory formulation of physicalism, it must yield a thesis (i) that is not obviously false, (ii) that is not analytic or in any other way trivial,[4] and (iii) that possesses content determinable

---

[4] We should note that a formulation of physicalism that includes a stipulatively defined use of the word "physical" can perfectly well meet this nontriviality condition; for example, the thesis that all properties are physical or physically realized, where the "physical" properties are stipulated to be just those properties known to Aristotle, is evidently nontrivial – and equally evidently false. That a term appearing in a statement has a stipulated meaning does not entail that the statement itself is trivial.

now by us. There are at least two reasons why an adequate formulation of physicalism must possess content determinable now by us. The first is that, if it does not, then, for all we now know, our putatively physicalist thesis might turn out not to exclude from existence such items as souls, entelechies, and ghosts, items that do not qualify as physical on even the broadest interpretation of "physical," and which have traditionally been viewed by physicalists as *entia non grata*. But the second, and more important, reason is that, if our formulation of physicalism lacks content determinable now by us, then we would have no warrant for taking any scientific findings *actually* available to us as evidence for (or evidence against) physicalism, and no way, indeed, of telling what *would* count as evidence for (or against) the thesis.

However, there is a dilemma, apparently owed to Hempel (see Hempel 1969, 180–3; 1980, 194–5; also Smart 1978 and Chomsky 1972, 98), that is sometimes thought to show that no physicalist definition of "physical" can meet conditions (i) and (iii) simultaneously (see, e.g., Crane and Mellor 1990, 188; Crane 1991, 34; Van Fraassen 1996, 163–70 and 173–4; Daly 1998, 209). It is nicely expressed by Geoffrey Hellman:

> [C]urrent physics is surely incomplete (even in its ontology) as well as inaccurate (in its laws). This poses a dilemma: either physicalist principles are based on current physics, in which case there is every reason to think they are false; or else they are not, in which case it is, at best, difficult to interpret them, since they are based on a "physics" that does not exist – yet we lack any general criterion of "physical object, property, or law" framed independently of existing physical theory. (1985, 609)

So if "physical" entities and properties are those mentioned as such in the laws and theories of *current* physics, then physicalism is probably false, which obviously sounds like very bad news for the physicalist.[5] But if they are those mentioned as such in the laws and theories of *completed* physics, then, since we currently have no idea what completed physics will look like, the resulting formulation of physicalism will lack content determinable now by us, which is also bad news for the physicalist.

Can a physicalist go between the horns of Hempel's dilemma? Not easily, as the failure of two recent attempts to do so will illustrate. Jeffrey Poland defines "physical" in terms of physics but characterizes physics as

---

5 Notice, since the point will eventually, in Chapter 5, matter, that neither "probably false" nor even "very probably false" is the same as "certainly false."

the science that, to put it very crudely, provides true answers to certain questions that, plausibly, it is the business of physics to answer (1994, 124–6). Poland therefore avoids the first horn of the dilemma, because he need not identify physics with current physics; but physicalism formulated in terms of his definition of "physical" still possesses determinate content. However, the trouble is that, as he himself admits when he concedes that "No one knows" what theory it is that answers to his characterization of physics (126), this content is not determinable now by us; so he runs into the second horn of the dilemma.[6] He does add that "the best guess that can be made is that [what answers to his characterization of physics] is current physics or some suitable elaboration" (126); but how much help is this if, as the first horn of Hempel's dilemma alleges, current physics is probably false?

Similarly, Frank Jackson says that "physicalists have three reasonable things to say by way of explaining what they mean by physical properties and relations – they are those we need to handle the non-sentient, they are broadly akin to those that appear in current physical science, they are those we need to handle the relatively small" (1998a, 8). But if the "physical" is defined as what is needed to handle the nonsentient and/or the relatively small, *and* it is left entirely *open* what those properties and relations might be, the resulting formulation of physicalism will lack content determinable by us now, in which case Jackson runs into the second horn of the dilemma; if, on the other hand, it is assumed that those properties and relations are the ones mentioned as such in current physics, then, if the first horn of Hempel's dilemma is sharp, Jackson is also in trouble. That leaves him with his suggestion that the "physical" properties and relations are those "broadly akin to those that appear in current science" (see also Ravenscroft 1997). But "broadly akin" is very vague; and to the extent that it is interpreted liberally, Jackson will end up with a formulation of physicalism to that extent lacking in content determinable now by us, so that we will have corresponding difficulty in telling what would count as evidence for it and correspondingly reduced warrant for taking scientific findings actually available to us as evidence for it. In any case, those who take the first horn of Hempel's dilemma seriously hold that the track record of physical theorizing makes it likely not merely that current physics is just a little bit off target but that it is way off

---

6 However, since Poland advocates physicalism as a program worthy of pursuit, and is for independent reasons doubtful that much evidence now supports the theses of physicalism, this criticism will presumably leave him unfazed. For references, see note 1.

target, in which case a physics "broadly akin" to current physics is probably false too.

Physicalists who hold, as I do, that current scientific findings provide support for physicalism must at the least have a formulation of physicalism whose content is determinable by us now. But it is hard to see how else they can get one other than by defining "physical" by appeal to current physics; so that is what I shall do. Of course, if one defines "physical" by appeal to current physics, then although one's definition will clearly meet conditions (ii) and (iii), one must have some way of blunting the first horn of Hempel's dilemma and, hence, of showing either that the proposed definition of "physical" conforms to condition (i) despite appearances or else that for some reason its failure to do so does not matter. I do indeed have a way to blunt the first horn of Hempel's dilemma, though it is best presented in Chapter 5, when the dilemma is revisited in the context of critical discussion of potential evidence against realization physicalism. Until then, I beg the skeptical reader to suspend disbelief.[7]

Understanding physicalism by appeal to current physics does have the possibly unsettling consequence that, say, Hobbes was not a physicalist, since he had no notion of current physics. But this consequence is bearable, because, consistently with it, we can still insist that Hobbesian materialism nevertheless has much in common with physicalism. The most important commonality is the idea that some science distinct from the bare conjunction of the many sciences is in some metaphysical sense basic; but there is also the fact that Hobbes picked as the basic science something that turned out to be, sociologically and historically speaking, the ancestor of current physics. For the same reason, if tomorrow new evidence forces a revision of physics, it will be possible to formulate a new rival to physicalism as I am understanding it, by letting tomorrow's (superior) physics take the place of current physics in our formulation; and if the evidence for taking tomorrow's physics to be basic is as good as the evidence for taking current physics to be basic, which is highly likely,

---

7 A very quick preview: I argue, first, that we must distinguish sharply between the issue of how to formulate physicalism and the issue of characterizing what is involved in *endorsing* physicalism; and, second, that it is perfectly possible to endorse *any* scientific hypothesis, including therefore physicalism, and indeed to endorse it rationally, while acknowledging that it has only a very low probability of being true. (Notice that the poor track record of physical theorizing that the first horn of Hempel's dilemma emphasizes can at most show that current physics, and hence physicalism formulated by appeal to current physics, is *very probably* false, not that it is *certainly* false.) I realize that this view must initially seem a bit of a stretcher, but I promise that it will be argued for in detail in Chapter 5, Section 4.

the resulting doctrine will be superior. Now, strictly speaking, it will not be the doctrine I am calling physicalism. It will, however, have much in common with it; specifically, it will implement the generic idea that there is a basic science distinct from the bare conjunction of the many sciences, and the science it identifies as basic will be an immediate sociological descendant of current physics. So if we are looking for something to serve as "the spirit of physicalism," something that transcends particular formulations, then the commonality that I have just characterized might be a good candidate, in which case, however, the spirit of physicalism would not be attitudinal, as Bas Van Fraassen alleges it would have to be, but cognitive (see Van Fraassen 1996, 169–70). Moreover, existence of a spirit of physicalism, understood in this way, also serves to refute the charge made by Seth Crook and Carl Gillett that a hypothesis of physicalism formulated by appeal to current physics is incapable of progress (Crook and Gillett 2001, 342). For if tomorrow new evidence forces a revision of physics, and a new rival to physicalism can then be formulated, the new rival will still exhibit the spirit of physicalism; the situation will therefore not be one in which physicalism has been discarded and replaced with a view entirely alien to it.[8]

What, exactly, is to count as current physics, for the purpose of defining "physical"? My proposal is to identify current physics with those theories that are the object of *consensus* among current physicists (so not all theories that are merely being proposed or discussed by current physicists will count); and I think that in practice we can discover which theories these are by examining the contents of physics textbooks that are widely used in undergraduate and graduate teaching. There is admittedly *some* vagueness

---

8 A potential objection of a different sort to formulating physicalism by appeal to current physics can be dealt with here. Chris Daly (1998, 206–7) objects, to a certain proposal for defining "physical," that it implies that certain uninstantiated properties are not physical, even though, were they instantiated, we would be inclined pretheoretically to classify them as physical (e.g., certain nomologically possible *masses* possessed by no actual object in the history of the universe). My proposal to define "physical" by reference to current physics *may* have this implication too. But even if it does, Daly's objection has little force against it. For the proposal to define "physical" by reference to current physics does not purport to be a conceptual analysis in the first place, and so it does not *need* to be answerable to our pretheoretical intuitions. Moreover, the ability of the proposal to assist in the formulation of a thesis that meets the three conditions mentioned in the text is not compromised by the fact (if it is one) that the proposal has the implication in question. Admittedly, it is arguable that any thesis formulated with the help of the proposal must also meet a further condition, that of articulating what physicalists or materialists have typically had in mind by "physicalism"; but surely physicalism formulated with the help of the proposal to define "physical" by reference to current physics meets this condition rather well.

in characterizing current physics in this way, but the fact is that if one looks through the course offerings of physics departments, or peruses textbooks in some one branch of physics, one will be struck by the high degree of consensus one finds. It will be perfectly clear, for very many theories, whether they fall within the consensus.[9] And there is no reason to think that such vagueness as remains will be more problematic in this connection than in any other scientific or philosophical connection in which some degree of vagueness arises.

Thus understood, current physics will include branches such as condensed-matter physics, which deals with relatively macroscopic phenomena, and not just such branches as particle physics and quantum mechanics, which are usually thought of as treating the very small. As a result, this understanding provides realization physicalism with insurance against the possibility that some branches of current physics dealing with relatively macrolevel phenomena should turn out to be *strongly emergent* relative to microphysical phenomena, that is, derivable from microphysical phenomena only via micro-macro physical laws that are fundamental in the sense of being in no way explainable in terms of other laws. Some philosophers take such a possibility seriously; for example, Paul Humphreys mentions the possibility that solid-state physics may be "more than just advanced elementary particle physics" – and he does not mean merely that applying elementary particle physics to complex macrosystems may be a practical impossibility (Humphreys 1997a, 17).[10] But if current physics is construed broadly, as I have proposed, then even if some branches of current physics do turn out to deal with phenomena that are emergent in the relevantly strong sense, realization physicalism will not thereby have been refuted; for the strongly emergent phenomena will in that case count as physical in their own right. And if, on the other hand, no branches of current physics turn out to deal with strongly emergent phenomena, then, although I will have identified a broader physical basis as fundamental than I really needed to, realization physicalism will at least not for that reason be rendered false, and such small harm as will

---

9 So appeals to the so-called anthropic principle, or to the irreducible role of consciousness in accounting for the collapse of the wave function, are surely not part of current consensus physics.

10 But one must beware of concluding too hastily that such possibilities are actual. Paul Humphreys (1997b, 343), for example, mentions phase transitions and dissipative processes as possible examples of emergent phenomena. But condensed matter physics has had much success in accounting reductively for one kind of phase transition, superconductivity, and some success in accounting for others (Chandrasekhar 1998, ch. 12).

have been done can easily be put right by appropriately narrowing the basis.

The broad construal of current physics that I have proposed does assume, however, that it is unproblematic for physicalists to treat physics itself as disunified – that is, to treat some kinds of physical phenomena as strongly emergent relative to other kinds of physical phenomena. But is it really unproblematic? I think that it is (apparently *contra* Crane and Mellor 1990, 190; and Poland 1994, 28 and 170). Realization physicalism certainly entails that all the many sciences are unified – in the specific sense that the tokens postulated by, and described in the respective proprietary vocabularies of, the special sciences all stand in the realization relation to things that are physical in the narrow sense currently being explicated. But it is just a non sequitur to *deduce* from this that physicalism must therefore regard *physics itself* as similarly unified with regard to some proper part of itself. For the world may simply be such that the many sciences really are unified exactly as realization physicalism says that they are, while physics itself includes some branches that are strongly emergent relative to other branches. Realization physicalists need hope for no more. An analogy may help to bring out the unobjectionability of a physicalism that tolerates the disunity of physics itself. Given the evidence actually available, evolutionists conclude that all species are descended from a *single* ancestor species; but they might have had different evidence, and concluded instead that all species are descended from *several* ancestor species, none related to any of the others, so that life on earth must have arisen independently on several different occasions. Now this many-origins version of the hypothesis of evolution certainly finds less unity in the world than does the familiar, single-origin version that is supported by the actual evidence; but it is in no sense self-contradictory, there *might* have been excellent evidence for it, and the claim it makes would not have been much less controversial than the claim made by the single-origin version. Likewise, I suggest, for physicalism, to the extent that physics itself is disunified. To be sure, such disunity as the *physical* realm exhibits constitutes weak inductive evidence for supposing that the world *in general* is disunified. But evidence of this sort is not the only evidence there could be, and, being weak, it could easily be outweighed by contrary evidence to the effect that the world in general exhibits precisely the unity physicalism says it does. Indeed, there is a strong case for saying that it *is* so outweighed, as we shall see in Chapter 6.

For the purposes of the rest of this book, then, and unless otherwise indicated, I use the word "physical" (and, mutatis mutandis, the word "nonphysical") in the following way. I call a token *physical* iff it is a token of a type that is physical, where the types in question are assumed, as noted earlier, to be properties, object kinds, and event kinds; and I call a property, object kind, or event kind physical iff *either* it is expressed by some positive predicate (e.g., "is an electron," "has charge") used in the formulation of the theories of current physics *or* it is expressed by some predicate constructible out of the positive predicates of current physics via the use of such predicate-forming machinery as the language of physics already contains, as well as of (possibly infinitary) conjunction and disjunction, and negation, so long as (i) the constructed predicate does not express a necessary property (e.g., that of either being a quark or not being a quark) and (ii) the constructed predicate is not entirely negative. Clause (i) is included in order to avoid having to say that a Cartesian ego has a physical property just because it satisfies the predicate, "is a quark or is not a quark."[11] Clause (ii) is included in order to avoid having to say, implausibly, that the number 5 has a physical property just because it satisfies the (entirely negative) constructed predicate, "does not have charge" (for the problem, see Post 1987, 178–80; for the solution, see Poland 1994, 128; Klagge 1995, 63).[12]

Three consequences of this definition of "physical," in the narrow sense, are especially noteworthy. First, it implies that certain types – unimaginably complex kinds of microphysical systems, for example, or the properties possessed by them – will count as physical (since expressible by some suitably constructed predicate), even though they are macroscopic and working physicists may have neither the occasion nor the practical ability to speak of them as such.[13] Second, certain properties can count

---

11 Thanks to Barbara Montero for alerting me to this danger.
12 Poland (1994) fears that the linguistic approach to specifying the physical that is embodied in the second disjunct of my definition encounters certain cardinality objections (48–52, 56-7, 129–30), and prefers an approach that appeals to certain object- and property-forming operations (131–2). But the cardinality objections he mentions smell fishy to me; and in any case I am not yet clear how a switch to object- and property-forming operations that mimic the predicate-forming operations I invoke can amount to anything more than a cosmetic change.
13 My definition of "physical" implies not only that these types are physical but also that they are genuine types (properties, object kinds, event kinds, or whatever). That is, it assumes that there is *such a thing* as the (kind of) thing expressed by so-and-so predicate, constructed in accordance with the second disjunct of the definition, just because there are such things as the (kinds of) things expressed by the *simple* predicates employed in the construction. This assumption raises difficult and abstract metaphysical issues that I cannot adequately discuss here. For example, the assumption seems to imply that for any two physical

as physical by this definition that are emergent in the *weak* sense that they are possessed by wholes but are not possessed, and perhaps cannot be possessed, by any, still less all, of the wholes' constituent parts; examples would be the property of being a two-particle system, or that of having a mass of one kilogram. So a version of physicalism formulated in terms of this definition of "physical" is not committed to any doctrine of "atomism" that would deny the existence of physical properties that are emergent in this weak sense. Finally, as already noted, certain types can count as physical by this definition that are emergent in the strong sense given earlier. Such types may be expressible by simple predicates of some branch of macrophysics or, as routinely happens in the case of the examples that quantum entanglement apparently supplies (Teller 1986), by a constructed predicate of the sort specified in the definition's second disjunct; either way, the current definition counts such emergent types as physical. Moreover, the tokening of such types by a complex physical system might confer causal powers on the system that are *novel*, in the sense that they could not be derived, even in principle, from knowledge of the system's physical components, of those components' physical interrelations, and of the physical laws governing their local interactions in local circumstances. As a result, the system's *components* might behave differently from how they would behave when not composing such a system or when composing complex systems of different types; but this is unproblematic for physicalism so long as the novel causal powers of the system can be characterized as physical according to the definition given, and so long as these powers arise in accordance with physical laws of *some* sort (e.g., holistic laws of composition that take into explicit account

> entities that exist there exists a physical entity that exists iff the two physical entities first mentioned merely exist, regardless of how these entities are arranged; thus, it seems to imply a restricted version of the controversial metaphysical doctrine of *universalism* (for criticism, see Van Inwagen 1990; for defense, see Rea 1998). However, even if metaphysical inquiry should in the end prove that universalism is false, the assumption licenses the existence of many (complex) physical entities that do *not* exist *solely* in virtue of the sheer existence of certain (simple) physical entities because the physically specifiable *relatedness* of the (simple) entities in question matters too (for example, a hydrogen atom is a complex physical system that does not exist solely in virtue of the sheer *existence* of a proton and an electron); and it may turn out that complex physical entities of this sort are all that realization physicalism needs to serve as physical realizers of macroscopic entities. In that case, the second disjunct of my proposed definition of "physical" could surely be modified so that it no longer implies that any two physical entities *automatically* (i.e., regardless of physical relations) compose a third physical entity, though getting the details right might be tricky.

the possibly very wide physical context within which a complex physical system exists).[14]

3. A CANONICAL FORMULATION

As already noted, realization physicalism claims that everything (i.e., every actual token that is contingent or causal) is either physical, in the sense just now given, or else physical in a broader sense expressible by saying that it stands in a certain special relation to what is physical in the first sense. The most distinctive feature of realization physicalism is that it takes the central notion required for characterizing this special relation to be neither identity nor supervenience but *realization*.[15] But what is realization? And how exactly should we use the notion of realization to characterize this special relation? The answers to these questions require a little space.

Let us begin by construing realization as a relation between two tokens of distinct types. The token that gets realized must be a token of a *functional* type, that is, a higher-order type such that, necessarily, it is tokened iff there is a token of some or other lower-order type that plays some particular role or – more generally – meets some particular condition.[16] This condition, for a particular functional type, we may call the functional type's *associated* condition; it is the condition, C, such that, necessarily, there is a token of that functional type iff there is a token of some or other type that meets C. Functional types differ from one another with regard to their associated conditions, and in the next section I display some of the wide variety of possible associated conditions that may be invoked in characterizing a functional type.

The token that does the realizing, on the other hand, that realizes (say) some particular token of a particular functional type, F, does so by being a token of some or other type that in fact meets the associated

---

14 See my subsequent discussion of how I understand "physical law."
15 That the notion of realization might be so usable gains some plausibility from the suggestion that English contains an "is" of *constitution*, in addition to an "is" of existence, an "is" of predication, and an "is" of identity (see Wiggins 1980, 30–5). Constitution is not a precise idea, of course, but *one* way to make it precise is to identify it with realization as I elucidate it later; so my account of realization should be treated as a candidate analysis of constitution (for other analyses of constitution, see Baker 1999 and Thomson 1998).
16 Note that, *pace* Kim (1998, 20), I do not require that the lower-order types belong to some specified set.

condition for F, whatever that may be. I propose the following definition of realization:

> Token *x realizes* token *y* iff (i) *y* is a token of some functional type, F, such that, necessarily, F is tokened iff there is a token of some or other type that meets condition, C; (ii) *x* is a token of some type that in fact meets C; and (iii) the token of F whose existence is logically guaranteed by the holding of condition (ii) is numerically identical with *y*.[17]

Note that, even though this definition employs the notion of numerical identity, it does not entail that if token *x* realizes token *y*, then token *x* = token *y*. As far as this definition goes, then, it is an open question whether a realized token is identical with its realizer. Furthermore, a realizing token can be of any type, even a functional type, so long as the type meets the requisite associated condition.[18] And, of course, tokens of very different types (e.g., very different physical types) can realize distinct tokens of the same functional type, F, so long as the different types have in common that they meet the associated condition for F.

It will be recalled that, at the end of Section 1, I announced my intention to limit consideration to types that fall into the three categories of properties, object kinds, and event kinds. Accordingly, we can regard any functional type as falling into one of the three categories of functional properties, functional object kinds, and functional event kinds. A *functional property*, P, is a property such that, necessarily, there is an instance of P iff there is a token of some type or other (e.g., an instance of some property or other) that meets condition C. Note that on my account the bearer of a functional property need not be the same individual as the bearer of the property that realizes it, *pace* Jaegwon Kim (1998, 82). Examples of functional properties plausibly include transparency, having currency, and being an analgesic. A *functional object kind*, O, is an object kind such that, necessarily, there is an object of kind O iff there is a token of some type or other (e.g., an object of some or other object kind) that meets condition C. Examples of functional object kinds plausibly include

---

17 Ernest LePore and Barry Loewer offer an apparently quite different account of realization as a "necessary connection which is *explanatory*" (1989, 179; emphasis in original). But, as we shall see in Chapter 3 when the relationship between realization physicalism and reductionism is explored, realization as I understand it is intimately connected with explanation, so that their account is closer to mine than initially appears.

18 The discussion in Chapter 4 vindicates the idea that tokens of functional types can be singular causes, and that functional types can be causally relevant. The way is therefore clear for functional types to meet associated conditions by playing appropriate causal roles.

can openers, digestive systems, and cells. A *functional event kind*, E, is an event kind such that, necessarily, an event of kind E occurs iff there is a token of some type or other (e.g., there occurs an event of some kind or other) that meets condition C. Examples of functional event kinds plausibly include storms, births, and extinctions. We can now see that the account of the two-place realization relation just given obviously applies to tokens of functional properties, to tokens of functional object kinds, and to tokens of functional event kinds — that is, it applies to functional property instances, objects, and events.

But how exactly should we employ the realization relation, as just defined, to characterize the special relation in which something must stand to what is physical in the narrow sense specified in the previous section in order for it to count as physical in the broad sense? The most obvious first thought is to attempt a formulation of realization physicalism as follows:

> (R_0) Every property instance (object, event) is *either* an instance of a physical property (an object of a physical kind, an event of a physical kind) *or* an instance of some functional property (an object of a functional object kind, an event of a functional event kind) that is *realized by* an instance of a physical property (an object of a physical kind, an event of a physical kind).

In line with the policies announced earlier, the domain of quantification should be restricted to actual tokens, past, present, or future, that are contingent or causal, and "physical" should be taken in the special sense explained in Section 2.

But this tempting formulation will not quite do (see, in effect, Poland 1994, 55–7). The realization physicalist wishes to express the idea that all tokens that are not themselves physical nevertheless owe their existence entirely to the way things are physically and wishes to do so by saying that all nonphysical tokens are, as we might put it, *realized by the physical*. But while it is certainly a *necessary* condition for a nonphysical token to be "realized by the physical" that it should be realized by a physical token, it turns out not to be a *sufficient* condition. The point can be made in two ways. First, consider a token of a functional type, F, whose associated condition is some role, R, and suppose that this F-token is indeed realized, in the sense defined earlier, by a certain token of a physical type that plays role R. Still, if this physical type's playing of role R is *miraculous*, in the sense that in playing R it behaves in ways not required by, or even contrary to, the laws of physics, then, intuitively, the F-token is not realized by the physical, even though it *is* realized by a physical token.[19] Alternatively, consider a token of a functional type whose associated condition is such that the functional type is tokened only if there is a token of some or other type *such that so-and-so conditions obtain* (where the obtaining of these conditions cannot naturally be regarded as something that a type *does*). If the obtaining of these conditions is not itself a physical or physically realized affair (e.g., perhaps their obtaining requires the presence in Australia of five angels), then the functional token may be realized by an entirely law-abiding token of a physical type, but still fail, intuitively, to be realized by the physical.

In order to rule out such cases as these, and therefore to articulate the intended sense of a functional token's "being realized by the physical," a realizationist evidently needs to define a more demanding relation than that of being realized by a physical token. I propose that we identify a functional token's being realized by the physical with a functional token's being *physically realized*:

> A token x of a functional type, F, is *physically realized* iff (i) x is realized by a token of some physical type, T, *and* (ii) T meets the associated condition for F solely as a logical consequence of the distribution in the world of physical tokens and the holding of physical laws.

In both of the hypothetical examples given in the previous paragraph, clause (ii) is not met by the functional token imagined. For in neither example does the physical realizer meet the relevant associated condition solely as a logical consequence of the distribution in the world of physical tokens and the holding of physical laws. So, in both examples, the functional token imagined does not count as physically realized.

Let me clarify this definition by explaining what I mean by "physical law." I mean any lawlike regularity, universal or statistical, that is *either* expressed by a law statement standardly used in some branch of current physics *or* expressible by a law statement logically derivable in principle from law statements standardly used in any of the branches of current physics.[20] Because some of the law statements standardly used in current

---

19 If it is *essential* to a physical token's identity that it should only behave in strict accordance with all physical laws, then this imagined state of affairs is incoherent. But I am inclined to doubt the antecedent here. While plausible for physical simples like electrons, it seems to me that it is *not* essential to the identity of a very *large and complex* physical entity (recall that my official definition of "physical" allows such entities to count as physical) that it should behave only in strict accordance with all physical laws; it might behave in accordance with laws that are *strongly emergent* relative to physical laws.

20 For an account of what makes a regularity lawlike, see Chapter 4.

23

physics will express physical laws of composition (i.e., laws describing the physical properties had by relatively complex physical systems given that they are composed of relatively less complex physical systems), this disjunctive definition of "physical law" leaves open the possibility that unimaginably complex physical systems (e.g., those realizing blood cells) should nevertheless behave in accordance with physical laws (i.e., laws that meet the second condition in my disjunctive definition of "physical law"), even though these laws are expressed by no law statements standardly used in any branch of current physics.

Surprisingly, perhaps, it does not follow from this account of a physical law that every lawlike regularity concerning phenomena that are physical in the sense defined in Section 2 counts as a physical law. Suppose that there is a lawlike regularity in the behavior of some unimaginably complex physical system, but that a statement of this regularity cannot be derived, even in principle, from a complete physical description of the system's components and their physical organization plus the standardly used laws of physics *unless* you also include as a premise a law of composition that, although expressible in purely physical terms, is expressible *neither* by a law statement standardly used in some branch of current physics *nor* by a law statement derivable from such law statements. (Perhaps this regularity is fundamental and holds *only* for unimaginably complex physical systems that physicists *qua* physicists do not standardly talk about.) In that case, this lawlike regularity fails to satisfy the account of "physical law" given earlier, even though it concerns phenomena that are physical in the sense defined in Section 2. The intuition that explains my preference for this more restrictive account of "physical law" is this: if some unimaginably complex physical system met the associated condition for (say) being a blood cell even partly in virtue of the holding of such a regularity as I have just described, then, I say, the cell in question would not be realized by the physical in a sufficiently strong sense. But readers who do not share this intuition are at liberty to broaden their definition of "physical law" so as to include as a physical law *any* lawlike regularity concerning phenomena that are physical in the sense defined in Section 2; and in any case the issue is moot, since there is, as far as I know, no evidence that there are any such regularities.

In formulating realization physicalism, therefore, let us employ the notion of a functional token's being physically realized, because no weaker construal of the notion of being realized by the physical seems adequate to rule out intuitively unacceptable cases. Yet employing the notion of being physically realized has an unexpected consequence. For clause (ii) of the definition of being physically realized requires that a physical type's meeting the associated condition, C, of a given functional type must be a logical consequence of physical facts alone. But if a physical type's meeting condition C must *follow logically* from physical facts alone, then condition C cannot just be characterized any old way, else there will be no valid derivation, even in principle, of the conclusion that C has been met from premises that specify purely physical facts; indeed, for the derivation to be valid, condition C must be characterized in terms that are either physical or quasi-logical or a mixture of both.[21] (Quasi-logical terms are terms that, though not logical in any traditional sense, are nevertheless not part of the proprietary vocabulary of any particular science or honorary science. Examples are "cause," "property," and "is nomically associated with." The use of quasi-logical terms in addition to physical terms in specifying associated conditions is acceptable because quasi-logical terms are linked to physical terms via analytic trivialities such as "If something has charge, then it has at least one property." But nonphysical terms of no other kind than quasi-logical ones are linked to physical terms via analytic generalizations [e.g., no biological or psychological terms are so linked]; so no other kind of nonphysical term is acceptable.) In that case, however, the only functional types whose tokens are even *capable* of being physically realized turn out to be those whose associated conditions can be specified in physical or quasi-logical terms.[22] Given the understanding of "physical" that I am using, this is an unexpectedly strong requirement for the acceptable specification of associated conditions for physically realizable types, even though its rationale is clear. As shown in the next section, however, this requirement is not problematic.

We are very nearly in a position to present a canonical formulation of realization physicalism. But we must first note an important point. Realization physicalism makes a claim about the broadly physical character of *all* causal or contingent tokens. But in order for this claim to be

---

[21] In the context of characterizing legitimate specifications of associated conditions, I mean by "physical" terms those that are either positive predicates used in the formulation of the theories of current physics or else predicates constructible out of the positive predicates of current physics via the use of such predicate-forming machinery as the language of physics already contains, (possibly infinitary) conjunction and disjunction, negation, the "... is such that..." predicate-forming operator, and also higher-order quantification. Note that types that are expressible by terms that are physical in this sense form a *larger* class than those that are physical in the sense given in the text, where higher-order quantification is *not* permitted as part of the predicate-forming machinery.

[22] The tokens of functional types whose associated conditions are characterizable in physical or quasi-logical terms do not, of course, *have* to be physically realized; but they can be.

true, its domain of quantification must be restricted so as to *exclude* tokens of certain types. For example, tokens of what might be called *superlative types* (e.g., being the *tallest* building, being the *worst* war) must be excluded. For even if the tallest building – that very building – is physically realized, its status as the *tallest* building would be jeopardized by the existence of an even taller building that was realized *nonphysically*. So part of what makes it the case that a certain building is in fact the tallest building is the nonexistence of any nonphysically realized taller building; but the nonexistence of any nonphysically realized taller building is not itself a physical fact. Indeed, tokens of certain other types must be excluded too. For example, every dog is a token of the type, *kind of entity such that every actual member of the kind is physically realized*, at least according to realization physicalism. But tokens of this type exist partly in virtue of the nonexistence of any ectoplasm that might serve as the realizer of nonphysically realized dogs; and the nonexistence of ectoplasm is not itself a physical fact. Such restrictions as these, however, on realization physicalism's domain of quantification no doubt complicate the formulation of realization physicalism, but surely they pose no threat to its spirit. For although they are motivated by cases of actual tokens that are not physically realized, the explanation of *why* they are not physically realized is that they are realized in part by certain *absences*, and the role that these absences play provides no encouragement whatever to any familiar sort of antiphysicalist.

Here at last, then, is a canonical formulation of realization physicalism. The domain of quantification is restricted to actual tokens, past, present, or future, that are contingent or causal, and that are not of the types, partially constituted by absences, noted in the preceding paragraph; and the terms "physical" and "physically realized" are to be understood as defined above:

> (R) Every property instance is *either* an instance of a physical property *or* a physically realized instance of some functional property; every object is *either* an object of some physical object kind *or* a physically realized object of some functional object kind; every event is *either* an event of some physical event kind *or* a physically realized event of some functional event kind.

According to realization physicalism, then, the world contains a certain distribution of physical tokens, a certain distribution of physical property instances, objects, and events; but because some of these tokens are of physical types that, as a logical consequence of physical facts alone, meet a huge number and variety of associated conditions, $C_1, C_2, \ldots, C_n$, these tokens realize, and so the world also contains, a certain number of tokens of various functional types; however, the physical tokens, together with the functional tokens that some of them realize, are the *only* causal or contingent tokens that the world contains; there are no causal or contingent tokens that are *neither* physical *nor* physically realized. Let me conclude this section with five comments on realization physicalism as now canonically formulated.

First, realization physicalism is a contingent thesis, true at those possible worlds at which the only causal or contingent tokens are either physical or physically realized, but false at those worlds containing tokens that are neither physical nor physically realized. (Tokens that are neither physical nor physically realized might be *either* tokens of nonfunctional types unknown to current physics *or* functional tokens that are not physically realized.) In consequence, because empirical investigation is obviously required to determine what sort of causal or contingent tokens the actual world contains, empirical investigation will be required to determine whether realization physicalism is true – that is, to determine whether the actual world contains any realizationism-falsifying causal or contingent tokens that are neither physical nor physically realized. In Chapter 5 and Chapter 6, of course, we examine what sort of empirical evidence bearing on this issue we currently have.[23]

In fact, realization physicalism is not merely contingent but is *strongly* contingent, in the sense that it is true just so long as every token in the *actual* world is either physical or physically realized, regardless of the character of other possible worlds; it may be contrasted, therefore, with the thesis Kim calls "physical realizationism" (1998, 19), which claims that mental properties not only are but *must* be physically realized. Is the strong contingency of realization physicalism too much contingency? I confine myself to two remarks.

1. It would not be plausible to turn realization physicalism into a lawful thesis by claiming that, as a matter of natural law, every token is physical or physically realized. For *what law* could it be that would guarantee the physicality or physical realization of every token? Certainly not a law of physics, or else physicalism would *follow* from the laws of physics, which surely it does not, since nonphysicalist worlds in which the laws of physics

---

23 My inference from contingency to a posteriority may seem too swift, in light of Kripke's famous argument that some claims, though contingent, are nevertheless knowable a priori (1980). But although David Chalmers and Frank Jackson both try, in effect, to exploit Kripke's arguments in the interests of showing that physicalism *is* knowable a priori, I think they fail. For a sketch of their attempts, plus the gist of my response, see note 36.

are fully respected seem perfectly possible. But then what other kind of law? Certainly no law of any special science, either, for the same reason. There is some plausibility to the idea that if physicalism is true in the actual world, then it should also be true in nearby worlds. But this idea may simply reflect the thought that the nearness of a world to the actual world is a matter of resemblance in respect of important truths that hold in the actual world, so that if realization physicalism is an important truth about the actual world, then it is a truth in nearby worlds too, and so the truth of realization physicalism is *not* a mere accident. (Equivalently, perhaps, the universal generalization that expresses realization physicalism may on the same grounds be treated as being *itself* a law.)

2. Still, it *may* be true that realization physicalism, as canonically formulated, is too contingent. For consider a possible world in which every token is in fact physical or physically realized, but in which it is an (uninstantiated) law that if certain physical conditions *were* to obtain, which in fact they never do, though they might easily have done so, then certain tokens neither physical nor physically realized *would* exist; perhaps it is a world in which, if there were a sphere of gold one hundred meters in diameter (though in fact there never is), then an angel would spring into existence. One might judge that physicalism is not entirely true of such a world, as David Chalmers apparently does (1996a, 363–4). But even if one shares Chalmers's judgment, and even if one has no qualms about the very idea of uninstantiated laws of the sort that the example appeals to, the proper response is not to reinforce realization physicalism by modalizing it. One should instead simply add to the still unmodalized (R) an explicit denial that any uninstantiated laws of the troublesome sort in fact hold, a denial that is surely very plausible empirically, since we have no reason whatever to believe in any laws like the imagined law about a golden sphere. If someone wished to amend realization physicalism in this way, by conjoining (R) with such a denial, then I would have no strong objection.

Before I can make my next three comments about (R), I must introduce a distinction between three senses in which we may speak of the *realizer* of a functional token; the distinction is not perfectly precise, but it is useful all the same.[24] Suppose that a token of functional type, F, with associated condition, C, is physically realized; so it is one and the same as the token of F whose existence is logically guaranteed by the existence of a certain

---

24 This threefold distinction is inspired, of course, by Sydney Shoemaker's twofold distinction between the core and total realizations of a functional property (1984, 265).

token of some physical type, P, that meets C, where P's meeting C is a logical consequence only of the obtaining of external or historical physical conditions and the holding of physical laws. Let us call this realizing P-token the *narrow realizer* of the F-token in question, just so long as the type, P, of which it is a token is the *simplest* physical type (given the physical laws and the external or historical physical conditions) still sufficient to meet C. Intuitively, the narrow realizer is located just where we would ordinarily locate the F-token in question.[25] Let the *broad realizer* of the F-token in question be the narrow realizer, *plus* the fewest external or historical physical conditions needed to ensure (given the physical laws) that P meets C. Finally, let the *very broad realizer* of the functional token in question be the broad realizer, *plus* the holding of the fewest physical laws needed to ensure that P meets C.

Now for the second comment about (R): although realization physicalism requires that every nonphysical token should have a narrow realizer that is physical, it does not impose any requirement to the effect that every nonphysical token must be *composed of (chemical) atoms* in the sense of having atoms as current spatiotemporal parts; it is *consistent* with every nonphysical token's having atoms as current spatiotemporal parts, but it does not require it. To see why realization physicalism does not impose this requirement, recall, first, that my favored definition of "physical" allows a token (e.g., a complex system) to qualify as physical even though it is large ("macro"), and/or working physicists need never speak of it as such, and/or it is emergent in the sense that its existence is not derivable from putatively more basic physical phenomena unless appeal is made to contingent micro-macro laws of composition that are in no way explainable in terms of other laws. Note, second, that, for all that (R) says, such a physical token can perfectly well serve as the narrow realizer of a functional token (e.g., a particular cell). However, and this is the point, such a physical token need not have as current spatiotemporal *parts* the atoms from which, as *ingredients*, it might have been made. Such a physical token would presumably *have* spatiotemporal parts, but these parts would

---

25 The motivation for imposing the requirement that a narrow realizer be a token of the simplest physical type still sufficient to meet C is as follows: if a given physical type, of which t is a token, meets C, then quite likely some more *complex* physical type, of which t' is a token, where t' includes t as a proper spatiotemporal part, will also meet C. Intuitively, however, t', the "bigger" physical token, will include parts that are *redundant* when it comes to explaining why the functional token in question is realized where it is realized. So the "smaller" physical token, t, seems a better candidate to be the realizer of the functional token in question.

not be atoms (although they would surely be characterizable in physical terms). Such a physical token might also be *made from* atoms, in the sense that it came into existence when certain atoms were brought into suitable physical relations with one other; but those atoms might have lost their essential properties and hence passed out of existence when the physical token came into existence. An (imperfect) analogy might be drawn with the two ingredient eggs from which a cake is made: the cake is certainly made *from* the eggs, but once the cake has been made the eggs no longer exist (if someone asks me for two eggs, I can hardly hand them the baked cake and say, "Here you are; have these two"); so the baked cake is not made *of* eggs.[26]

Third, nothing in (R) commits realization physicalism to the idea that reality constitutes a neat and tidy hierarchy of "levels," in which each level is the bailiwick of a particular branch of science. Indeed, the notion of "levels" is not even mentioned in (R). So when philosophers point out difficulties with the "levels" idea, the realizationist can happily agree – on condition, of course, that the difficulties raised provide no reason to think that any actual token is neither physical nor physically realized. For example, John Dupré claims that the constituents of an aardvark include both cells and hormones, things that appear to belong to *different* "levels" (1993, 102); but even if his claim be granted, it evidently casts no doubt on the realizationist thesis that cells and hormones are in fact physically realized. In fact, nothing in (R) even commits realization physicalism to the idea that physical realizers are at a different ("lower") "level" than the tokens they realize. For if "levels" are defined in terms of *scale* (as talk of "microlevel" and "macrolevel" suggests), then a physical token serving as the narrow realizer of a nonphysical token (e.g., a cell) will presumably be on the same scale, and hence at the same "level," as the token it realizes. It will count as physical in virtue of meeting the definition of "physical" presented in Section 2, but that definition allows physical tokens that are as large as you like. I can agree with Jaegwon Kim, then, when he says

---

26 In this paragraph I have been trying to show that realization physicalism is not committed either to what Paul Humphreys calls "ontological minimalism," which includes a compositionalist claim (1997b, S337–8), or to what he calls "atomism" (65); and also to accommodate the possibility that some macrophysical phenomena are emergent in Humphreys's sense (61 and 65). But I may easily have misunderstood him. In particular, if his true view is that emergent macrophysical phenomena that come into existence when appropriate microphysical entities are brought into suitable physical relations with one another have no proper parts *at all*, so that they are metaphysical *simples*, then realization physicalism cannot be squared with his view. (On the other hand, it does not need to be, since such a view is very implausible.)

that "the realization relation does not track the micro-macro relation" (1998, 82; emphasis removed) and that "Physicalism... should not be identified... with microphysicalism" (1998, 117).

Fourth, as inspection of (R) and of the definition of "physically realized" will reveal, realization physicalism does not require that the physical type to which a token that narrowly realizes a functional token belongs should fall into the same ontological category as the functional type to which the functional token being realized belongs. It does not require, for instance, that a token of a functional *object* kind should be realized by a token of a physical *object* kind; its narrow physical realizer might be a token of a physical type falling into a different category – for example, it might be a token of a physical *event* kind. The absence of this requirement leaves the realization physicalist free to claim, perhaps with greater plausibility, that living organisms, for instance, are realized by tokens of physical *processes* (perhaps to be understood as causally related sequences of events), rather than physical *objects*.

Finally, realization physicalism entails that, for every nonphysical token that falls within the scope of (R), there are physical conditions – the token's very broad realizer – that in the strongest sense necessitate the nonphysical token's existence: the nonphysical token exists in *all* possible worlds in which the very broad realizer exists.[27] For suppose that a token of some functional type, F, with associated condition, C, is physically realized, so that, by definition, it is realized by a certain token of a physical type that meets C, and which indeed meets C as a logical consequence of physical facts alone. Then, given certain physical facts (i.e., the existence of this physical token, the holding of certain physical laws, and perhaps also the holding of certain external or historical physical conditions), there *must* exist a token of a type that meets C. But given the existence of a token of a type that meets C, there *must* exist a token of F, since for there to be a token of F just *is* for there to be a token of some type that meets C. Moreover, by the definition of "realized," *this* token of F is one and the same as the F-token we were talking about in the first place. So, given the physical facts first mentioned, the F-token we were talking about in the first place *must* exist.[28] Realization physicalism

---

27 A token falls within the scope of (R), it will be recalled, iff it is an actual token, past, present, or future, that is contingent or causal, and that is not of any of the types, partially constituted by absences, noted immediately prior to the presentation of (R) in Chapter 1, Section 3.

28 In the next chapter, we look more closely at the nature of these very strong *must*s.

entails, therefore, that the physical nature of the world necessitates the nonphysical nature of the world in a very strong sense, a sense strong enough to rule out the idea that the nonphysical nature of the world is *strongly emergent* from the physical nature of the world. For, as we have just seen, the necessitation of the nonphysical by the physical that is entailed by realizationism requires no fundamental physical-to-nonphysical bridge laws. By contrast, of course, the strong emergence of the nonphysical from the physical would require precisely that the nonphysical be derivable from the physical *only* via physical-to-nonphysical bridge laws that are fundamental.

4. REALIZATION PHYSICALISM AND RETENTIVENESS

According to realization physicalism, then, the totality of what exists that is contingent or causal is certain physical tokens, plus whatever functional tokens are guaranteed to exist by the fact that the physical tokens belong to types that meet certain conditions, the meeting of which by tokens of some kind or other logically suffices for the existence of those functional tokens. Now let us call a version of physicalism *retentive* if, and to the extent that, it does not require denying the existence of tokens of special-scientific or honorary-scientific types – those types which are spoken of as such in the special sciences or in the honorary sciences such as folk psychology, folk physics, and other bodies of folk knowledge developed historically as parts of various practical arts and crafts.[29] An obvious question arises: is realization physicalism retentive? Perhaps surprisingly, the canonical formulation of realizationism in the previous section does not by itself entail an answer. For even if realizationism is true, the tokens of functional types guaranteed to exist by whatever physical tokens the world contains might, or might not, be identical with tokens of special- and honorary-scientific types. Realization physicalism will turn out to be retentive only if, and to the extent that, certain functional types whose actual tokens are physically realized turn out to be *identical* with special- and honorary-scientific types.

---

29 Obviously it is less than ideally clear what is to count as an honorary science (though it is quite clear that scientific knowledge, strictly so-called, is not the only knowledge worth retaining). But if commonsense moral claims should turn out to be knowledge, then moral discourse would also qualify as an honorary science. On some interpretations of its subject matter, mathematics would qualify, though the ontology of a platonistically construed mathematics, being neither contingent nor causal, will presumably fall outside the scope of realization physicalism entirely.

Before investigating the prospects for retentive realizationism (i.e., realization physicalism conjoined with the thesis that special- and honorary-scientific types *are* identical with certain functional types whose actual tokens are physically realized), let us pause to notice that such a view would possess two notable attractions. First, it would nicely honor what I shall call the Truthmaker Intuition about physicalism:

> (TI) If physicalism is true, then there must be some sense in which all the true descriptions of the world framed in the proprietary vocabularies of the special- and honorary-sciences are *made true* by the distribution in the world of physical tokens (given the physical laws).

According to (TI), then, physicalism implies that if it *is* true that kidneys, elephants, chairs, itches, and hurricanes exist, then what *makes* it true is, at bottom, the physically lawful doings of physical things; so the very same conditions in the world that make true all manner of physical claims *also* make true all manner of special-scientific and honorary-scientific claims. But (TI), though compelling, can easily seem puzzling; for how *could* propositions formulated in special- or honorary-scientific terms possibly be made true by the antics of physical things, especially if no a priori conceptual analysis can be given of special- or honorary-scientific terms in physical terms? Retentive realizationism, however, not only entails the Truthmaker Intuition; it does so in way that removes this puzzle. For if realization physicalism is retentive, then, by definition, the special- and honorary-scientific types are identical with certain functional types whose actual tokens are all physically realized. But if *any* token of a functional type is physically realized, then, as we have already seen, there are physical facts – the token's very broad realizer – that necessitate in the strongest sense that the token exists, and which therefore make it true that it exists. So if retentive realizationism is true, there must be physical facts that necessitate, and hence make it true, that there exist *all* the tokens of functional types that are identical with the special- and honorary-scientific types. And the reason why the antics of physical things can serve as truth makers for claims expressed in special- or honorary-scientific terms is, of course, the a posteriori identity of special- and honorary-scientific types with certain functional types. So if retentive realizationism is true, then God, having instituted the right physical facts (i.e., the appropriate very broad realizers), and having thereby ensured the truth of certain physical claims, would need to do nothing more in order to ensure the truth of certain special- and honorary-scientific claims also.

The second, and related, attraction of retentive realizationism is that it would not require the postulation of fundamental (i.e., primitive and inexplicable) one-way laws asserting the sufficiency of conditions specified in physical terms for conditions specified in special- or honorary-scientific terms (*pace* Daly 1995, 139). Certainly retentive realizationism entails the existence of one-way laws asserting the sufficiency of conditions specified in physical terms for conditions specified in special- or honorary-scientific terms; for it entails that, for every actual condition specifiable in special- or honorary-scientific terms, there is a condition specifiable in physical terms – its broad realizer – that, as a matter of (physical) law, is sufficient for it.[30] But retentive realizationism does not entail that these one-way laws are primitive and inexplicable. For, according to retentive realizationism, the fact that the broad realizer of a given special- or honorary-scientific condition is physically sufficient for it can be explained as the consequence of (i) the physical sufficiency of the broad realizer for a certain *functional* condition, plus (ii) the (metaphysical) sufficiency of this functional condition for the special- or honorary-scientific condition with which it is identical.[31]

So retentive realizationism is an attractive formulation of physicalism. But in order for it to be true, of course, special- and honorary-scientific types must in fact be identical with functional types whose actual tokens are physically realized.[32] However, as we saw in the previous section, a token can be physically realized only if it is a token of a functional type whose associated condition can be specified in physical or quasi-logical terms. So the truth of retentive realizationism requires that special- and honorary-scientific types should be identical with functional types of this special kind. Now this requirement certainly looks ridiculously hard to meet (especially since "physical" is defined by reference to serious physics) if you assume that the statements reporting the requisite identities must

---

30 The entailment arises as follows. Given retentive realizationism, every actual condition specifiable in special- or honorary-scientific terms is identical with some or other functional condition that is physically realized. But any functional condition that is physically realized has a broad realizer that, as a matter of (physical) law, is sufficient for it. So if a particular functional condition turns out to be identical with a certain special- or honorary-scientific condition, the functional condition's broad realizer must also be, as a matter of (physical) law, sufficient for the special- or honorary-scientific condition.
31 Chapter 2 elaborates the claims made in this paragraph and its predecessor.
32 Statements reporting such identities are presumably what Jeffrey Poland has in mind when he speaks of the "realization theories" required by the working out of the physicalist program as he understands it (1994, 210–16).

be obvious, or discoverable a priori, perhaps in virtue solely of one's competence with the relevant terms or one's grasp of the relevant concepts. But in fact there is no reason to assume any such thing. Statements reporting the requisite identities, if discoverable at all, will only be discovered a posteriori, nondemonstratively inferred from empirical premises, and even then perhaps only with great difficulty. Here is one way – Chapter 6 describes others – in which we might discover empirically that an a posteriori identity statement is true. First, by observation, we might discover that special-scientific type, P, is tokened in a given location when and only when functional type, F, is tokened in that same location; then, since the hypothesis that $P = F$ would, if true, arguably provide the best explanation of the perfect coincidence (within our experience) of P-tokens and F-tokens, we could argue by inference to the best explanation from our observational finding to the conclusion that in fact $P = F$ (see Hill 1991, 22–6). And conversely, of course, we might have empirical evidence *against* the identity hypothesis that $P = F$: observation of P-tokens in the *absence* of F-tokens would provide such evidence, since the hypothesis that $P = F$ entails that P is tokened at a time in a place iff F is tokened at the same time in the same place.[33]

It might be objected that, whatever empirical evidence might be obtainable for or against the identity statements required by retentive realizationism, we can still know a priori that such statements are false: we know that P *cannot* be F, because we can readily *conceive* that something has P but not F (or vice versa), from which it follows that it is really possible for something to have P but not F and hence that P cannot be (necessarily) identical with F. But the nonidentity of P with F cannot be proved in this way, and here is why. Even though it is surely conceivable that something should have P but not F, in the sense that we can entertain the thought that this is so without explicit contradiction or any sense of conceptual blockage, the real possibility that something should have P but not F just does not follow. Someone competent with the concept of table salt could gain competence with the concept of NaCl in a chemistry class that failed to mention that NaCl is the same stuff as table salt. It would

---

33 Empirical reasoning in favor of an identity hypothesis of the sort here described incidentally shows that, *pace* Frank Jackson (1998a, 57–60), the empirical discovery of a scientific identity statement can proceed entirely without benefit of a priori conceptual analysis; it also shows that what he calls "serious metaphysics," of which he takes defending physicalism to be a prime example, need involve no a priori conceptual analysis at all.

then be conceivable for this person, in the sense specified, to believe that his food could be sprinkled with salt but not with NaCl: he could entertain the thought that this is so without explicit contradiction or any sense of conceptual blockage. But it is not really possible that his food could be sprinkled with salt but not with NaCl, since salt and NaCl are the very same stuff and it is not possible that his food be both sprinkled and not sprinkled with the very same stuff. So the conceivability, in the sense specified, of a proposition does not in general entail its possibility.

The explanation for this failure of entailment is that the reference of our concepts is not an a priori matter: one does not know on the basis *merely* of one's competence with a concept what property that concept picks out.[34] Accordingly, one might be competent with two concepts without realizing that in fact they pick out the very *same* property. (It might be objected that sophisticated thinkers obviously do know simply on the basis of their competence with the relevant concepts that "salt" refers to salt, that "NaCl" refers to NaCl, and so on; maybe, but metalinguistic platitudes such as these evidently provide no hint that "salt" and "NaCl" both refer to the very same stuff.) Someone might therefore entertain the formally consistent thought, "My food is sprinkled with salt but not with NaCl," and in doing so feel no sense of conceptual blockage, even though, given that "salt" and "NaCl" corefer, and that no food is both sprinkled and not sprinkled with the same stuff, this thought expresses no possible state of affairs. Similarly, someone might entertain the formally consistent thought, "Something has P but not F," and in doing so feel no sense of conceptual blockage, even if, because P is the same property as F, and it is impossible that something should both have and not have the very same property, it is impossible that something should have P but not F. So it is because the reference of our concepts is an a posteriori matter that conceivability (in the sense specified) does not

---

34 The reason is simply that, as well-known examples owed to Hilary Putnam and Saul Kripke show, competence with a concept requires so little by way of knowledge about its referent. For those unmoved by such examples, however, I should add that adopting a descriptivist theory of predicative concepts does not guarantee a priori knowledge of the coreferentiality of two concepts one is competent with. Suppose competence with a concept requires associating it with some description uniquely satisfied by the referent. Then if two concepts have different, but consistent, associated definite descriptions, it is not a priori whether or not the two concepts corefer. For the very same referent might satisfy both unique descriptions. This point applies with especial force against a descriptivist, like Frank Jackson (1998b), who allows such descriptions as "is the appropriate (actual) causal origin of uses of term T." Who knows – a priori – what other terms' uses the object that meets this description might also be the appropriate (actual) causal origin of?

entail possibility.³⁵ Someone can infer that her consistent and blockage-free thought that something has P but not F expresses a genuine possibility only if she makes an a posteriori assumption that conceptual competence alone does not guarantee, namely, that "P" and "F" do not pick out the very same property. But this assumption begs the question against retentive realizationism, since it is tantamount to assuming that P is not the same property as F.

So there is, I suggest, no good a priori reason for denying that special- and honorary-scientific types might turn out to be identical with functional types whose associated conditions are specifiable in physical or quasi-logical terms, and hence no good a priori reason for denying retentive realizationism; whether the required identity statements are true can be settled only a posteriori, by seeking relevant empirical evidence.³⁶ On

---

35 Might conceivability nevertheless provide prima facie support for possibility? Only if, and to the extent that, it is reasonable to make the empirical presumption about our minds that distinct concepts generally pick out distinct properties; but I cannot recall ever having seen any evidence for this presumption. Notice that even if, as I am inclined to think, conceivability is no guide at all to possibility, we can still have reason to think that x, which *in fact* has F and G, *might* have had F but not G – by having empirical evidence for the distinctness of F and G (e.g., observational evidence that F and G are not always co-instantiated). A. D. Smith remarks that if, as I recommend, "we sever our beliefs in possibility entirely from conceivability, we shall simply land ourselves with an extreme Megareanism, where the possible and the necessary collapse into the actual" (Smith 1993, 243). Not so, as we have just seen. And, in any case, how could an *epistemological* premise about our knowledge of modality possibly support a *metaphysical* conclusion like Megarianism (unless via an implausible verificationism)?

36 This is a very strong claim, of course, and is denied by both the antiphysicalist David Chalmers and the (now) physicalist Frank Jackson (Chalmers 1996a, ch. 2; Jackson, 1998a, ch. 3; see also A. D. Smith 1993, 248–9). Both philosophers, despite allowing that the references of concepts we are competent with are not known to us a priori, nevertheless hold that we can determine a priori the truth of retentive physicalism. Their reason, roughly, is that retentive physicalism is true iff (in Chalmers's case) it is *inconceivable* that the world should be exactly the way it is physically but differ from how it is nonphysically, or (in Jackson's case) any nonphysical description of the world is in principle *deducible a priori* from a complete physical description of it. But this reason rests on the assumption that what Chalmers calls the *primary intensions* (and Jackson the *A-intensions*) of the concepts we are competent with are accessible to us a priori (even though their actual-world referents are not). But there is no obvious reason to make this assumption about primary (or A-) intensions, and hence no reason to expect the truth of retentive physicalism to be determinable a priori (see Melnyk 2001).

My very strong claim might also be denied by someone who holds that we can know by conceptual analysis, and hence a priori, that P and F fail to have all their properties in common, and hence (by Leibniz's Law) that P ≠ F. Derek Parfit seems to intend some such argumentative strategy when he retains a negative role for conceptual analysis in ruling out certain identity hypotheses. We may not be able to say a priori what heat and experiences *are*, but, he insists, we know a priori what they are *not*. He claims, for example,

the other hand, the retentive realizationist has at least one ground for optimism: because functional types, on my usage, are really just higher-order types, there can be many different *kinds* of functional types, corresponding to the many different kinds of associated conditions in terms of which a functional type can be defined, and so special- or honorary-scientific types that seem poor candidates for identification with functional types of *one* kind may yet turn out to be identifiable with functional types of some *other* kind. One familiar kind of associated condition, of course, is that of playing a certain causal role: to meet the condition, a type must be such that its tokens cause and are caused in certain, specified ways. But an obvious variation would be the playing of a noncausal nomic role: to meet a condition of this sort, a type must be such that, as a matter of law, it is tokened iff (but not *because*) some other, specified type is tokened.

The laws invoked in specifying an associated condition, then, might be causal or noncausal; and we can add that laws of either kind need not be strict and deterministic, but might also be probabilistic or hold only ceteris paribus (however that should turn out to be understood best). Similarly, a lower-order type's meeting of an associated condition might be a matter of its tokens' standing in other relations than nomic ones (e.g. spatiotemporal relations).[37] Again, a type's meeting of an associated condition might require the holding of certain, specified circumstances that are external to, and/or earlier (or indeed later) than, tokens of that type. Consider, for example, genuine coins, whose narrow realizers need to be regarded in a certain way by some population (e.g., desired not for use but exchange) and to have had a certain historical origin (e.g., to have

---

that "heat could not have turned out to be a shade of blue, or a medieval king," and that "experiences could not turn out to be patterns of behavior, or stones, or irrational numbers" (Parfit 1997, 122). But these examples are unconvincing, since, although they are certainly all denials of spectacularly implausible identity hypotheses, we do not need to explain their spectacular implausibility as resulting from our a priori recognition of conceptual impossibilities. (Indeed, perhaps we *cannot* so explain them: none of what Parfit denies strikes *me* as conceptually impossible.) We can explain our high confidence that heat is neither a shade of blue nor a medieval king, and that experiences are not patterns of behavior, stones or irrational numbers, by noting that it is part of our common knowledge, gained a posteriori, that heat, unlike any medieval king, in fact exists today, and that heat is in fact sometimes instantiated where blueness is not; and that experiences in fact have properties that patterns of behavior, stones, and numbers rather obviously lack. In short, there is sound reasoning against the implausible identity hypotheses that applies Leibniz's Law to premises that are, though clearly true, still entirely a posteriori.

37 Here I part company with Kim, in whose terminology a functional type is a second-order type "defined in terms of causal/nomic relations" (1998, 20).

been manufactured in the royal mint). So special- or honorary-scientific types whose tokens do not supervene upon simultaneous and local physical conditions might still be functional types in my sense. Biological types, for instance, might yet be functional types, even though, because they are sometimes defined in terms of a Darwinian selectional history of a certain sort, an atom-for-atom duplicate of (say) my heart that formed by accident in interstellar space would not be a heart. Finally, functional types, and their associated conditions, may be specified in clusters, by means of the technique of Ramsification (see, e.g., Hill 1991, 50–6). The realizationist toolbox, then, contains many tools, usable alone or in combination, for specifying the associated conditions of functional types, and no doubt there are more. That each special- and honorary-scientific type should turn out to be identical with a functional type of *some* kind or other does not seem at all unlikely.

Let me say a little more about one especially interesting kind of associated condition. A paradigm example of a functional property with an associated condition of the kind I have in mind is the computational property of *running program P*. Think of P as a set of rules that relate input states, internal states, and output states to one another in a particular way; but because these states are abstract mathematical states, think of it, not as describing the features, not even the high-level features, of any concrete system, but instead as characterizing a complex, structured mathematical object. We can then say that the property of running P is instantiated iff the following condition holds: there is some (concrete) object and some set of (concrete) state types that it can occupy such that (i) there is a one-one mapping between the abstract states mentioned in P and the members of the set of (concrete) state types, (ii) the object is in a token of one of the state types in that set, and (iii) the tokenings, both actual and counterfactual, of the state types in that set are related to one another in a way that exactly parallels the relations specified to hold (by the rules of P) among their abstract-state correlates (in P).[38]

Now the particular computational properties characterized when "P" has its place taken by particular, specified programs may well be of no special interest in their own right. But they do illustrate the possibility of an associated condition such that a type meets it iff its tokens exhibit a certain *pattern*, constituted by tokens of various types' being related to one

---

38 This way of spelling out what it is for a concrete system to be running or implementing a program is convenient but controversial (see Chalmers 1996b, Copeland 1996, and Melnyk 1996b).

another in mathematically specifiable ways; let us call a functional type defined in terms of such an associated condition a *purely structural* functional type. Physical realization, for a purely structural functional type, would therefore be a matter of pure isomorphism – sheer sameness of abstract structure – between some, presumably very complex, physical thing, on the one hand, and some mathematically describable thing, on the other; and characterization of its associated condition would obviously be in purely quasi-logical terms, with no physical terms required at all. Purely structural functional types are interesting because one aspiration of the emerging field of artificial life and related disciplines investigating complex systems is that of uncovering interesting similarities between complex phenomena in apparently unrelated domains, for example, political systems and the origin of life from nonlife (see Boden 1996). But since these similarities consist in precisely the sort of pure isomorphisms that characterize the associated conditions I am discussing, there is the intriguing possibility that artificial-life research will uncover purely structural functional types that are good candidates for identification with certain special- or honorary-scientific types.

As it happens, there are various special- or honorary-scientific types of traditional philosophical interest that it is somewhat plausible even now to regard as functional in character, even if we certainly do not yet have the details right; and brief discussion of three examples of such types may add verisimilitude to what might otherwise appear a bald and unconvincing narrative. The associated conditions of the functional types with which these three examples may plausibly be identified are not all specified in the exclusively physical or quasi-logical terms that we saw are required for their tokens to be physically realized. Nevertheless, they still represent progress toward identities with functional types whose associated conditions are thus specified. For a functional type whose associated condition is not *now* specified in purely physical or quasi-logical terms need not be unacceptable to realizationism, because the types mentioned in the specification of the associated condition might turn out *themselves* to be functional ones whose associated conditions can be specified in exclusively physical or quasi-logical terms, which would then permit (by substitution) a specification of the associated condition of the *original* functional type in exclusively physical or quasi-logical terms. Or maybe there is a longer chain running downward from a functional type whose associated condition is not specified in exclusively physical or quasi-logical terms to functional types that are so specified; still the result will be that the associated condition of the original functional type is specifiable in exclusively physical or quasi-logical terms, thus allowing for its tokens to be physically realized.

1. What makes it the case that a brain state has the property of representing that there are Ps? Jerry Fodor's asymmetric nomic dependence theory of mental representation purports to answer this question, claiming (approximately) that tokens of a state type, S, represent that there are Ps if (i) it is a ceteris paribus law that Ps cause tokens of S, and (ii) if it is a ceteris paribus law that tokens of any other type cause tokens of S, then this law depends asymmetrically upon the law that Ps cause tokens of S, in this sense: if the nomic link between Ps and Ss were broken, then any nomic link between non-Ps and Ss would be broken too, whereas if any nomic link between non-Ps and Ss were broken, the nomic link between Ps and Ss would not be broken (Fodor 1990). But Fodor's theory can easily be turned into an account of a functional property that it would not be too implausible to identify with the property of representing that there are Ps: something possesses this functional property if something has some or other property, Q, such that (i) it is a ceteris paribus law that Ps cause Q-instances, and (ii) if it is a ceteris paribus law that tokens of any other type cause Q-instances, then this law depends asymmetrically upon the law that Ps cause Q-instances. Obviously Fodor's theory is highly controversial (see, e.g., Adams and Aizawa 1994); but it surely has enough plausibility to make it seem really possible – no mere fantasy – that representing should turn out to be a functional property.

2. Consider now genes. Many philosophers have suggested identifying genes with (something like) segments of DNA, but Michael Levin has proposed treating the gene for, say, heights that fall within a specific range as a correlation (or mapping) between, on the one hand, environments (e.g., dietary regimes) and, on the other, phenotypes (e.g., specific heights). He also makes the less radical proposal that this gene should be regarded as that thing in the organism, whatever it is, which *explains* the capacity of the organism to reach different heights under different dietary regimes, that thing turning out, as it happens, to be a certain DNA segment (Levin 1997b, 83–4). But there is an attractive functionalist proposal intermediate between his two suggestions: the gene for heights that fall within a specific range should be identified with that functional object kind which is exemplified iff an object of some or other object kind is exemplified that, under dietary regime, D_1, produces height, H_1; under dietary regime, D_2, produces height, H_2; and so forth. This identification would leave open the possibility of genes not realized by segments of DNA; but, on the other hand, it would make genes more robust than mere

correlations. A more satisfactory version of the proposal would, of course, take into account the fact that what phenotype a given gene produces is affected also by what other genes are possessed by the organism to which it belongs.

3. Finally, consider the property of being alive. Inspired presumably by Aristotle, modern biologists find it plausible to treat a thing as alive if it possesses some, or all, or perhaps most, of some range of capacities, capacities for such things as nutrition, growth, stability, purposeful behavior, and reproduction. A functional understanding of the property of being alive naturally suggests itself: it is the functional property that is instantiated iff an object of some or other kind exists that possesses properties of some or other kind that enable it to take in resources from the environment and convert them into parts of itself, to make (approximate) copies of itself, and to sustain itself in existence in the face of some, though not all possible, changes in its environment. Something along these lines is surely very plausible (for critical discussion, however, see, Bedau 1996).

So far, I have been optimistic about the prospects of realization physicalism in retentive form. But we should now consider how heavy a blow for realization physicalism it would be if it turned out, despite my optimism, that special- and honorary-scientific types could *not* be identified with functional types, as required by retentive realizationism. Because a realization physicalist must deny the existence of tokens belonging to any special- or honorary-scientific types that cannot be identified with functional types of the requisite sort, the crucial question becomes how implausible those denials of existence would be. The answer to this question, I claim, depends upon what else, in addition to the denials, the realizationist could plausibly say.

Suppose it turns out that, for some reason or other, the property of being alive cannot plausibly be identified with any functional type of the required sort. Then the realizationist must go nonretentive, at least about life, and therefore deny that anything is ever alive. Now at first blush, of course, it sounds like a damning indictment of realizationism that it should require such a maneuver. But the matter is a little more subtle than that. It would certainly be very implausible to claim that nothing is alive, *if* such a claim were taken to imply that there is no important distinction whatever between paradigmatically living things, like trees, tigers, and dolphins, and paradigmatically nonliving things, like mountains and stars; or if such a claim were taken to imply – even worse – that volumes of space ordinarily thought to contain such paradigmatically living things as trees, tigers, or dolphins are in fact *empty*. Compare, perhaps, the claim that there are no gods, a denial that *does* imply both that there is no important distinction between paradigmatic gods (e.g., Jesus) and paradigmatic nongods (e.g., Quine), and that volumes of space (e.g., the upper atmosphere, Mount Olympus) thought to contain gods are in fact empty.

But the realizationist who denies that anything is ever alive need not be committed to either implication. On the one hand, the realizationist can consistently maintain that such paradigmatically living things as trees do differ in interesting and systematic ways from such paradigmatically nonliving things as mountains, in that the former but not the latter instantiate various functional properties (e.g., the capacity to make approximate copies of oneself) that we strongly associate with being alive and that may even serve us as criteria for judging that something is alive (even if, because of certain nonparadigmatic cases, the property of being alive cannot be *identified* with possession of those properties). On the other hand, the realizationist can consistently maintain that all the volumes of space ordinarily thought to contain living things do in fact contain physically realized objects of some kind or other, perhaps even objects that instantiate the functional properties just mentioned. As a consequence, a realizationist can deny that anything is alive while at the same time (a) finding *some* truth in the erroneous conviction that there are living things (for a falsehood may still imply many truths); and (b) explaining how the conviction nevertheless *is* erroneous, to the extent that it is (the explanation is that there do exist things importantly *like* living things in all the places where we took living things to be, so that our ordinary distinction between living and nonliving things tends to track a genuine distinction in the world, and our error in supposing that there really are living things is entirely understandable). So although denying that anything is alive does require convicting ordinary believers of error, it does not require convicting them of total or unintelligible error. It cannot therefore be dismissed as just *obviously* misguided. Indeed, if the nonretentive realizationist can find, for each type that is eliminated, a good enough *replacer,* as we might call it, nonretentive realizationism may emerge as scarcely less plausible intuitively than the retentive realizationism that (we are assuming) cannot be true.

Can an antirealizationist renew the attack on realization physicalism in the face of this sort of response? Yes, but only by arguing that tokens of the eliminated special- or honorary-scientific type T exist *in addition* to whatever replacers the realizationist acknowledges exist, so that realization physicalism has still left something out; for example, by arguing that trees, tigers, and dolphins possess a nonfunctional property of being alive *in addition* to whatever functional properties they may possess. Arguing this, however, will require doing something that may not be very easy, namely, producing evidence for the existence of tokens of T – the genuine article – that cannot be accounted for equally well by the hypothesis that only tokens of T's replacer exist. For example, it may seem as obvious as anything could be that trees are alive; but what evidence could you produce to show that trees possess the property of being alive, where this property is explicitly understood as a property entirely over and above their having the capacity to grow, to make approximate copies of themselves, to turn components of their environment into parts of themselves, and so forth? From the comfort of your armchair, at least, none at all.

Let me turn now to a different concern. The worry that realizationism might require the elimination of many special- and honorary-scientific types is the worry that it is committed to *less* than commonsense sanctions; but one might also worry that it is committed, objectionably, to *more* than commonsense sanctions. One form of this second worry is a version of Peter Unger's problem of the many (Unger 1980).[39] Suppose we consider a chair-shaped volume of space that we ordinarily take to be occupied by one, and only one, chair. Then, if retentive realizationism is true, this volume of space must contain some physical system – call it P – that plays the chair role. The trouble is, however, that this volume of space seems to contain any number of *other* physical systems that share nearly all of their microphysical parts with P but which are numerically distinct from it and from one another. For the volume of space containing the chair will contain many other systems that count as physical by the second clause of our definition of "physical" – that is, many other systems of types that are expressible by some predicate constructible out of the positive predicates of current physics via the use of such predicate-forming machinery as the language of physics already contains, as well as of (possibly infinitary) conjunction and disjunction, and negation, so long as (i) the constructed predicate does not express a necessary property (e.g., that of either being a quark or not being a quark) and (ii) the constructed predicate is not entirely negative; and it is hard to see a reason for denying the existence of these other physical systems that would not *also* be a reason for denying the existence of *any* physical system that could possibly serve as a physical realizer of the chair (e.g., system P). But since, by hypothesis, P plays the chair role, then so also does each of these other systems; for they

---

39 It was first expressed to me several years ago by Terry Horgan; but a similar worry has recently been formulated by Trenton Merricks (1998) as part of an argument against a form of supervenience physicalism.

differ from P only in respect of a few microparticles, the presence or absence of which surely could not make the difference between playing and not playing the chair role. But since each such numerically distinct physical system plays the chair role, and since the playing of the chair role by some or other physical system is sufficient for there to be a chair, retentive realization entails that the volume of space that we took to contain just one chair actually contains many chairs; indeed, it entails that, as you read this, you are sitting on countless chairs.

To begin with, let us not exaggerate how embarrassing a consequence for retentive realizationism this result is, even if it is accepted at face value. It certainly does not show retentive realization to be false beyond any possible doubt, for any commonsense opinion, even if universally held, might conceivably be false. Nor is this a case in which a view entails a consequence that is incredible in the literal sense that one cannot get oneself to believe it: for once it is made clear that the putatively many chairs on which one is sitting share nearly all of their parts, rather than being, say, stacked up on top of one another, it is easy to believe that one is sitting on indefinitely many chairs. Nor, third, is this a case in which the evidence of one's senses is outrageously defied. For suppose that there *were* indefinitely many chairs occupying some volume of space we ordinarily take to contain only one, but that, as envisaged, they differed from one another only in microphysical ways that unaided human vision cannot detect; then our visual and tactile experience of the occupant(s) of that volume of space would be introspectively indistinguishable from how it actually is, so that if you *were* sitting right now on indefinitely many chairs, though in the way envisaged, it would feel and look to you exactly as if you were sitting on one chair. Nor, finally, has retentive realizationism been shown to have committed any offense against Ockham's razor. For since each of the many chairs has a very broad realizer, and since, if a token is physically realized, its existence is logically necessitated by its very broad realizer, the existence of each of the many chairs is logically necessitated by the way things are physically. So even if retentive realizationism is *committed* to many chairs, it does not postulate them as *fundamental* items in addition to the physical reality it is already committed to; and to offend against Ockham's razor, properly understood, you must postulate *fundamental* entities beyond necessity. Biting the bullet, then, is a defensible option for the retentive realizationist.

In fact, the potentially embarrassing result should not be taken at face value; for the reasoning that generates it can be used to generate an equally embarrassing result for a view that nearly everyone would accept (compare Lewis 1993, 24–5; Merricks 1998, 66). Surely there is a sense of "constituted by," acceptable to nearly everyone, according to which your car is constituted by a certain system of macroscopic, fully observable components, a system located where your car is located. But exactly the same system of components, minus a bolt or two, or minus even a large subsystem like the air-conditioner, would also constitute a car. So, because the volume of space containing your car also in fact contains this shrunken system, it turns out to contain two numerically distinct constituters of cars, and hence two cars. Notice that the view embarrassed by this reasoning could be combined with the idea that auto components are made of *ectoplasm*; and with a construal of "constituted by" as reflecting the holding of brute laws of emergence whereby the existence of suitable systems of auto components brings into existence certain entirely independent objects (viz. cars) that might conceivably exist while no auto components do – so the view embarrassed need not be physicalist or, even in a very mild sense, reductionist.

But if the potentially embarrassing result should not be taken at face value, because the reasoning that generates it also threatens very plausible views that need not entail physicalism, then what exactly is wrong with that reasoning? It may trade on an equivocation between different ways of counting (see Lewis 1993, 33–4). Retentive realizationism has the consequence that I am now sitting on more than one chair only if we count by numerical identity, that is, only if we take it as a sufficient condition of there being more than one chair that some x is a chair and some y is a chair and $x \neq y$. In everyday life, however, at least much of the time, we do not take the sheer numerical distinctness of x and y, even if x and y are both Fs, as sufficient for there to be two Fs. For example, if you and I enter a cafe and I say, "There's a table with two chairs," then you will understand me to have said something that implies that we can each have a chair to ourselves; if there turn out to be two numerically distinct chairs that nevertheless share 99.99 percent of their microphysical parts, you will rightly feel that you have been made the victim of a poor philosophical joke. In everyday life, then, we often seem to count by some such principle as this: there are two Fs only if some x is an F and some y is an F and $x \neq y$, *and* x and y have no (or at least very few) parts in common. And it is easy to see why for practical purposes the sheer numerical nonidentity of x and y, where both are Fs, is of no interest to us: we may wish to take x and y to opposite ends of the earth, which we cannot do if they share most of their parts. So what common sense asserts when it asserts that there is just one chair may be this: at least one chair is there, and every chair that is there is either identical with it *or else* shares nearly all its parts with it. But in that case, what common sense asserts and retentive realizationism entails are consistent. For what retentive realization entails is merely that at least one chair is there, and not every chair that is there is identical with it. And this does not exclude the possibility that all the distinct chairs nevertheless share nearly all their parts.[40]

A second form of the worry that realization physicalism is committed to more than is sanctioned by common sense claims that it is committed to an excess, not of tokens, but of types. The worry is that we can give stipulative definitions of functional types that are distinct from any of the special- or honorary-scientific types but whose tokens are in fact physically realized. The realizationist must then allow not only that tokens of these gerrymandered functional types exist but that they are every bit as real as tokens of those physically realized functional types that *can* be identified with special- or honorary-scientific types. For example, the realizationist must allow that *glurbiness* can be stipulated to be the property of being within a meter of either a photon or an object whose mass exceeds 0.34 kilograms, that glurbiness is therefore a perfectly respectable functional property, and that in fact the world is certain to contain many items that really are glurby, just as it contains many items that really are red, toxic, or exploding.

This objection, however, has little force. Everyone, and not just the realizationist, must allow that the world turns out to contain items that really are glurby, and for a very simple reason: that some things are glurby *follows logically* from the definition of "glurby" plus the undisputed physical facts, just as it follows logically from the definition of "grue" plus the fact that my lawn was often observed before 2000 to be green that my lawn was grue in 1999. In neither case does one have a choice, logically speaking, about whether to acknowledge the truth of certain predications and hence whether to acknowledge the existence of instances of the property in question.[41] Moreover, because, in merely acknowledging a commitment

---

40 Although I borrow this line from Lewis, I should point out that he (1993, 28–31 and 34–6) holds that for its complete solution the problem of the many requires in addition a supervaluationist response.

41 The operative assumption here is that every truly applied predicate expresses a property, but only in the *modest* sense of "property" introduced in Section 1, according to which talk of properties is not meant to imply that properties are *universals*, but merely to serve as a way of talking about what it is in the world that makes true predications objectively true. I do not claim that this modest sense of "property" is the only, or even an ordinary, sense of the term.

forced upon one, one has not strictly speaking *postulated* anything at all, in neither case is one guilty, *contra* Ockham, of postulating property instances *beyond necessity*.

But even if the reality of glurbiness is admitted, what of the further objection that, implausibly, realizationism makes glurbiness *equally* as real as (say) toxicity? To begin with, it is not *obvious* that glurbiness is any less real than toxicity. Doubtless there are many differences between glurbiness and toxicity: glurbiness is expressed by no familiar word of any natural language; it lacks both practical and theoretical interest to us; it presumably stands in few interesting nomological relations to other properties; and, for all we know, it may turn out to be something of a strain for minds made like ours to represent. But why suppose that these differences entail that glurbiness is any less *real* than toxicity? Moreover, it is not even clear that the very idea of *degrees* of reality – as presupposed by the charge that glurbiness is *less* real than toxicity – makes any sense. But, finally, even if it does, then, in order to produce an objection to realization physicalism, evidence would still be needed for holding that special- and honorary-scientific types (like toxicity) are *in fact* more real, in the specified sense, than glurbiness and its ilk. (Without such evidence, of course, the realizationist can just say that part of what we discover when we discover the truth of physicalism is that the special- and honorary-scientific types are not as real as we had previously thought, because they turn out to be no more – though no less – real than glurbiness.) Thus, suppose it were proposed that, even though certain objects really are glurby, and hence glurbiness is a property (albeit in a modest sense of "property"), glurbiness is still less real than toxicity because glurbiness is not, while toxicity is, a genuine *universal*. There would still be no objection to realization physicalism until and unless evidence were provided that toxicity *is* a genuine universal. And it is not even clear what such evidence *could* be, given that it would need to show *more* than that some things really are toxic. I conclude, then, that although realizationism is indeed committed to the existence of tokens of all kinds of bizarrely unfamiliar functional types, there is as yet no cause for concern.

2

But Why Not Supervenience?

1. REALIZATIONISM, SUPERVENIENCE, AND PHYSICAL NECESSITATION

The recent literature on the problem of formulating physicalism has construed physicalism as, or as importantly including, some thesis of global supervenience to the effect, roughly, that any possible world that is indiscernible from the actual world physically is indiscernible from the actual world *simpliciter*. The exact role that the supervenience thesis is intended to play in the formulation of physicalism varies from author to author and is sometimes left rather obscure. John Haugeland (1982) seems to take an appropriate global supervenience claim to constitute the whole of physicalism, as do David Lewis (1983a), Terry Horgan (1987), and Frank Jackson (1998a). Geoffrey Hellman and Frank Thompson (1975) and John Post (1987) hold that at least some additional claim of physical exhaustion is required, but I do not know what exactly they regard as sufficient; perhaps they regard a supervenience thesis (or equivalent claim) as expressing physicalism about *properties*, whereas other claims are required to express physicalism about *particulars*.

As we saw in the previous chapter, however, realization physicalism departs from this recent tradition by making no explicit claim of supervenience.[1] But such a departure requires explanation. For

---

[1] It also departs from tradition in eschewing claims of type and token identity with the physical. Although it is *consistent* with indefinitely many claims of type identity with the physical, it does not *require* the identity of every (or even any) type with some or other physical type, even in its retentive form. It does not even appear committed to the identity of every *token* with some or other physical token. So it promises to be a version of physicalism that avoids commitment to customary physicalist identity claims concerning both types *and* tokens. Of

realizationism, especially in its retentive guise, is committed to a posteriori identity claims that, despite my best efforts, may strike even physicalist readers as implausibly strong, or at least as needlessly risky; moreover, it will be no surprise to learn that, as I argue in Chapter 3, retentive realizationism has consequences that are reductionist – or, if not reductionist, then just as likely as reductionism to be found offensive by those who find reductionism offensive. So why not formulate physicalism in terms of global supervenience – and in doing so avoid the strong and perhaps offensively reductionist commitments of (retentive) realizationism? The answer I defend in the second section of this chapter is that it is very doubtful that global supervenience *can* provide an alternative (i.e., non-realizationist) way of formulating physicalism that avoids commitments as strong, and allegedly objectionable, as those of realizationism. But before I get to that, let me first clarify the relationship between realizationism and a variety of modal claims, including claims of supervenience, so as to provide a clear backdrop for the critical discussion to follow.

As we saw in Chapter 1, realization physicalism entails that, for every nonphysical token that falls within the scope of (R), there are physical conditions – the token's very broad realizer – that necessitate the existence of that token.[2] For consider some particular nonphysical but physically realized token that falls within the scope of (R), and suppose that it is a token of nonphysical type F, with associated condition C; then, given the existence of a physical narrow realizer, the holding of certain physical laws, and also the holding of any external or historical physical conditions that are relevant, there must exist a token of a type that meets C; but given the

---

course, it does not follow from the fact that two things are numerically distinct that they stand in no interesting ontological, and more than purely causal or nomological, relation to one another; one might realize the other, or constitute it (on constitution, see Baker 1999 and Thomson 1998).

As it happens, there may be positive reason to deny that every nonphysical token is identical with a physical token. Considerations of modal discernibility tell against identifying every object with a physical object (see, e.g., Baker 1997 and Melnyk 1995a) and every event with a physical event (see, e.g., Boyd 1980 and Burge 1993), although it is not obvious that the essentialist metaphysics assumed by such arguments can be made plausible, especially for physicalists. As for property instances, it is plausible that, like events in Kim's sense, "two" property instances can be one and the same only if each is an instance of the *same* property; but then instances of nonphysical properties cannot be identical with the instances of distinct physical properties that realize them.

2 A token falls within the scope of (R), it will be recalled, iff it is an actual token, past, present, or future, that is contingent or causal, and that is not of any of the types, partially constituted by absences, noted immediately prior to the presentation of (R) in Chapter 1, Section 3.

existence of a token of a type that meets C, there must exist a token of F, since for there to be a token of F just *is* for there to be a token of some type that meets C; moreover, by the definition of "realized," *this* token of F is one and the same as the F-token we were talking about in the first place; so, given the physical facts first mentioned, the token of F we were talking about in the first place must exist. Now an immediate consequence of this claim is that if realizationism is true, then (given the physical laws that hold in the actual world) the distribution in the actual world of physical tokens necessitates the existence of all the tokens of nonphysical types, falling within the scope of (R), that the actual world contains. For consider any possible world that has exactly the same distribution of physical tokens as does the actual world, and in which exactly the same laws of physics hold as hold in the actual world. Because the physical tokens in such a world will evidently meet exactly the same (physical or quasi-logical) associated conditions as they meet in the actual world, it follows that they will realize in such a world all the tokens of nonphysical types that they realize in the actual world. But because, given realizationism, *all* actual tokens of nonphysical types, falling within the scope of (R), are physically realized, it follows that such a world will therefore contain *all* the tokens of nonphysical types, falling within the scope of (R), that the actual world contains (i.e., it will at least contain, for every token of a nonphysical type, falling within the scope of (R), that the actual world contains, an identically located token of the same nonphysical type). Realization physicalism is therefore committed at least to the following modal claim:

> (M) Any possible world that (a) has exactly the same distribution of physical tokens as does the actual world and in which (b) exactly the same laws of physics hold as hold in the actual world contains all the tokens of nonphysical types, falling within the scope of (R), that the actual world contains.[3]

Four closely related points about this result require emphasis. First, although (M) is a consequence of realization physicalism, and hence true if realizationism is true, it is arguably an unimportant consequence from the point of view of the metaphysical project of rendering

---

3   Robert Kirk (1996a and 1996b) has offered a formulation of physicalism *directly* in terms of a claim to the effect that the physical necessitates everything else, in the hope thereby of avoiding some of the difficulties with, and explicitly as an alternative to, supervenience formulations. In fact, however, his formulation runs into precise analogs of the problems I go on in this chapter to raise for supervenience formulations (see Melnyk 1998).

transparently intelligible the nature of the relations between physical entities, on the one hand, and special- and honorary-scientific ones, on the other. For we can distinguish between an explanatory factor and what *follows* from an explanatory factor; and surely it is the realizationist thesis that every special- and honorary-scientific token is either physical or physically realized that throws metaphysical light on the relationship between physical entities and special- and honorary-scientific ones, rather than the modal claim, (M), that follows from the realizationist thesis.

To appreciate the second point, we should first note that (M) provides an attractive way of articulating the intuitively compelling idea that if physicalism is true, then the physical facts *determine* the (positive) nonphysical facts. The second point, then, is that realizationism, by entailing (M), can plausibly be seen as *explaining* why (M) is true – that is, as explaining *why* the physical facts determine the nonphysical facts. The explanation, in a nutshell, is that the physical facts entail (syntactically or analytically) the existence of tokens of certain functional types; but because these functional types are (necessarily) identical with the special- and honorary-scientific types, the existence of the functional tokens in turn metaphysically necessitates the existence of the special- and honorary-scientific tokens.[4] Furthermore, as we noted in the previous chapter, since (because an explanation of this sort is available) realization physicalism does not have to treat the determination of the (positive) nonphysical facts by the physical facts as brute and inexplicable, it is not committed to the existence of *fundamental bridge laws* that specify, for each condition characterized nonphysically, some condition characterized physically that is physically sufficient for it (i.e., logically or metaphysically sufficient for it, given the physical laws).

Third, a realizationist can also provide an attractive account of the *necessity* recorded by (M). To see how, let "P" be a complete physical description of the actual world (not including the physical laws), let "L" express all the laws of physics that hold in the actual world, and let "N" be a statement, framed in the proprietary vocabularies of the special and honorary

---

4   Note that the identities invoked here, like identities in general, do not seem to need explanation. Of course, we might want to explain how, if "a = b" is true, "a" and "b" manage to be coreferential; and we might want justification for believing that "a = b" is true in the first place; but it seems misconceived to ask why a = b (when it is). Presumably this is so because identities hold necessarily, and it makes sense to explain why something is the case only if it might not have been the case.

sciences, that asserts the existence of all those tokens of nonphysical types, falling within the scope of (R), that actually exist. Then (M) entails that:

(M*) Necessarily, if P and L, then N.

The necessity operator here expresses the strongest sort of necessity, since it has to express the idea, made explicit in (M), that *any possible world whatever* in which it is true that P and L is one in which it is also true that N. But what, if anything, *explains* the strong necessity of "If P and L, then N"? Realizationism answers that the conditional's strong necessity need not be treated as a brute modal fact, for it has an explanation of the following sort. From the claim that P and L, it follows, via rules of natural deduction, together with analytic trivialities of the sort mentioned in the previous chapter (e.g., "If something has charge, then it has at least one property"), that there exist many tokens of certain functional types whose associated conditions are specifiable in physical or quasi-logical terms; let "F" assert their existence, specifying exactly which tokens they are and of what types. Now "F" does not immediately entail that N, either analytically or via rules of natural deduction, because while "F" is expressed in physical or quasi-logical terms, "N" is by contrast expressed in the proprietary terms of the special and honorary sciences, and there are, I take it, no analytic connections between physical terms and those of the special and honorary sciences. However, retentive realizationism claims that every (tokened) special- and honorary-scientific type is *identical* with some or other functional type whose associated condition is specifiable in physical or quasi-logical terms; moreover, given realizationism, it is precisely these functional types whose tokening follows from the claim that P and L. But if, given the claim that P and L, it follows that F (i.e., that tokens of these functional types exist), and if these functional types just *are* those special- and honorary-scientific types asserted to be tokened by the claim that N, it follows intuitively that, given the claim that P and L, it *must* be true also that N.

So the very strong necessity of "If P and L, then N" can be explained by a combination of syntactic and analytic entailments, plus the (metaphysical) necessity of identity. The role of the necessity of identity in this explanation can be specified a little more formally. Because "F," the claim that there exist tokens of certain functional types whose associated conditions are specifiable in physical or quasi-logical terms, is expressed in a disparate vocabulary from that employed in formulating "N," necessarily true bridge principles connecting the disparate vocabularies are needed in order to permit the derivation of the claim that N from the claim that F; and to ensure the very strong necessity of "If P and L, then N," these bridge principles had better be necessary in the same strong sense. But such bridge principles exist, given the necessity of identity and retentive realizationism's a posteriori identity statements asserting the identity of every special- and honorary-scientific type with some or other functional type whose associated condition is specifiable in physical or quasi-logical terms. For suppose that special-scientific property S is, hence is necessarily, functional property G; it follows that, necessarily, there exists a token of S iff there exists a token of G. So if we have derived from the claim that P and L the claim that there exists a token of G, we can further derive that there exists a token of S. So, given that P and L, there *must* be a token of S.

Furthermore, the necessity of identity statements formed using rigid designators can itself be explained in a metaphysically unmysterious way. For example, one might explain it, following Michael Levin (1987; see also Sidelle 1989), as a consequence of the "sociolinguistic truism" (Levin 1987, 285) that certain terms are rigid designators – that we treat certain terms, whenever we are using them to describe counterfactual states of affairs, as referring to what they refer to in the actual world. So suppose, for example, that $S = G$, and that "S" and "G" are rigid designators. Then, in considering and describing any counterfactual state of affairs (in which either term refers at all), we will take each term to refer to its actual-world referent; but because both terms have the same actual-world referent, because $S = G$, it follows that we will take the terms to be coreferential, no matter what counterfactual state of affairs we are considering, so that in no counterfactual state of affairs whatever is it true that $S \neq G$.[5]

Fourth, and finally, although realizationism entails (M) – that is, that the physical way things are necessitates the existence of all the nonphysical tokens, falling within the scope of (R), that exist – it does not entail

---

5 Notice that both the explanation of (M) and the explanation of the nature of the modality involved in (M) succeed perfectly well without the supposition that special- and honorary-scientific terms must in any way be analyzable a priori in physical or quasi-logical terms. Although we will see in Chapter 3 that realization physicalism does require the reductive explainability of special- and honorary-scientific facts, it does not require their reductive explainability *via a priori analyses* (apparently contrary to Chalmers 1996a, 47–51, and Jackson 1998a).

that we could figure out a priori which tokens they are, merely on the basis of assuming that P and L, even if we were fully competent with all the relevant special- and honorary-scientific concepts. That is, although realizationism entails that

(M*) Necessarily, if P and L, then N.

it does not also entail that the conditional, "If P and L, then N," can be discovered to be true a priori, *even* by someone who can understand it and hence who grasps all its constituent terms (or concepts). The reason, of course, is that "N" is a necessary consequence of "P and L" in virtue, partly, of the identity of every special- and honorary-scientific type with some or other functional type whose associated condition is specifiable physically or quasi-logically; and such identities will presumably be a posteriori, to be discovered empirically if at all, and hence not knowable on the strength of conceptual or linguistic competence alone. So, according to realizationism, learning the truth of "If P and L, then N" will very probably require not only a grasp of special- and honorary-scientific concepts or terms but also the *epistemic* ability to *recognize instances* of the corresponding properties in the world. For without having actually recognized such instances, one could not be in a position to assemble the *empirical evidence* needed to support the a posteriori identity claims required to licence the inference of "N" from "P and L," via "F."[6]

To this point, we have seen that realizationism entails (M) – that any possible world indiscernible physically from the actual world contains all the nonphysical tokens, falling within the scope of (R), that the actual world contains. But this modal consequence is not yet a claim of global supervenience as normally understood; for a claim of global supervenience would require that any possible world of some suitably specified sort should contain all *and only* the nonphysical tokens, falling within the scope

---

6 Recent work by David Chalmers (1996a) and Frank Jackson (1998a) argues that if physicalism is true, then a complete physical description of the world entails a priori a complete (positive) description of it *simpliciter*, so that, just given one's grasp of the relevant physical and nonphysical concepts, one could in principle work one's way a priori from the physical description to the (positive) nonphysical description. But, even granting physicalism, we get the a priori entailment of all (positive) facts by the physical facts only if we assume that if one is competent with a concept, one automatically has a priori access to the concept's primary intension (as Chalmers calls it). But this assumption is at best unsupported, as I show in Melnyk 2001. For other objections to the Chalmers/Jackson claim, see also Block and Stalnaker (1999) and Byrne (1999).

of (R), that the actual world contains. So let us ask whether realizationism entails the global supervenience claim that

> (GS) Any possible world indiscernible physically from the actual world is indiscernible *simpliciter* from the actual world (i.e., contains all and only the nonphysical tokens, falling within the scope of (R), that the actual world contains).[7]

But the answer is that it does not. Realizationism entails that every *actual* nonphysical token, falling within the scope of (R), is physically realized. But because it entails nothing at all about how nonphysical tokens, falling within the scope of (R), are realized in *other* possible worlds, it does not entail, in particular, that every such token in every world indiscernible physically from the actual world be physically realized. It therefore allows the existence of possible worlds that are indiscernible physically from the actual world, but which contain nonphysical tokens, falling within the scope of (R), that are *not* physically realized, nonphysical tokens that are additional to those that the actual world contains; such worlds, though indiscernible physically from the actual world, are therefore *not* indiscernible *simpliciter* from the actual world.

But is there a claim of global supervenience different from (GS) that realization *does* entail? There is certainly one. Let the *R-worlds* be those possible worlds in which all the nonphysical tokens that exist and that fall within the scope of (R) are physically realized, that is, those possible worlds in which realizationism is true. Then realizationism entails that

> (GS) Any R-world that is physically indiscernible from the actual world is indiscernible from it *simpliciter*.

Given realizationism, every actual nonphysical token that falls within the scope of (R) is physically realized; that is, it is (necessarily) identical with a token (of a functional type whose associated condition is specifiable physically or quasi-logically) whose existence is logically derivable from certain physical facts, via certain analytic trivialities. Given realizationism, then, any possible world (including therefore any R-world) in which the physical facts are exactly as they are in the actual world must contain *all* the nonphysical tokens, falling within the scope of (R), that the actual world contains. But in R-worlds, of course, the *only* nonphysical tokens,

---

7 Purists will notice that the account of indiscernibility *simpliciter* that I am here assuming faces certain difficulties – as indeed do all other accounts (see McLaughlin 1995, 30–7). But I hope that its relative clarity sufficiently outweighs them, at least for present purposes, and that the correct account, when it is discovered, will leave the substance of my claims unchanged.

falling within the scope of (R), are the physically realized ones; so R-worlds contain no "extra" nonphysical tokens, falling within the scope of (R), that are nonphysically realized, that is, no nonphysically realized nonphysical tokens, falling within the scope of (R), additional to those the actual world contains. Of course, R-worlds physically indiscernible from the actual world contain no "extra" nonphysical tokens, falling within the scope of (R), that *are* physically realized, either. So, given realizationism, any R-world physically indiscernible from the actual world contains all and *only* the nonphysical tokens, falling within the scope of (R), that the actual world contains.

That realizationism entails (GSR) occasions three comments that closely parallel the first three of the four comments occasioned by the fact that realizationism entails (M); but because the parallels are so close, the comments can be brief. First, although realizationism does entail (GSR), it does not follow that (GSR) helps to render transparently intelligible the relations between physical entities, on the one hand, and special- and honorary-scientific ones, on the other. On the contrary, indeed, and as we noted earlier, it is the realizationist thesis itself, that every token falling within the scope of (R) is either physical or physically realized, that seems to be throwing light on the character of such relations.[8] (We might also add that it is the realizationist claim, rather than (GSR), that seems to be doing the work in honoring our physicalist intuitions.) Second, because realizationism entails (GSR), it can provide an explanation of why (GSR) is true, so that the supervenience that (GSR) records need not be construed as the holding of a brute modal fact (e.g., construed as an inexplicable covariation across worlds). Third, (GSR) articulates the modal claim that, given the physical way things are, there is a nonphysical way that things *must* be; but because this modal claim is entailed and explained by realizationism, the nature of the necessity it records can also be explained, along the lines of the earlier explanation of (M), as a combination of syntactic and analytic entailments, plus the necessity of identity.

2. CAN GLOBAL SUPERVENIENCE PROVIDE A SUPERIOR ALTERNATIVE TO REALIZATIONISM?

Because realizationism entails the global supervenience claim (GSR), I have to concede that at least one claim of global supervenience is a

---

8 A deflationary view of the pretensions of supervenience claims is also taken by Paul Snowdon (1989, 150), David Charles (1992, 277, n. 15), and Jaegwon Kim (1993, 147–8 and 167–8). See also Melnyk (1997a).

logically *necessary* condition of physicalism. But is there a claim of global supervenience that (i) is a logically *sufficient* condition for physicalism (at least physicalism about properties) but which (ii) does not have commitments as strong – or allegedly bad – as those of realizationism? Only if there is such a claim, of course, will global supervenience provide a formulation of physicalism that is superior to that provided by realizationism (i.e., superior from the point of view of avoiding realizationism's distinctively strong commitments). But I doubt that there is. For, as we shall now see, it turns out to be much harder than one might have thought initially to find a claim of global supervenience that simultaneously meets conditions (i) and (ii).

Let us begin by considering again the claim that

(GS) Any possible world indiscernible physically from the actual world is indiscernible *simpliciter* from the actual world.

I will show that (GS) does not suffice for physicalism – by showing how it could be true while physicalism is false – and hence that it fails to meet condition (i). Suppose, then, that the actual world were as follows. It contains both physical tokens and nonphysical tokens that fall within the scope of (R); but the latter are not tokens of functional types that are always, as it happens, physically realized (so realizationism is false at this world). However, the way things are physically still necessitates the way things are nonphysically: the distribution of physical tokens necessitates that there be the nonphysical tokens that there are, distributed as they are, and also that they be the *only* such tokens that there are (the physical way things are therefore has a certain *exclusionary* power). Moreover, this necessitation is to be understood as necessitation of the strongest possible sort: *all* possible worlds physically indiscernible from this world also have exactly the same distribution of nonphysical tokens, falling within the scope of (R), as this world does. But, and here is the crucial point, this necessitation is to be understood as some sort of *primitive and irreducible modal fact*, not to be explained in terms of anything more fundamental. Not only is it inexplicable in terms of the identity of non-physical types either with physical types or with functional types that are always, as it happens, physically realized, but it cannot be explained at all.[9]

---

[9] Lest anyone suppose this "brute metaphysical necessitation" view to be too absurd to be worth considering, I should point out that at least one philosopher actually endorses it (Zangwill 1993 and 1997).

Upon reflection, it is very plausible intuitively that physicalism would be *false* if the actual world were as just described (Schiffer 1987, 153–4; Horgan 1993). But I think we can say a little more about *why* it would be false. It would be false, I suggest, because, if the actual world were as just described, then two important intuitions concerning what must be the case if (retentive) physicalism is true would not be honored. The first I have called the Truthmaker Intuition. Let me reintroduce it here by means of two remarks made by Robert Kirk: he says that, if physicalism is true, then "when we are talking about the mental states of actual organisms, we are talking only about the physical – not *as* physical, of course" (1996a, 159); similarly, he claims that, for all physicalists, "(in fact) there is nothing there to talk about but the physical" (1996b, 245). Now the wording of Kirk's first remark perhaps implies, infelicitously, that when we are talking about the mental states of organisms, we are not talking about the mental; and the wording of the second, that the mental is not there to be talked about. But the remarks still go some way toward expressing the Truthmaker Intuition, at least as it applies to (true) talk of the mental. Formulated to cover (true) special- and honorary-scientific talk of any kind, and freed from unintended suggestions of eliminativism, it can be expressed as follows:

> (TI) If physicalism is true, then there must be some sense in which all the true descriptions of the world framed in the proprietary vocabularies of the special- and honorary-sciences are *made true* by the distribution in the world of physical tokens (given the physical laws).

Note that (TI) does not prevent a physicalist from granting that there is *also* a sense in which all the true descriptions of the world framed in the proprietary vocabularies of the special- and honorary-sciences are made true by the distribution in the world of special- and honorary-scientific tokens that are quite real.

So, according to (TI), if (retentive) physicalism is true, descriptions of the world framed in the proprietary vocabularies of the special- and honorary-sciences are capable of being, and often are, perfectly true; but when they are, there is some sense in which they are made true by the very same tokens that, given the physical laws, make true those true descriptions of the world framed in the proprietary vocabulary of physics. But if the actual world were as described earlier, then (TI) would not be honored – that is, there would be no sense in which (say) a true ascription to the world of a certain special-scientific property would be made true by the way things are physically. For if the actual world were as described earlier, then the special-scientific property instance ascribed would certainly be necessitated by the way things are physically; but because this necessitation would be a primitive and irreducible modal fact, what would make the ascription true would only be the special-scientific property instance; nothing physical would be making the ascription true, notwithstanding its brute necessitation of what would (*pace* Jackson 1998a, 13–14). And the bruteness of the necessitation is the crux. For if the necessitation of the special-scientific property instance by the way things are physically were explainable, perhaps in a realizationist way by identifying the property with a functional property always physically realized, then (TI) *would* be honored; but if the actual world were as described, the necessitation would not be explainable, in either this or any other way, and that is why we would be left with no sense in which the way things are physically makes it true that the world contains the special-scientific property instance in question.

But there is – arguably – a second intuition that would not be honored if the actual world were as described earlier: the Constitution Intuition. It is admittedly vague, but not so vague as to lack teeth:

(CI) If physicalism is true, then the nonphysical is somehow entirely constituted by the physical.[10]

Whatever is or should be meant by "entirely constituted by," it is at least clear that if something nonphysical is entirely constituted by the physical, then it has something physical as a part (though not necessarily a proper part). That being so, it is easy to see that, were the actual world as described earlier, the nonphysical would not be entirely constituted by the physical. Consider any token of a special- or honorary-scientific type that the world would contain; then, for it to be entirely constituted by the physical, it would have to have something physical as a part. But although the token would be necessitated by the presence of some physical token or tokens, because the necessitation would be the holding of a primitive and irreducible modal relation, the token would not have anything physical as a part. As before, the bruteness of the necessitation is the crux. For if it were explained (e.g., in a realizationist way by treating the special-scientific token as functional but realized by some physical token), then the special-scientific token *would* have the physical token as a part. But if the actual world were as described, the necessitation would not be explainable, in

---

10 David Charles (1992, 274) expresses a similar intuition: "[T]he physical is what the mental is *composed of.*"

either this or any other way, and we would therefore be left with no sense in which the nonphysical is entirely constituted by the physical.

If the actual world were as described earlier, therefore, physicalism would be false. But if the actual world were as described earlier, (GS) would be *true*, since the fact that the physical way the world is would necessitate the nonphysical way it is would ensure that any possible world indiscernible from the actual world physically would be indiscernible from it *simpliciter*.[11] So, because there is a possible state of affairs in which (GS) is true while physicalism is false, (GS) is not logically sufficient for physicalism, and hence fails to satisfy condition (i) for being a superior alternative to realizationism.[12] Now it may be objected that because (GS) is a stronger claim than any prudent supervenience physicalist has ever actually advocated, this result is irrelevant. But the result can be extended. For if (GS) fails to entail physicalism, then any weaker supervenience thesis entailed by (GS) also fails to entail physicalism. Suppose, for example, that (GSR), which (GS) entails, itself entailed physicalism; then, by the transitivity of entailment, so would (GS); but (GS) does not entail physicalism, so neither does (GSR).[13] Supervenience theses entailed by (GS) will include

---

11 Readers familiar with the literature on supervenience and physicalism know that it is usual to treat (GS) as false. For a world that is, in the sense given, physically indiscernible from the actual world may yet contain tokens that are neither physical nor physically realized–ectoplasmic tokens, if you like – which, by playing the right roles, manage to realize tokens of nonphysical (e.g., psychological) types that do not exist in the actual world; and, a less familiar point, these ectoplasmic realizing tokens might be property instances as well as individual objects or events (see Jack 1994). Notice, however, that, on the supposition in the text about what the actual world is like, there just is no possible world that, although indiscernible from the actual world physically, is still discernible from it because it contains tokens that are neither physical nor physically realized but that realize special- or honorary-scientific tokens not present in the actual world; for we are assuming the way things are physically to possess a certain exclusionary power in respect of the way things are nonphysically.

12 Alternatively: if (GS) entailed physicalism, then, given (TI) and (GI), (GS) would entail *both* that there must be some sense in which all the true descriptions of the world framed in the proprietary vocabularies of the special- and honorary-sciences are made true by the distribution in the world of physical tokens (given the physical laws) *and* that the nonphysical is somehow entirely constituted by the physical. But since (GS) entails neither claim, it does not entail physicalism.

13 If the actual world were a brute-necessitation world as described earlier, then (GSR) would still be true (while physicalism was false), but its truth would be *trivial*, since its antecedent would be necessarily false. For if the actual world were a brute-necessitation world, *no* R-world would be physically indiscernible from the actual world, since if a world were physically indiscernible from the actual world it would have to contain nonphysical tokens that were not physically realized (given the brute necessitation of the nonphysical by the physical), but if it were an R-world, it could not contain any nonphysical tokens that were not physically realized.

all those patterned on (GS) but quantifying over some *subset* of all possible worlds indiscernible physically from the actual world; such theses will therefore also fail to satisfy condition (i).[14]

But if this conclusion is correct, and claims of global supervenience are *not* logically sufficient for physicalism (even physicalism about properties), what explains the popularity of attempts to formulate physicalism in terms of supervenience? What led philosophers to *expect* that a supervenience thesis would be logically sufficient for physicalism (or at least physicalism about properties)?[15] Reason to suppose that supervenience might play *some* role in formulating physicalism surely stems from acceptance of the attractive Fixing Intuition that

> (FI) If physicalism is true, then there is some sense in which the way things are physically *fixes* (or *determines*) the way things are nonphysically.

For a claim of supervenience looks like a good way to articulate the idea that the physical "fixes" everything else. But all that follows thus far is that a suitable claim of supervenience expresses a logically *necessary* condition for physicalism; acceptance of (FI) provides no reason to think that a suitable claim of supervenience expresses a logically *sufficient* condition for physicalism. However, it may be that some writers attracted to (FI) have *also* felt attracted to the converse of (FI), namely

> (FI*) If there is some sense in which the way things are physically *fixes* (or *determines*) the way things are nonphysically, then physicalism is true;

and from (FI*) it certainly follows, if supervenience indeed articulates the "fixing" idea, that a suitable claim of supervenience expresses a logically

---

14 For different ways of specifying this subset, see Lewis (1983a), Post (1987), and Horgan (1987). The supervenience claims of these authors are not quite patterned on (GS), since they begin, "*Any* two physically indiscernible worlds that are ... are indiscernible *simpliciter,*" thus making no reference to the actual world; but this does not affect my point in the text, which could easily be elaborated to apply to their claims.

15 The only explicit argument known to me in the literature for thinking a supervenience thesis to be sufficient for physicalism is given by Jackson (1998a, 14). But it works only by assuming that our world is not in fact a brute-necessitation world as described in the text. Now I agree that it is not, but (a) how does this contingent, empirical point reinstate a supervenience thesis as stating a logically sufficient condition for physicalism? And (b) do we have any evidence for denying that our world is a brute-necessitation world that is not at the same time evidence for saying that it *is* a realizationist world? If not, then constraint (ii) on providing a superior alternative to realizationism is not satisfied.

sufficient condition for physicalism. But (FI*) does not, of course, *follow* from the plausible (FI). Nor, upon reflection, is (FI*) plausible in its own right; for, as we have just seen, the way things are physically might indeed fix – in the sense of necessitate – the way things are nonphysically, but in the wrong sort of way to make it the case that physicalism is true.

Now I have to admit that my argument so far has rested on something like a willful misunderstanding of extant versions of supervenience physicalism: plainly, no flesh-and-blood supervenience physicalists intend their claims of supervenience to express the kind of brute metaphysical necessitation my argument has invoked – indeed, they would almost certainly repudiate this interpretation of their claims, were they presented with it. But to complain of this willful misunderstanding would be to miss the point. For my contention concerns the logic of supervenience claims, not the psychology of their proponents; and if my arguments are correct, allegedly physicalist global supervenience claims really are open to the willful misunderstanding according to which they fail to suffice logically for physicalism. The only interesting question is what (if anything) might be done, by someone who hopes that a suitable supervenience claim can yield a superior alternative to realizationism, to remedy this deficiency in supervenience claims.

An answer to this question is suggested by noting that, although claims of global supervenience articulate the intuitive idea that the way things are physically more-than-nomologically necessitates the way things are nonphysically, they say nothing at all by way of *explanation why* this relation of necessitation holds. And it is this silence, of course, that opens the door to the possibility of construing the necessitation as a brute modal fact, and hence to the possibility that a claim of global supervenience should be true while physicalism is false. We can see, too, exactly why those who expect supervenience to yield a formulation of physicalism superior to realizationism *must* offer some explanation or other of why supervenience holds. It is not because we cannot abide any brute facts at all, for we can, and sometimes, of course, we must. Nor is it, more subtly, because we might hope by explaining why supervenience holds to *reduce* the total number of brute facts we accept[16] – although if we explain supervenience partly in terms of identities we might succeed in doing so, because identities seem not to call for explanation and hence not to be brute if left unexplained.

---

16 So the demand for an explanation of why supervenience holds is not necessarily shown to be inappropriate by noting that any purported explanation of supervenience must *itself* take something as brute (*pace* Ernest Sosa, quoted by Kim 1993, 159, n. 51, and Zangwill 1997).

Nor is it, finally, because the brute necessitation relation might *itself* be thought to exceed the legitimate ontology of physicalism, although this difficult issue is one I have deliberately avoided by restricting the scope of physicalism to *contingent* features of the world. Rather, those who expect supervenience to yield a formulation of physicalism superior to realizationism must explain why supervenience holds because, unless they do so, and indeed in such a way as to honor physicalist intuitions, especially (TI), it is at best an open question whether what they offer us is even a formulation of (hence logically sufficient for) physicalism at all.[17] Given that this is so, however, perhaps those who hope that a suitable claim of supervenience may yield a superior alternative to realizationism can overcome the objection that claims of supervenience are not logically sufficient for physicalism – by providing an explanation of why supervenience holds that, when conjoined with the supervenience claim itself, *is* logically sufficient for physicalism.[18]

But if this strategy is adopted, there looms the new threat of falling out of the frying pan into the fire, that is, of satisfying condition (i) at the cost

---

17 Jessica Wilson (1999) makes the interesting suggestion that supervenience physicalists can avoid the kind of difficulties I am raising *without* explaining why their favored claim of supervenience holds – by conjoining the claim of supervenience with the requirement that "Each individual causal power associated with a supervenient property [be] numerically identical with a causal power associated with its base property" (Wilson 1999, 42). But I am not yet ready to abandon my claim in the text. For until various pressing questions about Wilson's suggestion are adequately answered, it will remain unclear whether the imposition of her requirement *does* succeed in avoiding the difficulties I raise while not providing an explanation of why supervenience holds. Among the pressing questions are: what are causal powers in the intended sense? Are they entities enough that we may speak of numerical identity in connection with them? Are the causal powers mentioned in her requirement associated with properties as types, or with property instances? In connection with a given supervening property, what is "its" base property? What must be assumed about the nature of supervening properties and about their relation to base properties for it even to be *possible* for the causal powers associated with a supervenient property to be identical with (a subset of) those associated with its base property? For example, must something at least as reductionist as realizationism be assumed?

18 Overcoming this objection is not their only task, of course. They also need to solve the problem that there seem to be worlds just like ours physically that nevertheless differ from our world by containing nonphysically realized (e.g., ectoplasmically realized) tokens of special- or honorary-scientific types. Can it be solved? Yes, and (GSR) is the result. But can it be solved another way? What is required is the specification of a sense of "nothing in addition to the physical" that allows one to say that any world just like ours physically, *in which there is nothing in addition to the physical*, is just like ours *simpliciter*. The problem is to do this without in effect glossing the italicized clause as "in which physicalism is true," thus making the supervenience claim presuppose, rather than constitute, a formulation of physicalism.

of failing to satisfy condition (ii) – by providing an explanation of why supervenience holds whose commitments are as strong, or as allegedly bad, as those of the realizationism which a supervenience formulation of physicalism is intended to supplant. Let me elaborate on how this threat arises, and on how it is not easily evaded.

All extant supervenience physicalists, we should note, endorse a thesis of the form

> (G) Any two possible worlds that are physically indiscernible and that meet condition C are indiscernible *simpliciter*,

although they differ over how to specify condition C. But because the actual world is a possible world, a claim of the form of (G) entails a claim of this form:

> (GA) Any possible world that is physically indiscernible from the actual world and that meets condition C is (if the actual world meets C) indiscernible from the actual world *simpliciter*.

But a claim of the form (GA) entails a claim of the following form, where "P" expresses a complete physical description of the actual world (including its physical laws), where "N" expresses a complete nonphysical description of the actual world, and where "necessarily" must be read as expressing the strongest grade of necessity, something like truth in all possible worlds:

> (NA) Necessarily, if P, and if condition C is met, then N.

What a claim of the form of (NA) expresses, then, is that, given that it is true that P and that condition C is met, it *must* also be true that N. But *why* must it also be true that N? It will not do to say that it just must, and there's an end on it; for if the metaphysical necessity of the conditional is thus treated as a brute and inexplicable modal fact, then physicalist intuitions, especially (TI), are left unhonored. So I ask again: why must it be true that N, given that it is true that P and that condition C is met? What explains this necessity? The question, I hasten to add, is not unanswerable; in fact, various answers naturally suggest themselves. The trouble with them, from the point of view of one who hopes that a suitable claim of supervenience may yield a superior alternative to realizationism, is that their commitments are at least as strong, and allegedly bad, as those of realizationism; they make it impossible to meet condition (ii). To see why, let us now examine the answers that suggest themselves most naturally.

Might the necessity in question be explained as analyticity? Not if all analytic truths are knowable a priori, since conditionals of the form, "If P, and if condition C is met, then N," do not appear, at any rate, to be knowable a priori.[19] But, in any case, even if the necessity were explained as analyticity, we surely would not have a superior alternative to realizationism, since we would then be committed to claiming that every nonphysical term is analytically definable somehow in physical terms, which is a translational reductionism surely more offensive (to those affronted by reductionism) than anything to which realizationism is committed. Might the necessity be explained as purely logical, reflecting the deducibility in accordance with some natural deduction system of the claim that N from the claim that P and that condition C is met? No, because the formulation of the claim that P will employ predicates that do not appear in the formulation of the claim that N (and vice versa). Nor might the necessity be explained as a combination of logical with analytical necessity, reflecting the syntactic deducibility of the conditional's consequent from its antecedent, given analytically true bridge laws connecting the distinctive predicates of physics with those of the special and honorary sciences. For no one who aspires to a physicalism less reductionist than realizationism can believe in such bridge laws.

What other options are there?[20] It looks like the only other way to explain the necessity in question would be to treat it as reflecting a combination of logical necessity with some species of Kripkean *metaphysical* necessity (Kripke 1980). But how? It is hard to see how the (alleged) necessity of *origin* could help. An appeal to the (alleged) necessity of *constitution*

---

19   The necessity in question might be what Chalmers has called 1-necessity (1996a, ch. 2). And if so, then, according to Chalmers, the conditional, "If P and condition C is met, then N," *will* be in principle knowable a priori. (For references, see note 6.) But I doubt that anyone who finds realizationism offensively reductionist will regard Chalmers's view as an improvement.

20   Peter Forrest's Grand-Property Hypothesis (1988) appears to be another option, but in fact it is merely another way of leaving supervenience a brute modal fact. According to his hypothesis, we can explain supervenience by claiming that supervening properties are properties *of the properties* on which they supervene; but (it turns out) this hypothesis can explain global supervenience only if the supervening properties are had *essentially* by the properties they supervene on (see Melnyk 1991, 582–3). In that case, however, the existence of a brute modal fact gets not avoided but merely relocated – to the *essential* possession by physical properties of the nonphysical properties that supervene on them. Furthermore, if supervening properties are essential properties of physical properties, and *that* is why they supervene upon physical properties, then, intuitively, we have been given no sense whatever in which they are physical; certainly the physicalist intuitions (TI) and (CI) are not honored. For a worry similar to this last, see Brian Loar (1992, 247).

initially sounds more promising, for it sounds plausible to construe physicalism as the claim that every actual token is entirely physically constituted. But in that case the notion of being "entirely physically constituted" would need to be spelled out in detail – partly to make it clear that the notion was truly capable of doing the required explanatory work, partly to make it clear that the resulting formulation of physicalism respected important physicalist intuitions like (TI) and (CI), and partly to make it clear that the resulting formulation of physicalism avoided reductionist commitments of precisely the sort that motivated the search for a superior alternative to realizationism in the first place. But whether the notion of being "entirely physically constituted" *can* in fact be spelled out so as to meet these three constraints is far from obvious. After all, it is tempting to regard realizationism *itself* as articulating the intuitive claim that everything is entirely physically constituted.

A better bet would be to try to explain the necessity in question by exploiting the metaphysical necessity of *identity*. But obviously we could not appeal to *type* identities. Not that the resulting explanation would be defective: we could certainly treat every type, a token of which is said to exist by the claim that N, as identical either with some physical type or with some functional type whose associated condition can be specified physically or quasi-logically; and we could then explain why, given that it is true that P and condition C is met, it *must* also be true that N by noting (i) that the types whose tokens are asserted to exist by the claim that N just *are* physical types or functional types whose associated conditions are specifiable in physical or quasi-logical terms, and (ii) that suitable tokens of these types are logically guaranteed to exist by the fact that P and that C is met.[21] The trouble, of course, with this explanation of the necessity in question is that the claims of type identity that it requires amount to a form of reductionism at least as strong, and allegedly bad, as anything to which realizationism is committed. So if these claims of type identity were conjoined with a claim of global supervenience, then, although condition (i) on using supervenience to formulate a superior alternative to realizationism would be met, condition (ii) would not be.

So to exploit the metaphysical necessity of identity in order to explain the necessity in question, the identities appealed to would have to be *merely*

---

21 It is worth noticing that when supervenience is explained in this way, via the identification of supervening properties with physical properties or with functional properties whose associated conditions are specifiable physically or quasi-logically, there is no room for the kind of possibility that Jessica Wilson exploits in objecting that Terry Horgan's superdupervenience is not superduper enough (Wilson 1999, 39).

token, that is, token identities that hold in the absence of corresponding type identities. But it is not clear how merely token identities *could* explain the necessity in question.[22] To see the problem, suppose that every (say) mental event is identical, and necessarily so, with some physical event, and hence that in every possible world containing all the physical events that the actual world contains there exist the very mental events with which those physical events are identical. This supposition, however, does not entail the supervenience claim that every world physically indiscernible from the actual world is also mentally indiscernible from it; hence the supposition fails to *explain* this supervenience claim. It does not entail the supervenience claim for two reasons.

The first is that not every world physically indiscernible from the actual world is one that contains *those very physical events* that the actual world contains: some worlds physically indiscernible from the actual world contain physical events that are *distinct* from the physical events in the actual world, even though they are physically indiscernible from them. Because the supposition that every (actual) mental event is a physical event does not prevent such worlds from being mentally discernible from the actual world, the supposition that every mental event is a physical event does not entail that *every* world physically indiscernible from the actual world is also mentally indiscernible from it. The second reason why the supposition does not entail the supervenience claim is this: from the fact that a merely possible world contains an event that in the actual world is a mental event it does not immediately follow that this event is a mental event in the merely possible world. For there might be possible worlds (a) that contain every physical event the actual world contains and also therefore every event that in the actual world is mental, but (b) in which nothing is a pain or a thought, just because being a pain and being a thought are not *essential* properties of any actual pain event or thought event. Some suitable account of the essential properties of events is therefore required

---

22 Nor is it clear, by the way, that merely token identities would suffice for physicalism: how, for instance, would the identity of every mental event with some physical event yield the result that the claim that my current mental state is a pain is *made true* by physical conditions (thus honoring the Truthmaker Intuition)? The problem here is a consequence of the fact that, if we have token event identities only, but no type identities of mental properties either with physical properties or with functional properties whose actual tokens are physically realized, then it is unclear why any particular physical event that is also a mental event *deserves* to be counted as a mental event. (The identity of every mental event with some physical event certainly suffices for physicalism about the mental if we covertly assume Kim's view that events are identical only if their constitutive properties are identical; but what if we consciously deny that assumption?)

if the token identity explanation of supervenience is to work. But it is not easy to see how to construct such an account. One obstacle to doing so is that, if we are restricted to token identities (so that every actual mental event is some physical event, but mental types are not identical with either physical types or physically realized functional types), then it is unclear what it is that *determines* whether a randomly selected physical event is one of the lucky ones that is also a mental event; for it cannot be the physical event's being a token of some physical type identical with some mental type, or its being a token of some type that plays a suitable functional role.

But we now seem to have exhausted the options for explaining the necessity of claims on the pattern of (NA). At this point, however, a philosopher who still hopes that a suitable claim of supervenience may yield a superior alternative to realizationism might protest as follows: "I am not sure that this idea of brute metaphysical necessitation of the nonphysical by the physical makes any sense, but even if it does, let me concede that a supervenience claim does not suffice for physicalism if it expresses this brute necessitation. But all I then need do in order to formulate physicalism in terms of supervenience is to present my supervenience claim and then tack on a denial that the necessitation of the nonphysical by the physical that it expresses is brute. In that case, however, I do not *need* to say *how* to explain the necessity of claims on the pattern of (NA); it suffices for me say *that it has* an explanation – something I have in effect already done by denying that it is brute." But one who hopes that a suitable claim of supervenience may yield a superior alternative to realizationism *does* need to say *how* to explain the necessity of claims on the pattern of (NA). For it might be that the only explanations possible are explanations of the kinds that we have already considered – in which case physicalism formulated in terms of supervenience will have consequences at least as strong, and allegedly bad, as those of realizationism, and so condition (ii) on providing a superior alternative to realizationism will not be satisfied. On the other hand, it might be that other kinds of explanation *are* possible; but in that case, unless we are told how they go, we will have no reason to think that they make it possible for a supervenience formulation of physicalism to satisfy condition (ii); so the aspiring supervenience physicalist must tell us how to explain the necessity of claims on the pattern of (NA) in order to *show* that condition (ii) on providing a superior alternative to physicalism can be met.

I conclude, therefore, that supervenience does not now provide a superior alternative to realizationism, and hence that we now have no reason for rejecting realizationism as a formulation of physicalism on the grounds that there is already available some less heavily committed supervenience formulation. Might things change in the future? Of course, but I am seeking only to obtain a license for the realizationist research program, not also to revoke that of the supervenience physicalist.

3

*Realizationism and R*d*ct**n*sm*

1. INTRODUCTION

The purpose of this chapter is to defend answers to a pair of questions of which the first is this:

(1) Is realization physicalism reductive? That is, does it entail the reducibility of the nonphysical to the physical (given plausible additional premises concerning, say, the character of reducibility)?

My answer to question (1) is that we need to distinguish between importantly different senses of "reduction" and its cognates and that, although realizationism turns out to be nonreductive in some of these senses, it turns out to be reductive, and importantly so, in others. If this answer is right, then realization physicalism opposes the drift of nearly all the pro-physicalist literature of the past twenty-five years, which has been toward a version of physicalism intended not to be reductive in any important sense (see, e.g., Fodor 1974, Boyd 1980, Post 1987).

There is, however, an almost universal consensus within professional philosophy that reductionism of pretty much any kind is false; there is also passionate opposition to reductionism from a wider intellectual public. Hence, given my answer to (1), I need also to address this second question:

(2) How *damaging* are the reductionist commitments of realization physicalism?

My answer to question (2) is that the forms of reductionism to which realizationism is committed are at least not open to *armchair* objections – objections that are a priori or based on empirical evidence available to a casual observer. These forms of reductionism may yet be open to a posteriori objections based on relatively recondite scientific evidence, but that is a question for Chapter 5. (In fact, of course, I there argue that they are not open to such a posteriori objections, but I do not assume this result in the present chapter.)

For reasons I do not fully comprehend, the issue of reductionism arouses intense passion, especially in nonphilosophers. Consequently, I begin by answering my two questions in relation to notions of reductionism plausibly attributed to nonphilosophical antireductionists, in a conciliatory attempt to do their concerns some justice. I hope to convince these antireductionists that there is a substantive issue of reductionism over which intelligent, informed, and well-meaning people may disagree, and that reductionists are neither fools who have missed the obvious nor demons who wish to strip the world of value. Then I address my two questions in relation to various notions of reductionism assumed by philosophers, at every point conceding as much as I can consistently with my conviction that the current antireductionist consensus in philosophy, especially among physicalists, is very poorly based. I hope to win over at least the physicalists, because I will be conceding that realizationism is nonreductive in the particular sense that has (though unmeritedly) dominated the literature on physicalism; and they may be quite happy, once all the distinctions are in place, to accept the substance of my position, even if they still bridle at the name. But if my hope goes unfulfilled, I shall still be content if I merely provoke antireductionist physicalists into providing a clearer explanation than I have yet been able to find or understand of (a) what exactly they take the autonomy enjoyed by the special and honorary sciences to consist in and (b) how exactly the enjoyment of this autonomy is supposed to be consistent with the truth of an adequately formulated physicalism. And such an explanation is sorely needed, because if nonreductive physicalism is to be possible, then nonphysical phenomena must be dependent enough on physical phenomena to count (in some suitably broad sense) as physical, but not so dependent on physical phenomena as to be reducible to them. It is not obvious how, or even whether, this can work.

2. MORE-OR-LESS NONPHILOSOPHICAL REDUCTIONISM

Among nonphilosophers, there may be some who use "reductionism" in no clear descriptive sense at all: it is, on their lips, *merely* a term of (strong) disapprobation. But there are others who appear to use "reductionist" to describe any view that denies the existence of something that, perhaps rather obviously, does exist, especially if they regard the something as morally or aesthetically significant. A view that is reductionist in this sense need not *explicitly* deny the existence of something that does exist; the denial may merely be an upshot, of which its proponent is unaware, of an attempt to do something else (e.g., to represent the thing in question as existing wholly in virtue of something else). So, for example, a reductionist in this sense about the mind is someone whose views about the mind, either explicitly or by possibly unnoticed implication, deny some aspect of mental reality (e.g., consciousness) that is deemed morally significant. One advantage of interpreting the usage of certain antireductionist nonphilosophers in this way is that we can thereby explain why they treat reductionism as automatically an error, as something that just could not be true. For since it is automatically an error to deny the existence of something that does exist, and since reductionism in the current sense, by definition, denies the existence of something that does exist, reductionism in the current sense *is* automatically an error.

But precisely because reductionism in this sense is by definition false, the question whether realizationism entails it boils down immediately to the question whether realizationism is *false* – that is, whether realizationism, in holding that every token that falls within the scope of (R) is either physical or physically realized, has left out something real, something whose existence it must therefore mistakenly deny. So is realizationism false? Well, the answer to this question obviously cannot just be "read off" the canonical formulation of realizationism, even on the assumption that special- and honorary-scientific tokens do indeed exist. For, as we saw in Chapter 1, realizationism might be *retentive*, and hence consistent with the existence of special- and honorary-scientific tokens, since it might identify special- and honorary-scientific types with functional types whose tokens are physically realized. Moreover, as we also saw in Chapter 1, because retentive realizationism stands or falls with the functionalist type-identity hypotheses that it requires, and because these identity claims are a posteriori, the question whether retentive realizationism is true cannot be settled a priori (e.g., by conceivability arguments). Of course, these identity hypotheses might still turn out a posteriori to be false, in which case, except by going eliminativist, realizationism could no longer evade the (fatal) charge of being reductionist in the current sense; but to discover whether they do turn out a posteriori to be false requires looking at some scientific evidence, as we do in Chapters 5 and 6.

Other nonphilosophers, and also some philosophers (e.g., Parfit 1984, 210; 1997, 108), appear to use "reductionism" slightly differently, to denote any view that, while not denying the existence of something (perhaps especially something regarded as morally or aesthetically significant), nevertheless claims that it exists entirely in virtue of the (simultaneous) existence of something else; contrast the case of, say, fundamental physical particles, whose existence is presumably not beholden to the (simultaneous) existence of anything else. Thus, a reductionist in this sense about the mind holds that minds really do exist but that their existence is somehow derivative from, or dependent on, or constituted by, the existence of something else, so that minds are not among the basic, independent constituents of the universe.

In this new sense, of course, retentive realizationism is obviously reductive. For it holds precisely that the special- and honorary-scientific tokens, though perfectly real, are physically realized and hence in that precise sense owe their entire existence to the physical. Indeed, all formulations of retentive physicalism have to be reductive in this new sense, since if they allowed any nonphysical tokens that fall within the scope of (R) to enjoy a nonderivative existence on an exact par with that of electrons, they would have supplied no broad sense of "physical" in which those tokens were physical. The only question of interest, therefore, is whether a commitment to reductionism in this new sense is a liability. But it is surely not a *conceptual* truth that it is; surely it is not a conceptual truth that tables, thoughts, and tragedies enjoy a basic existence, for if it were, then the claim that tables exist only derivatively would strike us as some kind of nonsense, which patently it does not. Likewise, casual observation, while no doubt able to assure us of the sheer existence of tables, thoughts, and tragedies, cannot assure us that their existence is nonderivative in the sense relevant to realizationism. For the question whether tables, thoughts, and tragedies exist nonderivatively in the sense relevant to realizationism is just the question whether they are physically realized; and this question, in turn, is (part of) the question whether retentive realizationism is true, a question that, as we lately noted, should not be expected to be answerable from the armchair, and on which, as we will see in Chapters 5 and 6, many uncontroversial scientific findings bear evidentially. Conceptual competence and casual observation leave the question of reductionism in this second sense open.

Let me now consider a third sense of "reductionist," inspired by a remark of Brian Loar. One condition that an interesting version of nonreductive physicalism must meet, he suggests, is that, according to it, "Mental truths should be *not second string*" (1992, 241). In similar spirit, one might take a view to be reductionist in a third sense if, while it does not deny the existence of something (perhaps especially something regarded as morally or aesthetically significant), it allows it only a second-class sort of existence, reserving first-class existence for some privileged group to which the item in question does not belong. So realizationism is reductionist in this sense just in case it grants second-class existence to the special- and honorary-scientific tokens, and first-class existence only to the physical.

Two arguments might be offered for holding that realizationism is indeed reductionist in this third sense. The first argument claims that because, as we have just seen, (i) realizationism, like all forms of retentive physicalism, is committed to treating the special- and honorary-scientific tokens as owing their entire existence to the physical, and because (ii) such derivative existence is merely second-class, realizationism, like all forms of retentive physicalism, is committed to according the special- and honorary-scientific tokens merely second-class existence. But it is not clear that premise (ii) of this argument is true – that derivative existence *is* merely second-class. For derivative existence is not a different *kind* or *caliber* of existence, any more than inherited wealth is a different or better kind of wealth than earned wealth; derivative existence is still *existence*. And in any case, do we really think that the fact that a dry-stone wall owes its entire existence to certain suitably arranged stones in any way impugns the reality of the wall, either absolutely or in comparison to that of its constituent stones? Nonetheless, it is still hard to rid oneself of the quasi-Anselmian intuition that basic existence is better, and that nonderivative existence, especially of oneself, would be more desirable, derivative existence rather less so; and if that intuition is correct, then realizationism, like all forms of retentive physicalism, is indeed committed to reductionism in the third sense. But even if it is, so what? To the extent that the totality of available empirical evidence makes realization physicalism credible, to that extent the same evidence makes it credible (*if* basic existence is better) that the special- and honorary-scientific tokens (including ourselves) *do* enjoy an inferior, merely second-class existence. And *if* they do, then we should simply try to accept the fact with as much humility as we can muster, perhaps indeed with some of the "natural piety" that antireductionist emergentists have occasionally urged upon us. It would hardly be the first time that science had revealed humans as occupying a less important place in the universe than they had previously supposed.

The second argument concludes that realizationism is committed to second-class existence for special- and honorary-scientific tokens on the grounds that, according to realizationism, all (tokened) special- and honorary-scientific types are higher-order functional types, and hence necessarily such that something *else* (namely, the realizers of their tokens) must exist in order for them to be tokened, whereas physical types are first-order types, with at least the possibility of being tokened alone. Now this argument assumes that the necessary ontological dependence of higher-order types entails a kind of second-class existence for their tokens, and such an assumption is hardly obvious. Even if this assumption is false, however, the argument still usefully reminds us that realizationism is committed to an important ontological distinction between special- and honorary-scientific types, on the one hand, and physical ones, on the other; and this commitment alone may well disappoint the ontologically egalitarian aspirations of some philosophers attracted to the idea of nonreductive physicalism. For example, suppose that metaphysicians are able to prove that only first-order types can be *genuine universals*, and hence that higher-order types cannot be; then realizationism entails that the only genuine universals must be *physical* types, and hence that special- and honorary-scientific types are in danger of relegation to second-class status. But this consequence, although it would perhaps expose realizationism as rather more revisionary than either expected or hoped, would surely provide no reason to think that it is *false*.[1]

Certainly, once the question has been raised, the assumption that all types enjoy the same ontological independence as physical types is a natural one to adopt, at least in the absence of any pertinent empirical evidence. But it cannot plausibly be held to be part of common sense, for it answers a question that has simply not occurred to most of humanity. And if realizationism entails that it is false, and realizationism is credible in light of the totality of available empirical evidence, then the assumption should surely be abandoned. Once again we are returned to the potentially laborious question of whether realization physicalism *is* supported by the totality of available empirical evidence.

---

1 Here I take issue with an anonymous reader for the Press who suggested that my "entire enterprise" would be "broken-backed from the start" if "we can find no serious place in an ontology of properties for the notion of a 'higher-order' property."

3. TWO PHILOSOPHICAL REDUCTIONISMS

One reductionist thesis fairly prominent in the philosophical literature, though usually discussed only to be rejected, has been *translational* reductionism. It is a thesis concerning the proprietary vocabularies of different theories, or of different branches of science. According to it, the special and honorary sciences are reducible to physics in the sense that all special- and honorary-scientific terms are translatable, without loss or change of meaning, into physical terms, the correctness of the translations being determinable a priori by anyone competent with all the terms in question. Translational reductionism entails, then, that every special- or honorary-scientific term is analytically definable in physical terms, where the definitions could at least in principle be discovered a priori by anyone competent with the relevant terms, and where these definitions could in principle serve as bridge laws by means of which all special- and honorary-scientific truths could be derived from physical truths. However, as is already no doubt quite clear, realization physicalism, which is not a linguistic or semantic thesis, is not committed to translational reductionism, which is. Realizationism, if in retentive form, is certainly committed to the identity of every special- or honorary-scientific token with a physically realized token of some functional type whose associated condition is specifiable in physical or quasi-logical terms;[2] but such identities can perfectly well be a posteriori, and hence not discoverable a priori even by someone competent with all the scientific terms in question.[3]

Perhaps the most prominent reductionist thesis in the philosophical literature, however, has been what I call reductionism in the *received* sense, a version of reductionism descended from, though not identical with, the version famously articulated by Ernest Nagel in 1961 (Nagel 1979); and it is commitment to reductionism in this sense that nonreductive physicalists in the recent tradition have desired most strongly to avoid. It is usually expressed as a thesis concerning different theories, and hence, since it construes theories as sets of law statements, between different sets of law statements; it can also concern whole branches of science, so long as a branch of science is construed as a cluster of theories. Accordingly, reductionism in the received sense about a theory,

---

2 The notion of quasi-logical terms was introduced in Chapter 1, Section 3. It will be recalled that they are terms that, though not logical in any traditional sense, are nevertheless not part of the proprietary vocabulary of any particular science or honorary science.
3 *Contra* Frank Jackson and David Chalmers. See note 36 in Chapter 1.

T_1, is the claim that T_1 is reducible to some theory, T_2, in the sense that the law statements of T_1 are deducible from the law statements of T_2 by means of bridge principles taking the form of statements that assert the identity of every T_1-type with some or other T_2-type.[4] Now let us call *physical reductionism* the thesis that every theory of every special and honorary science is reducible in the received sense to some theory of physics. Is realization physicalism committed to physical reductionism?

Apparently not. For physical reductionism is true only if every special- and honorary-scientific type is identical with some or other physical type; otherwise the requisite bridge principles are false. But realizationism, even in its retentive form, is committed only to the identity of every special- and honorary-scientific type with some or other functional, not physical, type.[5] Admittedly, as we saw in Chapter 1, these functional types must have associated conditions that are specifiable in physical or quasi-logical terms; but that does not make them physical. For one thing, the associated conditions of some of these functional types might be specifiable entirely in quasi-logical terms, so that by no conceivable stretch could these types be regarded as physical types. But even in the case of functional types whose associated conditions are wholly or partially specifiable in physical terms, it seems wrong to count them as physical. Suppose that the object kind, mousetrap, is a functional type of this sort. Then in some possible world there are mousetraps whose narrow realizers are complex systems of psychons, the smallest possible units of ectoplasm, and which therefore have no physical parts whatsoever. But it seems wrong to call an object kind physical if objects of that kind could exist without any physical parts whatsoever (even if they could not exist in a world *completely* devoid of physical things).[6]

Jaegwon Kim (1993, 323–4), however, has claimed that, if a functional type is such that its tokens are always physically realized, then it should

---

4 There exist more sophisticated variations on this basic theme; but the additional complications do not matter here.
5 Recall that, according to the definition of "physical" in Chapter 1, Section 2, the machinery of higher-order quantification, which the characterization of functional types would require, is not permitted.
6 As elsewhere in this book, my argument here assumes the metaphysical possibility of ectoplasm, i.e., stuff that is neither physical nor physically realized. But should it turn out to be impossible, presumably because it turns out that existents just *are* physical things, then a more aggressive physicalism than I defend in this book will have turned out to be true. So my assumption should be welcomed with gratitude by antiphysicalist readers.

be identified with the disjunction of the physical types whose tokens realize its tokens. But if Kim's claim is right, then, because realizationism entails that *every* special- and honorary-scientific type is such that its tokens are always physically realized, realizationism entails that every special- and honorary-scientific type is identical with some disjunction of physical types. And, although opponents of reductionism might deny that a disjunction of physical types is itself a physical type, good reasons for this denial are not easy to uncover (see Block 1997). So if Kim is right, realizationism arguably does entail statements asserting the identity of every special- or honorary-scientific type with some or other physical type, thus ensuring the deducibility of special- and honorary-scientific laws from those of physics and hence physical reductionism. Moreover, the resulting physical reductionism would be immune to the standard multiple realizability objection, since it is quite consistent with multiple realizability.

Now great care must be taken if a functional type is to be identified with a disjunction of its physical realizer types. In the first place, the disjuncts must surely include not just all those physical types whose tokens ever *actually* realize tokens of the functional type, but also all those physical types whose tokens physically could do so but in fact never do. For consider a physically possible physical object kind that is never actually tokened, but which is such that if it were tokened, the token would play the mousetrap role; surely we want to say that, if it were tokened, there would be a mousetrap. But if we have identified the object kind, mousetrap, with a disjunction only of those physical object kinds whose tokens *actually* realize mousetraps, then we must deny that if the physical object kind in question were tokened, there would be a mousetrap, since the tokens of this physical object kind are never actual mousetrap realizers. Second, in the case of a functional type that has broad physical realizers distinct from its narrow ones, the disjuncts will obviously have to be (at least) its broad physical realizer types (Antony and Levine 1997, 89). Finally, however, whether or not a functional type has broad physical realizers distinct from its narrow ones, each disjunct will typically have to be one of its *very* broad physical realizer types, that is, it will have to be a certain physical type (possibly such that certain physical historical or environmental conditions obtain) *and* such that so-and-so physical laws hold. The reason is that, in the case of some pairs consisting of a physical type and a functional type, tokens of the former realize tokens of the latter only if certain laws hold. Consider a physical object kind whose actual tokens, given the actual physical laws, realize mousetraps; if it is tokened in a possible world where the physical laws are different, its tokens there may not realize mousetraps. So being a token of that physical object kind is not metaphysically sufficient for being a mousetrap; that physical object kind cannot therefore be the whole of a disjunct in any disjunction allegedly identical with the object kind, mousetrap.

But none of this amounts to an *objection* to identifying functional types with disjunctions of physically possible physical realizer-types; such an identification would certainly require a liberal conception of "physical type," but the conception of "physical type" defended in Chapter 1 would be liberal enough. The real difficulty with identifying functional types with disjunctions of physically possible physical realizer types is that functional types do not have, metaphysically, to be physically realized. So *if* we are going to identify a functional type with any disjunction of realizer types, it would have to be with a disjunction of all *metaphysically* possible realizer types; for why should we privilege *physically* possible realizer types with special treatment? But in that case, because a disjunction of all metaphysically possible realizer types would include some *nonphysical* realizer types, we would not have identified the functional type with a *physical* type, even if we do not scruple to count a disjunction of types as itself a type. And what was required for physical reductionism, of course, was precisely the identity of every special- and honorary-scientific type with a *physical* type.

The same point also undercuts such argument as Kim provides for identifying functional types with the disjunctions of their physical realizers in the first place. He writes that "the property of having property P is exactly identical with P, and the property of having *one* of the properties, $P_1, P_2, \ldots, P_n$, is exactly identical with the disjunctive property, $P_1 \vee P_2 \vee \ldots \vee P_n$. On the assumption that N_h, N_r, and N_m are all the properties satisfying specification H, the property of having a property with H, namely pain, is none other than the property of having either N_h or N_r or N_m – namely, the *disjunctive* property, $N_h \vee N_r \vee N_m$!" (1993, 323–4). But why suppose that pain is the property of having either N_h or N_r or N_m just because N_h, N_r, and N_m are all the *actual* physical realizer types? Presumably because it is assumed that pain is the property of having any property that *in the actual world* meets H, so that pain is the property that a thing has in a world, w, iff it has in w any property that, in the *actual* world, meets H. But, on the authentic realizationist view, pain is the property that a thing has in a world, w, iff it has in w any property that, in w, meets H. There is no implicit reference to the actual world.

4. REDUCTIONISM IN THE CORE SENSE

Reductionism in the *received* sense is a modification of a detailed account of reductionism famously proposed by Ernest Nagel (1979, ch. 11). But Nagel prefaces his detailed account with these words: "Reduction, in the sense in which the word is here employed, is the *explanation* of a theory or a set of experimental laws established in one area of inquiry, by a theory ... for some other domain" (338; emphasis added). Nagel's whole discussion is guided, therefore, by this intuitive conception of reduction as a special kind of explanation, explanation of facts expressible in one theoretical vocabulary by appeal to facts expressible in another; and his subsequent detailed account of the formal and informal conditions of reduction – the account that generated reductionism in the received sense – is evidently intended to keep faith with this conception. Now reductionism in the *core* sense, as I shall be calling it, aims to articulate the intuitive conception of reduction that guides Nagel (though without commitment to the details of his formal and informal conditions). It will shortly receive a more careful formulation, but for the moment we may think of it as asserting, roughly, that contingent facts of some kind, K_1, can be noncausally explained by appeal *merely* to approximately simultaneous contingent facts of some other kind, K_2, plus necessary truths.

Now realizationism has not turned out so far to be very interestingly or importantly reductive. But I argue in the next section that realizationism in its retentive form (better: realizationism, to the extent that it is retentive) is committed to reductionism in the core sense. And this conclusion, if correct, does make retentive realizationism importantly reductive. For, as we have just seen, reductionism in the *core* sense expresses the intuitive idea of which reductionism in the *received* sense is a fuller and more rigorous development. So if my conclusion is correct, retentive realizationism still honors the *spirit* of reductionism in the received sense; my earlier concession that it is not committed to the *letter* of reductionism in the received sense will therefore turn out to be a merely Pyrrhic victory for nonreductivists, who have won a battle only to lose the war.[7]

---

7 Other philosophers who have suggested that we need to distinguish the spirit from the letter of Nagel's account of reduction, that the spirit of reductionism is the explainability of higher-level phenomena in terms of physical phenomena, and that the prospects for the spirit of reductionism thus understood brighten considerably are C. Kenneth Waters (1990), Peter Smith (1992), and D. H. M. Brooks (1994). But though the views of Brooks are closest to my own, none of these authors gives a really clear and detailed account of how reductive explanations are supposed to work, especially in the face of the standard multiple-realizability objections to reductionism.

The conclusion that retentive realizationism is committed to reductionism in the core sense is also important because there are two reasons to think that reductionism in the core sense expresses the notion of reductionism intended by certain practicing scientists. The first reason is that it is faithful to their explicit pronouncements about reductionism. Steven Weinberg, for example, understands reductionism as "the perception that scientific principles are the way they are *because* of deeper scientific principles (and, in some cases, historical accidents) and that all these principles can be traced to one simple connected set of laws" (1994, 52; emphasis added). Murray Gell-Mann writes that "the process of *explaining* the higher level in terms of the lower is often called 'reduction'" (1994, 112; emphasis added). And Francis Crick defines reductionism as "the idea that it is possible, at least in principle, to *explain* a phenomenon in terms of less complicated constituents" (1994, 277; emphasis added). Certainly these three scientists are not all saying exactly the same thing; and none of them addresses the difficulty with reductionism that looms largest in philosophers' minds, namely, whether appropriate bridge principles can be found to make *possible* the explanation of facts expressed in one vocabulary by facts expressed in a quite different vocabulary. But

> Jeffrey Poland, although he officially repudiates reductionism, includes among the theses of physicalism both the claim that all instantiations of nonphysical things are "vertically explainable" (1994, 208) and the claim that all regularities (and exceptions to them) are explainable in terms of physically based phenomena (218). These claims certainly sound like reductionism in the core sense. However, Poland treats them as self-standing theses of physicalism apparently independent of any other theses of physicalism (e.g., claims of realization), whereas I argue that reductionism in the core sense is a *consequence* of the thesis that everything is physically realized. Furthermore, Poland does not give us any details about how exactly his "vertical explanations" are supposed to work; so I cannot say how closely his view really does resemble mine. They will certainly appeal to what he calls "realization theories" (1994, 210–16), which sometimes sound like they might be the nonphysical-to-functional-type identity claims on which reduction on my account depends; but since he explicitly denies that realization theories are identity statements, he presumably must have something else in mind (213).
>
> A recent defense of reductionism that does not understand reduction as reduction in the received sense but which also lays no stress at all upon the idea that reducibility is a special sort of explainability is provided by John Bickle (1998). However, although the structuralist formalization of reduction that he develops rather obscures its ontological import, his account is, I think, consistent with mine in the sense that it can accommodate it; at any rate, the extended example of an accomplished psychoneural reduction that he provides (ch. 5) beautifully exemplifies my conception of reduction as well as his. But reduction as he construes it is broad enough to include cases of replacement, which mine is not, and he officially claims (ch. 2) that it does not require bridge laws, again contrary to my account (though for doubts that he can consistently claim this, see Endicott 1998). More generally, since he gives little explicit consideration to a psychofunctionalist metaphysics of mind, Bickle's attitude toward realizationism is not clear.

they are united in conceiving of reduction as a special kind of noncausal, synchronic explanation.

The second reason to think that reductionism in the core sense expresses the notion of reductionism intended by at least some practicing scientists is that to assume that they understand reductionism in this way helps explain their generally enthusiastic attitude toward reductionism. For if, in line with reductionism in the core sense, proreductionist scientists understand reducibility as (a special kind of) explainability, and if they hold, as most scientists do, that it is in general a very good thing to be able to explain things, then they can be expected to hold also that it is in general a very good thing to be able to reduce things, hostility to reduction being tantamount, in their view, to hostility to the central scientific goal of explanation. Indeed, if reductionism in the core sense is *true*, which it must be if retentive realizationism is true and entails it, then the assumption that proreductionist scientists like the three Nobel laureates just quoted understand reductionism as reductionism in the core sense can help explain, without any need for an implausible attribution of gross error, why they all think (as they do) that reductionism is turning out to be true.

But before I show that retentive realizationism is committed to reductionism in the core sense, I must first formulate this version of reductionism with more precision, and with particular reference to the case in which we are currently interested, that of the reducibility of special- and honorary-scientific facts to physical facts:

> (CR) All nomic special- and honorary-scientific facts, and all positive nonnomic special- and honorary-scientific facts, have an explanation that appeals only to (i) physical facts and (ii) necessary (i.e., entirely noncontingent) truths.

By "special- and honorary-scientific facts," I mean facts expressible in the proprietary vocabularies of the special and honorary sciences.[8] And

---

8 The requirement that what gets reduced be *facts* entails that, according to (CR), only *true* generalizations and *real* tokens can get reduced in the core sense. This is harmless, because reduction in the core sense is meant to help only with the *synchronic* problem of interscience relations, which assumes that each of the many sciences is, or at least might be, speaking the truth about the world and which aims to say how these different accounts relate to one another; reduction in the core sense is not meant to address any *diachronic* problem of intrascience theory succession. However, many philosophers of science writing about reductionism have been addressing the diachronic problems and have therefore been anxious for their accounts of reduction to leave room for the possibility of the reduction of theories that are not strictly correct. To extend my account of reductionism in the core sense to cover

by "nomic special- and honorary-scientific facts," I mean the holding of such counterfactual-supporting regularities as can be expressed by generalizations couched in the proprietary vocabularies of the special and honorary sciences. However, these regularities may be few in number, they may be statistical only, they may hold only ceteris paribus, their scope may be restricted to certain spatiotemporal regions only, their scope may be restricted to special- and honorary-scientific tokens whose physical realizers are of approximately the same physical type, and they need not amount to laws in any metaphysically very demanding sense (e.g., they need not be relations among universals). By "positive nonnomic special- and honorary-scientific facts," I mean, paradigmatically, the existence of tokens of special- and honorary-scientific types; the qualification, "positive," is intended to exclude both such *explicitly* negative facts as that there is no zebra in my office and such *implicitly* negative facts as that there are exactly n zebras, which can hold only if it is a fact that there is no $n+1$th zebra. By "physical facts," I mean to include two classes of facts: first, nonnomic facts expressible in the proprietary vocabulary of physics, where this vocabulary consists of both the positive predicates used in the formulation of the theories of current physics and the predicates constructible out of the positive predicates of current physics via the use of such predicate-forming machinery as the language of physics already contains, (possibly infinitary) conjunction and disjunction, negation, and also the "... is such that..." predicate-forming operator;[9] and, second, the holding of physical laws as defined in Chapter 1, that is, all lawlike regularities, universal or statistical, that are either expressed by law statements standardly used in any branch of current physics or expressible by law statements logically derivable in principle from law statements standardly used in any of the branches of current physics.

Four features of (CR) deserve comment. First, (CR) does not claim that, in order for the special or honorary sciences to be reduced to physics, explanations of special- or honorary-scientific facts that appeal only to

---

such cases, it suffices, I think, to adopt Kenneth Shaffner's (1967) suggestion and treat the reduction of a strictly false but approximately true theory as, properly speaking, the reduction in the core sense of a *corrected* version of the false theory.

9 We should also add the qualifications that (i) the constructed predicate does not express a necessary property (e.g., that of either being a quark or not being a quark) and (ii) the constructed predicate is not entirely negative. Note that, in the characterization of physical facts given in the text here, higher-order quantification is not included among the permissible predicate-forming machinery – as it was not in the definition of "physical" in Chapter 1, Section 2.

physical facts and necessary truths should *replace* nonreductive explanations of those same facts that appeal to other special- or honorary-scientific facts. Certainly (CR) claims that all special- and honorary-scientific facts of the specified kinds have *an* explanation that appeals only to physical facts and necessary truths; but, for all that (CR) claims, it remains an entirely open question whether these facts *also* have *other* explanations (e.g., nonreductive ones citing other special- or honorary-scientific facts).[10] Moreover, we should be clear *why* (CR) leaves this question open. The reason is not that physical explanations of special- and honorary-scientific facts leave some part of those facts unexplained; the idea is not, for instance, that there are physical explanations only for the *physical* features of events, with special-scientific explanations therefore required to account for the *special-scientific* features of those same events. For (CR) entails that literally *every* special- or honorary-scientific token has an explanation that appeals only to physical facts plus necessary truths; hence (CR) entails that every special- or honorary-scientific *feature* of every event has such an explanation, since special- or honorary-scientific features of events (however exactly we understand "features") would be special- or honorary-scientific tokens too; so physical explanations of (positive) special- and honorary-scientific facts do not leave *any* parts of those facts unexplained. The true reason why (CR) leaves open the possibility that the relevant special- and honorary-scientific facts should have nonreductive as well as reductive explanations is that (CR) neither states nor implies that it would be in any way objectionable for one and the same token to have *more than one* explanation. The assumption that it would be objectionable for one and the same token to have more than one explanation is not trivial, and I argue in Chapter 4 that, in fact, it is false. The point for now, however, is only that (CR) does not make this assumption and can therefore allow

---

10 Thus Gell-Mann (1994, 111–20) takes commendable pains to emphasize that even though, as he believes, chemistry and biology can in principle be explained in terms of fundamental physics, additional explanations of chemical and biological phenomena in chemical or biological terms are both possible and desirable. Contrast, however, the antireductionist Harold Kincaid, who assumes an intuitive account of reduction according to which a reducing theory "can in principle do all the explanatory work" of the reduced theory (1997, 3 and 71); his meaning becomes very clear when he gives as a reason for holding that biochemistry has not reduced biology the fact that "it has not replaced biological explanations," a reason obviously presupposing that reduction requires replacement of explanations (10). Notice that although he connects reduction with explanation, as I do, what the reducing theory must explain, for him, is whatever the reduced theory seemed able to explain, rather than, as for me, certain facts, including nomic ones, expressible in the vocabulary of the reduced theory.

that one and the same special- or honorary-scientific token should have *both* a nonreductive explanation (in special- or honorary-scientific terms) *and* a reductive explanation (in physical terms).

Second, according to (CR), a nomic special- or honorary-scientific fact counts as reducible to physics so long as it has an explanation that appeals only to physical facts (plus necessary truths); but those physical facts can include *particular* physical facts (e.g., the initial physical conditions of the universe) as well as physical laws.[11] By contrast, reductionism in the received sense does not count a special- or honorary-scientific law as reducible to physics unless it has an explanation that appeals only to physical *laws* (plus certain necessary identities). Reductionism in the core sense does not impose this needlessly strong requirement.

To appreciate the third comment on (CR), note that it allows reductive explanations to appeal to necessary truths, in addition to physical facts; and the purpose of these necessary truths, of course, is to serve as bridge principles, connecting special- and honorary-scientific facts with physical facts so that the former can be explained in terms of the latter. Now according to reductionism in the *received* sense, bridge principles take the form of a posteriori necessary identities holding between each and every special- or honorary-scientific type, on the one hand, and some or other *physical* type, on the other. By contrast, however, and this is the third comment, (CR) does not require bridge principles of exactly that form. Indeed, I try to show in the next section that the bridge principles employed in a reduction can perfectly well take the form of a posteriori necessary identities holding between each and every special- or honorary-scientific type, on the one hand, and some or other *functional* type, on the other.

Finally, however, (CR) insists that these bridge principles be necessary in the strongest sense of being entirely noncontingent, that is, true in all possible worlds. (So merely nomologically necessary bridge principles, such as those permitted by Nagel's detailed account of the conditions of reduction, would not suffice, since merely nomologically necessary bridge principles would still be contingent.) Why this insistence that bridge principles be entirely noncontingent? The intuitive reason is that, unless the bridge principles are entirely noncontingent, (CR) gives us no sense in which special- and honorary-scientific facts are *reducible* to physical facts: if

---

11   Both Weinberg (1994, 32–8) and Gell-Mann (1994, 110–11, 113–14) explicitly allow that physically reductive explanations of the sort they believe to exist may have to appeal to very local physical conditions as well as physical laws.

the bridge principles are at all contingent, special- and honorary-scientific facts might still be explainable in *some* sort of way by physical facts, but not explainable in the *special* sort of way required for them to count as *reducible* to physical facts. And what is that special sort of way? Our intuitive idea, I suggest, is that an *explanation* of some special- or honorary-scientific fact by physical facts counts as a *reduction* of it to physical facts only if the only *contingent* facts appealed to in the explanation are physical facts; other explanatory factors may be cited, but they cannot be contingent. Contingent bridge principles, however, would *not* be purely physical facts; they would be "mixed" facts, as much special- or honorary-scientific as physical. So they cannot be employed in any explanation that is to count as a reduction to physical facts. Allowing them into an explanation putatively amounting to a reduction of some fact to *physical* facts would in effect yield the result that the special- or honorary-scientific fact was reduced, not to physical facts, but to a *mixture* of physical facts and special- or honorary-scientific facts.

You might fairly ask, of course, *why* an explanation of some special- or honorary-scientific fact by physical facts should count as a reduction of it to physical facts only if the only contingent facts cited in the explanation are physical facts. The answer is an even more basic idea we have about reduction: acknowledging the reducibility of some fact (or kind of fact) should effect an overall decrease in the ontological commitments of our total world view, these ontological commitments, indeed, being precisely what gets reduced (in the ordinary sense of *lessened*) in a reduction. Reducibility is not eliminability, of course; if a fact is reducible, its existence is undiminished; indeed, if reducibility is (a special kind of) explainability, then, since explanation is necessarily of genuine facts, a fact acknowledged to be reducible *cannot* coherently be denied.[12] Nevertheless, acknowledging the reducibility of some fact still effects an overall decrease in the ontological commitments of our total world view, not by requiring the outright repudiation of the reducible fact, but by showing that we can acknowledge the reducible fact as perfectly genuine but without construing it as *logically additional* to the facts to which it is reducible, facts that, of course, we already acknowledge.

---

12 Obviously a fact can be explained *away*. But to explain away a fact is to explain the *appearance* of the fact, not the fact itself, and indeed to explain the appearance of the fact consistently with the nonexistence of the fact, thus rendering postulation of the fact explanatorily gratuitous.

If the reducible fact can thus be treated as an ontological free lunch, then whereas formerly we took the reducing facts *plus* the reducible fact to be basic, independent existents, we need now take *only* the reducing facts that way, and so our overall world view is simplified.[13] But, and here is the point, we can avoid construing the reducible fact as logically additional to the reducing fact (i.e., we can treat the reducible fact as an ontological free lunch) only if the bridge principles that secure the reduction are entirely noncontingent. Indeed, in order to achieve the ontological simplification that is essential to reduction, a further requirement must be imposed on the bridge principles required by (CR): not only must they be entirely noncontingent, but they must also not express the kind of brute metaphysical necessitation mooted in Chapter 2 in connection with the adequacy of a pure supervenience formulation of physicalism. For if they express the *brute* metaphysical necessitation of special- or honorary-scientific facts by physical facts, that is, a necessitation inexplicable by appeal to type identity claims of any kind, then, intuitively, the facts to be reduced *are* logically additional to the reducing facts, contrary to the idea that what gets reduced in a reduction is overall ontological commitment. However, it suffices to avoid this "brute necessitation" problem if we add to (CR) the requirement that the entirely noncontingent bridge principles involved in a reduction must reflect the holding of certain *necessary identities*, as explained in Chapter 2.

5. RETENTIVE REALIZATIONISM'S COMMITMENT TO REDUCTIONISM IN THE CORE SENSE

My case for the conclusion that realization physicalism in its retentive form is committed to (CR), and is therefore in that important sense reductive, falls into two stages. In the first, I argue that, if retentive realizationism is true, then propositions of two sorts are in principle *derivable* from propositions expressing physical facts, plus necessary truths: (i) every proposition asserting the existence of one of the special- and honorary-scientific tokens that actually exists; and (ii), in the case of each regularity holding among special- and honorary-scientific tokens, every proposition asserting the holding of an *instance* of that regularity. (An instance of the regularity that every F-token is followed by a G-token is the fact that some particular F-token exists and is followed by a G-token.) In

---

[13] Reductionism in the core sense therefore entails reductionism in the second sense distinguished in Section 2.

the second stage, I argue that this derivability of propositions of types (i) and (ii) from propositions expressing physical facts, plus necessary truths, amounts to the *explainability* of nomic and positive nonnomic special- and honorary-scientific facts by appeal to physical facts (plus necessary truths). Because such explainability suffices by definition for the truth of (CR), it follows that, if retentive realizationism is true, then (CR) is true too.

Let me now embark on the first part of the first stage, and show that, if retentive realizationism is true, then every proposition asserting the existence of one of the special- and honorary-scientific tokens that actually exists is in principle derivable from propositions expressing physical facts (plus necessary truths). Let us begin by reviewing the metaphysical position. As we saw in Chapter 1, if retentive realizationism is true, then the existence of every special- or honorary-scientific token falling within the scope of (R) is necessitated in the strongest sense by certain physical facts. For consider a particular such token of special-scientific type, F. If retentive realizationism is true, then it is physically realized; that is, by the definition of "physically realized," there is a token, p, of some physical type, P_1, which, purely as a logical consequence of certain other physical facts, including physical laws, meets condition, C, where the tokening of some or other type that meets C just is the tokening of F. But then, given the physical facts that p exists, that it is of type P_1, that relevant historical or environmental conditions obtain, and that the laws of physics hold, it logically must be true (given certain analytic trivialities) that there exists a token of some or other type that meets C; and given that, and the metaphysically necessary identity of the tokening of F with the tokening of some or other type that meets C, it must metaphysically be true that there is a token of F; but since this token of F exists, and since, by the definition of "physically realized," this token is necessarily identical with the token of F that we were originally considering, it must be true that the token of F that we were originally considering exists. So if retentive realizationism is true, certain physical facts necessitate in the strongest sense the existence of the token of F that we were originally considering. But since there is nothing special about this case, we can generalize our conclusion to say that, if retentive realizationism is true, then certain physical facts necessitate in the strongest sense the existence of *all* special- or honorary-scientific tokens that fall within the scope of (R).

But we can now see how the truth of retentive realizationism would provide the resources to ensure that every proposition asserting the existence of one of the special- and honorary-scientific tokens that fall within the scope of (R) is in principle derivable from propositions expressing physical facts (plus necessary truths). The following schema, for the case of an arbitrarily selected token of F, crudely captures the form of the derivation for every case:

(1) There is a token of P_1.

(2) Certain physical environmental or historical conditions obtain.

(3) So-and-so laws of physics hold.

∴ (4) A token of some or other type that meets condition C exists.

(5) Necessarily, a token of F exists iff a token of some or other type that meets condition C exists.

∴ (6) A token of F exists.

(7) The token of F mentioned in (6) = the arbitrarily selected token of F.

∴ (C) The arbitrarily selected token of F exists.

If retentive realizationism is true, so that the arbitrarily selected token of F is physically realized, then there must be ways of filling out premises (1), (2), and (3) so that they are true and, with the aid of analytic trivialities, logically entail subconclusion (4); there must also be some proposition identifying F with some functional type whose associated condition is specifiable in physical or quasi-logical terms, some proposition that, given the necessity of identity, entails a way of filling out premise (5) so that it is true; and, finally, given the definition of "physically realized," there must be some true proposition identifying the arbitrarily selected token of F with the token of F mentioned in (6), so that premise (7) is true. But (C) obviously follows from (1), (2), (3), (5), and (7). So if retentive realizationism is true, the proposition that there exists a certain token of F is in principle derivable from propositions expressing physical facts, that is, premises (1), (2), and (3), plus necessary truths, that is, (5) and (7). Of course, the proposition is no doubt not derivable in practice, since we are quite unable to determine and then state the appropriate fillings for the premises, and even if we could, the derivations would be intractably complex, even with computer assistance; but the proposition must be derivable in principle.

Let me now show that, if retentive realizationism is true, then, in the case of each regularity holding among special- and honorary-scientific tokens that fall within the scope of (R), every proposition asserting the holding of an instance of that regularity is in principle derivable from propositions expressing physical facts, plus necessary truths. As before, let us first clarify the metaphysical position. Suppose that F and G are special- or honorary-scientific types, and that the following regularity holds among their tokens: every F-token is followed by a G-token.[14] Now, if retentive realizationism is true, *every* F-token must be physically realized and therefore have a narrow realizer of some physical type that, given the physical laws, meets the associated condition for F and hence necessitates the existence of the F-token. (Assume for simplicity's sake that each F-token has only a narrow realizer and a very broad realizer, but not a broad realizer.) So, if retentive realizationism is true, then, given the physical laws, the existence of certain physical tokens necessitates the existence of all the F-tokens that there are. But now suppose that some of these physical tokens – some of the narrow realizers of the F-tokens – were *not* such that, given their respective physical circumstances and the laws of physics, they are followed by some physical token that realizes and hence (given the physical laws) necessitates a G-token. It would then follow, contrary to the assumption of the example, that some F-tokens are *not* followed by G-tokens; for these F-tokens would not be followed by *physically* realized G-tokens and, given realizationism, there *are* no *nonphysically* realized G-tokens. So, if retentive realizationism is true, and if every F-token is followed by a G-token, then the (physical) narrow realizer of *every* F-token must be such that, given its physical circumstances and the laws of physics, it is followed by some physical token that realizes and hence (given the physical laws) necessitates a G-token.[15]

It should now be clear that, and how, if retentive realizationism is true, the holding of every instance of the regularity that every F-token is followed by a G-token is necessitated in the strongest sense by the physical facts. For the holding of every instance of the regularity just is the fact that every actual F-token is followed by a G-token. But, given

---

14 I use this simple schematic example of a special- or honorary-scientific regularity for the sake of convenience, but I do not hold that all special- or honorary-scientific regularities have to resemble it in being universal and unhedged.

15 Notice that this claim is consistent with the possibility that the physical circumstances that the narrow physical realizer of the F-token is in should be physically sufficient *all by themselves* for the existence of a narrow physical realizer of a G-token; the narrow physical realizer of the F-token would in that case not be *necessary* for the existence of the G-token, even though it was sufficient *in the circumstances* for it. This possibility will assume considerable importance in the account of causation and causal relevance that I present in Chapter 4.

realizationism, the only F- or G-tokens that exist are physically realized ones whose existence is therefore necessitated in the strongest sense by the physical facts. So, given realizationism, if every actual F-token is followed by a G-token, then certain physical facts, including physical laws, must necessitate the existence of each F-token that exists; and certain *other* physical facts, including physical laws, must necessitate that each F-token is followed by a G-token. Physical facts therefore necessitate in the strongest sense the holding of all the instances of the regularity that make it up.

Let me now show how the truth of retentive realizationism would provide the resources to ensure that, in the case of each regularity holding among special- and honorary-scientific tokens, every proposition asserting the holding of an instance of that regularity is in principle derivable from propositions expressing physical facts, plus necessary truths. I do so by presenting in highly schematic form the derivation of a proposition asserting the holding of just one instance of a single regularity, and by showing that, if retentive realizationism is true, it must be possible to fill in this derivation so as to make it sound. It will obviously be possible to generalize from this schematic example to reach the same conclusion about every instance of every special- or honorary-scientific regularity.

The schematic regularity we consider is that every F-token is followed by a G-token. Let us begin by considering a particular F-token. Given retentive realizationism, it must have a narrow physical realizer that is a token of a physical type we may decide to call "P_1"; our first premise can therefore be the (physical) proposition that

(1) A token of P_1 exists.

We are also entitled, independently, to the (physical) premise that

(2) The laws of physics hold.

But now, because the token of P_1 mentioned in (1) has been assumed to be the narrow physical realizer of the F-token, and for simplicity's sake we are assuming that no historical or environmental conditions are necessary for it to realize the F-token, it logically follows (given analytic trivialities) that

(3) A token of some or other type that meets condition C exists,

where "C" is what we decide to call the associated condition for F. That F is identical with *some* functional type whose associated condition can be specified physically or quasi-logically is guaranteed by retentive realizationism. But then we are also entitled to the (metaphysically necessary) premise that

(4) Necessarily, a token of F exists iff a token of some or other type that meets condition C exists,

from which it follows, given (3), that

(5) A token of F exists.

But we are assuming, of course, that this F-token, like all others, is followed by a G-token; and we have already seen that, given retentive realizationism, this can be so only if some physical token that realizes a G-token is the invariable consequence of the physical token that is the narrow realizer of this F-token, given the laws of physics and certain possibly very complex physical circumstances simultaneous with and subsequent to it. If we call these physical circumstances the "enabling" circumstances, then we can add the (physical) premise that

(6) The enabling physical circumstances obtain.[16]

But from (1), (2), and (6) it follows that

(7) A (later) token of P_2 exists,

where P_2 is the physical type tokened by the narrow realizer of the G-token that follows our F-token. But precisely because this later token of P_2 is the narrow realizer of the G-token, it must follow from (2) and (7) that

(8) A (later) token of some or other type that meets condition D exists,

where "D" is what we decide to call the associated condition for G. That G is identical with *some* functional type whose associated condition can be specified physically and/or topic-neutrally is guaranteed by retentive realizationism. But then we are also entitled to the (metaphysically necessary) premise that

(9) Necessarily, a token of G exists iff a token of some or other type that meets condition D exists.

---

16 As pointed out in note 15, it could happen that the enabling physical circumstances *alone* are sufficient for the physical token that realizes the G-token – in which case the description of them as "enabling" would be something of an understatement.

It then follows from (8) and (9) that

(10) A (later) token of G exists.

Finally, from (5) and (10) it follows that

(C) A token of F exists, and a (later) token of G.

In this way, then, given the truth of retentive realizationism, a proposition asserting the holding of one particular instance of the regularity that every F-token is followed by a G-token is derivable, in principle, from propositions expressing physical facts, that is, (1), (2), and (6), plus necessary truths, that is, (4) and (9). Moreover, because no special assumptions were made about the F-token and the G-token that were the subject of the schematic derivation just given, we can generalize to the conclusion that, if retentive realizationism is true, then, for *every* particular F-token, a proposition asserting that it exists and is followed by a G-token can in principle be derived from physical premises plus necessary truths in the way indicated earlier. Indeed, we can obviously generalize again to reach a parallel conclusion about the derivability of every proposition reporting an instance of *any* universal special- or honorary-scientific regularity. Five comments on such derivations are in order.

The first comment concerns the status of such *necessity* as special- or honorary-scientific regularities can enjoy if propositions reporting their instances are derivable in the way just indicated. As we see from the presence of premise (6), derivations of such propositions are permitted to appeal not only to physical laws, but also to the holding of particular physical circumstances, circumstances that might result ultimately from entirely accidental physical conditions that characterized the beginning of the universe (if it had one). Therefore, such necessity as special- or honorary-scientific regularities can possess if propositions reporting their instances are derivable in the way just indicated may reflect not only such necessity as *physical* regularities enjoy but also brutely contingent physical particularities. So although it may be quite true that every F-token not only is but *must be* followed by a G-token, this necessity may be a consequence of the necessity of physical laws only given particular physical circumstances that are not themselves required by physical law.

Second, derivations of the sort just indicated do not make the presumably false assumption that the laws of physics are universal and nonprobabilistic; and, perhaps surprisingly, they do not make this assumption even if the special- or honorary-scientific regularity whose instances are being derived is *itself* universal and nonprobabilistic. A simple example makes the point. Suppose that every F-token is realized by a token of either physical type P_1 or physical type P_2; and suppose that every G-token is realized by a token of either physical type Q_1 or physical type Q_2. Then the regularity that every F-token is followed by a G-token might be underwritten by a physical law to the effect that (i) a P_1-token has a 90 percent chance of being followed by a Q_1-token and a 10 percent chance of being followed by a Q_2-token, and another physical law that (ii) a P_2-token has a 10 percent chance of being followed by a Q_1-token and a 90 percent chance of being followed by a Q_1-token. Neither law (i) nor law (ii) is a universal, nonprobabilistic physical law, and yet their joint operation, given realizationism, would ensure that every F-token without exception is followed by a G-token.

The third comment concerns the character of the *bridge principles* that derivations of the sort just indicated presuppose or entail. These derivations obviously presuppose bridge principles, patterned on (4) and (9), that affirm the identity of special- or honorary-scientific types with *functional* types; and *if* those functional types have associated conditions specifiable (even partially) in physical terms, these bridge principles entail in their turn that there are certain *physical* states of affairs (namely, those referred to in specifying the associated conditions) for which tokenings of special- or honorary-scientific types are metaphysically sufficient. But do these derivations entail any further bridge principles linking the physical with the nonphysical? It is logically necessary that, if (1) and (2) are true, then (3) is true; and it is metaphysically necessary that, if (3) is true, then (5) is true; so it is necessary in the strongest sense that if (1) and (2) are true, then (5) is true, that is, that if a certain physical token exists, and the laws of physics hold, then there is an F-token. So derivations of the sort indicated earlier certainly entail bridge principles that run in the physical-to-nonphysical direction, and that assert the sufficiency (in the strongest possible sense) of certain physical conditions, given the laws of physics, for the tokening of certain special- or honorary-scientific types (equivalently: the *physical* sufficiency of those same physical conditions for the tokening of the same special- or honorary-scientific types). But derivations of the sort indicated earlier do not entail bridge principles that are the converse of these bridge principles.

And it is good that they do not, for such bridge principles, running in the opposite, nonphysical-to-physical direction, are very probably false. It is certainly not necessary in the strongest sense that if there is an F-token, then some narrow physical realizer for it exists, since the existence of a *nonphysically* realized F-token is at least metaphysically possible.

It is probably not even necessary in the strongest sense that *if the laws of physics hold* and there is an F-token, then some narrow physical realizer for the F-token exists. For the laws of physics apparently do not rule out the possibility of nonphysically realized F-tokens. How could they? They could not rule out nonphysically realized tokens of functional types whose associated conditions are specifiable entirely noncausally (e.g., quasi-logically). For nonphysical and nonphysically realized realizers of such functional tokens would not be required to interact causally with physical tokens, and only if they did is it plausible to think that there might therefore be some conflict with the laws of physics. But what about nonphysical and nonphysically realized realizers that *would* be required to interact causally with physical tokens in order to meet the associated conditions of the functional types they were realizing? The laws of physics would rule out the possibility of nonphysical and nonphysically realized realizers of this kind only if they ruled out the possibility of causal interaction between physical tokens, on the one hand, and tokens that are neither physical nor physically realized, on the other. But traditional attempts to show that physical conservation laws do precisely that have few advocates today; and it is hard to believe that physics itself could lead quite so swiftly to a refutation of (nonepiphenomenalist) dualism.

The fourth comment answers the following question that may have occurred to some readers: if it is true, as I have argued, that if retentive realizationism is assumed, then, for *every* particular F-token, a proposition asserting that it exists and is followed by a G-token can in principle be derived from physical premises plus necessary truths, then why not simply *conjoin* the premises of all these derivations and then derive from their conjunction the generalization that *all* F-tokens are followed by G-tokens? The reason why not is simply that from the conjunction of the premises of all the individual derivations the desired conclusion just does not follow. To make it follow, we would need to add as an explicit premise the claim that the F-tokens mentioned in the instance-reporting propositions (i.e., the physically realized F-tokens) are all the F-tokens that there are. (A logically analogous situation is this: if there are exactly one thousand ravens and we know from observation that each one of them is black, it does not follow from our observations that all ravens are black, even though we have observed every raven there is and found it to be black; we may deduce this conclusion only if we add to our observations the explicit premise that the ravens we have observed are all the ravens there are.)

Now the missing premise here – that the physically realized F-tokens are all the F-tokens that there are – must in fact be true, if retentive realizationism is true, because retentive realizationism entails that every F-token is physically realized; so retentive realizationism indeed guarantees us the missing premise we need. Why not then use it, you might wonder, to derive the generalization that all F-tokens are G-tokens? The reason is that this premise, though true, would be neither a physical truth (for it must mention F-tokens as such) nor a necessary truth (for in some possible worlds F-tokens are nonphysically realized).[17] So were we to use it in a derivation of the generalization that all F-tokens are G-tokens, we would only have shown the derivability of that generalization from contingent physical propositions, plus necessary truths, *plus* a proposition (expressing the truth of realizationism) that was contingent but nonphysical. It would then be impossible to construe this derivability as the reducibility in the core sense of the regularity in question. For, according to (CR), reducibility in the core sense requires the explainability of what gets reduced by appeal *only* to contingent physical facts, plus necessary truths.[18]

Finally, my earlier schematic example concerns the universal, unhedged regularity that every F-token is followed by a G-token; and, as already noted, the conclusion drawn from it obviously generalizes to all cases of universal, unhedged regularities. But the conclusion can easily be seen to generalize also to special- or honorary-scientific regularities that are either hedged or statistical. In the case of regularities that hold only ceteris paribus, the key point is that, given realizationism, any *cetera* must be physical or physically realized; so if a regularity holds ceteris paribus, then, given realizationism, physical conditions must be such that, when (and only when) the physical *cetera* (or their physical realizers) are *paria*, narrow realizers of F-tokens are followed by narrow realizers of G-tokens. So it will still be possible in principle to derive a proposition reporting each instance of the regularity from physical premises plus necessary truths, although the fact that the physical *cetera* (or their physical realizers) are *paria* must be mentioned in an explicit premise. In the case of statistical regularities, the key point is that if it is a regularity that $n\%$ of F-tokens are followed by G-tokens (where $n < 100$), then, given retentive

---

17 Notice that the thesis of realization physicalism itself, that everything is physical or physically realized, is not entailed by the totality of physical facts. Since it is nevertheless, if true, contingently true, a physicalist must take care not to claim that *every* contingent truth holds solely in virtue of the way things are physically.

18 The point made in this paragraph is one that I missed in my earlier article (1995b), which was written before I had articulated the idea of reductionism in the core sense.

realizationism, physical conditions must be such that n% of narrow realizers of F-tokens are followed by narrow realizers of G-tokens. So for each F-token that *is* in fact followed by a G-token (each *instance* of the statistical regularity), a proposition asserting that it exists and is so followed will be derivable in principle from physical premises plus necessary truths. This completes my defense of the claim that if retentive realizationism is true, then, for every special- or honorary-scientific regularity, every proposition asserting the holding of an instance of the regularity is in principle, though only in principle, derivable from propositions expressing physical facts, plus necessary truths.

Now for the second stage of my case for holding that retentive realizationism is committed to reductionism in the core sense: having shown, on the assumption of retentive realizationism, the in-principle derivability from propositions expressing physical facts, plus necessary truths, of (i) every proposition asserting the existence of one of the special- and honorary-scientific tokens that actually exists and (ii), in the case of each regularity holding among special- and honorary-scientific tokens, every proposition asserting the holding of an instance of that regularity, I need now to show that the derivability of such propositions amounts to the *explainability* of nomic and positive nonnomic special- and honorary-scientific facts by appeal only to physical facts, plus necessary truths. If it does, then, given (CR), retentive realizationism is committed to reductionism in the core sense.

The ideal strategy for showing that the derivability of the relevant propositions amounts to the explainability of the facts they report would no doubt start with a well-developed account of explanation demonstrably superior to all rival accounts. Regrettably, however, I have no such account to offer. A less ideal strategy would start with an account of explanation that was at least widely accepted. But no consensus among philosophers exists on a positive account of explanation; consensus has formed only around the negative point that the derivation of a proposition reporting some fact does not automatically count as an explanation of the fact. So my strategy has to be different. I begin by attempting, on the basis of what I hope are plausible intuitions, to establish a defeasible presumption that the derivability of the relevant propositions amounts to the explainability of the facts they report; I then argue that this presumption is as yet undefeated.

Let me start with the in-principle derivability of every proposition asserting the existence of one of the special- and honorary-scientific tokens that actually exists. I have four points to make. The first is that although not all derivations of propositions are explanations of the facts they report, everyone allows that very many *are*; and this surely provides *some* reason, albeit inductive, to think that actual derivations on the pattern I outlined here would be explanations of the special- or honorary-scientific tokens their conclusions report to exist. Second, an actual derivation on that pattern would certainly *sound* like an explanation: "Why is there a can opener there? Well, there's a swarm of physical particles there that plays the can opener role, and all it takes for there to be a can opener there is that *something* there should play the can opener role." Surely this sounds like an explanation, like *an* explanation, of why there is a can opener in a certain place. At the very least it counts as what David Chalmers aptly calls a *mystery-removing* explanation (1996a, 48–50): if it were a complete mystery to you why a can opener was there, then it would no longer be a complete mystery after the remarks about a swarm of physical particles. Of course, there would obviously still be much more you might like to know, for example, how the swarm of particles got there; but it is true of *all* explanations that they leave some of the factors they invoke unexplained, even thought we might want those factors explained.

Third, actual derivations on the pattern I outlined here would meet certain conditions that we strongly associate with explanations. They would cite factors relative to which the fact reported in the conclusion is *no accident*: given the swarm of physical particles, the laws of physics, and the relevant honorary-scientific/functional type-identity claim, it is no accident, indeed it is inevitable, that there should be a can opener. The derivations' premises would be such that knowledge of them would have led one to *expect* the fact reported in the conclusion: on the basis of knowledge of the swarm of physical particles, the laws of physics, and the relevant honorary-scientific or functional type-identity claim, one could have *predicted* that there would be a can opener. And the derivations would exhibit the facts reported in their conclusions as *instances* of a more *general* phenomenon, namely, as special- or honorary-scientific facts that are necessitated by physical facts, given the physical laws and relevant honorary- or special-scientific/functional type-identity claims.

Finally, an actual derivation on the pattern outlined earlier would closely resemble a kind of explanation that scientists routinely offer. Here is an example: "Why is that gas sample transparent? Because its atoms are such that they do not absorb photons at a frequency within the visible range; and transparency just *is* the property of not absorbing photons at a frequency within the visible range." We must surely count this as an explanation; but in view of its close similarity to actual derivations on the pattern I outlined earlier it is not clear how we could consistently do so while denying that those derivations would also count as explanations; so I think we have to count those derivations as explanations.

I take it that the combined effect of these four points is to establish a defeasible presumption that actual derivations on the pattern I outlined earlier would amount to explanations. But can this presumption be defeated? Is there any good reason to *deny* that such derivations would amount to explanations? One reason might be that their premises provide no information about the *causal ancestry* of the particular facts their conclusions report: physical realizers evidently do not *cause* the special- or honorary-scientific tokens they realize, at least not as Aristotelian *efficient* causes. But although many explanations of particular facts do in fact provide information about the causal ancestry of the facts, no one, to my knowledge, has ever shown that they *have* to.[19] And there seem to be clear cases of noncausal explanations of particular facts. One is the gas transparency example given earlier. Here is another: "Why did allowing that blue flame to play upon the surface of that cool beaker produce droplets of *water*? Because allowing that blue flame to play upon the surface of that cool beaker produced aggregates of H_2O molecules in a liquid state, and aggregates of H_2O molecules in a liquid state just *are* droplets of water." Here, we explain why a certain action produces water, but without saying anything about *what caused* that action's production of water.

Here is a second possible objection to holding that an actual derivation on the pattern I outlined earlier would amount to an explanation of the fact its conclusion reports: the *real* explanation of a fact cites *earlier* facts characterized in the *same sort of vocabulary* as that used to characterize the fact to be explained; so what really explains (e.g.) why there is a can opener in a certain place is not some bizarre derivation from particle physics, but the fact that the chef put one there (see, e.g., Putnam 1975, 295–8). But this objection frames the issue in a way that we need not accept: it assumes that a particular fact can have only one explanation, so that if a bizarre derivation from microphysical premises were accepted as even *an* explanation of why the can opener is there, we would then be forced to say that the causal explanation adverting to the chef was no

---

19 David Lewis (1986), for example, offers no argument for his version of this view, contenting himself with trying to show that it is not refuted by any intuitively plausible case of an explanation of an event. I might add that, although Lewis's paper inspired the objection in the text, his account (1986, 223–4) of the explanation of Walt's immunity suggests that he might well not endorse it.

explanation at all. However, if a particular fact can have *more* than one explanation, then we need not decide whether the bizarre derivation from particle physics would be *the* explanation, but only whether it would be *an* explanation; and, indeed, if the derivation from particle physics is no longer treated as a *rival* to the commonsense explanation, so that we are no longer forced to choose between them, then we will perhaps be readier to allow that it is at least *an* explanation. In the next chapter, I argue at length that it is quite unobjectionable for a particular fact to have *more* than one explanation, and hence for it to have *both* a nonreductive, causal explanation *and* a reductive one. For now, I merely note that allowing both a reductive explanation and a nonreductive, causal explanation of the same particular fact at least poses no threat of *causal overdetermination*, since a reductive explanation, as lately noted, is not a *causal* explanation.

Admittedly, if I reply to someone who asks me why there is a can opener in a certain place, "Well, there's a swarm of physical particles there that plays the can opener role, and all it takes for there to be a can opener there is that *something* there should play the can opener role," then I am sure to get the response, "Yes, but..." Such a response, however, would show only that I had exhibited the kind of uncooperativeness in communication with which philosophers enjoy irritating their friends and relations. It would not show that I had failed to provide an explanation; indeed, the "Yes" in "Yes, but..." would be tantamount to an admission that I *had* provided *an* explanation. However, the "but" in "Yes, but..." would indicate that I had not provided an explanation of the kind expected or desired. What the questioner wanted to know all along was how the can opener got to be where it was, that is, what *caused* it to get there; and almost certainly, too, the questioner wanted an explanation that cited a cause of a familiar, everyday, potentially alterable kind. But you need not request an explanation against that sort of background of assumptions and interests, common though it is. Suppose that, against a background that includes the assumptions that you have in mind no practical purpose whatever and that the region of space occupied by the can opener is also occupied by a swarm of physical particles, you ask why – or perhaps *how come* – there is a can opener there; then the bizarre derivation from particle physics would be just the ticket, and the nonreductive, causal explanation would be communicatively uncooperative.[20]

---

20 Notice that we can give a reductive explanation of why there is a *can opener* there (rather than, say, a *cat*) by noting that the appropriately located swarm of particles meets the associated condition for can openers but not for cats; and that we can give a reductive explanation

A third objection to treating an actual derivation on the pattern I outlined earlier as an explanation of the fact its conclusion reports is that such a derivation would bring in masses of irrelevant microphysical detail. But to what, exactly, would this microphysical detail supposedly be irrelevant? If to the fact to be explained (so that the charge in effect is that the detail would be irrelevant *explanatorily*), then no *reason* is being given for holding that the derivations in question would not be explanatory; that conclusion is simply being reaffirmed in slightly different language. Actually, however, what advocates of this sort of objection seem to have in mind is that the microphysical detail would be irrelevant to *the explanation* of the fact to be explained, that is, to its nonreductive explanation: either the microphysical detail would be irrelevant if *added* to the nonreductive explanation or it would be a gratuitously obscurantist way of *representing* the facts appealed to by the nonreductive explanation, one that tended to conceal important explanatory patterns (see Putnam 1975, 295–8; and perhaps Kitcher 1984, 348). But, either way, this third objection rests on the same contestable assumption as did the second, namely, that a single fact can properly have one and only one explanation. For if an actual derivation on the pattern I outlined earlier could be an explanation of the fact its conclusion reports *in its own right*, and *in addition* to the same fact's nonreductive explanation, then there is no reason to evaluate it by asking how well it would supplement, or represent, the same fact's nonreductive explanation. So if the case to be made in the next chapter for the unobjectionability of plural explanations of the same fact is sound, then this third objection to treating actual derivations on the pattern outlined earlier as explanatory also fails.[21]

Let me turn now to the in-principle derivability, in the case of every regularity holding among special- and honorary-scientific tokens, of

---

of why there is a can opener *there* (rather than, say, a meter to the right) by noting that a swarm of particles meeting the associated condition for can openers is there but that there is none a meter to the right.

21 Harold Kincaid (1997, 88–90) rebuts two further possible objections. The first claims that an actual derivation on the pattern I outlined earlier would not state a necessary condition for the fact to be explained. But it *would* state a *token* condition that is necessary in the circumstances for the fact to be explained; and explanations *need not* state *type* conditions that are necessary for effects of the sorts in question. The second objection claims that a derivation on the pattern I outlined earlier would be ungraspable by humans. But that correct observation would entail that the derivation was nonexplanatory only given an implausibly strong pragmatic account of explanation (one that would imply that in a possible universe in which the evolution of intelligent life was *impossible*, nothing would have an explanation, since no explanation in such a universe would be graspable by anything).

every proposition asserting the holding of an instance of that regularity. I need to argue for two new premises. The first new premise states that the in-principle derivability, on the pattern indicated earlier, of a proposition reporting a particular instance of a regularity amounts to the explainability of that instance. When this premise is added to what has already been shown, the conclusion follows, given retentive realizationism, that every instance of every regularity holding among special- and honorary-scientific tokens is explainable by appeal only to physical facts plus necessary truths. The second new premise is that if *every instance* of some regularity has an explanation, then the regularity *itself* has an explanation. From this premise, plus the reductive explainability of every instance of every regularity holding among special- and honorary-scientific tokens, it follows that, given retentive realizationism, every regularity holding among special- and honorary-scientific tokens has an explanation that appeals only to physical facts plus necessary truths – namely, that reductionism in the core sense about nomic special- or honorary-scientific facts is true.

The first new premise I need to defend, then, is that the in-principle derivability, on the pattern indicated earlier, of a proposition reporting a particular instance of a regularity amounts to the explainability of that instance. The explanation that an actual such derivation would provide would go like this: this F-token exists and is followed by a G-token because – and here I simply sketch the derivation informally – there is a physical token that necessitates (in the strongest sense) the F-token, and this physical token is sufficient, given the actual physical circumstances and the physical laws, for a later physical token that necessitates (in the strongest sense) a G-token. (So the F-token exists and is followed by a G-token because the very thing that gives rise to the F-token is so circumstanced physically that, given the physical laws, it must be followed by something else that gives rise to a G-token.) But why hold that an actual derivation on this pattern *would* constitute an explanation of the instance its conclusion reports? A presumption in favor of doing so is provided by the first three of the four points earlier made to support treating actual derivations of propositions reporting particular facts as explanations: there is an inductive reason for thinking that such a derivation would be an explanation, because many derivations *are* explanations; such a derivation would sound like a (mystery-removing) explanation; and such a derivation would meet the three conditions mentioned earlier as strongly associated with explanations (it would render the explanandum no accident; prior knowledge of it would have enabled you to predict the explanandum;

it would exhibit the explanandum as an instance of a more general pattern).

Let me give a new reason, however, that applies only in the present case. An actual derivation, on the pattern indicated earlier, of a proposition reporting an instance of a regularity is strongly analogous to a kind of explanation that we all accept in everyday life. In an explanation of this kind, we explain why one thing is followed by another by identifying a *common cause* (token) of both things. For example, we explain why a child developed a rash and then a fever by citing a viral infection that first caused a rash and then (presumably via the mediation of further processes) a fever. The strong analogy between everyday explanations of this kind and derivations on the pattern indicated earlier lies in the fact that in each case there is a common factor that is responsible for both the earlier and the later member of some pair of events. (The infection is responsible for both the rash and the fever; the narrow physical realizer of the F-token is responsible for both the F-token and the subsequent G-token.) In view of this strong analogy, what could justify a refusal to treat derivations on the pattern indicated earlier as explanations too? Certainly there is one disanalogy between the two cases: the narrow physical realizer of the F-token does not *cause* the F-token, whereas the viral infection does cause the rash (and indeed the fever).[22] But in the absence of any good reason to hold that all explanations are causal explanations, it is obscure why that disanalogy should matter. I conclude, then, that the derivability on the pattern indicated of a proposition reporting an instance of a regularity entails that the instance has an explanation, an explanation that appeals only to physical facts plus necessary truths.

The second new premise I need to defend claims that if *every instance* of some regularity has an explanation, then the regularity *itself* has an explanation. So it claims that it *suffices* for explaining a regularity to explain every one of its instances; because it makes no claim about what is *necessary* for explaining a regularity, it is consistent with the existence of other possible ways of explaining a regularity, say, by deducing the regularity from a further regularity plus boundary conditions. Despite this clarification, however, the premise will no doubt arouse some immediate

---

22 You might wonder whether the narrow physical realizer of the F-token causes the G-token and/or the G-token's narrow physical realizer. According to the theory of causation I advance in the next chapter, it might or might not, depending on the circumstances of the case. The determining factor will be whether the enabling physical circumstances (as I earlier called them) are sufficient *by themselves* for the narrow physical realizer of the G-token; if they are, then the F-token is no cause.

suspicion, but it must be admitted to have some initial plausibility. For what part of a regularity could have been left unexplained, if every instance of it has been explained? Furthermore, in everyday life we do allow that a regularity can be explained, and explained completely, by explaining each of its instances. Suppose that, within a single month, all six of the 747 Jumbo jets manufactured by Boeing in 1995 crash. Now although we might immediately suspect some systematic defect in the jets produced that year, it might turn out as the result of extensive investigation that the cause of each crash was quite different: one was due to pilot error, another to metal fatigue, a third to sabotage, and so on. It might turn out also that these different causes did not stem from any interesting (i.e., nontrivial and nondisjunctive) common cause further back in the causal chains culminating in the crashes. Now so long as we have explained why each of the six jets crashed, no one in everyday life will deny that we have explained why all six crashed. Everyone will agree, for example, that the investigation is complete. In a case of this sort, then, an explanation of each instance of a regularity apparently suffices for an explanation of the regularity. The explanation may not be the loveliest we might have hoped for, but it is certainly *an* explanation, in light of which it is certainly no longer a mystery why all six jets crashed; and in any case we have to settle for it, because it is all that the evidence warrants. So there is a prima facie case for thinking that if we can explain every instance of some special- or honorary-scientific regularity using derivations on the pattern outlined, then we have at least *an* explanation of the regularity.

Admittedly, if the regularity that all F-tokens are followed by G-tokens *is* explained via the separate explanation of every one of its instances, and if F- and G-tokens are both realized by physical tokens belonging to widely differing physical types, then the separate explanations of all the instances of the regularity will have nothing physical in common, and so the explanation of the regularity *as a whole* will lack a certain unity, a unity that we normally find desirable in explanations. But while unity in an explanation of a regularity is desirable, we are sometimes obliged to accept an explanation of a regularity that lacks unity – just because, as in the 747 example, it is not there. Indeed, it is possible that all that certain physicalist antireductionists have ever wanted to insist on is that, given multiple realization, special- or honorary-scientific regularities will turn out to have only highly disunified explanations in physical terms; and if their point has really been so modest, then I happily concede it. But it obviously does not entail the falsity of reductionism in the core sense. For even if a unified explanation is better, ceteris paribus, than a disunified one, a disunified explanation is still an explanation; and reductionism in the core sense requires only that special- and honorary-scientific regularities should have *an* explanation that appeals only to physical facts plus necessary truths. Could antireductionists reply that reductionism requires more – that these regularities should have *unified* explanations? They could, but at best it would be an unwarranted attempt to monopolize the word, "reduction" and at worst a definitional sulk.

Similarly, in the 747 example, we wish pretheoretically to say that the crash of the six jets within the space of a single month turned out to be a *coincidence*. Therefore, if special- or honorary-scientific regularities are only as well explained as the crash of the six jets in this example, we will also have to say that special- or honorary-scientific regularities are coincidences if they are explained via the separate explanation of each of their instances and turn out to be multiply realized. As before, however, there is no difficulty, for there is no tension between being a coincidence and being explained. In calling a regularity a coincidence, we mean, I suggest, not that it lacks an explanation of *any* kind, but that it has an explanation of the following special (and perhaps rather unsatisfying) kind: roughly, the explanations of each of its instances had nothing (interesting) *in common*, and did not in their turn stem from a *common* explanatory factor.[23] On this understanding of a coincidence, then, a special-scientific regularity that is multiply realized can *both* be a coincidence *and* have a reductive physical explanation: the regularity need only be such that the separate physical explanations of all its instances have nothing (interesting) physical in common and stem from no common physical explanatory factor.

But do we really want to say that special- and honorary-scientific regularities are coincidences at all? It certainly sounds wrong, but in fact it is possible within my overall position to accommodate our sense that many special- and honorary-scientific regularities are not coincidences. For suppose, in line with the idea that it is unobjectionable for a single fact to have more than one explanation, that a special- or honorary-scientific regularity also has in addition to its physical explanation an

---

23 Obviously it will not always be a clear-cut matter whether a regularity is a coincidence. For example, I run into you at the bookstore sale, so there is a modest regularity: you are there and I am there. Coincidence? Well, no agreement to meet caused us both to be there. But wait! We are both bibliophiles who love a bargain, and this *is* the annual half-price sale.

explanation of another kind; then this other explanation might be one in which there *was* something in common (albeit not something *physical*) among the explanations of each instance of the regularity, so that, relative to this other explanation of the regularity, the regularity was *not* a coincidence. For instance, an additional explanation of why every F-token is followed by a G-token might be that every F-token *causes* a G-token. Such an explanation is not trivial. For suppose that an increase in the rate of ice-cream consumption is followed by an increase in the murder rate; then, although it might turn out that some chemical in ice cream actually makes people more aggressive, so that the increase in ice-cream consumption *causes* the increased murder rate, it might also turn out that some common cause explains both increases (e.g., perhaps summer heat causes both increased desire for ice cream and also murderously shorter tempers). But then if every F-token is followed by a G-token because every F-token *causes* a G-token, the separate explanations of all the instances that make up the regularity *will* have something in common with one another (viz., the F-token cause), so that, on the suggested account of a coincidence, the regularity will not be coincidence – at least from the point of view of that kind of explanation.[24] Therefore, as long as nothing in realization physicalism rules out the possibility that physically realized tokens should be causes (a central issue to be addressed in the next chapter), reductionism in the core sense can be squared with our sense that special- and honorary-scientific regularities are often not coincidences.

When contemplating the idea that a regularity can be explained via the explanation of each of its instances, one is nevertheless strongly tempted to suppose that such an explanation leaves something about the regularity unexplained. But what? Not any instance of the regularity, because, by hypothesis, each instance has been explained. Perhaps the fact that the regularity holds *of necessity*? But according to the explanation of why every F-token is followed by a G-token, every F-token is such that, given the actual physical circumstances, its physical realizer *must* be followed by a physical realizer of a G-token, as a matter of whatever necessity

---

24 It is worth noticing that the regularity that every coin in my pocket today is a quarter emerges as a coincidence not only from the point of view of reductive physical explanation (as in the examples I envisage in the text) but *also* from the point of view of nonreductive, causal explanation, since being in my pocket does not *make* a coin a quarter. I mention this to make it clear that realizationism is not committed to treating all special- and honorary-scientific regularities as on a par with the paradigmatically coincidental regularity concerning coins in my pocket.

(if any) the laws of *physics* possess; so the suggested explanation of the regularity does (or at least could) entail that every F-token *must* be followed by a G-token. Perhaps we feel that what has been left unexplained by the explanation of every instance is the fact that the regularity sustains *counterfactuals* – for example, the counterfactual that, if there had been an F-token in a certain location (as in fact there was not), then it would have been followed by a G-token. But if it really is a counterfactual-supporting regularity that every F-token is followed by a G-token, and if retentive realizationism really is true, then we just have to suppose that, had there been an F-token that the actual world lacks, then it would have been realized by a physical token that, given the physical circumstances and laws, would have been followed by a physical realizer of a G-token. This is not a wild supposition to make. For, on the usual semantics, the counterfactual in question is true iff in all the closest worlds in which there is an F-token that is absent in the actual world it is followed by a G-token. But if realizationism does hold at our world, then that seems like an important fact about our world, as does the holding of the special- and honorary-scientific laws; they both seem like the kinds of fact we might well hold fixed in evaluating counterfactual suppositions. If so, then all the closest worlds to the actual world are worlds that resemble the actual world in respect of its being true at them that realizationism holds and that every F-token is followed by a G-token; hence every F-token in such worlds must be realized by a physical token which is sufficient, given the physical laws and surrounding circumstances, for a G-token.

How, indeed, could matters be otherwise in a physicalist world? How *could* any more strongly autonomous special- or honorary-scientific necessity hold among tokens all of which are physically realized by physical tokens governed entirely by the laws of physics? The bottom line, I fear, is that philosophers reluctant to admit that a special- or honorary-scientific regularity is explained if each of its instances is explained are assuming a metaphysical conception of what it is for such a regularity to hold according to which there is more to the holding of such a regularity than the holding of each of its instances – more, indeed, than any adequately formulated physicalism can allow. Admittedly, someone might then say, "Well, shame on realization physicalism if it can allow only for special- and honorary-scientific regularities that are but a pale shadow of their true selves." But that reply assumes an affirmative answer to a crucial empirical question: do we have any *evidence* for interpreting the special- and honorary-scientific regularities as involving more, metaphysically, than realizationism can allow? The realizationist's negative answer, as we shall see in Chapter 5, is that we do not.

I conclude, then, that, if every instance of some regularity has an explanation, then the regularity itself has an explanation. So since, given retentive realizationism, every instance of every special- and honorary-scientific regularity *does* have an explanation, it follows that, given retentive realizationism, every such regularity has an explanation. And, though perhaps not frequently, we might on occasion *want* such an explanation: suppose we want to know why a certain special- or honorary-scientific regularity holds, given our shared assumption that the regularity holds among tokens that all possess an exhaustive decomposition into physical parts. The reductive physical explanation whose existence is assured by retentive realizationism is certainly not the only possible explanation that would account for the holding of this regularity, for the special- or honorary-scientific tokens among which it holds might conceivably possess novel causal powers that would defeat any reductionist explanation; but the reductive physical explanation is certainly one possible explanation for it.

My case for holding that retentive realizationism is committed to reductionism in the core sense is therefore now complete. Retentive realizationism entails the in-principle derivability from propositions expressing physical facts, plus necessary truths, of (i) every proposition asserting the existence of one of the special- and honorary-scientific tokens that actually exists and (ii), in the case of each regularity holding among special- or honorary-scientific tokens, every proposition asserting the holding of an instance of that regularity. But the derivability of such propositions entails that all nomic and positive nonnomic special- and honorary-scientific facts have an explanation that appeals only to physical facts (plus necessary truths). So retentive realizationism entails reductionism in the core sense. And that it does so, let me add, provides some small encouragement that realization physicalism in its retentive guise faithfully articulates the inchoate but still influential form of materialism that many practicing scientists seem to assume in their working lives. For the claim that all nomic and positive nonnomic special- and honorary-scientific facts have explanations that appeal only to physical facts (plus necessary truths), *if* these explanations take the form retentive realizationism implies they must, provides an attractive way of articulating a metaphysical claim that practicing scientists with materialist inclinations often make in order to express their materialism, namely, that everything that goes on at any special- or honorary-scientific level is sustained by an *underlying physical mechanism*, the description of which would *explain how things work* at those levels.

6. HOW DAMAGING IS THE COMMITMENT?

Are there any good armchair objections to reductionism in the core sense (and hence to the retentive realizationism that entails it)? One objection to reductionism, rarely articulated but perhaps still influential psychologically in motivating the exceedingly brisk dismissals of reductionism one sometimes encounters, is simply that, at least off the tops of our heads, we cannot even begin actually to formulate the bridge principles that reductionism requires. For this objection to apply to the form of reductionism that retentive realizationism entails, of course, the bridge principles that we cannot formulate off the tops of our heads must be bridge principles that assert the identity of every special- or honorary-scientific type with some or other functional type whose associated condition can be specified in physical or quasi-logical terms. But we should not expect such bridge principles to be discoverable a priori; so our admitted inability to generate them a priori does not tell against the reductionism that retentive realizationism entails. Moreover, if retentive realizationism is true, and contemporary science even approximately correct, then, even if bridge principles of the appropriate sort do hold, they would be quite extraordinarily complex, perhaps too complex for human minds to grasp, and such complexity would obviously defeat even an a posteriori attempt to discover them, if made from the armchair; so a failure to discover them a posteriori, but still from the armchair, provides no evidence for their nonexistence. It is to serious science that we must look for evidence that such bridge principles exist, and to such examples of them as we humans might be capable of formulating.

A second armchair objection to reductionism, and the one most commonly advanced, appeals to the *multiple realization* of special- and honorary-scientific types by physical types. But while multiple realization of a given special- or honorary-scientific type certainly rules out any bridge principle that identifies the type with some or other *single* (i.e., nondisjunctive) physical type, reductionism in the core sense, at least in the specific form to which retentive realizationism is committed, does not require bridge principles that identify special- or honorary-scientific types with single physical types, as inspection of the derivation schemata given earlier makes clear; it makes do with bridge principles asserting the identity of every special- and honorary-scientific type with some or other multiply realizable *functional* type. It is therefore fully consistent with multiple realization.

Although he does not address reductionism in the core sense, Jerry Fodor has recently attempted to revive the multiple realization objection to reductionism in the received sense (1997, 156). Accordingly, he tries to explain what would be wrong with allowing *disjunctive* bridge principles linking each special- and honorary-scientific type with some *disjunction* of physical types. For because multiple realization does not rule out disjunctive bridge principles, an obvious reply on behalf of reductionism in the received sense is to suggest that disjunctive bridge principles are all that reductionism needs; and it is far from obvious what would be wrong with such principles (Block 1997). Now, given multiple realization, retentive realizationism turns out to be committed, in particular, to physically necessary physical-to-special/honorary-scientific disjunctive bridge principles: if tokens of a special-scientific type, F, are always realized either by tokens of physical type P_1 or by tokens of physical type P_2, then it is necessary in the strongest sense that if either P_1 or P_2 is tokened, and if the laws of physics hold, then F is tokened (equivalently: it is physically necessary that if either P_1 or P_2 is tokened, then F is tokened).[25] In view of this commitment, it is worth asking how much force Fodor's objection to disjunctive bridge principles has. In fact it has none. Fodor points out, quite correctly, that the antecedent of a disjunctive bridge principle would feature a disjunctive predicate that is not *itself* needed for the statement of purely physical laws (even though its disjuncts are so needed). But he gives no reason to hold that reduction *requires* bridge principles whose antecedents feature only predicates that are needed for the statement of purely physical laws. Now, he does speak of predicates that are needed for the statement of purely physical laws as "independently certified" to be projectible; so perhaps his argument is that disjunctive bridge principles are not proper laws, proper laws being those which feature only predicates "independently certified" to be projectible. If this is his argument, however, then to complete it he would need to show that reduction *requires* that bridge principles be proper laws in his proprietary sense; but he does not. And reduction does not *seem* to require that bridge principles

---

25 Recall, however, from Chapter 1, Section 4, that these disjunctive bridge principles, like all such bridge principles, are derivative from more basic truths; retentive realizationism is not committed to the existence of *basic* disjunctive bridge principles. Perhaps there *would* be something wrong with *basic* disjunctive bridge principles; at the least they would prompt the question why members of just *this* set of physical conditions, and not some slightly different set, should suffice for some particular special- or honorary-scientific condition.

be proper laws, for everyone thinks identity statements would make acceptable bridge principles, and identity statements, since metaphysically necessary, do not seem to be laws in any usual sense at all.[26] Moreover, bridge principles have a job to do: they enable the achievement of reduction's goal of intertheoretic (or interscientific) *explanation*. But bridge principles that fail to be proper laws in Fodor's sense would not, it seems, be any the less able to do this job.

A third objection to reductionism, at least as regards the mental or psychological, arises from Donald Davidson's (1980, chs. 11–13) argument in support of the anomalism of the mental – the thesis that there are no strict psychophysical or psychological laws. Because, as we have just seen, retentive realizationism is committed to the existence of physically necessary physical-to-special/honorary-scientific disjunctive bridge principles in general, and hence to physically necessary physical-to-*psychological* bridge principles in particular, and because these principles are neither probabilistic nor hedged, retentive realizationism is apparently committed to strict psychophysical laws of precisely the sort against which Davidson's argument is targeted. (The only residual doubt would be whether these bridge principles amounted to laws at all.) So is Davidson's argument any good? Unfortunately, its notorious obscurity makes it very hard to evaluate (see, e.g., Lycan 1988, ch. 2), and in any case I have nothing to add to the already large exegetical literature. Instead, I briefly discuss three reconstructions of the argument for psychophysical anomalism that are, if not Davidson's, (I hope) at least sufficiently Davidsonian to engage with the underlying concerns of those philosophers who are moved by Davidson's own presentations (e.g., Kim 1993, ch. 11; Cynthia Macdonald 1989, 87–99). All three reconstructions share the basic idea that, if there were strict psychophysical laws, then, intolerably, one could be justified in ascribing mental states to a person in the following way: one could have physical evidence for thinking that the person was in a certain brain state, and then justifiably infer, via a psychophysical law connecting brain states of that type with some type of mental state, that the person was in a mental state of that type.[27] The three reconstructions differ, however, on why exactly that result would be intolerable, though in each case the reason stems from

---

26   Here I neglect the minority view that laws of nature are metaphysically necessary.
27   Here, and in the discussion to follow, I ignore the fact that mental content is probably determined at least in part by environmental or historical conditions. The discussion is thereby simplified, and nothing is lost, since Davidson's opposition to strict psychophysical laws presumably applies also to putative psychophysical laws connecting mental states to brain states *plus* environmental or historical conditions.

certain "constitutive principles governing the application of predicates," principles allegedly peculiar to mental (propositional-attitude) predicates (Cynthia Macdonald 1989, 92).[28]

According to the first reconstruction, any would-be mental ascription that was inferred from a brain state via a psychophysical law could not be a genuine mental ascription, since it would have violated some *conceptual constraint* on mental ascriptions; hence any would-be mental ascription inferred in this way would amount to "changing the subject" (Davidson, 1980, 216; Cynthia Macdonald 1989, 95). But what conceptual constraint is it that we would violate if we were to (try to) ascribe a mental state to someone on the basis of an inference from a brain state via a psychophysical law? The only candidate plausible exegetically is the constraint expressed by the following claim, alleged by Davidsonians to be a conceptual truth of the first importance: if a person is in *any* (propositional-attitude) mental state, then (i) that person must also be in *other* such mental states and (ii) all the mental states that the person is in must be so interrelated as to exhibit some important degree of theoretical and practical *rationality* and *coherence*. But even if this claim does indeed express a genuine conceptual constraint on ascriptions of mental states – that is, a genuine conceptual constraint on what conditions a thing must meet to be in any mental state at all – the constraint need not be violated if there were psychophysical laws. For if a mental state were ascribed on the basis of an inference from a brain state via a psychophysical law, it would not follow that the mental state was *not* a member of a system of mental states so interrelated as to be rational and coherent; it might perfectly well be so, in which case, of course, the person would in fact be in *other* brain states from knowledge of which, via *other* psychophysical laws, someone could infer that the person was in various *other* mental

---

28 Kim suggests a different kind of reconstruction, an explicitly metaphysical one according to which "The mental system has a certain essential characteristic X and the physical system a certain essential characteristic Y, where X and Y are mutually incompatible. Laws linking the two systems, if they exist, would 'transmit' these characteristics from one system to the other, leading to incoherence" (1993, 201). But I confess to not understanding how this transmission is supposed to work. If system S1 has X essentially, then it has X in every world in which it exists; now suppose that in all nomologically possible worlds in which S1 has X, system S2 exists and has Y, and that S2 has Y in every world in which it exists. Why it is supposed to follow, incoherently, that S2 has X (as well as the incompatible Y) – or that S1 has Y (as well as the incompatible X)? However, when Kim presents a more formal rendition of the Davidsonian argument as he understands it (1993, 205–6), it does not appear to embody this explicitly metaphysical approach; it is much closer to one of the three reconstructions I consider in the text.

states, where the totality of the person's mental states exhibited precisely the rationality and coherence required by the conceptual constraint on the ascription of even one mental state. There might yet be something wrong with the idea of inferring mental ascriptions from brain states via psychophysical laws, but it is not that the putative ascriptions would inevitably fail to meet the constitutive conceptual constraint described earlier.

The second reconstruction is inspired by Davidson's remark that "there cannot be tight connections between [the mental and the physical] if each is to retain its allegiance to its *proper source of evidence*" (1980, 222; emphasis added). On this reconstruction, then, what would be intolerable about ascriptions of mental states based on inferences via strict psychophysical laws is that they would not be based on the "proper source of evidence" for mental ascriptions. But what is a "proper source of evidence" – both in general and for mental ascriptions in particular? It is presumably true that we ordinarily base ascriptions of mental states to a person on the evidence constituted by his or her overall gross bodily behavior, including verbal behavior; and we would obviously not be so basing them if we based them instead on inferences from knowledge of brain states via a strict psychophysical law; so if the "proper source of evidence" for some ascription is just the source of evidence ordinarily used to justify the ascription, then the "proper source of evidence" for mental ascriptions is overall gross bodily behavior, and strict psychophysical laws would indeed permit mental ascriptions not based on their "proper source of evidence." But what would be *wrong* with that? Chicken pox is ordinarily diagnosed on the basis of a distinctive, itchy rash, which is therefore its "proper source of evidence" in the current sense; but there would be nothing wrong with diagnosing it on the basis of something else (e.g., a blood test). So if a "proper source of evidence" for ascriptions of some kind is just the source of evidence ordinarily used as a basis for those ascriptions, then strict psychophysical laws would generate no objectionable result by implying that mental ascriptions could be based on something other than their "proper source of evidence." If, therefore, the current argument for anomalism is to work, then "proper source of evidence" must be given another, and stronger, interpretation, so that it means something like "source of evidence such that ascriptions of the relevant sort just *cannot* be based on evidence of any other kind"; and then, if mental ascriptions' "proper source of evidence" in this strong sense is overall gross bodily behavior, it will certainly follow that strict psychophysical laws cannot exist, since their existence would imply that mental ascriptions *can* be based on evidence on which, because it is not "proper," such ascriptions *cannot* be based.

But the very idea of a "proper source of evidence" in this strong sense is highly dubious. For, on the face of it, it is epistemically possible that types of any kind should turn out to be nomologically linked to types of any other kind, so that a token of the latter type could therefore be used as evidence for a token of the former type, and an ascription of the former type justified by appeal to a token of the latter type, which would then constitute nonstandard evidence. In the present case, then, precisely *because* we might discover strict psychophysical laws, we must disallow the idea that mental ascriptions have such a thing as a "proper source of evidence" in the strong sense: in effect, the appeal to a "proper source of evidence" for mental ascriptions begs the question against the believer in strict psychophysical laws. Nor can Davidsonians reply at this point by denying a priori the possibility of discovering strict psychophysical laws; for that would be to assume that they had *already* achieved, via some other argument, precisely what the appeal to a "proper source of evidence" in the strong sense was meant to accomplish in the first place, namely, an a priori proof of psychophysical anomalism.

In any case, how could it be *impossible* to base a mental ascription on a nonproper source of evidence? What would *stop* you? The Davidsonian answer would have to be a *conceptual* constraint – though not the conceptual constraint considered in the first reconstruction of the argument for anomalism, since, as we saw, that constraint need not be violated were psychophysical laws to exist. An appropriate conceptual constraint would have to constrain not what sort of thing can *be* in a mental state but what sort of *evidence* the ascriber must employ in ascribing it.[29] So the fundamental premise, on the second reconstruction of the argument for anomalism, would have to be something like this: it is a conceptual truth that no ascription would count as an ascription of a *mental* state unless it were based on the evidence of overall gross bodily behavior. But this is *not* a conceptual truth: ordinary people feel no sense of conceptual blockage when they entertain the idea that, say, an omniscient God could learn their deepest desires by looking directly into their minds, or that

---

29 Cynthia Macdonald (1989, 94) more than once uses the unfortunate expression "conditions of application," which hovers uncertainly between these two sorts of conceptual constraints. Kim's talk of "constitutive principles" (e.g., 1993, 205–6) is similarly unclear: do they express conditions that a *thing* must meet in order to *be* an X, or conditions that an *aspirant "X"-ascriber* must meet in order to be *warranted* in calling a thing "an X"?

a brain scientist of the future might be able to determine their thoughts with a brain scan. There just is no *conceptual* impossibility in the idea of a mental ascription that is not based on the evidence of overall gross bodily behavior. So the Davidsonian argument fails also on the second reconstruction.

According to the third reconstruction, what would be wrong with mental ascriptions based on inferences via strict psychophysical laws is that they would indeed violate an *evidential* conceptual constraint, a conceptual constraint on what evidence a mental ascriber may properly rely on (as in the second reconstruction), but this evidential conceptual constraint would be *justified* by appeal to the *constitutive* conceptual constraint specifying what conditions a thing must meet in order to *be* in any mental state at all (as in the first reconstruction). The justification would proceed via the following somewhat plausible principle: if, in order for a thing to be F, it is conceptually required that it also be G, then any evidence for thinking that something is F must also at the same time be *capable* of being evidence for thinking that the thing is G. For example, nothing could possibly be evidence that Smith is a bachelor unless there is some way in which it could be evidence for Smith's being male; if the putative evidence were *neutral* on the maleness of Smith, if it left it *open* whether or not he was male, then it could hardly be evidence for his bachelorhood.[30] Similarly, then, suppose that if a person is in any mental state, then, as a matter of conceptual necessity, (i) he or she must also be in other such mental states and (ii) all the mental states that he or she is in must be so interrelated as to exhibit some important degree of theoretical and practical rationality and coherence. It would follow via the somewhat plausible principle that nothing could be evidence for ascribing to someone the belief that, say, eggs float that was not *also* capable of being evidence for (i) ascribing to the same person various *other* mental states, other mental states such that (ii) the *totality* of mental states thus ascribed exhibited the requisite rationality and coherence. But evidence consisting of the fact that someone was in a certain brain state could not meet this condition; for it could tell us nothing about what *other* mental states the person was in, or about the rationality and coherence exhibited by the *totality* of the person's mental states. So evidence for the ascription to someone of even one mental state has to be at the same time evidence for ascribing

---

30 In fact, as Paul Weirich has pointed out to me, the principle seems false if the evidence in question is nonconclusive: Smith's being unmarried could surely be (nonconclusive) evidence that Smith is a bachelor, even though it is neutral on Smith's maleness.

many mental states – a condition that can be met by evidence consisting of someone's overall gross bodily behavior, but that cannot be met by evidence consisting of his or her being in a particular brain state.

However, this third reconstruction rests upon the tacit assumption that a strict psychophysical law would have to connect a type of *local* brain state, on the one hand, with just *one* type of mental state, on the other (e.g., highly localized neuronal activity, on the one hand, with the belief that eggs float, on the other); and were this assumption true, it would indeed follow from the other premises that someone's being in that local brain state could not provide evidence that the person was in such *other* mental states as the person must be in, given the holism of the mental that our concept of the mental allegedly guarantees. But the assumption is not true. A strict psychophysical law could perfectly well state that a *nonlocal* brain condition was nomologically sufficient for *many* mental states; such a physical condition would suffice for believing that eggs float but also for possessing such other mental states (their totality exhibiting the requisite rationality and coherence) as constitutive conceptual constraints require; such a physical condition, therefore, *could* provide evidence for the ascription of mental states other than the belief that eggs float. And if the mental is as holistic as Davidsonians say, then strict psychophysical laws of this sort will be the only ones there are. Thus the third reconstruction of the argument for anomalism also fails. In each of the three reconstructions, the suggested conceptual constraint on mental ascriptions is either not genuine or, though (perhaps) genuine, not such as to be violated by the existence of strict psychophysical laws. Either way, reductionism in the core sense emerges unscathed.

Let me end this chapter not by answering further armchair objections to reductionism but by showing that reductionism in the core sense does *not* entail two consequences, consequences whose apparent implausibility would certainly tell against it if it did. The first consequence that reductionism in the core sense does not entail is that the special and honorary sciences lack a certain kind of autonomy that arguably they do in fact enjoy. Autonomy of this kind is enjoyed just in case there are *realization-independent* special- or honorary-scientific laws, where a law to the effect that F-tokens are followed by G-tokens is realization-independent iff the law applies to all F-tokens even though their physical realizers are of significantly different physical types (and perhaps similarly for the G-tokens). So, for example, if it turns out to be true that once bitten, twice shy, and true of (say) humans, frogs, and octopuses, and if being bitten and being shy turn out to be very variably realized in these different creatures, then it is a realization-independent law that once bitten, twice shy; but if, on the other hand, it is true only of humans, and if being bitten and being shy turn out to have pretty uniform physical realizers in humans, then, though it is still a law that once bitten, twice shy, it is not a realization-independent one. Now it is far from obvious whether there really are any realization-independent laws, since plenty of special- and honorary-scientific regularities (e.g., that whenever I depress my gas pedal, ceteris paribus, my car goes faster) hold among special- or honorary-scientific tokens that have pretty *uniform* physical realizations; however, some philosophers have recently argued both that they do exist and that their existence is in any case to be expected (Antony and Levine 1997, 92–3; Block 1997; Fodor 1997). But their existence, and the autonomy for the special- and honorary-sciences that their existence constitutes, is *consistent* with reductionism in the core sense. For reductionism in the core sense only requires the complete explainability of every special- or honorary-scientific nomic fact by appeal to physical facts (plus necessary truths); and, if the arguments of the last section are correct, the nomic fact that every F-token is followed by a G-token can be explainable in this way, even if the F-tokens turn out to have physical realizers exhibiting great physical diversity. Admittedly, such realization-independent special- or honorary-scientific nomic facts will then be coincidences from the point of view of physical explanation, as we earlier noted, but, as we also noted, not thereby unexplained.

Some philosophers, however, may have in mind a stronger notion of the autonomy of the special and honorary sciences than the one just considered. According to the stronger notion, the special and honorary sciences are autonomous just in case there are special- or honorary-scientific laws that are realization-independent in the sense that they hold independently, not only of facts about multiple physical realization in the actual world but also of any facts about realization at all; for example, these laws would hold even among special-scientific tokens that were sometimes or always *ectoplasmically* realized. So if the law that F-tokens are followed by G-tokens is realization-independent in this stronger sense, then not only does it apply to all actual F-tokens even though their physical realizers are of significantly different physical types, it applies also to possible F-tokens that are not physically realized at all. It is presumably laws that are realization-independent in this strong sense that Margaret Boden has in mind when she claims that some people see artificial intelligence as "the science of intelligence in general," which would encompass "the entire range of possible minds" (1990, 1), and that Robert Van Gulick has in mind when he presents the "conjecture" that "in neighbouring worlds... which do not contain any physical matter... patterns exist that are very much like... patterns... in our world," so that "there is a sense in which even in our world the order of higher-level patterns is not dependent on the physical order of the world" (1993, 253).

How should a reductionist in the core sense reply to philosophers who take the special and honorary sciences to be autonomous in the sense that special- and honorary-scientific regularities are realization-independent in this new, strong sense? Well, *if* any special- or honorary-scientific regularities are realization-independent in this strong sense, then it is certainly very hard to see how they could possibly be given an explanation by appeal to physical facts (plus necessary truths); so their existence would, I agree, refute reductionism in the core sense. But the point is moot, since there is no reason to think that any special- or honorary-scientific regularities *are* realization-independent in the strong sense. There may well be evidence for thinking that special- or honorary-scientific regularities are realization-independent in the original, weaker sense, but such evidence is not automatically evidence for thinking that they are realization-independent in the new, strong sense. Indeed, it is hard to see how anything even could be evidence for thinking that special- or honorary-scientific laws are realization-independent in the strong sense without *also* being evidence for thinking that special- or honorary-scientific tokens are not physically realized at all, but instead are tokens of nonphysical and non-physically realized types that are merely connected to physical tokens by brute laws of emergence; and in Chapter 5 we conclude that there is no evidence for thinking that *any* special- or honorary-scientific tokens fail to be physically realized.

Similar points apply to the claim, frequently voiced by *soi-disant* physicalists, that the special and honorary sciences are autonomous in the sense that by using special- or honorary-scientific terms we can "capture" regularities that cannot be "captured" in physical terms (see, e.g., Pylyshyn 1984, 7). Reductionism in the core sense can allow that the special and honorary sciences are autonomous in this sense if "cannot be captured in physical terms" is charitably interpreted to mean merely "cannot be expressed in physical terms – except by the use of (among other things) intractably massive and unwieldy *disjunctions* of physical terms"; for on that interpretation the claimed autonomy might obtain given the holding of special- or honorary-scientific regularities that are realization-independent only in the original, weaker sense that reductionism in the core sense can happily acknowledge. But if "cannot be captured in physical terms" is intended to express some stronger idea, perhaps the idea that there are special- or honorary-scientific regularities that are realization-independent in the new, stronger sense, or maybe the idea that special- or honorary-scientific tokens, just in virtue of being such, are thereby endowed with causal powers in no way attributable to the causal powers of the physical tokens that underlie them, then the autonomy being claimed for the special or honorary sciences begins to sound like something that not only goes beyond what reductionism in the core sense can allow but is also inconsistent with physicalism (no matter how formulated) and unsupported by current evidence.

The second consequence that reductionism in the core sense does *not* entail is that the special sciences should be abandoned, special scientists fired, and their departments closed down! In fact, as we have already noted, because reductionism in the core sense asserts the *explainability* of the special-scientific tokens and the regularities that hold among them, it actually presupposes that they exist, and so would appear on the face of it to leave anyone who wishes to investigate them at perfect liberty to do so. Moreover, there is no reason why the scientists who do so should not enjoy full *confirmational* autonomy, in the sense of being free to propose and test their hypotheses in the usual scientific way without needing to know how, or even that, the special-scientific tokens their hypotheses concern are physically realized (though in practice they might *welcome* the independent tests of their hypotheses made possible by the truth of reductionism).[31] Admittedly, reductionism in the core sense does impose one methodological constraint on the special sciences: to the extent (if at all) that there is reason to hold that reductionism in the core sense is *true*, there is correspondingly *some* reason to dismiss any special-scientific hypothesis asserting the existence of a special-scientific fact that, if genuine, would clearly *not* be reducible in the core sense. But this reason would merely be an application of the general principle of methodological conservativism whereby newly proposed hypotheses should be judged, in part, by how well they fit in with background hypotheses enjoying some degree of support. And this reason would in any case only be a *defeasible* reason,

---

31 If they are seeking to confirm putatively realization-independent (weak sense) laws, then they must take care to avoid a problem raised by Kim. His worry is that if all the confirming positive instances of the realization-independent law that all F-tokens are followed by G-tokens are instances where the F-tokens are uniformly physically realized and the G-tokens are uniformly physically realized, then they will provide no reason to expect that actual F-tokens with physical realizers of quite *different* types will be followed by G-tokens. Obviously this is a risk, but, as Fodor (1997, 151–2) aptly points out, it is a kind of risk to which all inductions are prone.

with the ease of possible defeat inversely proportional to the strength of the evidence for reductionism. Even when faced with evidence for reductionism, then, special scientists would still remain methodologically free to discover that reductionism in the core sense (and hence realizationism) was *false*, by discovering the need to postulate special-scientific facts that were demonstrably not reducible in the core sense.

So why on earth would someone take the abandonment of the special sciences to be a proper consequence of reductionism in the first place? Certainly reductionism in the core sense does entail that any facts that the special sciences might uncover are all potentially explainable by appeal to physical facts (plus necessary) truths. But so what? Even if we took this to imply that the only explanations of special-scientific facts possible or worth having were the reductive ones, it would *still* not follow that the best way to discover these reductive explanations was by working from physics upward; the best, and almost certainly the only practicable, way would still be first to allow confirmationally autonomous special sciences to discover special-scientific regularities and then gradually work down, perhaps via more than one intermediate science, to physical explanations, with the baton being passed down through the levels. Nor, even if special scientists were allotted only this merely heuristic role, would it follow that their work must be less significant than that of physicists. For even if the significance of (pure) special-scientific research were properly judged solely by its heuristic contribution to the discovery of reductive explanations, it would remain quite possible that some piece of special-scientific research that opened the door to the discovery of reductive explanations of a wide class of interesting phenomena might by reason of its fertility be more significant scientifically than the tedious working-out of the microphysical details by some journeyman microphysicist armed with a huge computer.

But even though reductionism in the core sense does entail that any facts that the special sciences might uncover are all potentially explainable by appeal to physical facts (plus necessary truths), it does *not* further entail, except with an additional assumption, *either* that the only explanations of special-scientific facts possible or worth having are the reductive ones *or* that the significance of (pure) scientific research is properly judged solely by its contribution to the discovery of such explanations. The additional assumption is that a fact can have only one complete explanation, so that if a special-scientific fact has a complete reductive explanation, then there is no need for a second explanation to be supplied by the special sciences themselves. In the chapter to follow I argue that this assumption is unsupported and probably false. But the point now is that, *if* it is false, so that special-scientific explanations of special-scientific facts are both possible and desirable even if they are additional to reductive ones, then reductionism in the core sense is fully consistent with the antecedently plausible idea that the results of the special sciences, and in particular the explanations they discover, are independently worthwhile contributions to the scientific goal of understanding the universe, contributions on all fours with the explanatory results of physics. It remains true, of course, given reductionism in the core sense, that all the explanatory factors special scientists cite, inasmuch as they are special-scientific tokens or regularities, owe their existence entirely to conditions that it is the business of physicists to study, and this consequence may perhaps injure the pride of some especially sensitive special scientists; but if so, then they had better just get used to it, since the same consequence will follow from any view deserving the name of physicalism. If any special scientists regard the explanatory factors they cite as owing their existence to *nothing* else, and hence as on an ontological par with electrons and quarks, then their quarrel is with physicalism itself, and not with some gratuitously strengthened, reductive version of it.

4

Causation and Explanation in a Realizationist World

1. INTRODUCTION

In recent years, doctrines of retentive physicalism that eschew comprehensive claims of nonphysical-to-physical type identity have faced the charge that they *epiphenomenalize* both mental phenomena in particular and special- and honorary-scientific phenomena in general. Roughly, the objection is that if, for every special- and honorary-scientific phenomenon, there is a physical phenomenon sufficient for it (as physicalism requires), and if all such underlying physical phenomena are completely caused by earlier physical phenomena in strict accordance with physical laws, then special- and honorary-scientific phenomena are just riding piggyback on the physical phenomena; it is the physical phenomena that are doing all the real causal work, and the appearance of causation among special- or honorary-scientific phenomena is just an illusion. So, because special- and honorary-scientific causation is surely not an illusion, any doctrine of retentive physicalism that implies that it is thereby faces the apparently damning objection that it has to deny an obvious truth.

In fact, it is not clear just how damning such an objection would really be. Imagine a doctrine of retentive physicalism that is committed to repudiating special- and honorary-scientific causation as illusory, but which can nevertheless explain why we would still *believe* in such causation, even if it did not exist; suppose, for example, that this doctrine of physicalism can predict the holding, given the actual physical facts, of just those special- and honorary-scientific regularities that we do in fact observe, and suppose also that we have a strong psychological propensity to infer from such regularities the existence of special- and honorary-scientific causal relations. Then even if this doctrine of physicalism were true, and in consequence there really were no special- and honorary-scientific causation, it would still be predictable that, and explainable why, we would nevertheless mistakenly think that there was. So although this doctrine of physicalism would admittedly require the attribution to common sense of a large and systematic error, it would only require the attribution of an *explicable* error and hence, arguably, nothing especially implausible.[1] And retentive realizationism, in particular, can certainly be defended in this way against the charge of epiphenomenalizing special- and honorary-scientific phenomena. For, at least if the conclusions of the previous chapter are correct, retentive realizationism *can* account for the holding of the special- and honorary-scientific regularities that we observe; and it is surely true that in everyday life we can hardly help but construe such regularities as strong (if defeasible) evidence for the existence of causal relations among special- and honorary-scientific phenomena. But although retentive realizationism can be defended in this way, I shall pretend that it cannot in the discussion to follow, assuming instead that if retentive realizationism does turn out to epiphenomenalize the special- and honorary-scientific, then that is very bad news.[2]

Before I can state the conclusions for which I argue in this chapter, I must first distinguish two senses in which a view can be said to epiphenomenalize special- and honorary-scientific phenomena. A view can be said to epiphenomenalize the special- and honorary-scientific in one sense if it entails, perhaps in conjunction with additional truths about

---

1   A doctrine of retentive physicalism could live even more easily with a commitment to epiphenomenalism if, as seems likely, it could also account for all the intuitively correct *counterfactuals* expressible in the proprietary vocabularies of the special- and honorary-sciences. For the residual causation that it was still committed to denying would in that case strike many people as rather unimportant.
2   Paul Moser (1996) seeks to confront David Papineau's (1993) version of physicalism with a dilemma, one horn of which is that Papineau's physicalism must deny the causal efficacy of the mental; but Moser simply assumes without argument that it would be intolerable for Papineau to evade the dilemma by *accepting* this (alleged) consequence of his position and somehow explaining away its appearance of implausibility. (As it happens, the other horn of Moser's dilemma is also blunt. It claims that if Papineau's physicalism does *not* deny the causal efficacy of the mental, then it must deny that "the main goal of the actual physical sciences [is] to offer full, and not merely sufficient, explanations of all physical phenomena" [Moser 1996, 267], where the explanations will not be "full" unless they "affirm...the existence of every actual cause of physical phenomena" [266]. But I know of no retentive physicalists who wish to accept this view of the goal of the physical sciences, and Moser gives no reason why they should. On retentive realizationism in particular, of course, physics must indeed be able to affirm the existence of the *physical realizer* of every actual cause of every physical phenomenon, but its proprietary vocabulary will not permit it to affirm the existence of every actual cause itself, for example, every actual mental cause.)

(say) causation, that no special- or honorary-scientific token is ever (or hardly ever) a *singular cause* of any effect. Doctrines of nonreductive physicalism (e.g., Davidsonian anomalous monism) that entail the identity of every special- or honorary-scientific token with some or other physical token are not open to the charge that they epiphenomenalize the special- and honorary-scientific in this sense: since physical tokens are presumably unexceptionable singular causes, and since "... is a singular cause of —" is plausibly held to be extensional, the unquestioned status of physical tokens as causes is automatically transmitted to the special- or honorary-scientific tokens with which they are identical. Retentive realizationism, however, since it is apparently *not* committed to the identity of every special- or honorary-scientific token with some or other physical token, *is* open to this first charge of epiphenomenalizing the special- and honorary-scientific and must therefore confront it.

A view can be said to epiphenomenalize the special- and honorary-scientific in a second sense, however, if it entails, perhaps in conjunction with additional truths, that special- and honorary-scientific *types* are never (or hardly ever) *causally relevant*. But what is it for a type to be causally relevant? The term "causal relevance" is just a philosophical term of art; so let me explain how I use it, and why. The interest of the charge that realizationism precludes the causal relevance of special- and honorary-scientific types lies in the fact that, if correct, it entails that realizationism precludes the causal relevance of such types in some sense of "causal relevance" in which we ordinarily think that they *are* causally relevant; so that, if realizationism *does* preclude causal relevance in this sense, realizationism is thereby shown to entail a gross implausibility. By contrast, were we to use "causal relevance" in some proprietary, neologistic sense in which it was an entirely *open* question whether any special- or honorary-scientific type actually was causally relevant in that sense, the charge would presumably be of no interest whatever. In fact, of course, our high confidence that special- and honorary-scientific types are indeed causally relevant (in the intended sense) stems from our inclination to take as uncontroversially true certain everyday claims that are not ordinarily expressed using the term "causal relevance." So, on pain of losing contact with any issue of interest, we must only use "causal relevance" to express whatever feature of special- or honorary-scientific types it is that those everyday claims attribute to them.

Here is an example of such a claim. Suppose that a certain hurricane caused extensive damage, and that this hurricane was in fact predicted by the meteorological bureau. Then it strikes us as uncontroversially true to claim that

> the hurricane caused the extensive damage *because* it was a hurricane.

This claim paradigmatically attributes causal relevance, in the sense in which I shall be using the term, to the type, *being a hurricane*. Similarly, the claim that

> the hurricane didn't cause the extensive damage because it was predicted by the meteorological bureau

denies causal relevance in exactly the same sense to the type, *being a token predicted by the meteorological bureau*.

Let me now try to bring out four general features of causal relevance thus understood, as whatever feature it is that everyday claims of these sorts attribute (or deny) to types. First, the word "because" in "because it was a hurricane" is naturally construed as introducing an *explanation*. We might equally well have said that the hurricane caused the extensive damage *in virtue of* being a hurricane, but, significantly, "in virtue of" also denotes an explanatory relation (see McLaughlin 1989, 114–15). Second, the explanation introduced is an explanation not of the extensive damage (i.e., the effect), but of *why the hurricane caused the effect that it did cause* – of why a particular cause produced an effect of the type it did produce. Third, and in consequence, a type is causally relevant, not *simpliciter*, but rather on particular occasions, relative to a particular cause that produced a particular effect of a particular type. Finally, what follows the word "because" implies that it is somehow possible to explain why a particular cause produced an effect of the type it did produce simply by noting a type of which the cause is a token. Putting these four points together, then, we can say that, in the everyday sense in which we find it obvious that special- and honorary-scientific types are often causally relevant, a type T is causally relevant to token t_1's causing of token t_2 iff t_1's being a token of T explains why it caused t_2. This account of the sense of "causal relevance," however, leaves it entirely open *how* a cause's being a token of T helps to explain why it caused the effect it did; in due course, I address this question at length.

Now, in our example, we could also have expressed the causal relevance of *being a hurricane* by making the following counterfactual but still tolerably idiomatic claim: if there had *not* been a hurricane, there would *not* have been extensive damage (or, perhaps, by making the following counterfactual but rather stilted claim: if the *cause* had not been a hurricane, the *effect* would not have been extensive damage). But the causal relevance expressed by these counterfactual claims need not be treated as different from the kind already characterized (*pace* Lepore and Loewer 1987, who do treat it as different). For we can treat these counterfactuals as holding precisely *because* the hurricane's being a hurricane somehow explains why it caused the extensive damage in question: if there had not been a hurricane, then the actual hurricane would not have been one (or would perhaps not even have existed), so that, given the explanatory role of *being a hurricane*, the actual hurricane would not have caused any extensive damage. However, even though in *this* example it is in fact true that if there had not been a hurricane, there would not have been extensive damage, the truth of this counterfactual claim is neither a logically necessary nor a logically sufficient condition for the causal relevance of *being a hurricane*; it is at best a good proxy for causal relevance. It is not a logically necessary condition because circumstances might have been as follows: the hurricane caused the extensive damage, and did so because it was a hurricane, but some mischievous and omnipotent demon had earlier decided that, if there were no hurricane, he would still, by a miracle, cause extensive damage just as if there had been. Under such circumstances, despite the causal relevance of *being a hurricane*, the relevant counterfactual would have been *false*: if there had not been a hurricane, there would *still* have been extensive damage (see Worley 1993, 350–1). The relevant counterfactual is not a logically sufficient condition for the causal relevance of *being a hurricane* because the cause's being a hurricane might not itself be causally relevant, and yet it might be so intimately connected (e.g., nomologically) to the cause's being of some type that *is* causally relevant that the counterfactual nevertheless comes out as true (see, e.g., Kazez 1995, 82–4; Kim 1998, 71).[3]

To return to our example: we could have attributed causal relevance to *being a hurricane* in yet another way, by saying that there was extensive damage *because there was a hurricane*. But in this expression, we should note, the word "because" introduces an explanation of the extensive damage – of the effect produced – rather than of why the cause produced that effect. However, the explanation that follows does more than cite a cause of the

---

3 These considerations are not intended to show that a counterfactual account of causal relevance could not possibly succeed. The most promising such account is perhaps David-Hillel Ruben's (1994) account of causal explanation. However, such an account need be no rival to the nomic account that I shall eventually give, since the truth of my nomic account might be what *explains* the holding of the counterfactuals that a counterfactual account appeals to.

effect: had we said that there was extensive damage *because there was a certain event predicted by the meteorological bureau*, we would arguably have cited the very same event as a cause, but we would have said something false (or at best very misleading), even though the event cited was in fact predicted by the meteorological bureau. In "There was extensive damage because there was a hurricane," the explanation that follows the word "because" certainly cites a cause of the effect, but it does so in a way that also reveals that it is a token of a particular type, *being a hurricane*, which is privileged in some way; and there is no reason to reject the obvious suggestion that, at least in this case, the privilege thereby claimed for this type is its causal relevance in the sense already characterized – that is, its contributing to the explanation of why the hurricane caused the extensive damage.

It is now possible, at last, to state the three conclusions that this chapter aims to establish. The first is that retentive realizationism does not epiphenomenalize the special- and honorary-scientific in the first sense. That is, retentive realizationism is entirely consistent with the claim that the special- and honorary-scientific *tokens* that we ordinarily take to be *singular causes* (of special- and honorary-scientific effects) should turn out genuinely to be so. Out of deference to the literature on the problems of mental causation, I assume that the tokens in question are events, rather than, say, objects, even though we often speak of objects as causes; but what I have to say ought to be acceptable, mutatis mutandis, to those who deny that causes are events. The second conclusion is that retentive realizationism does not epiphenomenalize the special- and honorary-scientific in the second sense. That is, retentive realizationism is entirely consistent with the claim that the special- and honorary-scientific *types* that we ordinarily take to be *causally relevant* should turn out genuinely to be so. If both these conclusions are correct, then retentive realizationism does not itself require the revision of any of our commonsense judgments concerning the causal status of special- and honorary-scientific tokens and types.

The third conclusion is that, consistently with retentive realizationism, it is unobjectionable for one and the same special- or honorary-scientific token to have more than one explanation; in particular, given retentive realizationism, multiple explanations of one and the same token do not give rise to *overdetermination* of any objectionable kind. For example, it is unobjectionable in any way for one and the same special- or honorary-scientific token to have *both* a nonreductive, causal explanation in special- or honorary-scientific terms, of the sort claimed in the second conclusion to be consistent with retentive realizationism, *and* a reductive physical explanation of the sort discussed in Chapter 3. Thus, even if every case of extensive damage is physically realized, and therefore has a reductive physical explanation, it can *still* be true also, without any threat of unacceptable overdetermination, that the extensive damage in our example occurred because there was a hurricane. In arguing for this third conclusion, I am discharging an obligation incurred in Chapter 3, where I used it as a premise on several occasions. I am also assuming this third conclusion as I proceed now to argue for my first and second conclusions.

2. THE INTUITIVE ROOTS OF THE CHARGE OF EPIPHENOMENALISM

To the best of my knowledge, the thesis that doctrines of retentive physicalism without type identities epiphenomenalize the mental has never been argued for on the basis of a systematic and independently motivated theory of causation and causal relevance. Rather, the usual procedure has been first to present the doctrine of physicalism and then to invite the reader to share the author's intuitive reaction that, if it is true, then "all the causal work is being done at the physical level" or "the mental makes no causal difference." And certainly it is true of retentive realizationism in particular that, once its consequences have been grasped, our intuition that it epiphenomenalizes the special- and honorary-scientific is immediate and strong. Take any special- or honorary-scientific effect you like – for example, the extensive damage in our earlier example. Then if retentive realizationism is true, it is physically realized, that is, there is some set of simultaneous physical circumstances that, given the laws of physics, is sufficient in the strongest sense for its occurrence. But this set of physical circumstances that realizes the extensive damage has itself evolved out of *earlier* physical circumstances in strict accordance with the laws of physics. So these earlier physical circumstances, given the laws of physics, are sufficient in the strongest sense for the later-occurring extensive damage; hence no causal work appears to remain for the hurricane, *qua* hurricane, to contribute to its production.

My goal in this section is purely destructive: to try to undermine this sort of intuition-based support for the thesis that retentive realizationism epiphenomenalizes the special- and honorary-scientific, and hence to suggest that our intuitions do not unambiguously favor the charge of epiphenomenalism. (A positive vindication of the causal role of the special- and honorary-scientific must await my next section.) My argumentative strategy turns on the notion of an *epi-world*, a kind of possible world concerning which our intuitive judgment is spectacularly clear: in such a world, nonphysical phenomena are so related to physical phenomena that the former are epiphenomenal in both of the senses I earlier distinguished. An epi-world is an extreme case, of course, and perhaps no one has seriously thought that a physicalist world would literally *be* an epi-world. But the guiding assumption of my strategy is that what underlies our intuition that retentive realizationism epiphenomenalizes the special- and honorary-scientific is the thought that a retentive realizationist world would at least *resemble* an epi-world in the relevant respects, so that the reasons for judging special- and honorary-scientific phenomena to be epiphenomenal in an epi-world carry over to the case of a retentive realizationist world. If this guiding assumption is correct, then asking why we react as we do to an epi-world promises to throw into sharp relief the reasons why we fear that retentive realizationism would epiphenomenalize the special- and honorary-scientific.

Having described epi-worlds, and having diagnosed *why* we judge so readily that the nonphysical phenomena in them are epiphenomenal, I first point out that a retentive realizationist world would certainly not resemble an epi-world in *every* respect; then I argue that it is at best an open question whether it would nevertheless resemble an epi-world in the *relevant* respects. The upshot is that our reasons for judging that nonphysical phenomena in an *epi-world* are epiphenomenal cannot safely be assumed to carry over automatically to nonphysical phenomena in a *retentive realizationist* world. More is required to support the charge that retentive realizationism epiphenomenalizes the special- and honorary-scientific than the alleged intuitive obviousness of the charge. This section also makes it clear that, to the extent that the charge of epiphenomenalism against retentive physicalism without type identities has any merit, it applies to *all* nonbasic phenomena and not just to mental phenomena, so that, *pace* Kim (1998, 77–87), the problem of mental causation *does* generalize.

An epi-world, then, contains just two kinds of events, physical and mental, and no mental event is type- or token-identical with a physical event. All physical events succeed one another in accordance with physical laws that are fundamental and deterministic; one of these fundamental physical laws is that all P_1-tokens are followed by P_2-tokens. However, every mental event has a simultaneous *underlier* that is a physical event, and which (in an epi-world) underlies a mental event of a given type by being of some physical type such that it is a fundamental synchronic psychophysical law that if an event of that physical type occurs, there occurs a simultaneous event of the relevant mental type; one such fundamental psychophysical law is that if there is a P_1-token, there is a simultaneous M_1-token; another is that if there is a P_2-token, there is a simultaneous M_2-token. All the tokens of any given type of mental event are in fact underlain by simultaneous tokens of just one type of physical event. An epi-world contains no kind of *fundamental* law beyond the physical and psychophysical kinds of law already mentioned; but the description of an epi-world does entail that all M_1-tokens are followed by M_2-tokens, and that this is no accident. For because all M_1-tokens have simultaneous physical underliers, and P_1-tokens are their only physical underliers, all M_1-tokens must be underlain by P_1-tokens; but P_1-tokens are lawfully sufficient for later P_2-tokens, which are in turn lawfully sufficient for simultaneous M_2-tokens. A fragment of an epi-world can be depicted like this, where the regular arrows denote fundamental nomological connections and the double arrowheads denote derivative nomological connections:

$$\ldots \gg M_1\text{-token} \gg M_2\text{-token} \gg \ldots$$
$$\uparrow \qquad \uparrow$$
$$\ldots \to P_1\text{-token} \to P_2\text{-token} \to \ldots$$

Now, if our knowledge of an epi-world were restricted to knowledge *only* of the nonaccidental regularity that all M_1-tokens are followed by M_2-tokens, we would naturally be inclined to say that in an epi-world M_1-tokens *cause* M_2-tokens, perhaps adding that they do so *because* they are M_1-tokens. However, as we learned more about epi-worlds, we would surely change our minds, judging instead that M_1-tokens cause nothing in an epi-world, and that M_1 is not a causally relevant type. But why is that? Why, upon learning the full story about the fragment of an epi-world depicted earlier, would we entirely lose our previous inclination to construe the M_1-token as a cause of the M_2-token and M_1 as a causally relevant type?

The reason, I suggest, is that we recognize that the situation depicted is an example of a type of everyday situation in which, paradigmatically, the appearance of causation and causal relevance turns out to be illusory.[4] The type of situation I mean is one in which, for example, a distinctive kind of rash (i) is reliably followed by a fever, (ii) appears to the uninitiated

---

4 This diagnosis seems to be increasingly widely accepted. It is explicit in David Robb (1997, 181), and implicit in Gabriel Segal and Elliott Sober's objection to simple nomic accounts of causal relevance, that they just *assume* that special- and honorary-scientific laws are causal laws rather than merely noncausal laws of association (Segal and Sober 1991, 4–6; see also Kim 1998, 50).

to cause the fever and indeed to cause the fever *because* it is a rash of that kind, but (iii) in fact does not cause it at all because both the rash and the fever are *joint effects of a common cause*, namely, a viral infection. The situation depicted is an example of this everyday type because, in an epi-world, M_1-tokens are reliably followed by M_2-tokens, but the M_1-token and the M_2-token of each instance of this regularity turn out to be joint effects of a common cause, a certain entirely distinct P_1-token; it follows, then, that an M_1-token no more causes the M_2-token that succeeds it than any rash in our everyday rash-fever example causes the fever that succeeds it. And on this diagnosis of why an epi-world strikes us as one in which the mental is epiphenomenal, the fear that any version of retentive physicalism without type identities will epiphenomenalize the special- and honorary-scientific is simply the fear that any version of retentive physicalism without type identities is bound to reveal *every* instance of *every* special- and honorary-scientific regularity as having some physical common cause, namely, the physical token that *both* determines the first token in the instance *and* causes the physical token determining the second token in the instance; the fear, in effect, is that discovering the truth of physicalism would amount to discovering some analog of a viral infection for absolutely every special- and honorary-scientific event-sequence we ordinarily take to be causal.

Now suppose this diagnosis of why an epi-world strikes us as one in which the mental is epiphenomenal is correct: we recognize the similarity between epi-worlds, on the one hand, and everyday cases like the rash-fever case, on the other, in which an apparent cause turns out to be no cause at all. Still, what explains our judgment about the rash-fever case that the rash is not a cause of the fever after all? The answer here, I suggest, is that, in view of the role of the viral infection, it turns out that the rash *makes no difference* to the fever in the following specific sense: the rash turns out not to be a "topper-up" for a fever – not to be something that, if added to (the rest of) actual conditions, which by themselves would *not* have been sufficient for a fever, would have created conditions that *would* have been sufficient for a fever (see Mackie 1965). The rash turns out to make no difference, then, because something entirely distinct from the rash, the viral infection, turns out to be sufficient in the actual circumstances for a fever, and the rash, though indeed a part of the actual circumstances, is not an *indispensable* part of them in the sense that an infection under those same circumstances but minus the rash would fail to be sufficient for a fever. But if this answer is correct, then we should say the same about our reaction to epi-worlds: we judge that in an epi-world no M_1-token is a cause of an M_2-token because, it turns out, no M_1-token ever turns some set of actual conditions that by itself is *not* sufficient for an M_2-token into a set of conditions that *is* sufficient for an M_2-token; for the P_1-token, which is entirely distinct from the M_1-token, is *already* sufficient in the circumstances for an M_2-token, and the M_1-token, though a part of those circumstances, is not an indispensable part of them in the requisite sense.

It is worth pausing to ask whether the idea that M_1-tokens make no difference in this sense can be expressed with a counterfactual claim. It is initially tempting to suppose that the idea is expressed by the *falsity* of the counterfactual claim that had there been no M_1-token, there would have been no M_2-token (for the *truth* of such a claim is often taken as a sufficient condition of causal relevance). But the temptation should probably be resisted, since this counterfactual claim seems in fact to be *true* of the imagined situation: given that in the epi-world M_1-tokens are necessitated by, and only by, P_1-tokens in accordance with a fundamental law, it is at least plausible that, in the closest worlds in which there is no M_1-token, there is no M_1-token because there is no P_1-token, with the result that there is no subsequent P_2-token or M_2-token either. Similarly, in the rash-fever case, it is intuitively plausible that if a sick child had not had a rash, she would not have had a fever – even though the rash is no cause of the fever. Simple counterfactual dependence, then, can apparently hold between events that are not related as cause and effect.[5] A more sophisticated suggestion for expressing counterfactually the idea that M_1-tokens make no difference in the requisite sense is this: they make no difference iff it is *false* that, had there been no M_1-token *while the rest of the actual circumstances remained the same*, there would not have been an M_2-token. Now the embedded counterfactual claim here is indeed false of the imagined situation, as required: had there been no M_1-token while the rest of the actual circumstances remained the same, the P_1-token underlying it would still have existed and caused the P_2-token underlying the M_2-token. But the falsity of this counterfactual claim does not entail that the actual M_1-token made no difference. For it might be false even though the M_1-token *did* make a difference. Imagine that an M_1-token did cause an M_2-token (in virtue of a fundamental law linking M_1-tokens

---

5 *Pace* David Lewis, who denies the counterfactuals I here take to be true (see his 1986, 170–1). Terry Horgan, who defends a sophisticated counterfactual account of causal relevance, still allows that there could be counterfactual dependence between nonphysical events that are not related as cause to effect, but he says nothing to solve the problem (1991, 91).

with M_2-tokens), but that a mischievous demon stood ready to cause an M_2-token in case no M_1-token occurred; in such possible circumstances, had there been no M_1-token while the rest of the actual circumstances remained the same, there would still have been an M_2-token – and yet the M_1-token did make a difference.

So much for epi-worlds. Let me turn now to the crucial question: is a retentive realizationist world similar enough to an epi-world that, by parity of reasoning, we have to judge that nonphysical phenomena in a retentive realizationist world are every bit as epiphenomenal as nonphysical phenomena in an epi-world? Certainly a retentive realizationist world is not *exactly* similar to an epi-world. The difference lies in the nature of the relation between a nonphysical token (e.g., an M_1-token) and its simultaneous physical underlier (e.g., a certain P_1-token) in the two kinds of world. It is true that, in both an epi-world and a retentive realizationist world, a nonphysical token and its physical underlier are not numerically identical. But in a retentive realizationist world the *positive* relation between a nonphysical token and its physical underlier is more intimate than it is in an epi-world. In an epi-world, this positive relation is brute nomological determination: the M_1-token is nomologically determined by its physical underlier in virtue of the holding of a *fundamental* psychophysical law to the effect that, if there is a token of the physical underlier's type, then there is a simultaneous M_1-token. In consequence, in an epi-world, if an M_1-token is underlain by a particular P_1-token, it is logically possible, even given the physical laws and any other physical facts you care to add in, that the P_1-token should have existed while the M_1-token it underlies did not; this is not logically possible given the *psychophysical* laws, of course, but it is given the purely *physical* laws.

In a retentive realizationist world, however, the positive relation between an M_1-token and its physical underlier is that of realization – that is, the M_1-token is a token of (what is in fact) a functional type, M_1, such that (i) there is a token of M_1 iff there is a token of some or other type that meets associated condition C; (ii) the physical underlier of the M_1-token, purely in virtue of physical facts, is a token of some or other type that meets C; and (iii) the M_1-token guaranteed to exist by this physical token, given purely physical facts, just is the M_1-token originally considered. In consequence, in a retentive realizationist world, if an M_1-token is underlain by a particular P_1-token, it is *not* logically possible, given the physical laws and perhaps also other physical facts, that the P_1-token should have existed while the M_1-token it underlies did not: the existence of the P_1-token, given the physical laws and perhaps also other physical facts, necessitates in the strongest sense the existence of the M_1-token. Certainly, in a retentive realizationist world, it is a law that if there is a token of the physical underlier's type (perhaps given certain historical or environmental physical conditions), there is a simultaneous M_1-token; and although this law is a physical law in the sense that it holds in all worlds in which the actual laws of physics hold, it is a psychophysical law in the sense that it holds between physical circumstances, on the one hand, and psychological ones, on the other. But it is not a *fundamental* psychophysical law, since, as we saw in Chapters 1 and 2, it is a logical consequence of the (necessary) identity of M_1 with a functional type whose associated condition is necessarily met by P_1, given the physical laws and perhaps other physical facts.

That an epi-world and a retentive realizationist world are not *exactly* similar can hardly be denied, because it is a logical consequence of stipulative definitions of the two kinds of worlds. But does the difference between them matter for the issue at hand, so that our reasons for judging that nonphysical phenomena in an epi-world are epiphenomenal *cannot* safely be assumed also to apply automatically to special- and honorary-scientific phenomena in a retentive realizationist world? Let me now argue that the difference between the two kinds of worlds does matter. To begin, recall my earlier suggestion that the reason why we judge that nonphysical phenomena in an epi-world are epiphenomenal is that we recognize that in an epi-world every apparently causal regularity among nonphysical phenomena turns out to be strictly analogous to the sort of *noncausal* regularity exemplified in everyday life by the rash-fever regularity, a regularity that initially appears to be causal but which is subsequently revealed to be noncausal by the discovery of the viral infection that causes first a rash and then a fever. *This* reason for judging nonphysical phenomena to be epiphenomenal, however, does not *straightforwardly* apply to nonphysical phenomena in a retentive realizationist world. For, in such a world, any nonphysical token thought to be a cause would be underlain by a numerically distinct physical token that nevertheless *realized* it. By contrast, the viral infection that underlies a rash, while numerically distinct from it, merely *causes* the rash; it does not *realize* it.

Now this disanalogy between an epi-world and a retentive realizationist world certainly muddies the waters. But, I now suggest, it does more. Suppose I buy some Kwik-Gro fertilizer and apply it to my roses, which subsequently flourish as they have never done before; this is unsurprising, since, as more experienced gardeners inform me, Kwik-Gro can nearly always be relied upon to give roses a boost – which is why they buy it.

Suppose, however, that I make the following pair of discoveries: first, that Kwik-Gro is a mixture of two ingredients, an active ingredient, which is sufficient in the circumstances for boosting roses, and a filler, which plays absolutely no role in helping the active ingredient to work but is added only because customers have an irrational preference for putting *lots* of stuff on their roses; and, second, that the manufacturers of Kwik-Gro do not always use the *same* active ingredient in their product but instead make a monthly choice among several equally effective active ingredients, basing their decision on cost. Now before I made these discoveries I was naturally inclined to say that what caused my roses to do well this year was Kwik-Gro, and that Kwik-Gro caused them to do well *because* it was Kwik-Gro. But, intuitively, my discoveries throw no doubt whatever upon these claims. I may have discovered *how* Kwik-Gro makes roses do well, but surely I have not discovered that Kwik-Gro does *not* make roses do well.[6]

But it is puzzling that our intuitive judgments about this case do not change after we make our discoveries about Kwik-Gro's active ingredients, for our discoveries in the rash-fever case *do* lead us to revise our earlier judgments about the causal role of rashes, and the Kwik-Gro case obviously resembles the rash-fever case in the following way: in both cases we find something (a) that is numerically distinct from the putative nonbasic cause (the infection is nonidentical with the rash; the portion of active ingredient is nonidentical – because of the filler – with the sample of Kwik-Gro applied on the particular occasion) and (b) that is sufficient in the circumstances *by itself* for the putative nonbasic cause's putative effect (where the putative nonbasic cause is not a part of those circumstances). So what is the relevant difference between the rash-fever case and the Kwik-Gro case? Why is it that, in the rash-fever case, the viral infection excludes the rash from playing a causal role, whereas, in the Kwik-Gro case, the active ingredient does *not* exclude Kwik-Gro from playing a causal role? The answer, I suggest, is that even though in both cases the underlying condition that is sufficient for the putative nonbasic effect is numerically distinct from the putative nonbasic cause, in the Kwik-Gro case the underlying sufficient condition (i.e., the portion of active

---

6 This case serves, of course, as a counterexample to the exclusion principle formulated (though later rejected) by Stephen Yablo: if an event x is causally sufficient for an event y, then no event x^* distinct from x is causally relevant to y (1992, 247). The inspiration for the case derives from Terry Horgan and James Woodward (1985, 218, n. 16). For different examples but the same moral, see also Segal and Sober (1991, 14–15) and David Henderson (1994, 139).

ingredient) is nevertheless a *part* of the putative nonbasic cause (i.e., the sample of Kwik-Gro), whereas in the rash-fever case the rash is not even a part of the infection, being *entirely* and not merely numerically distinct from it. But if this answer is correct, then a retentive realizationist world differs in a highly relevant way from an epi-world. For if an M_1-token, rather than being nomologically necessitated by a P_1-token in accordance with a fundamental psychophysical law, is instead realized by a P_1-token, then the relation between the M_1-token and the P_1-token looks a lot more like the relation between Kwik-Gro and the active ingredient than that between the rash and the infection; indeed, it is tempting to say that if an M_1-token is realized by a P_1-token, then the P_1-token just *is* a part of the M_1-token. But if so, and if the relevant difference between the rash-fever case and the Kwik-Gro case lies, as I have suggested, in the presence or absence of a part-whole relation, then the discovery that a putative nonbasic cause has a physical realizer that is sufficient for the putative cause's nonbasic effect, in circumstances of which the putative nonbasic cause is not an indispensable part, need not undermine the causal status of the putative nonbasic cause.[7]

Consider, next, the second suggestion I made: that the underlying reason why we think that in an epi-world no M_1-token is a cause of any subsequent M_2-token is that in an epi-world the M_1-token turns out not to be a "topper-up" for an M_2-token – that is, it turns out not to be something that, if added to (the rest of) actual conditions by themselves not sufficient for an M_2-token, would have created conditions that were sufficient for an M_2-token. Let us grant that this suggestion is correct. Still, it does not entail that, in a *retentive realizationist* world, no M_1-token is a cause of any subsequent M_2-token. For if an M_1-token is *realized* by a P_1-token, then the M_1-token could still be a topper-up. Because the M_1-token is entirely constituted by the P_1-token, to imagine adding that very M_1-token to actual circumstances that lack it is surely to imagine adding it to actual circumstances *minus* the P_1-token – for how could we take away that very M_1-token without taking away the P_1-token that realizes and hence entirely constitutes it? But actual circumstances minus the P_1-token might easily be insufficient for a subsequent M_2-token.

---

7 As Sara Worley correctly notes (1993, 341–2), not every whole, one of whose parts causes X, is itself a cause of X; but, as she later notes (348), it may yet be that every such whole, so long as it meets some further condition, is itself a cause of X. Her suggestion as to this further condition – that it is the holding of "appropriate counterfactual-supporting generalizations" connecting the whole with X – resembles mine in the next section.

So the M_1-token might well top up to sufficiency (for an M_2-token) circumstances not sufficient by themselves.

Finally, let us consider the suggestion that the reason why we think that in an epi-world no M_1-token is a cause of any subsequent M_2-token is that we recognize that in an epi-world the following counterfactual claim is true: had there been no M_1-token while the rest of actual circumstances had remained the same, there would still have been an M_2-token. As we saw earlier, the truth of such a counterfactual at least provides a defeasible reason to judge that no M_1-token is a cause, even though it does not entail it. This counterfactual claim, however, is *false* of a retentive realizationist world, and false precisely *because* in such a world the M_1-token is realized by a P_1-token – rather than just nomologically determined by it in accordance with some fundamental psychophysical law. Because the M_1-token is realized by the P_1-token, the existence of the P_1-token necessitates (in the strongest sense) the existence of the M_1-token, given the laws of physics. So the closest possible worlds in which the M_1-token does not exist while the rest of actual circumstances, including the existence of the P_1-token, remain the same must be those in which the laws of physics do not all hold, so that the P_1-token fails to realize the M_1-token, through not playing the right nomic role to meet the associated condition for M_1. In such worlds, however, there might not be an M_2-token; for, given that the laws of physics do not all hold in them, the P_1-token might not cause a P_2-token, and even if it does, the P_2-token might not realize an M_2-token (through its failure to play the right nomic role for M_2).

In sum, then, my argument has been this. The powerful intuition that retentive realizationism epiphenomenalizes the special- and honorary-scientific arises from the possibly unconscious assumption that a retentive realizationist world would relevantly resemble an epi-world; and certainly if a retentive realizationist world would relevantly resemble an epi-world, then discovering that all special- and honorary-scientific phenomena have physical realizers would be just like discovering the role of viral infections in the rash-fever case, only writ very large, and so would force us to abandon our commonsense convictions about the causal role of special- and honorary-scientific tokens and types. But once the indisputable differences between an epi-world and a retentive realizationist world are made explicit, it is far from clear that a retentive realizationist world *would* be relevantly similar to an epi-world. Thus, the intuition that retentive realizationism epiphenomenalizes the special- and honorary-scientific is undermined.

Let me conclude this section, however, by stressing that in trying to weaken the intuitive roots of the charge of epiphenomenalism I have repeatedly appealed to the central claim of retentive realizationism that special- and honorary-scientific phenomena are *realized* by physical phenomena – in the specific sense of "realized" that was introduced in Chapter 1 – rather than merely *necessitated* by them in accordance with brute synchronic laws connecting the physical with the special- and honorary-scientific. However, any physicalist who holds that all special- and honorary-scientific phenomena *supervene* upon, and hence are necessitated by, how things are physically, but who either denies that this supervenience is explained by the realization of special- and honorary-scientific phenomena by physical phenomena or who refuses to say anything at all about how it is to be explained is not entitled to argue as I have been arguing. Indeed, it is not all clear that such a physicalist has *any* resources with which to distinguish an epi-world from a supervenience physicalist world, and hence to rebut the charge of epiphenomenalism. So if the response to the charge of epiphenomenalism that I have sketched in the current section and will develop in the next is on the right track, then there is another reason, in addition to those provided in Chapter 2, for doubting that an adequate formulation of physicalism can be given in terms of supervenience alone. Such a formulation seems to postulate an insufficiently intimate connection between the physical and the special- or honorary-scientific to enable an adequate response to the charge of epiphenomenalism.

3. A THEORY OF CAUSATION AND CAUSAL RELEVANCE

The goal of the preceding section was negative: to undermine the reason that intuition provides for thinking that retentive realizationism epiphenomenalizes special- and honorary-scientific phenomena. In this section, I turn to a positive argument for thinking that retentive realizationism does *not* epiphenomenalize special- and honorary-scientific phenomena.[8]

---

8 My theory is indebted to a valuable article by Gabriel Segal and Elliott Sober (1991, esp. 15), whose account of causal relevance closely resembles mine. However, there are important differences. First, though they conceive of the relation between nonbasic and physical phenomena as that of mereological supervenience (which sounds as if they want to take the part-whole relation seriously), they go on (10) to understand mereological supervenience merely as nomic necessitation, thus omitting the mereological dimension that is, on my account, crucial. Second, the official formulation of their account (15) just assumes that nonbasic laws are causal, which means that their own nomic account of relevance is left

Building on the ideas of the preceding section, I first present and defend a general account of causation and causal relevance, and then show how it implies that, even in a retentive realizationist world, special- and honorary-scientific tokens could perfectly well be causes of special- and honorary-scientific effects, and special- and honorary-scientific types could perfectly well be causally relevant. Unfashionably, however, my account is Humean; and although I do not regard myself as involved in a priori conceptual analysis, I emphatically do mean the account to be a reasonably accurate characterization – give or take a bit – of the relation we are in fact speaking of when in everyday life we use the word "cause" and its cognates, and not merely to be an account of the relation we *should* be speaking of in order to be epistemically responsible.[9] The undertaking is therefore highly ambitious, and you might well wonder whether it is really necessary. My answer is that, though perhaps not strictly necessary, it is nevertheless highly desirable. For thus far I have provided no positive vindication of the causal role of special- and honorary-scientific phenomena in a retentive realizationism world, and such a vindication will surely be considerably more convincing if it is based not merely upon questionable intuitions about causal relevance in particular but rather upon a general, explicit, and independently plausible theory of causation. Moreover, at least one objection to the nomological approach to causal relevance that I end up defending requires for its rebuttal an explicit account of the difference between causal and noncausal laws, something it would be hard to provide without a full theory of causation. I hope that these two advantages compensate for the exceedingly high probability that my theory is not quite right, just as it stands, and for the certainty that it is incomplete.

My account is Humean in two distinct senses. It is Humean, first, in claiming that an event that is a cause of some effect *counts* as a cause of the

---

open to the very charge they bring (4) against Fodor's simple nomic account of relevance, namely, that it assumes that all laws are causal laws. Third, their account of causal relevance is never explicitly connected with any general account of causation, which gives it (as it gives all accounts of causal relevance similarly unconnected to a general account of causation) the slight appearance of being cooked up merely to save (physicalist) intuitions about particular cases of relevance. For another account of causal relevance similar in spirit to mine, though based on a quite different account of causation, see David Henderson (1994). I have also profited from reading Jean Kazez (1995), especially her very interesting remarks (85ff.) comparing and contrasting the "method of differences" with counterfactual tests of causal relevance.

9 *Pace* David Papineau (1986, 211), who, despite his Humean sympathies, finds a Humean analysis of our ordinary causal talk implausible. However, he does not consider the strategies for defending Humeanism about ordinary causal talk that I deploy later.

later event *solely* in virtue of the event pair's instantiating some contingent regularity of a special kind; so if we look at an event pair related as cause to effect, and another event pair not so related, we will find nothing present just in the relation between the event tokens in the first pair, but absent in the relation between the event tokens in the second pair, to constitute the fact that the first event pair is causal and the second not. Now this first Humean feature of my account of causation entails that whether an event causes a second depends in part on the occurrence of, and relations among, *other* events, thus defying the intuition of some philosophers that causation is a relation intrinsic to an event and its effect. But we can dismiss such an intuition as an error. Precedent for doing so is provided by the fact that, when we acknowledge that the properties of weighing one ton and of moving at thirty miles per hour involve a hidden relativity, we happily dismiss our earlier intuition that an object's weight and speed are intrinsic properties of the object.

Does the intuition that causation is a relation intrinsic to an event and its effect have any support? It is true that we often judge that one event caused another (e.g., that a child's reaching for the ketchup knocked over the glass) on the strength of observation of the two events alone; but observation typically takes place against a rich theoretical background, so inferences from the contribution made to an act of observation by the immediate scene to a conclusion about the nature of the state of affairs observed are insecure. For an everyday example, consider the fact that we can often judge correctly that someone is a professor on the strength of her appearance and manner alone, without examining whether she stands in the special relations to other people in which she would need to stand in order to be a professor. It may also be true that our *concept* of causation is unanalyzable, and if it is, that would also tend to sustain the idea that causation *itself* is unanalyzable, and hence not relational. But it is perfectly possible, of course, to have an unanalyzable concept of an analyzable thing. For example, as most philosophers suppose, one's concept of oneself is simple even though oneself – the person that one is – is not. So recognition of the simplicity of the concept of causation (if it is simple) provides no reason to treat causation as simple and therefore nonrelational. More generally, it is worth recalling that my account of causation is not being advanced as a conceptual truth, if that is taken to imply that the plausibility of the account can be evaluated a priori, solely in virtue of one's competence with the concept of causation.

Precisely because my account of causation is Humean in this first sense, it naturally suggests an account of *causal relevance*. For, on any account of causation that is Humean in this sense, an event counts as a cause of its effect *because* it satisfies the antecedent of some suitable regularity. Moreover, since it satisfies the antecedent of that regularity, in turn, *because* it is a token of a certain type, it follows, on any such account of causation, that an event causes its effect *because* it is a token of a certain type. (The "because" should be taken to express something like Aristotelian formal causation, as in "Smith is a bachelor because he is an unmarried man.") Now our earlier analysis of causal relevance (in the sense expressed by various everyday claims we ordinarily take to be true) was that a type T is causally relevant to token t_1's causing of token t_2 iff t_1's being a token of T explains *why* it caused t_2; however, this left it open *how* a cause's being a token of T helps to explain why it caused the effect it did. But we can now see a natural way to specify how it does so. On my account of causation, since it is Humean in this first sense, the causal relevance of an event token's being of a certain event type can plausibly be identified with the fact that the event token caused its effect because (in Aristotle's formal sense of "because") it was a token of that event type and therefore satisfied the antecedent of a certain regularity.

Now for the second sense in which my account of causation is Humean: it assumes that a cause-constituting regularity – a regularity such that an event sequence counts as a causal sequence in virtue of instantiating it – is a species of pure, empirical regularity, involving no sort of natural necessity (necessity in the world) whatever. What distinguishes a pure, empirical regularity that is cause-constituting from one that is not is no simple matter, on my account; but it will turn out to lie, neither in the regularities themselves, nor in the minds of those who talk about them, but somewhere else.[10] That my account of causation is Humean in this second sense will be a sticking point for many readers. So it is worth recalling that any account of causation that is Humean in both the second and the first senses – that is, any account holding that an event sequence counts as causal solely in virtue of instantiating a pure, empirical regularity of a special kind – possesses a familiar but very large advantage, and one to which physicalists ought to be sympathetic: it answers the fundamental question in the philosophy of causation, explaining wherein lies the difference between event sequences that are causal and those that are not, but it does so without requiring commitment to the existence of something – causal or natural necessity in the world – that is neither

---

10 As detailed later, the distinction turns out to lie in the character of how, if at all, the regularities can be *explained*.

directly observed nor justifiably postulated on the grounds of its causal-explanatory power. Causal or natural necessity is notoriously something that we do not just see when we witness cases of singular causation, even if, as some philosophers maintain, we can just see that one event *caused* another. And a hypothesis to the effect that all Fs *must* be followed by Gs (where the "must" is meant to express some necessary connection in the world) cannot explain anything that cannot also be explained, but at a lower ontological cost, by the pure regularity that all Fs are *in fact* followed by Gs.[11]

However, for my account of causation to vindicate the causal role of special- and honorary-scientific phenomena, not to mention avoid standard objections to Humean accounts, it must incorporate three non-Humean (though not necessarily un-Humean) features. First, since types, on my account, can be causally relevant only if cause-constituting regularities hold among their tokens, and since almost certainly no strict and exceptionless regularities hold among the tokens of special- and honorary-scientific types, the account cannot *require* cause-constituting regularities to be strict and exceptionless – on pain of disallowing any special- or honorary-scientific types to be causally relevant. It can *allow* strict and exceptionless cause-constituting regularities, of course, but it must also allow that an event sequence can count as causal in virtue of instantiating a ceteris paribus regularity (i.e., a reliable regularity that nevertheless has, and is often known to have, exceptions). That it permits ceteris paribus regularities to be cause-constituting is the first non-Humean feature of my account of causation.

Everyday life is full of such regularities. For example, it is an everyday ceteris paribus regularity that hurricanes are followed by extensive damage (even though some are not); and that, of course, is why people are evacuated from areas where a hurricane is expected. Indeed, without knowledge of ceteris paribus regularities, it is hard to see how we could be as good predictors of everyday phenomena as we evidently are, for it is hard to formulate even one exceptionless regularity about items of everyday interest that might serve as an alternative basis for prediction. Furthermore, it is the discovery of ceteris paribus regularities that in everyday life we take to be *evidence*, strong though defeasible, of the holding of causal connections. Ceteris paribus regularities are also discovered in the special sciences; for example, regularities involving the curative powers

---

11 It cannot even do a good job, I would claim, of explaining the pure regularity itself.

of various medications that are never invariably effective. The existence – as opposed to the analysis – of ceteris paribus regularities ought not to be controversial.[12]

But can they be cause-constituting? There is no *special* objection to supposing that ceteris paribus regularities can be cause-constituting. Admittedly, the recent philosophical tradition has required cause-constituting regularities to be strict and exceptionless, which would obviously disqualify ceteris paribus regularities from playing that role. But this requirement is too strong to be part of our ordinary concept of causation: contrary to what it implies, we would surely *not* abandon the idea that everyday events are causes, were we to discover (as it is plausible to think we already have discovered) that no regularities among objects of everyday interest are strict and exceptionless. In any case, there is no decisive reason for requiring cause-constituting regularities to be strict and exceptionless. Certainly it is plausible that our ordinary idea of a singular cause includes some idea of *generality*; but this does not require cause-constituting regularities to be *universal*, for generality does not entail universality. Nor are ceteris paribus regularities disqualified from being cause-constituting on the grounds that, if retentive realizationism is true, then they are *nonbasic* regularities. For why should being nonbasic make a difference? An event sequence can be a perfectly good instance of some ceteris paribus regularity (thereby counting as a causal sequence) even though the regularity is nonbasic in the sense that it has a reductive explanation appealing just to physical facts plus necessary truths; we ought not to think that a regularity does not *really* have instances just because it is not a *basic* regularity. In a similar vein, if the fact that an event sequence instantiates a regularity helps explain *why* the event sequence constitutes a causal sequence, then this explanation still holds even if the regularity *itself* has an explanation; the general principle I am invoking here is that if X explains Y, then X *still* explains Y, even if some Z explains X.[13]

---

12 Sadly, I have no analysis of ceteris paribus regularities to offer.

13 My claim is not the same as Brian McLaughlin's claim (1989, 124–9; see also LePore and Loewer 1989, 183) that a single event-sequence might enjoy its causal status *both* in virtue of a strict physical law *and* in virtue of a nonstrict nonbasic law. My view is that there is no particular reason to suppose that strict physical laws *themselves* play *any* (positive) role in grounding nonbasic causation, even though they might *explain* the nonbasic regularities that do. Also, McLaughlin's claim is formulated on an assumption that I do not make, namely, that every nonbasic event is *identical* with some or other physical event, so that literally the very same event might be subsumed by both strict physical and nonstrict nonbasic laws.

So there is, I suggest, no good reason to deny that ceteris paribus regularities can be cause-constituting. However, the feeling that a nonbasic (i.e., reductively explainable) regularity cannot ground cases of singular causation may arise from a perfectly correct observation: as our rash-fever case illustrates, we sometimes *do* withdraw the claim that a regularity is causal because of something we discover about the underlying *explanation* of why the regularity holds. But it does not follow that we do or should withdraw such claims in *every* case where a regularity turns out to have an underlying explanation and therefore to be nonbasic. I return to this crucial point in due course.

The second non-Humean feature of my account of causation is that the antecedent of a generalization that expresses a cause-constituting regularity might refer to events that belong simultaneously to *several* event types; so a generalization expressing a cause-constituting regularity might state that any event belonging to *all* of types $C_1, C_2, \ldots C_n$ is followed by an E-type event. For example, a cause-constituting regularity is plausibly expressed by the generalization that all match strikings, *when in the presence of abundant oxygen and gasoline vapor*, are followed by explosions. Consequently, for an event to satisfy the antecedent of a generalization that expresses a cause-constituting regularity, it might not be enough for the event to be of a *single* event type; it might also be required that it belong to other event types too. Thus, to continue the example, a particular match striking will not fall under the relevant regularity solely in virtue of being a match striking, but also in virtue of the fact that it was a match striking in conditions of abundant oxygen and gasoline vapor.

This second non-Humean feature of my account of causation confers two advantages. First, it allows events to be singular causes, even though the types of which they are tokens are not by themselves sufficient conditions for the relevant effect types; these events can be singular causes just so long as they are *indispensable parts* of conditions that are sufficient for those effect-types, so this second non-Humean feature allows for singular causes that are only toppers-up for their effects (see Mackie 1965). This advantage is important, because few everyday causes are sufficient for their effects. Second, however, and more important still, this second non-Humean feature of my account of causation allows an event type of which a given cause is a token to be causally relevant to the cause's effect, even though the event type in question is not nomically sufficient – not even sufficient ceteris paribus – for the effect's event type (*pace* Fodor 1990, 143; for the problem, see Horgan 1989, 55). For example, suppose that I have cut my hand on a knife standing point-upward in the dishwasher.

Since, intuitively, the knife made me bleed because it had a sharp point, *having a sharp point* is causally relevant. But it is not even a ceteris paribus regularity that knives that have a sharp point (let alone sharp-pointed things in general) suffice for bleeding people. So if the causal relevance of an event type required its nomic sufficiency, even ceteris paribus, *having a sharp point* would not qualify as causally relevant. However, it plausibly *is* a ceteris paribus regularity that objects with sharp points, *whose points are brought into rapid contact with human flesh*, suffice for bleeding people (which is why we teach children not to run with scissors). So, since any type to which a cause belongs is causally relevant if it is even partly in virtue of belonging to that type that the cause falls under the antecedent of a cause-constituting regularity, such a regularity is enough to make *having a sharp point* causally relevant to my bleeding.

Before proceeding to the third non-Humean feature of my account of causation, let us pause to take stock. According to the account so far, event c caused (was a cause of) event e iff there are event-types $C_1, C_2, \ldots C_n$ such that

(i) c occurred and was of types $C_1, C_2, \ldots C_n$;

(ii) e occurred and was of type E;

(iii) it is a contingent regularity (possibly ceteris paribus) that $C_1, C_2, \ldots C_n$-type events are followed by E-type events.[14]

But the account as it currently stands, in order to be plausible, must overcome two standard objections.[15] The first objection is that the account so

---

14   Given clause (iii) as it currently stands, my account of causation implies that simultaneous causation is impossible. If this implication is found too troubling, then the account could easily be modified to avoid it. One possible way of doing so would be to replace (iii) with

   (iii*) it is a contingent regularity (possibly ceteris paribus) that $C_1, C_2, \ldots C_n$-type events are either followed by, *or merely co-occur with*, E-type events, so long as the instances of following outnumber the instances of mere co-occurrence.

   The virtue of this proposed modification is that while it allows for $C_1, C_2, \ldots C_n$-type events sometimes to cause simultaneous E-type events, their doing so is parasitic upon $C_1, C_2, \ldots C_n$-type events' causings of *later* E-type events; hence, it rules out the sort of situation with which a regularity theory apparently cannot cope, wherein $C_1, C_2, \ldots C_n$-type events *always* cause simultaneous E-type events.

15   An interesting nonstandard objection has been raised by Barbara Montero, who claims that we can speak of some kind of thing having a causal power to produce an effect even though there are in fact no regularities between the thing and the effect; maybe some never-synthesized chemical compound *would* be poisonous to humans if it were synthesized, or

far, since it would allow paradigmatically non-cause-constituting regularities, like the rash-fever regularity in our earlier example, to satisfy clause (iii), would imply that all sorts of event pairs are related as cause to effect that in reality are not. So some fourth requirement is obviously needed, in addition to clauses (i) through (iii), that would have the effect of disallowing non-cause-constituting regularities. But, it may be said, no account of the distinction between cause-constituting and non-cause-constituting regularities is even *possible* within the limits of a pure regularity theory of causation. And with no account of this distinction, it might turn out, for all that we can now say, that ceteris paribus regularities among special- or honorary-scientific events are *never* cause-constituting, in which case the causal role of the special- and honorary-scientific would obviously not be vindicated. The second standard objection is even more basic: it seems that, in order to be cause-constituting, a regularity must at least be lawlike, as opposed to merely accidental; but the distinction between lawlike and merely accidental regularities is another distinction that cannot be made within the limits of a pure regularity theory. Indeed, such a framework implies that *all* regularities are merely accidental, hence that none are lawlike.

The third non-Humean feature of my account of causation is designed to circumvent the first of these two objections. It consists in adding the following clause to the account:

> (iv) The (possibly ceteris paribus) regularity that C_1, C_2, ... C_n-type events are followed by E-type events has *no undercutter*.

So a cause-constituting regularity is simply one that (so long as clause (iii) is satisfied) has no undercutter; whereas a non-cause-constituting regularity, on the other hand, is one that does have an undercutter. As we will see, whether a regularity has an undercutter is a matter of whether, and if so how, the regularity may be *explained*. But even without a detailed account of what an undercutter of a regularity is, two consequences of this third non-Humean feature of my account of causation can be noted. The first consequence is that, according to the account, a regularity is

> maybe some actual chemical compound *would* be poisonous to humans if it were consumed (which, prudently, it never is, has been, or will be). Perhaps it suffices, in reply to this objection, to say that something has an unexercised causal power just in case it *would* exemplify an appropriate regularity that *would* hold, if circumstances were different in some specified way; and I presume that background knowledge of the composition of the thing, or actual experience with things of similar kinds, could justify a counterfactual claim of this sort.

cause-constituting not in virtue of possessing something *extra*, as an anti-Humean necessitarianism would have it, but in virtue of *lacking* something, namely, an undercutter. A second consequence is that, to the extent that claims about the existence of undercutters are mind-independently true or false, whether a regularity is cause-constituting or not emerges as a mind-independent matter; so cause-constituting regularities are not distinguished from non-cause-constituting regularities on my account by any difference in our *attitudes* toward them.

The incorporation of this third non-Humean feature into my account of causation is motivated by two observations. The first observation is that in practice we *revise* our judgments about whether a regularity is cause-constituting in response to discoveries about what *explains* the regularity. For instance, we abandon the judgment that the rash-fever regularity is cause-constituting, and with it the judgment that rashes cause fevers, in response to our discovery that the regularity holds *because* infections cause rashes and then, without help from the rashes, fevers. Conversely, suppose that we learn that an increase in a city's ice-cream consumption tends to be followed by an increase in its murder rate, and that, on the ground that there is, as we say, no underlying mechanism connecting ice-cream consumption with murders, we initially judge that this regularity is *not* cause-constituting; yet if we subsequently discovered that what *explains* the regularity is the presence in ice cream of an artificial flavoring that has the side effect of making some people very much more aggressive and, hence, more likely to commit murder, we would instead judge that the regularity *is* cause-constituting, surprising though that would be. The fact that we revise our judgments about whether regularities are or are not cause-constituting in the light of discoveries about what explains them provides some reason to think that what *makes* a regularity cause-constituting is (in part) some fact about how it is explained.[16]

The second observation motivating the incorporation of a third non-Humean feature into my account of causation is this: we are capable of taking any regularity that we think actually *is* cause-constituting and of *imagining* that it might have turned out *not* to be cause-constituting; and, in doing so, we imagine discovering something new about the *explanation* of the regularity. For example, given our current state of knowledge, we confidently judge the ceteris paribus regularity that hurricanes are followed by extensive damage to be cause-constituting. But, with effort,

---

16 Possibly including, as we shall see, the fact that, having no explanation, it is *not* explained.

we can imagine what it would be like for this regularity *not* to be cause-constituting. In doing so, however, we imagine some such bizarre scenario as this: whenever there is a hurricane, God temporarily and locally suspends the laws of physics so that fast-moving molecules of air can pass straight through solid matter, but he also causes roofs and so forth to fly through the air just as if they had been struck by rapidly moving masses of air. But what we are imagining here is precisely that the *explanation* of the hurricane-damage regularity is other than what we normally take it to be. The role that hypothetical alternative explanations of regularities play in imagining that actually cause-constituting regularities are non-cause-constituting also supports the suggestion that what *makes* a regularity cause-constituting is (in part) some fact about how it is explained.[17]

But in order for the inclusion of clause (iv) to succeed in saving my account of causation from the objection that it cannot distinguish cause-constituting from non-cause-constituting regularities, the crucial distinction between lacking and having an undercutter needs to be specified. Moreover, the distinction must be specified without making the overall account of causation of which it is a part *circular*, by explicitly characterizing the distinction in terms of causation, the very concept to be analyzed. I explain the distinction negatively, by explaining the (only) two ways in which a regularity can *lack* an undercutter; if a regularity does not lack an undercutter in either of these ways, then it *has* an undercutter.

Consider the regularity, R, that all events belonging to every type in the set $\{C_1, C_2, \ldots C_n\}$ are followed by E-type events. The first way in which R can lack an undercutter is for the regularity to be *basic* in the sense of lacking any explanation (e.g., a reductive or a causal explanation) at all *and* for it not to be the case, for any proper subset of the set $\{C_1, C_2, \ldots C_n\}$, that it is a regularity that all events belonging to every type in that proper subset are followed by E-type events (i.e., as I sometimes put it, for no "cut-down antecedent" versions of the regularity to hold).[18] Now,

---

17 Louise Antony (1991, 316ff.), though she too stresses the importance of underlying mechanisms, seems to think that a mere coincidence can be distinguished from a true law by the fact that the latter is grounded in an underlying mechanism. But, given retentive realizationism, *all* nonbasic regularities must be grounded in *some* underlying physical mechanism, as we saw in the previous chapter; we need a way to distinguish *among* such mechanisms if we want to distinguish between coincidences and laws – or between causal laws and noncausal laws.

18 Strictly speaking, for a regularity to be basic is for it to lack any *noncircular* explanation, where an explanation of a regularity is noncircular just in case no matter how far back you go in explaining what explains the regularity, explaining what explains what explains the regularity, and so on, you do not need to invoke the original regularity.

given realizationism, the only regularities that can meet these two conditions are certain *physical* regularities; given realizationism, all nonphysical regularities hold in virtue of physical phenomena that realize them, but certain physical regularities do not hold in virtue of phenomena at some yet deeper level of reality that realizes the physical (so they lack a reductive explanation), nor do they hold because something that is not physically realized, such as God, causally produces and maintains them (so they lack a causal explanation). On the present account of causation, it follows, given realization physicalism, that since these physical regularities have no explanation at all, they are (candidates to be) cause-constituting. It follows, further, that the physical types involved in these regularities are (candidates to be) causally relevant – which suggests that we are on the right track, since no one who worries about the causal relevance of special- or honorary-scientific types worries about the causal relevance of physical types.

It is worth noting that, on the present account, even if certain physical regularities, in virtue of their being basic, are in fact (candidates to be) cause-constituting, we can still make sense of the idea that they might *not* have been cause-constituting. For we can still make sense of the idea that they might *not* have been basic, and indeed have had a reductive or causal explanation that amounted to an undercutter. We can imagine, for example, that some form of *occasionalism* is true, whereby God separately brings every physical state token into existence from nothing, but does so very systematically, so that regularities emerge in the physical phenomena exactly like those we actually observe. On the present account, however, we cannot make sense of the possibility that these physical regularities might have failed to be cause-constituting *while remaining basic*. But this consequence of the present account is not at all embarrassing. On the contrary, it is antecedently plausible: perhaps I am alone in this, but the *only* way in which I find I can make sense of the possibility that actually cause-constituting physical regularities should have failed to be cause-constituting is by imagining that they are not explanatorily basic.

The second way in which the regularity R can lack an undercutter is for it to have an explanation (or explanations), but for the explanation not to be (or for none of them to be) an *undercutting* explanation. (Clearly, if a nonbasic, hence explainable, ceteris paribus regularity is to be cause-constituting, then it must get to be so in this way, by having only nonundercutting explanations.) But what makes an explanation of a regularity an undercutting or nonundercutting one? My answer arises from reflection on the difference between, on the one hand, cases of the sort illustrated by the Kwik-Gro or the ice-cream and murder-rate examples and, on the other, cases like the rash-fever example. In the Kwik-Gro case, we do *not* regard the ceteris paribus regularity that application to a rose of Kwik-Gro is followed by unusually vigorous growth as revealed to be non-cause-constituting by the discovery that the regularity holds because samples of Kwik-Gro always contain some active ingredient that is sufficient in the circumstances for the unusual growth of roses. Similarly, in the ice-cream and murder-rate case, we would judge the ceteris paribus regularity that increases in the rate of ice-cream consumption are followed by increases in the murder rate to be cause-constituting precisely *because* we discovered that what explained it was that ice cream contains an ingredient sufficient in the circumstances for some people to be more aggressive and hence likelier to kill. By contrast, of course, when we learn what explains the rash-fever regularity, we retract our judgment that the regularity is cause-constituting.

So here is the account of what makes the explanation of a regularity undercutting. Consider again the regularity, R, that all events belonging to every type in the set $\{C_1, C_2, \ldots C_n\}$ are followed by E-type events. An explanation of R is undercutting iff it entails, in the case of every instance of R, that, for some $C_i \in \{C_1, C_2, \ldots C_n\}$, *not even a part or constituent* of the earlier $C_1, C_2, \ldots C_n$-type event's tokening C_i is a cause of the later E-type event token in that instance, where "is a cause of" should be understood in the sense given by the account of which clause (iv) is a part – that is, roughly, as a condition sufficient in actual circumstances. According to this account, the explanation of the holding of the rash-fever regularity *is* undercutting. For it entails (i) that viral infections cause fevers, without any help from rashes, and (ii) that viral infections are not merely numerically distinct from rashes but also share no parts with rashes – with the result that not even a part or constituent of a rash turns out to be a cause of a fever.[19] By contrast, however, the explanation of the regularity in the Kwik-Gro case is *not* undercutting. For although it entails that the active ingredient of Kwik-Gro is a cause of increased rose growth, and although the active ingredient in any sample of Kwik-Gro is numerically distinct from that sample, the active ingredient is still a part or constituent of that sample – with the result that the explanation of the

---

19 There is also an undercutting explanation of the regularity that drinking holy water quenches thirst, ceteris paribus. For the reductive explanation of this regularity will entail that no part of the drunk water's being *holy* – having been blessed by a priest – is a cause of thirst-quenching. Thus we will not be forced to say, falsely, that my drinking of some water quenched my thirst because the water I drank was *holy* – on the grounds that the water I drank was in fact holy, and that drinking holy water quenches thirst, ceteris paribus.

Kwik-Gro regularity does *not* entail that no part or constituent of samples of Kwik-Gro is a cause of increased rose growth. Similarly, the explanation of the ice-cream and murder-rate regularity is *not* undercutting, because the cause of increased murder rates that it uncovers (viz. the aggression-increasing artificial flavor in ice cream) evidently *is* a constituent of the ice cream, even though numerically distinct from it.[20]

In the case of both undercutting and nonundercutting explanations of nonbasic regularities, then, we find, in each instance of the original regularity, that there is a condition, numerically distinct from the putative nonbasic cause, that is sufficient for the putative effect – sufficient, that is, in circumstances that do not include, or do not include the whole of, the putative nonbasic cause. (It is in precisely this sense that we do indeed find that "all the causal work" is going on "at a lower level.") But, in the case of a *nonundercutting* explanation, this condition, though *numerically* distinct from the putative cause, is not *entirely* distinct from it, since it (or some part of it) is still a *part* of the putative nonbasic cause. Indeed, when we learn how to explain a nonbasic regularity, and the explanation is nonundercutting, we naturally describe ourselves as having discovered the *mechanism* by which the putative nonbasic causes cause – *still* cause – their putative effects.

One might reasonably wonder *why* a nonundercutting explanation of a nonbasic regularity leaves the cause-constituting power of the regularity unaffected. The answer, I suggest, is that a cause of some effect, as we ordinarily understand it, is a topper-up for the effect – that is, a component of the actual circumstances that, if removed, would leave a certain subset of the actual circumstances insufficient for the effect, but that, if restored, would make them sufficient again. And this conception of a cause is clearly visible in the account of the condition under which a *basic* regularity lacks an undercutter. For if an event sequence meets conditions (i) through (iii) of the proposed account of causation, the relevant cause-constituting regularity is explanatorily basic, *and* no "cut-down antecedent" version of the regularity holds, then the earlier member of the event sequence is indeed a topper-up in this sense. But suppose now that the regularity is not explanatorily basic, but that its explanation is nonundercutting. Then, although, in the case of each instance of the regularity, no topper-up is

---

20 Strictly speaking, the fact that a nonbasic regularity has one nonundercutting explanation does not logically entail that it does not also have *another* explanation that *is* undercutting; but the conclusion that it does not will usually, I presume, be reasonable. It is hard to see, for instance, how the biochemical explanation of some cellular regularity might be nonundercutting while the microphysical explanation of it *was* undercutting.

numerically identical with the putative nonbasic cause, it is *still* true, since some topper-up is a *part* or *constituent* of the putative nonbasic cause, that (i) if the putative nonbasic cause *and therefore all of its parts* were removed from the actual circumstances, then a subset of the actual circumstances that previously was sufficient for the putative effect would cease to be so, and that (ii) if the putative nonbasic cause *and therefore all of its parts* were restored, then that subset of the actual circumstances would be topped up to sufficiency again. The nonundercutting explanation of a nonbasic regularity tells us *how* the earlier member of every event sequence that is an instance of the regularity gets to be a topper-up, but it casts no doubt upon the claim that each such event *is* a topper-up.

It might be objected, however, that the preceding account of what makes an explanation undercutting infects the overall account of causation to which it belongs with circularity. Certainly it appears to; for the account explicitly mentions *causes*, while the account itself plays a role in the overall account of what a cause is. This appearance, however, is illusory. For clause (iv) requires only that a cause-constituting regularity should *lack* an undercutter. But one way in which a regularity can lack an undercutter is by being explanatorily basic while no "cutdown antecedent" version of the regularity holds; and the specification of this sufficient condition for lacking an undercutter makes no mention of causes (given that explanatory basicness need not be defined in terms of causation). So one class of causes can be defined without even the appearance of circularity, and then all remaining causes can be defined in terms of those in the first class. Let me explain.

According to my overall account of causation, the explanatory basicness of certain physical regularities, in the absence of "cutdown antecedent" versions of those regularities, is sufficient for those regularities to be cause-constituting and, hence, for certain physical event sequences to be causal; and the account of what makes those physical event sequences causal will *not* mention causes. Nonbasic regularities, on the other hand, can then qualify as cause-constituting if every explanation of them in terms of the physical regularities and physical tokens that realize them is nonundercutting. Since nonundercuttingness is defined by reference in part to causes, the account of what makes *nonbasic* event sequences causal (when they are) *will* mention causes; but this is legitimate, since the causes mentioned will be physical causes that owe *their* status as causes to their falling under certain explanatorily basic physical regularities that hold in the absence of "cutdown antecedent" versions of those regularities. On my account, then, a nonbasic event can perfectly well be a cause in virtue (partly) of causes at a lower "level," and indeed these causes can perfectly well be causes in virtue (partly) of causes at some yet lower "level," and so on. But it cannot be turtles all the way down: the causal status of any non-basic cause must in the end "bottom out" in causes that owe their causal status not to causes at some lower "level" but to mere regularities that qualify as cause-constituting by being explanatorily basic in the absence of "cutdown antecedent" versions of those regularities. On my account of causation, then, and leaving aside for the moment the second standard objection noted earlier, a world in which the explanatorily basic regularities are bare, empirical regularities can be a world in which (i) there is genuine singular causation, in which (ii) some nonbasic regularities are cause-constituting, while others are not, and in which, in consequence, (iii) there really is a deductive fallacy of post hoc ergo propter hoc.

But it is no fallacy, of course, to take the regularity that all Fs are Gs as *inductive* evidence that Fs cause Gs. And indeed, by incorporating clause (iv), not only can my account of causation distinguish bare regularities that are cause-constituting from those that are not, but it also has the additional advantage of yielding a neat explanation of why, in both everyday and scientific life, we take the regularity that Fs are *followed* by Gs as strong inductive evidence that Fs *cause* Gs, even though the holding of the regularity does not deductively entail the holding of the causal relation. According to the account, in order for Fs to cause Gs it must at least be a regularity that Fs are followed by Gs; so the fact that such a regularity holds shows that at least it *might* be true that Fs cause Gs. But according to the account, the holding of such a regularity is also *sufficient* for Fs to cause Gs, so long as the regularity has no undercutter. Given that our epistemic policy is to assume (whether rightly or wrongly) that a regularity does *not* have an undercutter until we acquire positive evidence that it *does*, the discovery that Fs are followed by Gs provides presumptive evidence that Fs cause Gs.

The incorporation of clause (iv), however, does expose my account of causation to the objection that, with clause (iv) included, the account in effect implies that a cause must be necessary in the circumstances for its effect, whereas standard examples of causal overdetermination show that this implication is false. But my account does not entail that a cause must be necessary in *the* circumstances for its effect – that if the cause were removed from the *totality* of actual circumstances, its effect would not occur. It does entail that *among* the actual circumstances there must be *some* that it tops up to sufficiency for its effect, but these circumstances need not be the *totality* of actual circumstances. The squeezing of a trigger may top up to sufficiency for a death *one* part of actual circumstances, while the administration of a lethal poison might top up to sufficiency for a death *another* part of actual circumstances; so my account can allow that both a shooting and a poisoning might cause the very same death, even if the death is thereby causally overdetermined.

Let me turn now to the second standard objection to my account of causation, namely, that it lacks the resources to distinguish regularities that are genuinely lawlike (whether they are cause-constituting laws or non-cause-constituting laws of association) from regularities that are, as we say, merely accidental. This objection, I argue, can be met, and met indeed without any modification at all to the account of causation already presented. It can be met by adopting an account of the distinction between lawlike and merely accidental generalizations that meets three conditions: (i) it requires only resources that are consistent with a regularity theory of causation; (ii) it entails, given my account of causation, that all cause-constituting regularities are lawlike; and (iii) it accords with our pretheoretical classifications of regularities as lawlike or merely accidental. The account of the distinction results from taking two steps: the first step is to identify a regularity's being *merely accidental* with its being *coincidental*; the second is to identify being *coincidental* with *lacking a unitary explanation* (as suggested in the previous chapter). The account of what makes a regularity merely accidental therefore comes to this: a regularity is merely accidental iff it has no explanation according to which *either* all the individual explanations of its instances share some interesting common feature (e.g., they all cite explanatory factors of the same type) *or* all the instances of the regularity are revealed as stemming from some single common source.[21] This account, we see at once, meets condition (i): according to the account, the existence of regularities that are lawlike and not merely accidental requires nothing (e.g., no natural necessity) that is disallowed by a pure regularity theory of causation.

The account also meets condition (ii), since it entails, given my account of causation, that all cause-constituting regularities are lawlike and not merely accidental. For if a regularity is cause-constituting, then *one* way

---

21 The word "interesting" in the account is obviously doing important work. It is a gesture intended to prevent the analysis from being trivialized, as would happen if the explanations of instances of a regularity were allowed to have something in common because, say, they all appealed to causes, or they all appealed to tokens of some irreducibly *disjunctive* cause-type. Sadly, I have no account of interestingness to offer, though an account that made interestingness a matter of degree, or relative to highly contingent (e.g., anthropocentric) standards, would be quite acceptable.

of explaining it is to explain each of its instances by first explaining the earlier event in each instance and then citing each earlier event as a *cause* of the later event in that same instance; for example, the cause-constituting regularity that all C-type events are followed by E-type events could be explained in this fashion by first explaining, in the case of each C-type event, why it occurred and then noting that that C-type event *caused* an E-type event.[22] It follows that if a regularity is cause-constituting, then it has an explanation according to which the explanations of all its instances *do* have something interesting in common: they all cite a cause of the same type. So, according to the account of lawlikeness, the cause-constituting regularity qualifies as lawlike. On my overall view, then, it is certainly true that if a regularity is cause-constituting, then it must be lawlike; but this is not because, in order to be cause-constituting, a regularity must first, and independently, be certified as lawlike, and only then, in virtue of meeting some further condition, qualify as cause-constituting. In fact, that would get things exactly backward. On my view, a regularity qualifies as lawlike (or at least can qualify as lawlike) *because* it qualifies as cause-constituting. Accordingly, no modification to my account of causation is needed in order to respond adequately to the second standard objection to which neo-Humean theories of causation are liable.

The account of what makes a regularity lawlike or merely accidental also meets condition (iii), since it entails (a) that those regularities which we pretheoretically take to be lawlike are indeed lawlike, and (b) that those regularities which we pretheoretically take to be merely accidental are indeed merely accidental. We have just seen that the account entails that all cause-constituting regularities are lawlike – exactly as we pretheoretically judge. However, we also pretheoretically take certain *non*-cause-constituting regularities to be lawlike. For example, consider again the (imagined) regularity that increases in ice-cream consumption are followed by increases in the murder rate; but this time suppose that what turns out to explain the regularity is that increases in ice-cream

---

22 Such an explanation would admittedly be *circular*, in the sense that if you went on to explain (reductively) the fact that C-type events cause E-type events, you would need to invoke the regularity that you initially set out to explain, namely, that all C-type events are followed by E-type events. But why should circularity invalidate the explanation? (An explanation of the kind now being considered would not, of course, be attempting to explain a fact by deriving it from *itself*.) Suppose that an explanation aims to exhibit its explanandum as inevitable (or at least to some degree probable) relative to certain other facts; in doing so, it exhibits its explanandum as being, at least to some degree, no accident. Then an explanation of the kind now being considered can achieve that aim, in spite of its circularity; it really can help reveal the interconnectedness of things.

consumption are caused by warmer weather (people eat ice cream to cool themselves), while the very same cause – warmer weather – also makes people more irritable and hence more likely to get into fights, some of which end in murder. Though not cause-constituting, this regularity would surely still be lawlike, since it is hardly a mere accident. And the foregoing account entails that it would be. For although, as we have imagined things, increases in ice-cream consumption would not cause increases in the murder rate, there would still be an explanation of the regularity linking ice-cream eating to the murder rate according to which the explanations of each of its instances would have something interesting in common: a cause of the same type (viz., warmer weather) would be responsible for both the earlier and the later event in each instance of the regularity. Similarly, the account also entails the lawlikeness of the rash-fever regularity, even though this regularity is not cause-constituting; the common causal factor in this case, of course, would be a viral infection, a token of which would cause first the rash and then the fever in each instance of the regularity.

Finally, we pretheoretically judge certain regularities to be merely accidental. As our first example, consider the regularity that all the coins in my pocket are quarters. The current account entails that this textbook example of a regularity that we all judge to be merely accidental really is so. For, at least in the circumstances that we normally assume when we think about the example, the only explanation of the regularity is the set of explanations of each of its instances, *and* the members of this set have nothing interesting in common. Thus, perhaps one quarter got into my pocket because I bought a drink costing $1.75 and tendered $2 in payment; another quarter got into my pocket because my son wanted two dimes and I gave him two dimes and a nickel in exchange for a quarter; and so on. So the regularity that all the coins in my pocket are quarters has no unitary explanation and therefore qualifies as merely accidental. Interestingly, however, if we imagine this regularity as holding under rather different circumstances, we no longer judge the regularity to be accidental. Suppose we imagine that being in my pocket magically *causes* any coins placed there to *become* quarters; or that I superstitiously avoid having non-quarters in my pocket because, like walking on the cracks, they bring bad luck. Under each of these circumstances, we would judge the regularity that all the coins in my pocket are quarters *not* to be merely accidental. To its credit, however, the current account entails that, under these different imagined circumstances, the regularity would indeed not be merely accidental. For, under each of these different circumstances, there *would* be a unitary explanation of the regularity, which would therefore qualify as nonaccidental.

As a second example of a regularity that we pretheoretically judge to be merely accidental, consider the regularity that all gold spheres have a mass less than 100,000 kilograms. Wesley Salmon contrasts this regularity with the intuitively *lawlike* regularity that all enriched uranium spheres have a mass less than 100,000 kilograms (1990, 15). The difference between these regularities can be explained by the current account. It is not merely accidental that all enriched uranium spheres have a mass less than 100,000 kilograms, because the explanation of this regularity entails that there is a common factor in the explanations of all its instances, namely, the fact that the critical mass for enriched uranium is just a few kilogram. But it *is* merely accidental that all gold spheres have a mass less than 100,000 kilograms, because the explanations of why all gold spheres have a mass less than 100,000 kilograms presumably have nothing interesting in common. Interestingly, however, and as previously, we can imagine circumstances in which we would no longer judge the regularity about gold spheres to be merely accidental: suppose, perhaps, that lots of people *wanted* a gold ball with a mass greater than 100,000 kilograms, but that no one could *afford* it. But under those circumstances, of course, the explanations of why all gold spheres have a mass less than 100,000 kilograms *would* have something interesting in common, and so the current account would imply, in agreement with our pretheoretical judgment, that the regularity about gold spheres would be lawlike.

Salmon himself stresses that the statement expressing the uranium regularity differs from the statement expressing the gold regularity in that (i) it has "modal import," the negation of the uranium regularity statement reporting something "physically impossible," and (ii) it supports counterfactuals (1990, 15). But I think I can explain these features, consistent with my account of lawhood. (i) Suppose that a claim reports something physically necessary iff the claim is entailed by some or all of the laws of physics, and reports something physically impossible iff the claim is inconsistent with some or all of the laws of physics. Then, trivially, it follows that a claim reporting a regularity that is a physical law will report something physically necessary (since the claim entails itself), and that the negation of such a claim will report a physical impossibility (since the negation of a claim is inconsistent with the claim). (ii) As for counterfactual supportingness, we need only suppose that in evaluating counterfactuals the nonholding of laws is treated as a feature only of very distant possible worlds, while the nonholding of merely accidental regularities is not; and future research on the *psychology* of counterfactual thought might explain this difference in treatment. Given the supposition, however, if it is a law that F-tokens are followed by G-tokens, then, in the closest worlds in which there is an F-token that the actual world lacks, the law holds, and so the F-token is followed by a G-token; whereas if it is a merely accidental regularity that F-tokens are followed by G-tokens, then the closest worlds in which there is an F-token that the actual world lacks need not be worlds in which a G-token ensues. The counterfactual supportingness of law statements might therefore have no metaphysical implications at all.

The defense of my account of causation against the two standard objections that I earlier distinguished is now complete. To increase the account's plausibility further, I would need to confront further objections, and also develop the account in various ways.[23] I hope that nevertheless the account now seems plausible enough to make it worthwhile for me to turn to the second task of this section: showing that if this account is true, then retentive realizationism does not epiphenomenalize special- and honorary-scientific phenomena in either of the two senses distinguished earlier.

My account of causation implies, first of all, that retentive realizationism does not epiphenomenalize special- and honorary-scientific phenomena in the sense of entailing that no special- or honorary-scientific token is ever (or hardly ever) a singular cause of any effect. For, according to the account, all it takes for *any* event sequence to be causal is that it should meet conditions (i) through (iv); and it is consistent with retentive realizationism that a special- or honorary-scientific event sequence should do so. In the previous chapter, we saw that retentive realization is consistent with the holding of regularities among special- or honorary-scientific tokens; for the holding of such regularities in a retentive realizationist world is a logical consequence of appropriate physical facts (plus certain necessary truths). Moreover, and crucially, although retentive realizationism ensures that every such regularity has a reductive explanation that appeals only to physical facts (plus necessary truths), *this explanation need not be undercutting*, and so such regularities need not have undercutters. For the reductive explanation of the special- or honorary-scientific regularity that C-type events are followed by E-type events *might* imply that, in the case of each

---

23 In addition to the need for an account of ceteris paribus regularities and of "interesting" commonalities, which I have already mentioned, the account as a whole needs extending so that it covers the indeterministic case of quantum mechanics. The obvious suggestion would be to allow *statistical* regularities to count as cause-constituting, and to modify appropriately the notion of lacking an undercutter. But I have not worked this out.

instance of the regularity, the *narrow physical realizer* of the earlier C-type event was a cause of (i.e., a topper-up in some of the actual circumstances for) the later E-type event. And if the narrow physical realizer of the earlier C-type event *was* a cause of the later E-type event, then, since the narrow physical realizer of a C-type event is surely a part or constituent of that C-type event, the reductive explanation of the regularity would not meet the definition of being undercutting; for it would not entail that, in the case of every instance of the regularity, *not even a part or constituent* of the C-type event token in each instance was a cause of the E-type event token in that instance. So the power of a special- or honorary-scientific regularity to constitute certain event sequences as cause and effect might be undiminished even in a retentive realizationist world.

My account of causation implies, second, that retentive realizationism does not epiphenomenalize special- and honorary-scientific phenomena in the sense of entailing that special- and honorary-scientific types are never (or hardly ever) causally relevant. For, according to the account, the causal relevance of a special- or honorary-scientific type to a particular event's causing a particular effect is the type's being such that the cause falls under the regularity that makes it a cause *in virtue of* its being a token of that type; and since, as we have just seen, retentive realizationism is consistent with the holding of special- or honorary-scientific regularities that do not have undercutters, and hence with an event's being a cause in virtue of falling under a special- or honorary-scientific regularity, it follows that retentive realizationism is consistent with the causal relevance of special- or honorary-scientific types. Indeed, on my account of causation, retentive realizationism allows for nonbasic types to be causally relevant (and for nonbasic tokens to be causes) in the very *same* sense of "causally relevant" (and of "cause") in which we all agree that *physical* types are causally relevant (and *physical* tokens causes). On retentive realizationism, therefore, special- and honorary-scientific causation and causal relevance are neither sui generis nor second-rate.[24]

---

24 Notwithstanding the suggestion of David-Hillel Ruben that all theories in a class to which my account of causal relevance belongs must analyze macrocausal explanation differently from microcausal explanation (see his 1994, 469). The point in the text also suffices to undermine the argument made by Tim Crane (1995) to the effect that a certain line of prophysicalist reasoning is self-defeating, in that although it initially assumes that mental causation is causation in the *same sense* as physical causation, this assumption is contradicted by the physicalist conclusion it reaches, since physicalism must (allegedly) hold that mental causation is *not* causation in the same sense as physical causation. For an excellent rebuttal of Crane's argument on different lines, see William Child (1997).

So far, perhaps, so good. But can my defense of the compatibility of retentive realizationism with special- and honorary-scientific causation and causal relevance be extended to the case of special- and honorary-scientific types that are *wide* in the sense that, for a type of this sort to be tokened, the world has to be a certain way at *places* other than the place where, intuitively, the token is located, and/or at *times* other than the time when, intuitively, the token exists?[25] If wide types are functional types (as realizationism must assume), then we can say, using our earlier terminology, that wide types are types with broad, and not just narrow, realizers. Now tokens of wide types seem not only to be causes but also to cause their effects in virtue of being tokens of these wide types. For example, the availability for auction of a genuine Rembrandt requires much more than what is going on in the auction house when it is actually offered for sale; crucially, it requires also that the painting on offer have been painted by Rembrandt himself. But it might be true that the great flurry of interest at the auction house was *caused* by the availability for auction of a genuine Rembrandt, and that the availability for auction of this painting caused the great flurry of interest that it did *because* it was the availability for auction of a genuine Rembrandt. Similarly, a woman's now being the full-time caregiver of four young children requires not only that she behave in various caring ways, but also that those four young children now exist. But it might be true that a woman's permanent tiredness was *caused* by her being the full-time caregiver of four young children, and that her being the full-time caregiver of four young children caused her tiredness *because* it was her being the full-time caregiver of four young children.

So can retentive realizationism allow tokens of wide special- and honorary-scientific types to be singular causes and the wide types themselves to be causally relevant, *if* the account of causation presented here is correct? It can. The requisite ceteris paribus regularities seem to hold. An auction house that made available a genuine Rembrandt would *expect* great interest to be shown and might therefore make special preparations (e.g., put out extra seats); similarly, we would *expect* a woman to be permanently tired if we learned of her only that she was the full-time caregiver of four children. And such expectations must surely be grounded in knowledge of regularities of some kind, which must presumably hold only ceteris paribus. Moreover, it seems plausible that the relevant regularities need

---

25 For a discussion of this question with specific reference to mental content, as it arises for an account of causal relevance similar to mine, see Segal and Sober (1991, 16ff.).

not have undercutting explanations in the sense earlier given, according to which an explanation of the regularity that all events belonging to every type in the set $\{C_1, C_2, \ldots C_n\}$ are followed by E-type events is undercutting iff it entails, in the case of every instance of the regularity, that, for some $C_i \in \{C_1, C_2, \ldots C_n\}$, not even a part or constituent of the earlier $C_1, C_2, \ldots C_n$-type event's tokening C_i is a cause of the later E-type event token in that instance. For, in the auction house case, the availability for auction of a painting will fall under the relevant ceteris paribus regularity only if it is the availability for auction of a genuine Rembrandt; and the genuineness of the painting on offer must surely have played some causal role in producing the flurry of interest, perhaps via the reactions of those experts in art history whose knowledge of the provenance of the painting in question and recognition of Rembrandt's distinctive brushwork led them to judge the painting genuine. And, in the case of the caregiver's tiredness, surely the four young children must have played some causal role in producing the caring activities that were so fatiguing.

The account of causation presented in this section turns out to have a third interesting implication that I conclude this section by pausing to consider. The implication is that tokens of functional types that are defined in terms of the invariable causation of certain effects cannot be singular causes of those effects, nor can their being tokens of such functional types be causally relevant to their production of those effects. To see how this implication arises, imagine a functional type, F, so defined that there is an F-token iff there is a token of some or other type that *always in fact causes* an effect of type E. It follows from this definition, not merely that all F-tokens are *in fact* followed by an E-token, but that all F-tokens *must* (in the strongest sense) be followed by an E-token. According to the account of causation presented earlier, however, an F-token causes an E-token only if the F-token and the E-token instantiate some *contingent* cause-constituting regularity. (Allowing noncontingent regularities to be cause-constituting would apparently require us to say, implausibly, that a ball's being red *caused* it to be colored.) Since the only candidate to be a cause-constituting regularity between F-tokens and E-tokens is the regularity that all F-tokens are followed by an E-token, and since this regularity is necessary in the strongest sense and hence noncontingent, it follows that the F-token is not a cause of the E-token, and also that the functional type, F, is not causally relevant to any E-token. It might be supposed that this implication could be avoided by suggesting that the F-token and the E-token fall under some *other* cause-constituting regularity, in virtue perhaps of their identity with certain physical tokens. But realization physicalism is not committed to treating functional tokens as identical with their physical realizers; and in any case the *causal relevance* of the type, F, to E-tokens could only be supported by a regularity between F-tokens and E-tokens.

How serious a problem for retentive realizationism is this implication? Not very. It does admittedly provide reason to reject certain functionalist identity hypotheses. For example, it provides reason to reject the hypothesis that pain is the state of being in some or other state that, inter alia, always in fact causes wincing, since this hypothesis, coupled with my account of causation, will then imply the presumably false conclusion that pain never causes wincing. But retentive realizationism does not stand or fall with such particular hypotheses (apparently *pace* Kim, 1998, 51). For there are alternative functionalist hypotheses as to the nature of pain (e.g., the representationalist one in Tye 1995) that do not entail that being in pain requires being in some or other state that always in fact causes wincing, and which therefore do not entail that being in pain metaphysically necessitates wincing. Quite generally, indeed, although retentive realizationists must identify every special- or honorary-scientific type with some or other functional type, the associated conditions for these types need not be causal at all. And even if they are causal, they need not include the *invariable* production of certain effects. Moreover, even if the associated condition for a given functional type does include the invariable production of certain effects, all that follows is that tokens of this type cannot be singular causes of, and the type itself cannot be causally relevant to, effects of *those* kinds; tokens of such a type can perfectly well be singular causes of, and the type itself can perfectly well be causally relevant to, effects of *other* kinds.

An apparent problem is provided by such locutions as "I fell asleep because I took a sleeping pill." For although a sleeping pill appears, by definition, to be anything that if taken causes sleep, so that the regularity connecting the taking of a sleeping pill with falling asleep is noncontingent and hence non-cause-constituting, we seem nevertheless to offer a genuine and apparently causal explanation of why I fell asleep if we say, "I fell asleep because I took a sleeping pill." But the problem is more apparent than real. It is simply not true that a sleeping pill, in order to be one, must be something that if taken *always* causes (and hence is *always* followed by) sleep, for there are any number of reasons why someone who had taken a perfectly genuine sleeping pill did not fall asleep (e.g., excessive coffee consumption or being atomized by a nuclear blast). Therefore, since there does not *have* to be (and is not always *in fact*) a falling-asleep after every taking of a sleeping pill, the taking-of-a-sleeping-pill and falling-asleep sequence on a particular occasion does not instantiate a noncontingent (and hence non-cause-constituting) regularity; since it instantiates a contingent regularity, it might well be a causal sequence. However, it is not wrong to think that there is *some* sort of constitutive connection between sleeping pills and falling asleep. For it is somewhat plausible to claim that to be a sleeping pill is (at least) to be something that if taken causes sleep ceteris paribus. But the hedging clause here makes all the difference. For if the provisions of the hedging clause are not always met (as seems likely), then it just does not follow from the nature of a sleeping pill that every taking of a sleeping pill *must* be followed by a falling asleep. So the regularity connecting takings of a sleeping pill and fallings asleep can be quite *contingent*, and hence can serve as an acceptable candidate to be a cause-constituting regularity. Our original locution – "I fell asleep because I took a sleeping pill" – can therefore be treated as a standard and unproblematic example of an explanation of an effect by the citation of one of its causes, a cause referred to as belonging to the type in virtue of which it *is* a cause of that effect. And the contingency and genuine informativeness of the locution can be attributed to its implication that on the occasion in question the taking of a sleeping pill did, in fact, cause a falling asleep. The moral, perhaps, is that one must take care in handling the multiply ambiguous idea of being "defined in terms of certain effects."

4. THE UNOBJECTIONABILITY OF MULTIPLE EXPLANATIONS OF THE SAME THING

So much for the first two conclusions of this chapter. Let me now turn to the third, the conclusion that, consistently with retentive realizationism, it is unobjectionable for one and the same special- or honorary-scientific token to have more than one explanation, that is, a nonreductive, causal explanation in special- or honorary-scientific terms, and a reductive physical explanation of the sort discussed in the previous chapter. Now if the main argument of the previous chapter is correct, then retentive realizationism is at least *consistent* with the thesis that every special- and honorary-scientific token that falls within the scope of (R) has a *reductive* explanation; and if the previous two sections of this chapter are correct, then retentive realizationism is *also* consistent with the thesis that special- or honorary-scientific tokens have nonreductive, causal explanations, explanations that cite earlier special- or honorary-scientific causes and perhaps also cause-constituting regularities. So, as long as these two things are consistent with one another, retentive realizationism is consistent with both of them together: it is consistent with retentive realizationism for special- or honorary-scientific tokens to have more than one explanation, namely, a reductive physical one and a nonreductive, causal one. *Are* the two things consistent with one another? I assume that they are; and surely there is no *obvious* contradiction between them.

However, there may still be weighty objections (falling short of the charge of logical inconsistency) to the idea that one and the same special- or honorary-scientific token should have more than one explanation. In the remainder of this section, then, I show that three potentially strong objections to the idea turn out, when examined, not to work. I do not recall having seen these objections in print, but I suspect that nevertheless they underlie the common feeling that multiple explanations of the same token are unacceptable.

The first objection is *metaphysical* and alleges that allowing multiple explanations of the same token commits one, implausibly, to regarding the token as causally overdetermined. Suppose that some token is multiply explained in the way suggested. The nonreductive, causal explanation of the token will (or easily could) specify *special- or honorary-scientific* conditions that are causally sufficient for the token. But there will also be *physical* conditions, simultaneous with these special- or honorary-scientific conditions, that are also causally sufficient (or close enough) for the token; these conditions will be physical conditions causally sufficient (or close enough) for the physical realizer of the token. The upshot, then, is that, if multiple explanations are allowed, there will be numerically distinct simultaneous conditions, each of which is causally sufficient (or close enough) for the existence of the token – which surely amounts to causal overdetermination. And while isolated cases of such overdetermination might be credible, the ubiquity of nonreductive, causal explanations of special- and honorary-scientific tokens, coupled with the retentive realizationist assumption that every special- or honorary-scientific token that falls within the scope of (R) has a reductive physical explanation, entails that the overdetermination would be on an implausibly massive scale.

The second objection is *epistemological*. It alleges that we should not allow multiple explanations for the same token, not because doing so would commit us to metaphysical absurdity, but because it would violate the epistemic principle – Ockham's razor – that we should not multiply entities beyond necessity. Since, on the assumption of retentive realizationism, we already have a reductive physical explanation of every special- or honorary-scientific token that falls within the scope of (R), accepting special- or honorary-scientific explanations in addition would gratuitously expand our ontology.

The final objection is *methodological* (perhaps to be found in Paul Churchland 1981, 78–82, and Kim 1993, 260–4). The worry is that, once we grant the principle that the same token can have multiple explanations, the floodgates are opened for the acceptance of all sorts of bad explanations supplied by justly discredited old theories. A believer in the phlogiston theory of combustion, for example, could defend it by *first* fixing it up so that it can handle all relevant evidence (which could surely be achieved by the liberal use of ad hoc hypotheses), *then* pointing out that it is not strictly speaking contradicted by the oxidation theory, and *finally* saying that it constitutes a perfectly good explanation (of combustive phenomena) *in addition to* that supplied by the oxidation theory; and, if multiple explanations of the same tokens were allowed, no objection could be raised to the final step. In short, the idea that the same token can have multiple explanations threatens to abolish theoretical rivalry in those cases where two theories that purport to explain some single domain are not strictly inconsistent with one another and can both be made to handle the empirical evidence. There probably are such cases, but even if there are not, there clearly could be, and then the right thing to do would be to eliminate one of the explanations, not retain both.

Let me now examine these objections, beginning with the charge that if a single token has multiple explanations of the sort I have been countenancing, then it is causally overdetermined. The first thing to say is that, if we count a token as causally overdetermined just so long as there are at least two numerically distinct, simultaneous conditions, each of which alone is sufficient for it, then multiple explanations of the sort I have been countenancing do indeed entail the causal overdetermination of whatever is thus multiply explained. However, causal overdetermination in *this* sense can, it seems, exist in a situation that nevertheless *fails* a commonly accepted intuitive test for overdetermination; so causal overdetermination in this sense may not be our intuitive notion of causal overdetermination. According to the intuitive test, there is overdetermination only if, had either of the sufficient conditions occurred in the absence of the other, the overdetermined token would have occurred anyway. Now if the two simultaneous conditions, each sufficient for the multiply explained token, are not only numerically distinct from but also entirely independent of one another, then the intuitive test will be passed. But if retentive realizationism is true, then the two simultaneous conditions, though numerically distinct, are *not* entirely independent of one another. For since the special- or honorary-scientific condition is by assumption a cause, so that the relevant special- or honorary-scientific regularity cannot therefore have an undercutting explanation, the special- or honorary-scientific condition must be *realized* (in part) by (some part of) the physical condition. In that case, however, the situation seems to fail the intuitive test for causal overdetermination. If the special- or honorary-scientific condition had been absent, then it must have been the case either that its physical realizer was absent or that its realizer was present though the laws of physics were different; either way it is not at all clear that the multiply explained token *would* have occurred anyway. Similarly, if the physical condition had been absent, then the special- or honorary-scientific condition (which it partially realized) would have been absent too, in which case, as before, it is not at all clear that the multiply explained token would have occurred anyway.

But even if the causal overdetermination to which one is committed if one allows multiple explanations of the same token is not our ordinary notion of causal overdetermination, it is certainly *one* kind of causal overdetermination. Should we regard overdetermination of this kind as objectionable? Not, surely, because it is conceptually incoherent, since we are quite able to make sense of the idea, as we have just demonstrated. A better suggestion is that causal overdetermination of this kind is objectionable because, implausibly, it requires belief in a certain sort of cosmic coincidence. Suppose that for a particular special-scientific event there is, given the relevant special-scientific laws, a sufficient special-scientific condition; and also that its physical realizer (which suffices for it, of course) has, given the physical laws, a sufficient physical condition. Then the laws at each level – special-scientific and physical – must converge on the same result, in the sense that whenever the operation of the physical laws results in a physical such-and-such, which is sufficient for the (simultaneous) special-scientific so-and-so that it realizes, the operation of the special-scientific laws must *also* result in a special-scientific so-and-so. But how could this be just a fluke? Surely it would be intolerable to treat such harmonious cooperation as a mere coincidence; it is as if a platoon received separate orders from both the captain and the colonel, and yet the orders were always to do exactly the same thing – surely we would demand some explanation for this remarkable convergence. And if many tokens have multiple explanations of the sort I have countenanced, then there must be in general an implausibly coincidental harmony between the operation of physical and that of special- and honorary-scientific laws.

Let us begin our examination of this argument for the objectionability of (one kind of) causal overdetermination by asking what exactly is supposed to be the surprising thing that is a consequence of causal overdetermination in the current sense. The surprising thing cannot be that the consequences of the operation of special- and honorary-scientific laws are *consistent* with the consequences of the operation of physical laws, for it is no surprise that the world is consistent – it could not be otherwise and requires no explanation. Nor can the surprising thing be that whenever the operation of special- and honorary-scientific laws produces a given outcome, the operation of physical laws produces the *same* outcome; for, given that whenever a special-scientific law operates to produce an outcome, some or other physical law always operates, if the physical laws that operated produced a *different* outcome, we would have a logically impossible state of affairs, the absence of which, as before, is no surprise and needs no explanation. The surprising consequence of causal overdetermination in the current sense – the cosmic coincidence to which it leads – must therefore be the *very existence*, in addition to physical laws whose operation produces certain outcomes, of *another* set of laws, namely, the special- and honorary-scientific laws, whose operations produce the *same* outcomes.

But if retentive realizationism is true, there is no coincidence here. For, as we saw in the previous chapter, if retentive realizationism is true, then the holding of special- and honorary-scientific laws is actually a necessary consequence, in the strongest sense, of the holding of physical laws and the holding of particular physical facts, given that we add in as a premise the realizationist claim that every special- and honorary-scientific token is physically realized; the special- or honorary-scientific laws that actually hold, then, are just those regularities that (logically) emerge when physical laws hold under actual physical conditions. But if, given retentive realizationism, the holding of physical laws and of particular physical facts *entails* the holding of the special- and honorary-scientific laws that there are, then the existence of these laws, whose operation produces the same outcomes as does that of the physical laws, is *not* some sort of contingent, coincidental addition to the existence of physical laws and particular facts; rather, given the existence of the physical laws and particular facts, the existence of the special- and honorary-scientific laws could not have been otherwise and is therefore no surprise and needs no explanation.[26] So realizationists who believe in multiple explanations of the same token are committed to causal overdetermination in the current sense, but are *not* thereby committed to an implausible sort of cosmic coincidence.[27]

Another possible reason why causal overdetermination of the relevant kind might be thought objectionable is that it multiplies entities beyond necessity, repeatedly allowing two causes where one will do. But this suggestion is obviously equivalent to the second, epistemological objection to the acceptability of multiple explanations of the same token; so let us turn now to that.

Are we really being unparsimonious if we suppose that a single special- or honorary-scientific token can be explained not only by citing a sufficient physical cause but also by citing a simultaneous special- or honorary-scientific cause? We are not. For we are committed to the special- and honorary-scientific ontology *anyway*, that is, even if we choose never to mention it in explaining anything, and hence independently of its possible explanatory indispensability. A quick and dirty route to this conclusion

---

26 Perhaps it is still surprising that, given retentive realizationism, the physical facts and laws should have entailed any cause-constituting special- or honorary-scientific regularities *at all*; surely ours could have been a world in which the way things are physically should have failed to exhibit *any* abstract patterns of the sort that cause-constituting special- or honorary-scientific laws describe. Perhaps – though such judgments of surprisingness are notoriously hard to evaluate. But given that the physical facts and laws do entail some cause-constituting special- and honorary-scientific regularities, it is no coincidence in need of explanation that, given retentive realizationism, these regularities harmonize with physical regularities.

27 There is, it is worth noting, a possible position that *is* committed to the implausible cosmic coincidence (*pace* Crane 1997). It is an antiphysicalist position that accepts the holding of all the regularities and particular facts that realizationism accepts, but which (in the manner of an epi-world) construes each special- and honorary-scientific token as necessitated (not realized) by some physical condition in accordance with some fundamental physical/special- or honorary-scientific law. Such a position must concede that, for each special- or honorary-scientific token that has a nonreductive, causal explanation, there are two distinct simultaneous conditions, each of which is sufficient for it. But this position, precisely because it denies that special- and honorary-scientific tokens are physically realized, must treat these two conditions as not just numerically but *wholly* distinct from one another, related only via a contingent, fundamental law. According to this position, therefore, the existence of special- and honorary-scientific laws whose operation produces the very same outcomes as does the operation of physical laws is *not* logically guaranteed by the way things are physically; the harmoniously operating special- and honorary-scientific laws that do exist *need not* have existed, even if the way things are physically had been exactly as it is in actuality. The fact that these laws do exist does therefore seem, on this antiphysicalist view, to be an extraordinarily surprising coincidence. For further discussion, see the third line of reasoning in support of the physical realization of mental phenomena in Chapter 6, Section 7.

is to note that even to raise the issue of whether special- or honorary-scientific tokens can have multiple explanations presupposes that special- or honorary-scientific tokens are candidates for explanation and hence *exist*. But the crucial, and longer, consideration is this. If retentive realizationism is true, then, as we have seen in earlier chapters, every special- and honorary-scientific token that falls within the scope of (R) is physically realized and hence, given the laws of physics, necessitated in the strongest sense by the physical tokens that there are; so, given our commitment to the physical tokens that exist, we are thereby committed (whether we know it or not) to the existence of the special- and honorary-scientific tokens that exist. And since the special- and honorary-scientific ontology comes as a bonus gift in this sense, we are at perfect liberty, at least as far as parsimony is concerned, to cite it in explanations. So we are not violating Ockham's razor – postulating entities beyond necessity – when we allow multiple explanations of the same token. But the necessity to postulate special- and honorary-scientific entities, we should notice, has nothing to do with their explanatory indispensability, and the vindication of special- and honorary-scientific ontology does not require us to rack our brains for abstruse explanatory tasks that, physicalism notwithstanding, only the special or honorary sciences can accomplish. If we are retentive realizationists, we are committed to the special- and honorary-scientific ontology quite independently of considerations of explanatory power, as a result of our prior commitment to the physical ontology.[28]

We are now in a position to see that the third, methodological objection to allowing the acceptability of multiple explanations of the very same token also fails: allowing such acceptability would *not* enable one to defend the retention of, say, phlogiston-citing explanations alongside oxygen-citing ones. For, given realization physicalism, there is a crucial disanalogy between the relationship of the phlogiston theory to the oxidation theory, on the one hand, and the relationship of special- and honorary-scientific explanations to physical explanations, on the other. Whereas special- and honorary-scientific tokens are dependent on, in the sense of being realized by, physical tokens, the ontology of the phlogiston theory is quite independent of that of the oxidation theory: obviously phlogiston is

---

28 This not to say that we were not *originally* warranted in accepting the existence of special- and honorary-scientific entities by employing inference to the best explanation and judging the postulation of special- and honorary-scientific entities to be explanatorily necessary. (But the whole idea of inference to the best explanation really needs a thorough reworking in light of the possibility that a single phenomenon might have multiple explanations.)

neither identical with nor even realized by oxygen (nor realized, indeed, by any other stuff to whose existence we are independently committed). And this disanalogy evidently matters. For, since special- and honorary-scientific tokens are realized by physical tokens, accepting special-scientific explanations in addition to physical ones does not multiply entities beyond necessity: as lately noted, it does not even multiply entities, since we are independently committed to special- and honorary-scientific tokens already. By contrast, however, accepting phlogiston-citing explanations in addition to oxygen-citing explanations *would* multiply entities beyond necessity: it would multiply entities because phlogiston is neither realized by, nor in any other relevant way dependent on, oxygen (so one is not committed willy-nilly to phlogiston by one's prior commitment to oxygen); and it would do so beyond necessity, because it would explain nothing not already explained by oxygen.[29] Although, if retentive realizationism is true, Ockham's razor cannot legitimately be wielded against special- and honorary-scientific explanations, it can still be deployed against phlogiston-citing ones and their ilk.[30]

Someone might admit that these three objections to allowing multiple explanations of the same token all fail but still suspect that something is wrong with multiple explanation. "Let us admit," she might say, "that allowing multiple explanations of the same token commits no offense against Ockham's razor; it does not multiply *entities* beyond necessity. But doesn't allowing multiple explanations still multiply *explanations* beyond necessity? Even if more than one explanation for each token is permissible, why do we *need* more than one explanation for each token? Or, in case

---

29 That the acceptance of two explanations for the same phenomenon *can*, in circumstances of the kind specified, violate the *epistemic* principle of Ockham's razor is, I suggest, the grain of truth in, and explanation for the appeal of, Kim's putatively *metaphysical* principle of explanatory exclusion (see his 1993, ch. 13).

30 The points made in this paragraph tell also against Paul Churchland's famous complaint (1981, 78–81) that functionalism is an objectionably conservative doctrine that would enable the defense of properly discarded theories. In fact, it would not, since it is not a plausible empirical hypothesis that medieval thought and talk about (e.g.) humors was thought and talk about *functional* entities at all, still less functional entities realized by entities whose existence we are independently committed to today. Of course, we could decide today to *change* our usage of the word "humor," so that it *did* refer to some functional type whose tokens are in fact all physically realized. But in that case, although we would then have to say that humors do exist, we could hardly be described as defending the medieval theory of humors. (Incidentally, readers who assume that it must be a matter of a priori conceptual analysis how the scientific thought and talk of the medievals worked should consult the naturalistic discussion of the reference of terms from defunct scientific theories to be found in Philip Kitcher ([1993, 75–80 and 95–105]).

it is too strong to say that we ever *need* any explanation at all, what at any rate is the *point* of more than one explanation for each token? Even if it avoids objectionable overdetermination, ontological profligacy, and methodological catastrophe, what could be the point of explaining a token *twice*?"

But we are not giving the *same* explanation twice over when we give two explanations for the same token: we are giving two different explanations. Now explanations, I suggest, are supposed to reveal their explananda as *no accident*. The most satisfying way of doing so is to show that the explanandum *had* to happen, although showing that it was *probable* to some degree is also explanatory since it reveals the explanandum as *not entirely* an accident. Either way, however, the crucial point is that explanations do not reveal their explananda as inevitable (or probable) *absolutely*, but only *relatively* – relatively to some or other circumstance. (Failure to grasp this point generates the popular prejudice that X has not really explained Y unless X is itself explained, *its* explainer is explained, and so on.) But there is more than one circumstance relative to which a single token might be revealed to be no accident, and no one circumstance enjoys any unconditional privilege (though some circumstances may enjoy conditional privileges dependent on the contingent abilities, needs, and interests of people). It follows that there is no sense in which a *single* explanation of a token, no matter how splendid, can ever do "all the explanatory work," even in connection with just one token. A single explanation can certainly reveal a token to be no accident relative to *one* circumstance, but there will be *other* circumstances relative to which it might also be revealed to be no accident, and such revelations would be every bit as explanatory (and in exactly the same sense) as the initial explanation, even if added to the initial explanation. Accordingly, a reductive physical explanation of some special- or honorary-scientific token can reveal the token as inevitable, and hence no accident, relative to its physical realizer and given the physical laws; and a nonreductive, causal explanation of the same token can also reveal it as inevitable, and hence no accident, relative to some earlier special- or honorary-scientific cause and given certain special- or honorary-scientific laws. Each explanation therefore gives us some of what we want in wanting explanations. It is tempting to suppose that to explain an event is to show that it had to happen, and that once we have shown that it had to happen, our explanatory work is done; but *no* explanation, at least no scientific explanation, can show that an event was *absolutely* inevitable, and once it is seen that inevitability is always relative to circumstance, it becomes obvious that the point of a second (or a third, or a fourth . . .) explanation of a single token is exactly the same as that of the first, and is quite undiminished by the presence of other explanations.

Given retentive realizationism, of course, the nonreductive, causal explanation of a special- or honorary-scientific token that falls within the scope of (R) must hold entirely in virtue of certain physical facts. But these physical facts will not be exactly the same as those cited in the reductive physical explanation of the same token, not even if this reductive explanation is supplemented by citing a sufficient physical cause of the token's physical realizer. For, if multiply realized, the special- or honorary-scientific law that underwrites the special- or honorary-scientific causal sequence is bound to hold in virtue of physical laws not cited in the reductive physical explanation, physical laws that help to explain other, differently realized instances of the special- or honorary-scientific law. So the reductive physical explanation of a given token, even when supplemented by citing a sufficient physical cause of the token's physical realizer, does not merely restate in physical language the nonreductive, causal explanation; the two explanations are genuinely distinct.

Admittedly, given retentive realizationism's identification of every special- and honorary-scientific type that falls within the scope of (R) with some or other functional type whose associated condition can be specified in physical or quasi-logical language, it must be possible *in principle* to express every nonreductive, causal explanation of a special- or honorary-scientific token in physical or quasi-logical terms (given the necessary machinery for higher-order quantification).[31] But it does not follow that the nonreductive, causal explanation is after all dispensable. Never mind the merely pragmatic point that the physical or quasi-logical "translation" of the nonreductive, explanation would lie well beyond our cognitive powers to grasp. The crucial point is metaphysical: if the "translation" were done properly, it would represent *exactly the same state of affairs* as the version framed in special- or honorary-scientific terms. So this "translation" would be a mere notational variant of the original nonreductive, causal explanation, and the explanatory insight of the

---

31 So, given retentive realizationism, Harold Kincaid is right to say that "higher-level theories describe causal patterns that cannot be derived from the appropriate lower-level theory" if, but only if, the underviability in question is to be explained in terms of human cognitive limitations, rather than by the idea that certain physical systems, when they attain a certain kind and degree of complexity, thereby acquire novel causal powers that are not determined by the underlying physical facts (Kincaid 1997, 5). In fact, he probably favors the former explanation (75), which leaves his professed materialism (1) uncompromised, but he is not quite explicit about it.

original explanation would in no way have been abandoned; the original explanation would still constitute exactly the same cognitive achievement as it did before for the special or honorary science that generated it. Special scientists need have no fear that in a retentive realizationist world they would have nothing to contribute to science's central goal of explanation.

5

The Evidence against Realization Physicalism

1. INTRODUCTION

According to realization physicalism, every causal or contingent token – past, present, or future – that falls within the scope of (R) is either a token of a physical type or else a physically realized token of a functional type; so realization physicalism is false if there is even one causal or contingent token – past, present, or future – that falls within the scope of (R) and that is neither a token of a physical type nor a physically realized token of a functional type. Let *direct* evidence against realizationism be any evidence that there exists precisely such a token – any evidence that (a) there exists a causal or contingent token of some type, T, such that T is neither (b) a physical type nor (c) a functional type all of whose tokens are in fact physically realized.[1] And let *indirect* evidence against realization physicalism be any evidence against it that is not direct.

Whether there exists any direct evidence against realizationism is an entirely a posteriori matter. For it is obviously a posteriori whether there actually exists a causal or contingent token of some type, T. Moreover, as argued in Chapter 1, it is also a posteriori whether T is (i.e., is identical with) some physical or functional type; in particular, this issue cannot be settled by appeal to (e.g.) thought experiments intended to validate some claim of conceivability and thereby of metaphysical possibility. Finally, it is a posteriori, even on the assumption that T *is* a functional type, whether or not a particular token of T is physically realized. For the question turns,

---

1 Recall that, because the scope of realization physicalism is explicitly restricted to tokens that are causal or contingent, the existence of nonphysical objects (e.g., numbers or sets) that are neither causal nor contingent could not in principle refute it. Mathematics, therefore, even if construed platonistically, poses no direct threat to realization physicalism.

in part, on whether a certain spatiotemporal region contains a token of some physical type that meets T's associated condition; and *any* question turning on which physical tokens exist and what physical conditions they meet is evidently an a posteriori one.

In this chapter, I make a case for the conclusion that, as far as we now know, there is no direct evidence against realization physicalism; there is admittedly one piece of *indirect* evidence, but by no means does it settle the issue against realizationism. My case for the first part of this conclusion – that there is presently no direct evidence against realization physicalism – consists in examining various potential sources of direct evidence against realizationism and arguing that, as it turns out, they yield no actual evidence against it. The potential sources of direct evidence that I examine meet one or both of two conditions: they are salient to philosophers (perhaps for entirely accidental reasons), and they strike me as promising enough to warrant discussion. But because I obviously cannot examine all potential sources of direct evidence against realizationism, my case falls short of being demonstrative – as cases for negative conclusions are apt to do. Nevertheless, it clearly has some force. And if it merely goads antiphysicalists into indicating potential sources of direct evidence against physicalism that I have not considered, I shall be well pleased. I should also emphasize that the absence of any direct evidence *against* realizationism is logically consistent with the absence also of any direct evidence *for* it, since it is possible that, having no evidence either way, we should suspend judgment on the question of realizationism. Whether there is any evidence *for* realizationism is the subject of the next and final chapter.

So realization physicalism is in principle open to empirical refutation. But has it actually been refuted? Is there, indeed, any evidence against it at all? Let us see whether we can find any, looking in places where we would expect to find it if it exists, beginning with potential *direct* evidence against realizationism.

2. DIRECT EVIDENCE AGAINST REALIZATION PHYSICALISM: THE MIND

The traditional focus of philosophical disputes about physicalism has been, of course, on the human mind, and although nearly all active researchers in contemporary philosophy of mind claim to be physicalists of one sort or another, there remains a dissident minority of antiphysicalists; the writings of this minority may therefore seem a promising place to search for evidence against realization physicalism (see, e.g., Madell 1988; Foster 1991; Robinson 1993a; Chalmers 1996a). These dissidents generally identify three categories of mental phenomena as problematic for physicalism. First, there are the so-called *phenomenal* characters of certain mental states – for example, the *way it feels* to one to see (or to hallucinate seeing) the blue sky, or the *way it feels* to one when one has a throbbing headache. Second, there is the *intentionality*, or aboutness, of such mental states as thoughts, hopes, and fears. Finally, there is the phenomenon whereby we do things, or reach conclusions, *for a reason*.

However, for two reasons, I do not discuss these dissident writings in any detail. The minor reason is that, sadly, I have no big, original ideas to add to the physicalist accounts of these problematic mental phenomena that the literature already contains, accounts that I regard as either adequate or at least promising;[2] and, though it would not in most cases be hard, it would use much space, for the sake of very little illumination, to provide detailed rebuttals of antiphysicalist claims that these accounts, or accounts like them, cannot succeed.[3] But the major reason is that, by and large, these dissident writings simply do not contain – do not, indeed, even purport to contain – what I am looking for, namely, direct evidence against physicalism. They point out the existence of perfectly genuine mental phenomena, such as the three already noted, but the case they make for taking these phenomena to be neither physical nor physically realized is typically a priori, usually appealing liberally to precisely the sort of conceivability considerations that I argued in Chapter 1 to be incapable in principle of refuting realization physicalism. So, for example, in the volume edited by Howard Robinson, promisingly entitled, *Objections*

---

2   For physicalist accounts of phenomenal states, see Hill (1991), Tye (1995), Dretske (1995), and Lycan (1987; 1996). For physicalist accounts of intentionality, together with detailed critiques, see Stich and Warfield (1994). For physicalist accounts of reasoning, see Fodor (1986, ch. 1) on the computational account of rational deliberation, Laudan (1996, chs. 7–9) on the naturalization of epistemic normativity, Goldman (1986) on physicalism-friendly reliabilist epistemological theories in general, and Thagard (1988) for an introduction to the computational modeling of reasoning in science.

3   It is distressing to find how often antiphysicalists in the philosophy of mind underestimate or ignore the resources available to their physicalist opponents. One example: although both the editorial introduction and one of the papers included in Robinson (1993a) charge that there is no adequate physicalist account of intentionality, the rich, intriguing, and well-known physicalist theory propounded by Ruth Millikan (1984 and 1993) receives no critical attention whatever. A notable exception, however, whose grasp of the full range of physicalist possibilities cannot be faulted, is David Chalmers (1996a) – which helps explain why his defense of dualism about phenomenal properties has received so much more attention than earlier such defenses. See my detailed response to Chalmers's subtle argument (Melnyk 2001).

to *Physicalism*, the chapters by George Bealer and A. D. Smith (pretty explicitly) and those by Howard Robinson himself and Michael Lockwood (implicitly) assume that the conceivability of X without Y entails the distinctness of X and Y, which, as I argued in Chapter 1, it does not (Robinson 1993a). The closest the volume gets to empirical evidence against physicalism is in the chapters by Ralph Walker (1993, 79) and Grant Gillett (1993, 96). Both authors claim, not implausibly, that if their neo-Kantian views of the nature of theoretical and practical reasoning (respectively) are correct, then there must be some human behavior that cannot be given a complete explanation in purely neurophysiological terms; but neither author mentions, nor apparently even feels the need to mention, any empirical evidence for supposing that such neurophysiologically inexplicable human behavior actually occurs. This omission is striking, for such evidence would surely clinch their cases. It is especially striking in the case of Gillett, who, as a neurosurgeon, might therefore be expected to know of such evidence if in fact it exists.

One contemporary dualist philosopher who, perhaps uniquely, does offer a posteriori arguments against physicalism is Richard Swinburne (1987). In addition to an avowedly a priori argument,[4] Swinburne presents two so-called "Arguments from Brain Research" (1987, 35–8). Let us briefly examine them. The first starts from the well-known behavioral peculiarities exhibited by patients who have undergone cerebral commissurotomy, peculiarities that make it extremely difficult to answer the question of how many people are associated with each postoperative body (see Nagel 1971). Swinburne takes the apparently unresolvable controversy that these behavioral peculiarities engender to support his key premise that "we may know everything about the state of a human body and brain, and yet not know how many centers of consciousness, that is, persons, there are connected with that brain" (1987, 35–6). Swinburne

---

4   This argument (1987, 35 and 47) fails for at least two reasons. First, it employs the general metaphysical principle that it is not even logically possible for a thing to continue existing if you destroy every part of which the thing is made. But this principle is arguably false: a composite object, like the ship of Theseus, might survive the complete destruction of all its parts if these parts are destroyed and gradually replaced by others. Similarly, and consistently with realization physicalism, I could perhaps survive the complete destruction of my physical body if all my neurons, before being destroyed, were gradually replaced by artificial neurons made out of ectoplasm. Second, however, and crucially, in order to support the premise that it is genuinely possible (in some sense in which physicalism entails that it would not be possible) to survive the complete destruction of one's body, Swinburne's argument relies on an inference from conceivability to genuine possibility, an inference criticized in Chapter 1, Section 4, as being, at best, of a very weak inductive type.

proposes dualism as the best explanation of this state of affairs, for if centers of consciousness are nonphysical, as he supposes, then complete knowledge of merely *physical* facts about a person would obviously not yield knowledge of facts about that person's *nonphysical* consciousness. But this dualist explanation has a physicalist rival, and Swinburne gives no reason for preferring the former to the latter. The rival explanation is simply that there is no *conceptual* entailment, knowable a priori, between the physical *description* of a person, on the one hand, and the consciousness *description* of the same person, on the other. Now this rival explanation, like Swinburne's dualist explanation, would *also* lead us to expect that we could know all the physical facts about a commissurotomy patient without thereby knowing how many centers of consciousness were associated with the patient. For in the absence of a conceptual entailment that was knowable a priori, even a complete enumeration of the physical facts would leave us unable to say, a priori, what the consciousness facts were. Analogously, knowing that your food is sprinkled with NaCl would leave you unable to say whether your food is sprinkled with salt – unless you had the a posteriori knowledge that salt = NaCl. But this rival explanation would be consistent with the *physicalist* view that *being a center of consciousness* should turn out a posteriori to be one and the same thing as *being a token of such-and-such functional type*, so that there is nevertheless a *metaphysical* entailment between the physical facts about someone, on the one hand, and the (positive) consciousness facts about the same person, on the other, an entailment, however, that cannot be known a priori.

To this objection, Swinburne cannot reply that his initial premise – that "we may know everything about the state of a human body and brain, and yet not know how many centres of consciousness... there are connected with that brain" – should be construed more strongly, as reflecting the fact that there is not even a *metaphysical* entailment between the physical facts and the (positive) consciousness facts about someone. For that construal would either beg the question against the physicalist (by assuming the falsity of physicalism) or else (to avoid begging the question) require *independent* evidence against physicalism, thus rendering otiose the alleged evidence from commissurotomy.[5]

---

5 The dialectic here is obviously very similar to that generated by Jackson's (1982) infamous Knowledge Argument. In fact, both of Swinburne's "arguments from brain research" are best regarded as forms of knowledge argument; as such, of course, they are not really a posteriori at all.

Swinburne's second argument from brain research has the same form as the first, but is even less closely connected with actual neuroscientific facts. The key premise is that, if we were to transplant one of your cerebral hemispheres into one acerebral body, and your other cerebral hemisphere into another acerebral body, then even a complete knowledge of the physical facts in the situation would not tell us which new person (if either) would be you. And, as before, the best explanation of this state of affairs, according to Swinburne, would be that there is more to the situation than physical facts, and, in particular, that persons are nonphysical and nonphysically realized objects that are at most contingently related to brains. But this second argument fails for exactly the same reason as did the first. The dualist explanation of the relevant state of affairs must confront a physicalist rival that Swinburne provides no reason to judge inferior. According to the rival, there is no conceptual entailment, knowable a priori, between physical descriptions of humans and person-level descriptions of humans; but this explanation would be consistent with the physicalist hypothesis that to be a person is to be a certain sort of functional system, so that there is nevertheless a metaphysical, a posteriori entailment between the two sorts of descriptions.

A prominent dualist who, though not a philosopher, was still well known to philosophers of mind was the distinguished brain scientist and Nobel laureate Sir John Eccles. Surely, one might think, if there is a case to be made against mind-body physicalism on the basis of empirical results from the neurosciences, he would know about it. Let us therefore carefully examine his last book, the culmination of a lifetime's campaigning for dualism, to see what he has to offer (Eccles 1994).[6] The book is especially worthy of consideration because it moves beyond the rejection of physicalism to provide what is, to the best of my knowledge, a uniquely detailed *positive* account of dualism.

According to Eccles, "all mental events and experiences . . . are a composite of elemental or unitary mental events, which we may call psychons" (Eccles 1994, 101). "[Psychons] *are* . . . experiences in all their diversity and

---

6   Eccles takes pains to stress that the dualism he espouses is not the Cartesian variety but rather the Popperian kind involving Popper's World 1 and World 2 (Eccles 1994, 46, 161, and 181; Popper and Eccles 1977, 36–50). But unless he means merely that, on his kind of dualism, the mind does not operate on the brain via the pineal gland, I have no idea what he takes the difference between these forms of dualism to consist in, especially since he repeatedly speaks of the self as if he envisages it as a nonphysical substance. Eccles more than once presents a diagram to explain his favored kind of dualism, but I have been unable to interpret it (Eccles 1994, 10, 80, and 90).

uniqueness" and, though belonging to different types, evidently include intentions (101 and 103). The individual psychons involved in a single mind might number "about forty million" (102); but they are not, of course, physical. Each psychon, however, is associated with something that is physical, namely, a particular *dendron*, or small cluster of apical dendrites that project upwards through the layers of the cerebral cortex from certain pyramidal cells located lower down (93–9). And psychons interact causally with their associated dendrons. Because they do so "in a manner analogous to the probability fields of quantum mechanics," and because "in quantum physics... energy can be borrowed provided it is paid back at once," this causal interaction need not violate any conservation laws of physics (81 and 107); so dualism can avoid what Eccles apparently takes to be the only serious objection it faces. Moreover, the location and nature of this causal interaction can be specified in some detail. The dendrites making up a given dendron are covered with spines, onto which the axons of other neurons make synapses, and a psychon simultaneously acts on many such synapses in its associated dendron (100–7). Now the probability that, when an impulse propagates down an axon making a synapse with a dendritic spine, one of the presynaptic vesicles inside the bouton of the axon should undergo exocytosis (i.e., fuse with the presynaptic membrane of the bouton and empty its load of transmitter molecules into the synaptic cleft) is between 0.2 and 0.3 (134, 140, and 160). And this probabilistic character of vesicular exocytosis requires a quantum mechanical treatment, which can in fact be given (Eccles 1994, 154–9, in a chapter coauthored with F. Beck). But this quantum mechanical treatment opens up the possibility that a psychon should causally affect its associated dendron by *raising* the probability of vesicular exocytosis at the synapses within it – and doing so without violating any conservation law (Eccles 1994, 160).[7]

Thus, Eccles's detailed dualist hypothesis.[8] But what arguments does Eccles give for supposing that we need any dualist theory at all? Some are philosophical, borrowed from Popper: one is that the identity theory

---

7   I should point out that Eccles presents no evidence that rates of vesicular exocytosis ever *in fact* undergo any mysterious increases that promise to be inexplicable by reference to purely physical causes. Indeed, a recent survey on neurotransmitter release does not even discuss the possibility that neurobiologists might need to invoke quantum mechanical hypotheses to account for vesicular exocytosis (Staple and Catsicas, 1997).

8   Though to do so is strictly irrelevant to my goal of seeking direct evidence against physicalism, I cannot resist noting some difficulties in Eccles's admirably bold development of a positive dualist theory. First, it is quite obscure how Eccles's psychons are supposed to be related to

epiphenomenalizes the mental, so that if it were true, mentality could not have been selected for and materialism would then be inconsistent with Darwinism (Eccles 1994, 8; Popper and Eccles 1977, 72–88); another is that mental states such as beliefs, if identical with brain states, would result from physical causes and therefore could not also be held on rational grounds (Eccles 1994, 11; Popper 1972, ch. 6).[9] But Eccles also claims quite explicitly that experimental evidence provides strong support for dualism: "Thus extensive experimental studies establish that mental intentions (psychons) can effectively activate the cerebral cortex" (Eccles 1994, 138). What experimental studies are these? And how can it be argued that they "establish" that nonphysical psychons influence cortical events?[10]

the *self* (of which he speaks often and, indeed, in his very title). He seems dimly aware of the problem, for he candidly admits (Eccles 1994, 109) that he cannot currently account for the unity of consciousness, and resorts later to brute force, saying that "it is the very nature of psychons to link together in providing a unified experience" (136); but that is evidently no help. (Ironically, he earlier takes materialism to task for allegedly having no such account [22].) Second, whatever the merits of his account of causal interaction from psychons to dendrons, he has virtually nothing to say about causal interaction in the other direction, such as on his view occurs all the time in perception. At the crucial point he speaks vaguely of "a signal that is transmitted to the mental world"; and the little he does say commits him to holding, implausibly, that for a perception to occur one's attention must first be directed to some part of the body (108). Finally, he tells us nothing whatever about how psychons work. For example, since we are never actually in all the mental states that we might be in (e.g., we are not always enjoying red sensations), but since it does not seem to be his view that psychons pop in and out of existence as needed, psychons must at least be capable of being in "on" and "off" states; but we are given no hint as to how this might work. Similarly, those psychons that are beliefs and desires must interact causally with one another; but again we are offered no hint of a theory about this. Quite generally, he just assumes that – with no explanation how – selves (or psychons) possess characteristically mental capacities, for example, for attention, choice, and learning (20 and 172). Eccles's development of dualism, then, though it goes further than any other treatment I know, is still confined to the negative task of trying to meet objections. Despite his best efforts, we still have no positive theory of the nonphysical mind.

9   Another philosophical consideration – hardly an argument – is that Eccles evidently finds the identity theory utterly baffling, repeatedly calling it "strange" or "enigmatic" (e.g., 1994, 167). That he should find it so is unsurprising, given that he holds that its "key postulate is . . . an inner and outer aspect" (6). Regrettably, this confusion is typical of the quality of the philosophical portions of his book.

10 In the book coauthored with Popper, Eccles claimed that certain experimental results presented by Benjamin Libet (1973, 1978, and 1981) must be interpreted as supporting dualism (Popper and Eccles 1977, 364). For incisive and conclusive demolition of Eccles's and Libet's claims, see Chris Mortensen (1980) and Patricia Churchland (1981a and 1981b); see also Daniel Dennett (1991, 153–62). Eccles makes no mention of this alleged evidence for dualism in his later work, so perhaps by 1994 he had repudiated it.

Eccles cites more than one experimental result, but in each case the discovery is that subjects undergo a distinctive pattern of brain activity when they are engaged in some kind of silent thinking (e.g., mentally rehearsing a learned motor task, attending to an unstimulated body part, starting from fifty and successively subtracting three), even though no peripheral stimulation is occurring. Eccles infers that this brain activity must therefore be caused by some mental state entirely distinct from any brain state (Eccles 1994, 74–80). The following quotation, in connection with the experimental results he cites concerning directed attention, illustrates the same reasoning that he also employs in the case of the other experimental results:

[It is] a remarkable finding of Roland (1981) that, when the human subject was attending to a finger on which a just-detectable touch stimulus was to be applied, there was an increase in the rCBF [regional cerebral blood flow] over the finger touch area of the postcentral gyrus of the cerebral cortex as well as in the midprefrontal area. These increases must have resulted from the mental attention because *no touch was applied during the recording.* Thus, [this] is a demonstration that the mental act of attention [*sc.* a psychon] can activate appropriate regions of the cerebral cortex. (Eccles 1994, 78; emphasis in original)

But Eccles's reasoning here – encapsulated in his penultimate sentence – seems to be a gross non sequitur. That the recorded brain activity was not caused by an immediately preceding peripheral stimulation does not entail, or even suggest, that it had no physical cause at all. It is no more necessary to postulate a nonphysical causal agent to explain why there should be brain activity during silent thought in the absence of peripheral stimulation than it is necessary to postulate a nonphysical causal agent to explain why my computer chugs away for some time after I have stopped pressing the keys telling it to save my document. In the case of the computer, the continued chugging in the absence of peripheral stimulation is caused by the interaction of earlier internal states of the machine, modified by the keystrokes telling it to save. Similarly, the increased brain activity discovered to occur while attending to a fingertip might perfectly well be caused by earlier brain activity, no doubt modified by the *instructions* that the subject earlier *heard* from the experimenter.

Nor are the experimental results that Eccles cites from Roland capable even in principle of ruling out such a possibility. For, according to the original paper reporting these results, "subjects were asked to count the number of threshold stimuli to the index finger in a given period of time." But because "the real test [as opposed to training sessions] started

5s *before* the ^{133}Xe injection [without which recording of brain activity could not begin]," brain activity during the *onset* of attention to the fingertip was *not recorded* in these experiments (Roland 1981, 745 and 746; emphasis added). According to Eccles, however, it was precisely the onset of attention that caused the brain activity that was recorded. But how could these experiments tell us that it was the onset of attention that caused the recorded brain activity, rather than some alternative physical cause (e.g., earlier brain activity of some sort), if no brain activity was being recorded at the time of the onset of attention? Because they evidently could not, the experimental results from Roland that Eccles cites cannot tell us whether it was the onset of mental attention that caused the brain activity that was recorded. Roland's results therefore do *not* show that the brain activity associated with mental attention just arises out of the blue, as far as physical causes are concerned; and, indeed, Roland's own discussion contains no suggestion whatsoever that some nonphysical causal influence must be invoked in order to explain his findings. In fact, those findings rather appear to suggest construing the brain activity recorded as *realizing* mental attention directed onto one's finger, in line with realization physicalism. The experimental results Eccles cites certainly generate no pressure toward dualism.

However, perhaps Eccles does not mean to infer that episodes of brain activity during silent thinking are nonphysically caused *solely* from the fact that they occur in the absence of peripheral stimulation. For, in an earlier passage, he seems to say that there *is no* earlier *brain* activity that could cause such episodes, so that, in effect, the physical is not causally closed (Eccles 1994, 67–8).[11] But although such a claim would obviously save his inference and pose a major problem for physicalism, he himself presents no evidence for it. Moreover, the experimental studies he later cites, concerning the mental rehearsal of a learned motor task and other forms of silent thinking, are as incapable as the study concerning attention to a fingertip of supplying such evidence; for, as the original research reports reveal, in their case also the recording of brain activity began only *after* the silent thinking of the subject had begun (Roland et al. 1980, 121; Roland and Friberg 1985, 1221).

So flimsy is Eccles's empirical case for dualism that one wonders whether perhaps he approached the experimental studies he cites *already*

---

11 Oddly, he does not repeat this crucial claim when in the following chapter he goes on to describe in detail the experimental results concerning silent thinking in the absence of peripheral stimulation (Eccles 1994, 74–8).

convinced on philosophical grounds that dualism of some kind is true, hoping to learn from the empirical findings only *where* the nonphysical mind (assumed already to exist) operates on the brain. But it is hard to construe what he says in this way (e.g., Eccles 1994, 147 and 163–4); and so I offer an alternative hypothesis to explain his attraction to what certainly seems to be unsound reasoning. My diagnosis is that he makes a certain assumption about the character of *any* physical mechanism that produces outputs in response to inputs. The assumption is that any such mechanism must be describable by simple input-output laws according to which a given type of input (via the mediation of internal states) is necessary and sufficient for the production of a certain type of output, in just the way in which pressing the button of a doorbell is necessary and sufficient for the doorbell to produce a sound. From this assumption it follows that if a perceiving, thinking, and acting human is just a physical mechanism that produces outputs in response to inputs, then the internal states of a human that mediate his or her perception and behavior *must* have perceptual input states as causes. And so, as a corollary, if a human enters internal states that are *not* caused by perceptual input states, then it cannot be just a physical mechanism; there must be something *else* inside it that can trigger the internal states. (Imagine what you would think if the innards of your doorbell suddenly became active while no one was pressing the button!) But the assumption about the character of all physical mechanisms that produce outputs in response to inputs is false, of course, and a counterexample is provided by my desktop computer: on every occasion on which I press the keys instructing my computer to print out a document, it typically produces a *different* motor output (i.e., prints out a different document) – and for the perfectly obvious reason that its outputs depend not only on its inputs but also on its current internal states. But it seems quite possible that Eccles, who contemptuously dismisses the relevance of artificial intelligence to understanding the mind, should have missed this (176–7).

Why is it that, as my brief survey suggests, mind-body dualists are able to offer so little empirical evidence against physicalism? The reason, surely, is that historically, but especially over the past hundred years, things have not at all gone their way: potential evidence that might have emerged favoring dualism has not actually done so. To begin with something so basic that it is apt to be overlooked, we might have discovered that the human skull, which evidently contains at least the proximate causes of human behavior (since it is where muscle-stimulating motor neurons come from), was empty, or full of blood, or (less implausibly) that it housed an organ of relatively modest complexity; and had we discovered any of these things, the postulation of a nonphysical mind would surely have been irresistible. But what we have actually discovered, obviously, is that, on the contrary, the human skull contains the brain, which, when examined at the cellular and indeed subcellular levels, turns out to be perhaps the most complex object in the universe, made up of billions of specialized cells interconnected in extraordinarily complex ways, with the likelihood that important computation occurs within it *intra*neurally and not just *inter*neurally (see Barlow 1998, 143–5).

Of course, there is an obvious way for a dualist to accommodate the finding that motor neurons emerge from the brain: to adopt a version of dualism according to which, although brain activity may be causally necessary for the nonphysical mind to receive its input (in perception) and for it to produce its output (in the initiation of physical movement), there are various mental processes and activities – for example, enjoying perceptual qualia, planning an action, doing mental arithmetic – that occur entirely in the nonphysical mind, and for which, therefore, no brain activity of any special sort is required. Now we can easily imagine acquiring evidence that these mental processes and activities indeed enjoy independence from neural activity of exactly the kind indicated; for instance, we might have discovered that the brain activity of someone who has earlier had an arithmetical task explained to him or her and has now been asked actually to do it shows no significant change. But not only has no evidence *for* this version of dualism emerged, we have actually discovered that it is false: *every* kind of mental process or activity, no matter how apparently abstract or unworldly, seems to require brain activity of some specific sort in order for it to occur – as, ironically, is evidenced by, for example, the very studies of cerebral blood flow during silent thinking that Eccles cites in support of dualism.[12] These discoveries do not, of course, entail that every imaginable form of dualism is false; but they do represent another failure of potential evidence for dualism to manifest itself in actuality.

Similarly, it was possible a hundred or more years ago to argue for dualism on empirical grounds by claiming that no purely physical mechanism could in fact give rise to the sort of complex, flexible, and unpredictable behavior that humans routinely exhibit; and we might have enormously strengthened that argument over the intervening period by discovering that, as we learned more and more about matter, we gained no reason to

---

12 For further evidence, see Chapter 6, Section 7, in connection with the third argument for regarding mental phenomena as physically realized.

revise our earlier judgment about the strictly limited behavioral capacities of purely material systems. But in actual fact, of course, as we have learned more and more about "mere" matter over the past one hundred years, we have been able to develop technologies that vividly demonstrate that the behavioral capacities of purely material systems are very much *more* extensive than were imagined a century ago. In particular, of course, we are now all familiar with computers, which we see at work in guided missiles and in autopilots, in expert systems that outperform humans at medical diagnosis, and in thermostats that keep one's house at a constant temperature by switching on the heating *before* the temperature has dropped below its target, how *much* before determined by the device's earlier attempts to maintain a constant temperature. Even if in the end thought turns out not to be a special sort of computation, these artifacts, whose status as purely physical no dualist will deny, exhibit behavior that, even though nothing like as impressive as that of humans, would nevertheless have staggered our Victorian ancestors. Certainly they undermine any case for dualism that rests on the assumption that the behavioral capacities of mere matter are so limited as to make it impossible or unlikely that humans should be merely material. And in the specific case of linguistic behavior, which Descartes himself regarded as beyond the capacity of any mere machine (1985, 1:139–40), we have made so much progress in understanding distinctively linguistic capacities (including, of course, the capacity for the production and comprehension of novel utterances) as resulting from the unconscious following of *rules* that it is getting very hard to argue that even linguistic behavior lies beyond the capacity of a purely physical system. A responsible dualist position today has to be not that the remarkably complex behavior of humans *could* not be produced by a purely physical or physically realized mechanism but that in fact it *is* not so produced.

Here is another respect in which things have not gone the dualists' way, and evidence for dualism that there might have been has just not turned up. Nearly all contemporary dualists want to hold that mental states are nonphysical and nonphysically realized states that play an indispensable part in the causation of behavior: mental states may not be causally *sufficient* for behavioral outcomes but they are causally *necessary*. But if interactionist dualism of this sort were true, then there should be human behaviors for which no sufficient *neurophysiological* cause can be found by tracing efferent motor neurons back into the brain; and discovering such behaviors would clearly provide spectacular support for the dualist hypothesis. However, neuroscientists have as yet failed to discover any such behaviors, and my strong impression is that they do not expect to (e.g., Shepherd 1994).

Philosophers sympathetic to dualism sometimes darkly hint that they suspect that the physical is not really causally closed and that, in particular, there are physical behaviors that lack sufficient preceding neurological causes; but to my knowledge they have never provided a scintilla of evidence for supposing that this is true, or the slightest indication of where in the brain they imagine that the chances of physical events, given earlier events and laws, are not fixed by the chances of earlier *physical* events plus *physical* laws.[13]

A further prediction of the interactionist dualism outlined earlier is that it must be possible in principle to insert into the brain of a conscious person some sort of probe that is sensitive to causal influences from the nonphysical mind in the same way as are those parts of the brain on which the nonphysical mind allegedly acts, and thereby to find that this probe is stimulated in ways that cannot be wholly accounted for by the causal influence of brain states. As before, however, although the experimental discovery of such a result would provide striking confirmation for interactionist dualism, it has not in fact been made. Admittedly, it is possible that the reason why this produalist discovery, as well as the earlier one, has not been made is that no one has ever troubled to perform the requisite experiments, or that current experimental techniques are inadequate to the complexity of neural phenomena; either way, it would be overhasty to infer from these nondiscoveries that interactionist dualism is false. But I am not making that inference here. I am merely pointing out that, as things currently stand, two sorts of potential evidence for dualism (and hence against physicalism) have not in fact been uncovered; and no theory can be supported by nonexistent evidence, whatever might be the reason for its nonexistence.

---

13 John Dupré is a good example of an antiphysicalist who denies, but who supplies no empirical evidence against, the claim that every human behavior has a sufficient neurophysiological cause (1993, 166). In the same passage, he also expresses doubt that a scientist even could come to know such a claim, but he does not explain why. Finally, he asserts that to make the claim "is wholly to beg the question in favor of physicalism." But if he means that the claim that every human behavior has a sufficient neurophysiological cause *entails* physicalism (about the mind), then he is mistaken; for the claim is clearly consistent with epiphenomenalist dualism and even with interactionist dualism if systematic causal overdetermination of human behavior is logically possible. If, on the other hand, what he means is that the claim that every human behavior has a sufficient neurophysiological cause, *when and only when combined with other contingent premises*, yields a valid argument for physicalism (about the mind), then he may be correct; but even if he is, it will follow that the claim begs the question in favor of physicalism only if *every* premise in *any* valid argument for *any* conclusion begs the question in favor of the argument's conclusion.

Finally, it has long been recognized that the discovery of paranormal phenomena would bear directly upon the question of physicalism, as John Beloff (1989) has recently reminded us; and indeed the explicit aim, not only of parapsychology's founding fathers but also of many of its current practitioners, has been precisely to overthrow a materialistic and scientific world view in which no room remains for the human soul (see Humphrey 1996). The specific relevance of allegedly paranormal phenomena to realization physicalism is this: because the causal powers of anything that is physically realized in my sense must be in principle explainable in physical terms, if the mind were discovered to have causal powers (e.g., telepathic or psychokinetic powers) that it would be impossible, according to current physics, for a physically realized system to possess, then the mind could not be a physically realized system. So the discovery of (e.g.) telepathic or psychokinetic powers would simultaneously falsify realization physicalism and support dualism. But once again things have not gone the dualists' way, for no such powers have in fact been discovered. Indeed, even Beloff (1989, 167) has to admit that it is "still legitimate to doubt the existence" of paranormal phenomena – and for good reason.

First, despite strenuous and determined attempts for nearly seventy years to demonstrate paranormal phenomena in the laboratory, it is still true that no allegedly paranormal phenomenon can be reliably produced at will by any competent researcher who wishes to do so in a suitably equipped laboratory. Only very patchy positive results, in the form of statistical anomalies, have ever been obtained, and over even these results hangs the unfortunate shadow of parapsychology's appalling history of experimental incompetence and sometimes even fraud. Second, the persuasiveness of such positive results as parapsychology has achieved would be greatly increased if parapsychologists were to offer, as they have not, some sort of reasonably developed *theory* to explain these alleged results, some theory adequate to explain, for example, why paranormal phenomena are as elusive as they are, in just the peculiar ways that they are; why paranormal powers are as unequally distributed over people as they are; why they take the peculiar forms that they do; why even in apparently successful experiments the effects allegedly detected are so weak and capricious; why attempts to replicate apparently successful experiments have so often failed; and why standard scientific experiments work as well as they do, which is to say, very well, even though they do not control for the alleged paranormal variables. My point, however, is not that, in the absence of an explanatory theory for anomalous phenomena, we can have no good reason to believe in the genuineness of the phenomena, for we clearly can (though the credibility of allegedly anomalous phenomena is certainly *increased* by the availability of a unifying theory to account for them, and the case for paranormal phenomena does not enjoy this boost). Rather, my point is that parapsychologists' failure to provide a theory of the sort I outlined means that the *overall pattern* of allegedly paranormal phenomena is simply left unexplained. So even if normal science cannot account for the alleged phenomena, neither, apparently, can the envisaged alternative. Small wonder, then, that the positive findings of experimental parapsychology have failed to generate a consensus – beyond the small and highly incestuous community of parapsychological enthusiasts – that there are even any phenomena to explain.[14]

Finally, it is not clear, even if parapsychology's positive results do indicate the existence of phenomena that are paranormal in the weaker sense that they have no obvious or standard physical explanation, whether they also show the mind to possess powers that are paranormal in the fullblooded sense that it is physically *impossible* for a physically realized system to possess them. For if the results were to support this stronger claim, then the phenomena established would have to be incapable of being physically realized. But there is no reason to suppose that we currently know what all the phenomena are that might nevertheless be capable of being physically realized, and hence there is no reason to suppose that we currently know what nonobvious and nonstandard physical explanations there might be for such positive results as parapsychology has achieved (Paul Churchland 1988, 17).

3. DIRECT EVIDENCE AGAINST REALIZATION PHYSICALISM: BIOLOGY

Does anything in the biological sciences provide evidence against realization physicalism?[15] Let me begin by considering the following *argument*

---

14 For thorough critiques of parapsychological research, see Hansel (1989), Hyman (1989), and Alcock (1990). Susan Blackmore's (1996) remarkable account of her own failed attempts to discover paranormal phenomena, despite a powerful antecedent conviction of their reality, also sheds valuable light on the distinctive *culture* of parapsychologists.

15 Artificial-life research is rife with talk of the *emergence* of biological phenomena (see, e.g., Boden 1996). But whatever exactly artificial-life writers mean by "emergence," it is pretty clear that they intend nothing that would conflict with materialism (see, e.g., Langton 1996). Mark Bedau's (1997) interesting notion of "weak emergence" is certainly consistent with realization physicalism and may well capture part of what they do mean, the part to do with noncomputability. However, they seem to me often to call a feature of a complex system emergent merely when the feature is not invariant under all transformations of the

from functional ascription: "Practicing biologists routinely ascribe functions to biological entities, including whole organisms, their organs, cellular subsystems, cells, organelles, and even molecules: they claim that these biological entities have the *function* of doing (or being) so-and-so. Let us assume they are right. But something has the function of doing so-and-so only if it was *deliberately created* with the *intention* that it should do so-and-so (as a can opener is deliberately created with the intention that it should help with the opening of cans). So biological entities must have been deliberately created. However, no agent that is physical or physically realized has created biological entities.[16] So biological entities must have been created by some nonphysical and nonphysically realized creator, whose existence entails that realizationism is false." Now at first sight this argument seems to have an obvious weak spot: the conditional premise that something has the function of doing so-and-so only if it was deliberately created with the intention that it should do so-and-so. But Alvin Plantinga has recently revived the argument by defending precisely this premise. His strategy is to argue ingeniously *against* an assortment of proposals for understanding functional ascriptions *naturalistically*, that is, in such a way as at least *not* to imply the conditional premise (Plantinga 1993, 194–215); and on the strength of his critical survey, he concludes by suggesting that functional ascriptions not merely have not been but *cannot* be understood naturalistically (210).[17]

      system's parts and/or when it belongs to a system entirely composed of parts whose behavior is under no central control, but is instead guided by relatively simple rules that are "local" in the sense that what a part must do in order to conform to the rules depends only upon its own states and its *local* environment of other parts.

16 Conceivably, the biological entities we are familiar with, including ourselves, have been created by *alien* agents that *are* physical or physically realized – modestly competent alien superscientists, perhaps. But an advocate of the argument in the text will surely insist that the same problem of functional ascription would arise for these aliens, their organs, cellular subsystems, and so on, as arises for familiar biological entities. (On pain of regress, however, it cannot arise for the postulated *nonphysical* and *nonphysically realized* creator: neither God nor his parts [if any] can have functions, according to the present argument.)

17 Mark Bedau (1992) presents an account of functional ascriptions according to which they always invoke the idea that some result is *good*. And he wonders whether naturalism can accommodate such objective goodness (1993, 23–5). But even if his account of functional ascriptions is accepted, the notion of goodness that Bedau appeals to (1992, 791) seems a reasonably promising candidate for naturalistic (or physicalistic) treatment: it is neither a notion of moral goodness nor that of goodness, all things considered. Of course, a naturalistic (or physicalistic) treatment cannot, on pain of circularity, analyze goodness in terms of the promotion of proper functioning; and for the same reason, as Bedau himself points out (1993, 25), aspirant teleofunctionalists in the philosophy of mind had better not analyze goodness in terms of contentful mental states (e.g., desires). But he gives no reason to think

For all their ingenuity, however, Plantinga's arguments against extant naturalistic proposals may just be wrong: Michael Levin, for example, has forcefully argued that a modified version of Larry Wright's naturalistic account of functions can withstand a variety of objections, explicitly including Plantinga's (Wright 1973; Levin 1997a). Moreover, in arguing that certain naturalistic proposals state neither necessary nor sufficient conditions for the correct applicability of our *everyday* concept of function (which, as he notes [1993, 195], is most at home in connection with artifacts), Plantinga makes the implicit assumption that talk of functions is *univocal* across artifactual and biological contexts. But this assumption might well be false – indeed, it might well be false that talk of functions is even univocal across all *biological* contexts (see, e.g., Godfrey-Smith 1994, 344–5); and if it is false, then one of the naturalistic accounts of functional ascription that Plantinga rejects might still be perfectly correct as an account of functional ascription in biology.[18]

Nor would the only alternative to univocality be the admittedly awkward supposition that artifacts and biological entities have functions in entirely unrelated senses. For the senses may be different and yet still bear important resemblances to one another; the property ascribed to an *artifact* by saying that it has a function may be distinct from and yet still importantly similar to the property ascribed to a *biological* entity by saying that *it* has a function. Let me illustrate this possibility. Suppose that in ascribing the function of doing so-and-so to an *artifact* we are ascribing to it the property (roughly) of having been deliberately created with the intention that it should do so-and-so. Then, in ascribing a function to an artifact, we are thereby (a) making a claim about events that occurred *before* the function-bearer existed, (b) offering an *explanation* of the

---

that these pitfalls are unavoidable. Suppose, however, both that Bedau's analysis of functional ascriptions turns out to be correct and that the notion of objective goodness it employs cannot be given an adequate naturalistic treatment. The dialectic will parallel that in the text with regard to Plantinga: the naturalist will go eliminativist and, in response, Bedau will have to provide evidence that biological entities really do have functions in his sense, evidence, in effect, that nonnaturalizable objective goodness really exists – and the naturalist will protest that there is no such evidence. (Actually, it turns out that on Bedau's [1992] account of functional ascriptions biological entities only have functions in a second-class sense – *unless* they are construed as artifacts; so Bedau's function-based challenge to naturalism threatens to reduce to Plantinga's.)

18 Denying the assumption of univocality will not circumvent all of Plantinga's objections to naturalistic accounts of function. He also charges such accounts with circularity, a charge that does not rely on the assumption of univocality (1993, 204, 206, and 210); but this charge can be met, I believe, by appealing to Millikan's notion of Normal conditions (1984, 33–4).

function-bearer's existence, and (c) leaving open the possibility that the function-bearer should sometimes or always *fail* to do what it is its function to do. Now, caricaturing the views of Ruth Millikan, suppose that in ascribing the function of doing so-and-so to a *biological* entity we are claiming (very roughly indeed) that the entity is a member of a family of items such that doing so-and-so is whatever prior members of the family did that explains why its current members exist, including the one being ascribed a function (Millikan 1984, chs. 1 and 2; 1993, chs. 1 and 2; my caricature is indebted to Godfrey-Smith 1994, 347). Then, in ascribing a function to a biological entity, we are *also* thereby (a) making a claim about events that occurred before the function-bearer existed, (b) offering an explanation of the function-bearer's existence, and (c) leaving open the possibility that the function-bearer should sometimes or always fail to do what it is its function to do.

Indeed, there is a further similarity between artifactual and biological functions, understood as we have been supposing for the sake of the current illustration. If the existence of an *artifact* is explained by its having the function (in Plantinga's everyday sense) of doing so-and-so, then its existence is explained by someone's having created it with the intention that it should do so-and-so; but, typically, part of what explains *why* someone created something with the intention that it should do so-and-so is that the person *believed* that earlier tokens like it did *in fact* do so-and-so (the only exceptions being *prototype* artifacts), where this belief is itself in part explained by the fact that they really did; so it will *typically* be true that *part* of the explanation of the artifact's existence is that earlier tokens like it did in fact do so-and-so. But if the existence of a *biological* entity is explained by its having the function (in Millikan's sense) of doing so-and-so, then it will *always* be true that part of the (Darwinian) explanation of its existence is that earlier tokens like it did in fact do so-and-so. Artifactual and biological function, then, though not exactly the same, need not on that account be brutely different, like banks at the sides of rivers and banks that pay interest.

But what if Plantinga turns out to be right, and functional ascriptions cannot be given a naturalistic treatment? In that case, the realizationist must go nonretentive, and deny that ascriptions of function to biological entities are true. But would it not be very implausible to deny what so many people, biologists and the laity alike, find so obviously true? Not if there is an explanation of their error that makes it understandable and even tempting; and there is. For even if biological entities lack functions in the putatively univocal sense in which having a function requires having been deliberately created, they surely still have *functionlike* properties, namely, those properties expressed by the naturalistic accounts of function (e.g., Millikan's) that Plantinga rejects as inadequate renditions of "function" in the putatively univocal everyday sense; and these functionlike properties are sufficiently similar to true functions that their possession by biological entities can help explain why we erroneously suppose them to possess true functions. We might add that the error is sustained by two further facts. First, biological entities undoubtedly appear, at least superficially, as if they have been designed, and the natural-selectionist explanation of this appearance is both unobvious and unintuitive; the folk might therefore find it all but irresistible to treat biological entities as artifacts. Second, precisely because natural selection can produce entities that really do resemble artifacts in various ways, adopting the "design stance" toward biological entities can be an enormously useful heuristic for biologists, even if it is literally false that biological entities have been designed (Dennett 1987, 16–17).

How might Plantinga respond to this eliminativist line? One tack would be to argue that an eliminativist about biological functions is committed, implausibly, to *skepticism* (at least as regards humans). For suppose, as Plantinga argues, that knowledge is to be analyzed partly in terms of the notion of the proper functioning of one's cognitive faculties, where the appropriate notion of function is the *everyday* notion; then naturalists who deny that this everyday notion of function has any application to biological entities must deny that anybody's cognitive faculties even have functions, still less that those faculties function properly, and hence must deny that anybody knows anything (Plantinga 1993, 202 and 214). But this objection is weak, even if it be granted that Plantinga's account of knowledge is correct.[19] For while we must take Plantinga's word for it when he says that his analysis of knowledge appeals to proper function in the everyday sense, we can readily envisage an account of knowledge (albeit not a conceptual analysis) in which all mention of function in the everyday sense is replaced by talk of function in, say, Millikan's (different, we are supposing) sense. Such an account might nevertheless inherit all the advantages of Plantinga's original account, yet permit the naturalist

---

19 Which it may well not be; for critical discussion, see the chapters in Kvanvig (1996). Elsewhere, Evan Fales points out that if Plantinga's account of knowledge is correct, and if God has no designer, then God has no properly functioning cognitive faculties and hence knows nothing (Fales 1996, 433; for Plantinga's attempt to finesse the difficulty, see his 1993, 236, n. 26).

to avoid commitment to skepticism (compare, perhaps, Millikan 1993, ch. 12).

Against eliminativism about biological functions, then, there remains to Plantinga, as far as I can see, one and only one resort, which is to insist that, in addition to whatever merely functionlike properties biological entities may possess, they *also* possess *true* functions (i.e., functions as understood by Plantinga). But this insistence can hardly rest upon an appeal to intuition or self-evidence; so we must be given some *evidence* for it. But because something has the true function of doing so-and-so only if it was deliberately created with the intention that it should do so-and-so, this evidence for holding that biological entities have true functions must be, at the least, evidence for holding that biological entities (or their resembling ancestors) were deliberately created (by something neither physical nor physically realized, if the rest of the antiphysicalist argument is to go through). Now there is a problem for physicalism here only if there really *is* such evidence; but *if* there is, then surely something like a traditional *design argument* in the style of Paley must be correct. So the problem (for physicalism) of functional ascription turns out to constitute no *novel* problem for physicalism at all, since whether such a problem exists turns out to depend upon the plausibility of something like a traditional design argument (*pace*, perhaps, Plantinga 1993, 214–15). Unsurprisingly, however, my view is that design arguments are weak, and that the available evidence does not favor the hypothesis that biological entities (or their resembling ancestors) were deliberately created by something neither physical nor physically realized. Let me sketch three considerations that, if sympathetically amplified and elaborated, would justify this judgment.[20]

20 The discussion of traditional biological design arguments that follows in the text is the closest I get in this book to evaluating the important challenge to realization physicalism posed by all arguments for the existence of a god who is assumed to be neither physical nor physically realized. Regrettably, I have little to add to critical analyses of the sort to be found in, for example, Michael Martin (1990). For a critical discussion of the most recent biological design arguments, those of the self-styled "intelligent-design theorists," see Robert Pennock's book (1999).

I have omitted from the text discussion of design arguments that appeal to the alleged fine-tuning for life of the physical constants because, though interesting, these arguments have no detailed connection with biology, and it is direct evidence against realizationism that might emerge from biology with which I am currently concerned. Actually, I suspect that facts about fine-tuning in any case add precisely nothing to the case for theism, since there is an unacknowledged conditionality in the claim that the universe is fine-tuned. When it is claimed that, if a certain magnitude had varied only slightly, life would have been impossible, we must take this to mean that, *if certain general features of the universe were held fixed*, then, if the values of certain other magnitudes had varied only slightly, life would have been impossible.

The first consideration is that, although the biological world certainly presents an appearance of design, and although the hypothesis that it was deliberately created promises to account for this appearance, upon closer examination this promise turns out to be illusory. The difficulty arises from the fact that the biological world presents us with a dazzlingly varied array of apparently designed entities, ranging from literally hundreds of thousands of species of beetle alone to the extraordinary apparatus employed by the angler fish for catching its prey; and it presents us with an equally diverse array of facts about these entities, such as that most (but not all) bird species fly, while most (but not all) mammal species do not, that the tails of whales and fish are, respectively, horizontally and vertically oriented, that some species use the reproductive strategy of producing huge numbers of young, most of whom die, while other species make large parental investments, and so forth; facts such as these can be garnered from any good television nature show.

But now the hypothesis of deliberate creation faces a dilemma. If it includes no information whatsoever about the *detailed intentions* of the hypothesized creator(s), then it simply does not account for the biological phenomena as they actually are, and fails to provide an explanation of anything. If, on the other hand, the hypothesis of deliberate creation tries to do better, it is in grave danger of having to postulate something like a *distinct* creative intention on the part of the creator for each and every one of the apparently designed biological entities that there are, and for

> If we do not take it this way, then where do claims of fine-tuning come from? Surely they come, and can only come, from the calculations of scientists who ask themselves how the universe would have turned out if a certain constant had been different while various other things had stayed the same. We simply have no basis for saying how the universe would have turned out if a given constant had been different while everything else could have been absolutely any old way. So what fine-tuning comes to is this: with certain features of the universe already in place, as it were, there turns out to be less latitude than you might have imagined in determining the values of remaining magnitudes, given that life is to be possible. But all that follows from this is that the probability of a life-containing universe is low, given that the universe has the fundamental structure of the actual universe. What we need to know, though, is the probability of a life-containing universe, given that no God created it – which is not the same probability. So the overall position is as follows. The fact that the universe contains life is evidence that God created it only if the probability that it contains life, given that he created it, exceeds the probability that it contains life, given that he did not. But what is the probability that the universe contains life, given that God did not create it? We know this probability only if we know the ratio of life-containing possible universes to all possible universes, life-containing or not. But facts about fine-tuning do not tell us this ratio; they tell us only the ratio of life-containing universes to a subset of possible universes, namely those, whether life-containing or not, which resemble ours in certain fundamental respects.

each and every fact about them, thus becoming an almost ludicrously unparsimonious and arbitrary hypothesis, hardly less puzzling than the original biological phenomena we wanted explained, and providing no unified explanation at all for the *overall pattern* of apparent design. If this second horn is chosen, the hypothesis of deliberate creation becomes exactly as credible as would be a naturalistic explanation of the full diversity of biological facts that postulated the past existence of (a single token of) a new type of particle whose nature it was, via the operation of innumerable brute laws of diachronic emergence, to cause to come into existence exactly the range of apparently designed biological entities that we have in fact found to exist; since a naturalistic hypothesis of this kind would obviously be quite incredible, so too would be the analogous creationist hypothesis.

The second horn of the dilemma could in principle, of course, be avoided. But doing so would require the formulation of a hypothesis of deliberate creation in which the hypothesized creator was assigned some reasonably small set of *basic* creative intentions in light of which more *specific* intentions, to fashion biological entities in all their spectacular diversity and to create certain patterns among them, could be represented as *derivative*. To the best of my knowledge, however, no advocate of a design hypothesis has ever seriously attempted such a formulation. (The traditional Judeo-Christian idea that the creator intends to create a *good* world gets us nowhere at all, of course, unless we are prepared to make very strong and specific, but apparently quite arbitrary, claims about what a good world would be like – for example, that in a good world some swimming creatures would have vertically oriented tails, while certain others would have horizontally oriented tails.)

Moreover, the absence of attempts to fashion a design hypothesis that accounts for the biological facts in all their fullness while remaining attractively economical is entirely predictable. An example illustrates the general point. My highly specific intention to climb into my car each morning can certainly be represented as derivative from my more basic intention to acquire resources for my family and myself: I climb into my car in order to get to work, and I work in order to acquire resources for my family and myself. But my highly specific intention to climb into my car can be derived from my more basic intention to acquire resources for my family and myself only because the means at my disposal for the pursuit of my ends are distinctly limited – I cannot acquire resources simply by conjuring them into existence, and I cannot get to work by flapping my arms and flying. Were the means at my disposal for the pursuit of my ends not limited, so that, for instance, I could conjure resources into existence, then no sense could be made of my intention to climb into my car each morning by reference to my intention to acquire resources for my family and myself. But a being hypothesized to be powerful enough to create life on earth must face – to put it mildly – considerably fewer limitations of means than I do, and fewer yet if hypothesized also to have created the whole universe and instituted all the laws of nature. So it is not surprising that it should be hard to represent such a being's intentions to create the diversity of biological facts that we actually observe as derivative from some more economical set of more basic intentions.

The second consideration against biological design arguments is that abundant biological phenomena *fail* to present an appearance of design. For example, the fact that the history of life on earth has been punctuated by several mass extinctions (probably caused by meteor or asteroid impacts), and that, on the usual estimate, more than 99 percent of the species that have ever existed are now extinct does not cry out, "Design!" Other examples are the "botched jobs," like the notorious panda's thumb (Gould 1980), which look either undesigned or else designed by someone operating under bizarre and apparently inexplicable constraints. Relatedly, there are those features, like the peacock's tail or the stag's antlers, which are conventionally explained by biologists in terms of sexual selection; these features perhaps do look designed, but certainly not designed to assist their owners to live long and prosper. Not that the hypothesis of deliberate creation is incapable in principle of accounting for such phenomena as these; on the contrary, to do so it need only attribute to the hypothesized creator just the right mixture of incompetence and whimsy. The trouble is that, if it does, it risks being impaled on the second horn of the dilemma identified two paragraphs ago, and becoming so unparsimonious and arbitrary as to constitute no progress whatever toward a satisfyingly unified explanation of the phenomena requiring explanation.[21]

The third consideration against biological design arguments is that hypotheses of deliberate creation have a rival: the hypothesis of evolution caused in large part by natural selection. This rival can explain not

---

21 A further consideration, which tells only against a Judeo-Christian theistic version of the hypothesis of deliberate creation, is, of course, that the world contains natural evils – states of affairs that, were they the intended or foreseen results of *human* action, would be judged (by Judeo-Christian moral standards) to be very bad unless necessary for some greater good, but which are *not* logically or metaphysically necessary for any greater good that anyone has ever been able to think of. An omnipotent, omniscient, morally perfect creator could have no reason to produce or allow any such states of affairs.

only the appearance of design in those biological entities that do appear designed, but also biological phenomena, like those mentioned earlier, that do not especially give the appearance of design. Moreover, suitably supplemented with independently testable auxiliary hypotheses, this rival can explain many detailed biological phenomena (e.g., detailed biogeographical facts, detailed patterns of homology, detailed patterns in the fossil record). And it accomplishes all this in a wonderfully economical way, by appeal to the repeated operation of fundamentally simple processes of kinds whose existence is independently confirmed. Finally, and contrary to a widespread prejudice, the hypothesis of evolution has generated novel predictions subsequently found to be true (see Futuyma 1995).[22]

Despite Plantinga, then, ascriptions of biological function in the end present no problem for realization physicalism.[23] So let us look elsewhere in biology for evidence that there exist biological tokens that are neither physical nor physically realized. But where? An answer can be found by noting that, as we saw in Chapter 3, realization physicalism, to the extent that it is retentive, entails a certain form of reductionism, which I called reductionism in the core sense; since this is so, any evidence against reductionism in the core sense will therefore automatically constitute evidence against (retentive) realizationism. Let us therefore search for such evidence in the writings of *antireductionists* about biology. Although these biological antireductionists may not be *aiming* to discredit reductionism in the core sense (for their targets may well be logically stronger forms of

---

[22] Richard Swinburne holds that the basic constituents and laws of the universe were deliberately created by God so that, via Darwinian evolution (whose reality he does not challenge), life would be likely or certain eventually to come into existence (1996, ch. 4). This moderate form of creationism, while much more plausible than others inasmuch as it does not need to dispute the abundant evidence for Darwinian evolution, must still confront both of the first two difficulties I have raised, as well, of course, as the problem of evil. Also, it is perhaps not entirely clear that biological entities produced in such a roundabout way as this thereby acquire functions.

[23] Plantinga presents two other arguments against naturalism that, if cogent, would tell also against realization physicalism (1993, ch. 12), and they are biological in the sense that they both allege that naturalistic evolutionism in biology is in some sort of trouble in light of the general reliability of our cognitive faculties; but I shall not be discussing them, and for two reasons. First, in their present form they have already been refuted to my complete satisfaction, so that further discussion would be otiose (see Fales 1996; Fitelson and Sober 1998). Second, although a genuinely perplexing question lies behind Plantinga's arguments – the question how our capacities to engage in advanced scientific and mathematical reasoning can have evolved by natural selection given that our hunter-gatherer ancestors did not engage in either – his discussion provides no serious attempt to answer it. (For a fascinating attempt to do so, however, see Pinker 1997, 186–205.)

reductionism), the considerations they deploy may nevertheless have that effect.

I begin with two philosophers of science who are biologically informed, and who have recently voiced their opposition to reductionism in biology.[24] The first, Harold Kincaid, opposes in particular the claim that cell biology is reducible to biochemistry (Kincaid 1997, 49–67). His arguments, supported by empirical examples, boil down to three (50–63). First, the phenomena treated by cell biology are sure to be *multiply realized* biochemically. Second, whether a certain biochemical phenomenon gives rise to the cell biological phenomenon that it underlies often depends on the *cell biological context* in which it arises. Third, biochemical accounts of cell biological phenomena often *presuppose* other cell biological phenomena.

However, it turns out that nothing in these arguments or in the empirical examples that Kincaid offers in their support constitutes any evidence against reductionism in the core sense (and hence against realizationism).[25] Reductionism in the core sense, it will be recalled, is the thesis that all nomic special- and honorary-scientific facts, and all positive nonnomic special- and honorary-scientific facts, have an explanation that appeals only to physical facts and necessary truths. But, as we saw in the development of this thesis in Chapter 3, reductionism in this sense is *consistent*

---

[24] Earlier philosophical opposition to reductionism in biology, focusing on the claim that classical Mendelian genetics is reducible to molecular biology, is analyzed and critically evaluated by C. Kenneth Waters (1990). Perusal of his discussion (and indeed of the papers he criticizes) reveals that the grounds for this earlier opposition to reductionism pose no more of a threat to realization physicalism than do the grounds for the more recent opposition to reductionism that I discuss later. One family of objections turns on the fact that, because of such empirically discovered facts as pleiotropy, polygeny, and the multiple realization of various genetic processes, classical Mendelian genes stand in no neat or even tractably specifiable relationship to the molecular conditions that realize them (for instance, they cannot simply be identified with segments of DNA); but no reason is given for thinking, nor is it even claimed, that classical Mendelian genes are not *realized* by (extraordinarily complex) molecular conditions. A second family of objections claims that, even if a derivation of the relevant explananda from molecular biological premises were manageable, it would provide an *inferior* explanation to an explanation in terms of the mechanisms spoken of in classical Mendelian genetics. But this does not entail that it would not provide *an* explanation, which is all that reductionism in the core sense requires. Compare my earlier discussions in Chapter 3, Section 5, and in Chapter 4, Section 4 (on the unobjectionability of something's having more than one explanation).

[25] This conclusion might seem unsurprising in light of the fact that Kincaid appears to profess himself a physicalist (1997, 1). But matters are not so simple. For it is not entirely clear from his *positive* view of the nature of interscientific relations that he is *entitled* to call himself a physicalist (1997, 6 and 65–7). And even if he is, the possibility remains that his antireductionist fervor has led him to endorse considerations that *contradict* his physicalism.

with the multiple realization of special- and honorary-scientific types; so Kincaid's first antireductionist argument leaves reductionism in the core sense unscathed.

His second argument fares no better. The fact that a token of a given biochemical type underlies a given cell biological phenomenon only if, and because, it occurs in a certain context poses no threat to reductionism in the core sense so long as the context itself is either physical or physically realized; for if it is, then a physical specification of the context could in principle be included as part of the reductive explanation, and specifiability in principle is enough for reductionism in the core sense. But Kincaid provides no reason at all for thinking that in biochemical explanations of cell biological phenomena the context itself is *not* either physical or physically realized. The empirical examples he cites merely support the claim that in certain biochemical explanations offered to date of particular cellular phenomena the context typically includes other cellular phenomena. But this claim is fully consistent with the physical – indeed biochemical – realization of these other phenomena. For the reason why extant biochemical explanations of cell biological phenomena refer to a context consisting in part of other cell biological phenomena may simply be that we have not yet discovered reductive biochemical explanations of these other phenomena and/or that we are constitutionally incapable of doing so; and even if we currently possessed a reductive biochemical explanation of every single cell biological phenomenon, we might still be unwilling (because of our peculiar explanatory needs and interests) to give a reductive explanation of every cellular phenomenon *at once*. Obviously it is logically *possible* that the reason why extant biochemical explanations of cell biological phenomena refer to a context consisting in part of other cell biological phenomena is that these other cell biological phenomena are emergent in the sense of not even being physically realized, so that the explanatory role they play cannot, even in principle, be reductively accounted for in terms of physical facts and necessary truths. But that this is a logical possibility, and indeed one that currently available evidence does not conclusively rule out, is not in dispute. The question is whether any positive reason exists for thinking that this undoubted possibility is actual; and my answer is that Kincaid's discussion provides no such reason. And essentially the same objection, of course, can be made to his third antireductionist argument. That extant biochemical accounts of cell biological phenomena often presuppose other cell biological phenomena does not tell us *why* they do so; and Kincaid provides no evidence for holding that the reason why is that these other cell biological phenomena are not reducible, even in principle, to biochemistry in the sort of way that reductionism in the core sense requires. For all that Kincaid has said, we can expect biochemistry to yield as many new explanations of cell biological phenomena over the next ten years as it has over the past ten years (for details, see Chapter 6, Section 5).

The second biologically informed philosopher of science whose opposition to reductionism in biology I discuss is John Dupré (1993, 102–45); his case is especially interesting since he does not consider himself to be a physicalist in any interestingly strong sense (92–3). His main argument against reductionism is not at all clear in detail, but the central idea is that the reduction of a biological theory requires biconditional bridge principles connecting its terms to those of the reducing (physical) theory; that such bridge principles hold only if biological types have essences; and that essentialism about biological types is false, so that the reduction of biological theories is impossible (1993, 103–5). Since our question is whether this argument tells, in particular, against reductionism in the core sense, we must ask whether its premises are true when the reductionism in question is reductionism in the core sense.

Even though the official target of Dupré's argument is the reducibility of *theories*, whereas reductionism in the core sense, as we lately noted, concerns the reducibility of *facts*, we can still ask whether reductionism in the core sense requires biconditional bridge laws connecting biological with physical types. The answer, as we saw in Chapter 3, is that the only bridge principles it requires to connect *all* biological types with *physical* types are one-way physical-to-biological laws that hold in all worlds in which the laws of physics hold. As we also saw, however, these bridge principles are themselves the consequence of biconditional bridge principles connecting biological types with physical types or (more probably) with *functional* types whose associated conditions can be specified physically or quasi-logically, these principles in turn following from the *identity* of every biological type either with some or other physical type or with some or other functional type that has a physically or quasi-logically specifiable associated condition. So we must now ask, in the spirit of Dupré's argument, whether the holding of these biconditional bridge principles – and of the a posteriori identities from which they follow – entails any sort of essentialism about biological types, and whether, if it does, the essentialism entailed is open to objection.

To begin with, is there anything essentialist about the idea that biological types should turn out a posteriori to be identical either with physical types or with functional types that have physically or quasi-logically specifiable associated conditions? One might call the idea essentialist on the grounds that if a biological type, B, *is* identical with some physical or functional type, F, then it is *necessarily* identical with it, so that B not only is but *must* be F, and anything that tokens B *must* token F too; and those "must"s certainly sound essentialist. But I see no sign that Dupré wishes to challenge the necessity of identity; and indeed it is hard to see how, given Leibniz's Law and the necessity of self-identity, he *could* resist the conclusion that, if B is F, then B *must* be F, and the further conclusion that *necessarily* something is a token of B iff it is a token of F. In fact, however, Dupré would probably count as essentialist the very idea that biological types should turn out a posteriori to be identical either with physical types or with functional types that have physically or quasi-logically specifiable associated conditions. For, if this idea is correct, there are, for every biological type, necessary and sufficient physical or functional conditions for something to be a token of that type; and he often seems to count as essentialist *any* view holding that there are necessary and sufficient conditions for something to be a token of a given type.

But, now, does Dupré have any good objection to essentialism in this rather weak sense? Despite his claim that "many scientific kinds...lack *any*...necessary and sufficient condition on membership" (1993, 105; emphasis in original), he surely cannot be right. For, assuming that our scientific concepts have determinate reference, there is a *trivial* necessary and sufficient condition for membership in every scientific kind: a kind concept, K, applies to something iff the thing is a K.[26] So what Dupré must be interpreted as objecting to is the idea that certain scientific kinds have *nontrivial* necessary and sufficient conditions on membership, that is, conditions on membership expressible using *different* concepts from those used to pick out the kinds in the first place; he must be claiming that even if, trivially, something is a B-token iff it is a B-token, there is in many cases no type, F, such that something is a B-token iff it is an F-token. The crucial question, therefore, becomes whether Dupré has any good objection to essentialism in this sense; for the presupposition of reductionism in the core sense that biological types should turn out a posteriori to be identical either with physical or suitably functional types is obviously a special case of essentialism in this sense.

He has no good objection to it. Toward the end of his presentation of the antireductionist argument I am now considering, he claims that

---

26 It is even true that "bald" applies to something iff it is bald. But Dupré's objections to essentialism appear unrelated to difficulties about the vagueness of predicates.

he has *already* refuted the essentialism to which reductionism is committed, presumably therefore somewhere in his chapters 1, 2, and 3 (Dupré 1993, 105). But although he may indeed have refuted *something* in those chapters, he has not refuted the particular essentialist claim required by reductionism in the core sense, the claim that biological types are in fact identical with physical or functional types. To see this, however, we must review those chapters, starting with chapter 1. There he defends the thesis that "it is far from universally the case that the preanalytic extension of a term of ordinary language corresponds to *any* recognized biological taxon" (27); so, for example, contrary to what is assumed (Dupré thinks) by the Putnam-Kripke view of natural-kind terms according to which such terms will turn out to refer to some scientific kind, the ordinary language term "moth" turns out not to pick out a kind of creature that is also picked out by any standard classificatory term drawn from scientific biology – and it is none the worse for that fact.

Now I find Dupré's thesis about the relation between biological and ordinary language terms for plants and animals quite plausible, and I certainly agree that, if it is true, then the ordinary language term "moth" is not thereby shown to be defective, nor are moths (in the ordinary sense) thereby shown to be unreal. But this thesis does not entail the falsity of the putatively essentialist claim that (folk) biological types are in fact identical with physical or suitably functional types. For the fact that ordinary language terms for plants and animals do not pick out kinds of creature picked out by standard classificatory terms used in scientific biology to refer to recognized biological taxa does not entail that they do not pick out kinds of creature that can be specified *somehow* in the language of scientific biology (e.g., by the use of terms *constructed* from the proprietary vocabulary of scientific biology); by the same token, neither does it entail that ordinary language terms for plants and animals do not in fact pick out physical or suitably functional kinds (though perhaps ones not expressible by the use of *simple* physical terms). Consistently with Dupré's thesis, then, "moth" might still pick out a physical or suitably functional type, albeit one bizarrely heterogeneous from the point of view of physics (or of any other science).[27]

---

27   It is not clear whether Dupré actually endorses the inference that I have just criticized, but he does claim in chapter 1 that "Ordinary language has a variety of aims in distinguishing kinds of organisms, and these need not coincide on the same classifications," adding that "the same is true even for scientific taxonomy" (1993, 34). But though he is no doubt right that the different "aims" of ordinary language *need* not "coincide on the same classifications," they still *might* do so – for all that the diversity of aims by itself proves; for concepts introduced for

Let us now turn to chapter 2, in which Dupré defends "a radically pluralistic conception of species." According to this pluralism about species, different inquiries within biology "may require different classificatory schemes" (1993, 50–1). In consequence, within the different theoretical contexts constituted by these inquiries what appears to be the same talk of species (e.g., the same use of terms for particular species) in fact picks out different groupings of individual organisms, so that "an organism might belong to both one kind defined by a genealogical taxonomy and another defined by an ecologically driven taxonomy" (58). But Dupré takes this pluralism about species to be a premise in an argument against essentialism, for he adds that "A pluralist, by denying that there is *any* uniquely correct scheme of classification, is clearly committed to the denial of essentialism" (53; emphasis in original). So Dupré's argument is that since pluralism about species is true, it follows that essentialism about species (i.e., the claim that there are necessary and sufficient conditions for being a member of any given species) is false.

Dupré's conclusion appears initially to be much more damaging to realizationism than it turns out to be on closer examination. It initially appears quite damaging, because if there really are *no* necessary and sufficient conditions for being a member of the species (say) *Homo sapiens sapiens*, then there can be no physical or suitably functional such conditions, so that being a human cannot in fact be identical with being a token of any physical or suitably functional type, contrary to realizationism. But upon closer examination Dupré's conclusion is far less damaging, for it is open to the realizationist to go nonretentive, and to deny that species really exist (e.g., to deny that any individual creature really *is* a member of the species *Homo sapiens sapiens*). Nor need such a denial be all that implausible. For it does not require denying the existence of the *individual organisms* usually supposed to belong to a given species; nor does it require denying the existence of extensive and varied *similarities* among these individual organisms (e.g., similarities in respect of morphology, molecular biology, ecology, and evolutionary history). In order to reinstate an objection to realizationism in the face of this nonretentivist move, Dupré would need to claim that being a member of a given species is an objective fact about

very different purposes, by groups of people under very different circumstances and with very different interests, *may* still turn out to designate the very same types. Furthermore, even if they do not, it is still possible that a member of one family of concepts should designate a type picked out by some concept *constructible* out of concepts belonging to some different family.

205

certain individual organisms, *and* (since he denies that species membership is a physical or suitably functional property) an objective fact *over and above* the exemplification by individual organisms of any merely physical or physically realized properties. But what evidence could he produce to support this claim that individual organisms exemplify a certain nonphysical and nonphysically realized property? Once we had described the gross morphology, the cellular and subcellular constitution, and the relations of descent of every individual organism, noted every relation of similarity between each and every individual, and in addition had explained all of this, all without using any species concept, nothing would be left, it seems, for the postulation of nonphysical and nonphysically realized species membership to explain. We would be just as well off without it.

But in fact Dupré's argument rests on an unsound inference: antiessentialism about species simply does not follow from pluralism about species. For even if, as pluralism maintains, there is no uniquely correct scheme for classifying individual organisms, but only a plurality of schemes corresponding to the plurality of branches of biological inquiry, it does not follow that essentialism is false regarding the species concept associated with each scheme. It is fully consistent with pluralism about species that there should exist, for each inquiry-relative species concept, a necessary and sufficient condition for an individual organism to belong to a given species of that inquiry-relative sort; such a necessary and sufficient condition might well be nontrivial, and might even consist in being a token of some physical or suitably functional type, as required by realization physicalism.[28] Perhaps to be a member of the species *Homo sapiens sapiens* when the theoretical context is genealogy is to be a token of *one* physical or suitably functional type, whereas to be a member of the species *Homo sapiens sapiens* when the theoretical context is ecology is to be a token of *another* physical or suitably functional type.

Dupré supplements this argument against essentialism about species with a brief survey of various suggested characterizations of the essence of a species (apparently assumed, no doubt *arguendo*, to be a single kind of thing across all contexts of biological inquiry), with a view to showing that each suggested characterization is defective; the candidate

---

28 Relatedly, the premise that there is no *uniquely* correct way of classifying individual organisms does not entail that it is not an entirely mind-independent matter whether or not some particular organism belongs to a given species of a particular, inquiry-relative sort. However, Dupré does in effect acknowledge this point, when he affirms the consistency of his pluralism with realism (1993, 57–8).

characterizations are gross morphological, microstructural, reproductive-isolationist, and phylogenetic (1993, 54–7). But Dupré's critical survey falls far short of establishing the falsity of essentialism about species. He does not discuss the possibility of *combining* the candidate characterizations in ingenious ways, which might easily succeed where each individual candidate fails. Nor are the specific criticisms that he makes of particular candidates always very convincing as they stand. He rejects the idea that necessary and sufficient conditions for membership in a species (of any kind) can be given in gross morphological terms; but in fact in vertebrate paleontology it is standard to classify species by reference to certain features of organisms' skeletons (often the only part of the animal available for scientific study), although this practice may merely be a proxy for phylogenetic classification. Against the suggestion that membership of a species is the having of the right sort of genetic constitution, he presents three reasons for thinking that "natural selection might tend to generate species with a high degree of genetic variation" (54). But even if this is right, it obviously leaves open the possibility that some sort of (perhaps quite intractable) *disjunctive* specification of genetic constitution is necessary and sufficient for an organism to belong to a given species. His discussion of this suggestion is the closest he comes to considering the possibility that membership of a species (of each of the possibly several sorts) should be identified with the tokening of some physical or physically realized type.

Although I hold no brief for any particular view as to *which* physical or functional type should be identified with membership of a species (of each of the sorts of species that there turn out to be), I would stress that there is no shortage of candidates. In line with Dupré's pluralism, let us assume that, associated with each branch of biological inquiry, there is a particular species concept, picking out a particular kind of species; let us assume also that the practitioners of each of these branches of biology are reliably able to determine which individual organisms belong to which species, so that, for each kind of species, there is a reasonably determinate set of individual organisms that are and would be assigned to any given species of that kind. Now because, as even Dupré admits, all organisms are in fact made of physical stuff, these sets are sets of things made of physical stuff. It is at least a possibility, then, that what the practitioners in each branch of biology are in fact tracking, whenever they exercise their reliable abilities to determine species membership, is something *physical or physically realized* that is necessary and sufficient for membership of particular species of the kind spoken of in that branch of biology. This something may be bizarrely complex and heterogeneous from a physical, and even from a molecular biological, point of view; it may reflect peculiarities of human cognitive equipment (e.g., our peculiar propensities to rank respects of similarity); its character may be extraordinarily difficult to discover; and there may be no especial value, to biology or to anything else, in actually discovering it; but there are any number of candidates for it that Dupré's critical survey has not ruled out.

Because it is entitled "Essentialism," Dupré's chapter 3 certainly sounds the likeliest of his earlier chapters to contain a good objection to the form of essentialism (if such it be) to which reductionism in the core sense, and hence realizationism to the extent that it is retentive, is committed. But in fact it contains no such objection, for the simple reason that the form of essentialism which is there attacked is neither identical with nor entailed by the form of essentialism required by reductionism in the core sense. Reductionism in the core sense, it will be recalled, requires that every biological type be identical with some or other physical or suitably functional type, so that — and this is the putative essentialism — for every biological type there is a nontrivial necessary and sufficient condition for something to be a token of that type. But the essentialism that Dupré attacks in chapter 3 is a stronger doctrine, including also an *explanatory* component. Because it is precisely this additional explanatory component to which Dupré objects, the essentialism required by reductionism in the core sense emerges from his attack quite unscathed.

According to the essentialism that Dupré attacks in his chapter 3, natural kinds have essences that may well be nontrivial necessary and sufficient conditions on kind membership, but which are also, and crucially, conceived as "*explaining the nature and properties* of the members of the kinds that such essences are supposed to determine" (1993, 64; emphasis added). Now Dupré's objection to the existence of essences in this stronger, explanatory sense is that, if they existed, they would provide a certain sort of epistemological shortcut, but that, since this shortcut is not always available, they do not always exist. They would provide an epistemological shortcut, because knowledge of an essence, understood in the stronger, explanatory sense, apparently "entitl[es] us to anticipate the existence of *laws* governing the behavior of objects that partake of it," laws connecting the essence to other, more superficial properties of the objects, and perhaps also, derivatively, laws connecting some superficial properties of the objects to others (63; emphasis added); so, for example, having determined the essence of (say) German shepherds by examining twenty dogs, and assuming that the essence of German shepherds by definition *explains* various other, perhaps more superficial, properties that German shepherds possess, we can be confident, *without actually bothering to examine any other animals*, that, so long as other animals possess the German shepherd essence, they too will possess the other, more superficial, German shepherd properties (61). But, Dupré argues, this promised epistemological shortcut is not always available, thus proving that essences in the stronger, explanatory sense do not always exist. Using sex as his main illustration, he concedes that sex does have an essence in the weaker, nonexplanatory sense: "What it is to be male or female ... is ... [the] property ... of producing relatively large or small gametes" (68). But since "whatever genetically determined behavioral differences there may be [between the sexes] are not, in fact, caused by the sex of the organism [defined in terms of relative gamete size]" but rather by "the sex-determining genetic structure," and since, more generally, "It is very doubtful whether there are any very significant laws relating to males and females in general," he concludes that sex does *not* have an essence in the stronger, explanatory sense (69). Now I take no stand on whether this objection of Dupré to essentialism in the stronger, explanatory sense succeeds.[29] My point is that, even if it does, it leaves unharmed the claim that there are essences in the weaker, nonexplanatory sense; and it is only essences in the weaker, nonexplanatory sense to which reductionism in the core sense is committed.

So Dupré's chapter 3 also fails to support his main argument against reductionism – at least if his target is construed as reductionism in the core sense. For, according to that argument, reductionism requires certain bridge principles, those bridge principles require essentialism, and essentialism is false; but Dupré equivocates on "essentialism," and the weaker, nonexplanatory essentialism required by reductionism in the core sense is neither identical with nor entails the stronger, explanatory essentialism that he directs his argument against in chapter 3. Nor does he say a word to suggest – what is in any case quite implausible – that reductionism (in any sense) requires the truth of the stronger, explanatory essentialism.

So much, then, for Dupré's main argument against reductionism, which has turned out not to provide any direct evidence against realization physicalism. Dupré also devotes two chapters to criticizing biological

---

29 I note, however, that it rests almost entirely on a single example, drawn from a single science, and that he does concede that noting the membership of an individual in some classes is more predictive than noting their membership in others (Dupré 1993, 64). For exposition and defense of explanatory essentialism of the sort Dupré rejects, see Hilary Kornblith (1993).

reductionism in particular, and he describes their task as being "to go into much greater detail" than does his rather abstract main argument (1993, 105). Worryingly, however, he goes on to say that "What the more detailed discussions will aim to show is that the kinds of factors appropriate for determining classifications at higher levels in many cases have nothing to do with the structural properties of objects" (105). Now this claim is not at all worrying if by "factors appropriate for determining classifications at higher levels" Dupré means something like *metaphysically necessary and sufficient conditions* for something to *be* a token of a given "higher level" type; for in that case his claim harmlessly states the conclusion for which he needs to argue – namely, that there are no necessary and sufficient "structural" (i.e., physical) conditions for the tokening of "higher level" types. But I strongly doubt that this is what he does mean. For in the next sentence he speaks, with no contrast apparently intended, of "the *grounds* of appropriate classification," and in the next chapter he claims that "the core *concepts* of science are exposed to conflicting pressure... from different structural levels," offering this as a reason against the (presumably reductive) unity of science (105 and 118; emphasis added). These alternative locutions encourage the suspicion that Dupré's "factors appropriate for determining classifications at higher levels" are really *epistemological* or *semantical* factors, rather than metaphysical ones – something like *ways of telling* that something is a token of a given "higher level" type, or perhaps a priori accessible *ways of thinking* of tokens of a given "higher level" type.

But *if* Dupré's "factors" are meant to be either ways of telling or ways of thinking, then he is proposing to commit a fallacy. For even if the "more detailed discussions" of his later chapters *do* show in either of *these* senses of "factors" that "the factors appropriate for determining classifications at higher levels in many cases have nothing to do with the structural properties of objects," no metaphysically antireductionist conclusion follows. For from the fact that "higher level" scientists have a standard way of telling whether something is a token of type, B, and other, "structural level," scientists have a different standard way of telling whether something is a token of physical or functional type, F, it does not follow that B and F are distinct types – any more than the distinctness of table salt and NaCl follows from the fact that ordinary folks' standard way of telling whether a heap of white crystals is salt differs from professional chemists' standard way of telling whether a heap of white crystals is NaCl. In neither case does the metaphysical conclusion of distinctness follow from the epistemological premise: for a *single* type might be such that there are *two* ways, each standard in a different context of inquiry, of

210

telling whether something is a token of it. Similarly, from the fact that "higher level" scientists, in thinking of a type, B, employ a certain way of thinking of it, and other, "structural level," scientists, in thinking of physical or functional type, F, employ a different way of thinking of F, it does not follow that B and F are distinct; for one and the same type might be such as to have *two* ways of thinking of it.[30]

Be all that as it may, let us now look more closely at the first of Dupré's specialist chapters on biological reductionism, in which he alleges the irreducibility of ecology, understood as "the study of the determinants of the abundance, or relative abundance, of particular kinds of organism" (1993, 108). In particular, he claims to show that "laws concerning the dynamics of populations could not be derived from any amount of information about the properties of the individuals that constitute those populations" (114). Now this is a very strong claim, or at any rate sounds like one: it sounds as if Dupré is claiming to have found empirical evidence for holding that populations of real organisms wax and wane in some kind of irreducibly holistic fashion not explainable, even in principle, in terms of the properties, relations, and particular environments of the individual organisms that make up those populations, together with their interactions.[31] And certainly if Dupré *had* discovered such evidence, it would constitute evidence against reductionism in the core sense and therefore direct evidence against realization physicalism. But in fact he has discovered no such evidence, and appears, indeed, despite the thesis statement just quoted, never to have intended to do so.

In order to see this, we must examine the case Dupré actually makes for the irreducibility of ecology. Because it is a little obscure, we should begin with an extended quotation:

[T]he general failure of reductionism may be attributed to the following fact: the individuals that would have to be assumed for the derivation of the macrotheory cannot be identified with those that are the subjects of descriptive accounts at the next-lower level. . . . The possibility of this non-identity is to be explained by the fact that the individuals at both levels are idealizations.[32] Both models at the

---

30 I do not myself believe in "ways of thinking," if these are assumed to be accessible a priori to the thinker (see Melnyk 2001); but I use the expression because I suspect it corresponds to Dupré's own assumptions, and I wish to avoid needless controversy.

31 Contrast the following claim from the distinguished mainstream ecologist Robert May: "The behaviour of populations is inherently derivable from the behaviour of the underlying individuals" (1998, 194).

32 Despite Dupré's talk here of the nonidentity of *individuals* across levels, it is clearly the nonidentity of organism *types* that he is asserting. For, as earlier noted, Dupré holds that

macrolevel and descriptive accounts or laws at the microlevel involve abstractions. But the abstractions involved are not the same.... the idealized individuals that form the basis of models in population ecology are distinct from those that might be described by physiologists or behavioral psychologists. (1993, 116)

What exactly is the argument here? On one interpretation, when Dupré speaks of individual organisms at both levels as "idealizations," he means to imply that they do not really exist, just as idealized frictionless surfaces and ideal gases do not really exist. But in that case Dupré's argument, even if sound, cuts no ice against reductionism in the core sense. For reductionism in the core sense requires the reduction only of biological *facts* of certain kinds and does not require the reduction of *theories* (or models) if, properly construed, they are true at best of ideal, and hence unreal, entities. Of course, to the extent that such theories (or models) are supplemented or modified so that they generate true generalizations about entities that do exist, reductionism in the core sense requires that those generalizations should in principle have reductive physical explanations. But a separate and independent argument would be needed to show that they lack reductive explanations, and no such argument is offered.

On an alternative interpretation, however, when Dupré speaks of individuals at both levels as "idealizations," he merely means that, although both the reduced and reducing theories characterize perfectly real organisms, they each focus on only some of the totality of attributes that individual organisms in all their concrete richness possess, while neglecting others; and when he remarks that "the abstractions involved are not the same" in both theories, he is simply pointing out that each theory abstracts away from, and hence neglects, a *different* set of attributes. But does this point tell against reductionism in the core sense? I do not see how. It plausibly entails that the ecologist's (say) hare cannot be *type-identified* with the physiologist's hare, for a concrete animal may count as a hare in ecology in virtue of possessing different attributes from those in virtue of which the very same animal counts as a hare in physiology, so that *being a hare$_{ecol}$* is distinct from *being a hare$_{phys}$*. But reductionism in the core sense is unaffected, since it does not require type identity between the entities mentioned in the reduced theory and those mentioned in the reducing theory. It *does* require, of course, that the types mentioned in the reducing theory are such that their tokens are *realized* by tokens of types mentioned in the reducing theory – or, at any rate, are realized physically

<blockquote>reductionism requires *biconditional* bridge principles, which token identities in the *absence* of type identities would not guarantee.</blockquote>

somehow; so the interesting question is whether Dupré's point proves that *that* requirement cannot be met. But it does not. For even if ecology and physiology focus on different sets of attributes of such concrete organisms as hares, the attributes on which ecology focuses, as well as those on which physiology focuses, may all nevertheless be suitably functional, with their tokens physically realized. Perhaps *being a hare$_{ecol}$* is itself a functional object kind, and each actual object of this functional kind is in fact realized by an object of the distinct functional kind, *being a hare$_{phys}$*, embedded in a suitable environmental context; or perhaps hares$_{ecol}$ do not have hares$_{phys}$ as their narrow realizers, but are instead realized by tokens of physical or functional types that play no significant or standard role in any branch of any science, but which are nonetheless characterizable in purely physical or quasi-logical terms, albeit terms of mind-boggling complexity. Either way, Dupré's point is entirely consistent with realization physicalism.

Dupré, however, might at this stage protest that his point has been underinterpreted: when he claims that the reduced theory and the reducing theory focus, respectively, on different sets of attributes of concrete organisms, he means that these sets are different in a very strong sense. He means that, in line with his pluralism, *being a hare$_{ecol}$* and *being a hare$_{phys}$* are, though equally genuine features of reality, so completely independent of one another that object tokens of the former kind are not even *realized* by object tokens of the latter kind; indeed, object tokens of both kinds are basic, and hence not physically realized at all. But although this stronger reading of Dupré's point probably is an accurate representation of his metaphysics, it can hardly serve as a premise in a non-question-begging argument against realizationism unless he offers some substantive empirical evidence that tokens of ecological types are not in fact physically realized – evidence, perhaps, that populations of real hares behave in ways that are not explainable, even in principle, in terms of such physical (or physically realized) factors as the properties, relations, and particular environments of the individual hares that make up those populations; but, as already noted, such evidence is conspicuously absent. Where the appearance of such evidence might have been expected, we find instead an assortment of claims about the differing aims and interests of different branches of biology, and of the different pressures the concepts drawn from these respective branches face; but claims of this sort, as we saw a few paragraphs ago, are incapable of establishing the nonidentity of biological types with physical or suitably functional types, and hence incapable of falsifying realizationism.

Let us therefore turn now to the second of Dupré's specialist chapters on biological reductionism, in which he argues for the irreducibility to molecular genetics of (i) classical Mendelian (transmission) genetics, (ii) the study of the processes of ontogeny, and (iii) population genetics (1993, 121–2). Fortunately, it is easy to see that his case, at least as applied to reductionism in the core sense, is weak. For he writes that "the grounds of my antireductionist position are as follows: the genes described structurally by the molecular geneticist are not *the same things* as those referred to in the models of population genetics or even of classical transmission genetics" (122; emphasis added). Evidently, then, he is assuming that the reductionist theses he opposes require the holding of certain transtheoretic type-identities between genes as understood by the theory to be reduced and genes as understood by molecular biology. Reductionism in the core sense, however, does not require transtheoretic type-identities of this kind: it can allow the nonidentity of each *type* of (e.g.) classical Mendelian gene with some *type* of segment of genetic material, so long as each *token* of a classical Mendelian gene is in fact *realized* by a *token* of some type of DNA segment, suitably circumstanced in an appropriate biochemical environment.

The only remaining question is whether Dupré's *reasons* for denying that (e.g.) classical Mendelian gene types are identical with types of DNA segment *also* constitute reasons for denying that all classical Mendelian gene tokens are even realized by suitably circumstanced tokens of types of DNA segment. But the answer is that they clearly do not. For his reasons for denying the trans theoretic type-identity claims rest upon appeals to what is, in effect, the molecular-biological *multiple realization* of classical Mendelian genes (1993, 125–7); to what he calls a "broadly *functional* interpretation of... chromosomes" (128; emphasis added); and to the idea that "different kinds of enquiry will require different classifications *of chromosomes or chromosomal events*" (128; emphasis added).[33] And such

---

33 There is perhaps an additional appeal to *vagueness*, as when he claims that it might be arbitrary whether or not certain molecules should count as hemoglobin (Dupré 1993, 126); but he gives no reason to deny that, for every arbitrary precisification of "hemoglobin," the referent would turn out to be physical or physically realized. Similarly, in his "broadly functional" approach, Dupré *may* be appealing to the idea I called in Chapter 3 the *strong realization-independence* of special- and/or honorary-scientific generalizations, as when he alleges that psychological reductionism "fails to capture the *full scope* of... psychological generalizations" (1993, 128; emphasis added); but he presents no *evidence* for regarding psychological generalizations as being strongly realization-independent in my sense.

appeals are fully consistent with realizationism;[34] they neither provide nor even purport to provide evidence that classical Mendelian genes fail to be realized by suitably circumstanced tokens of types of DNA segment (e.g., they provide no evidence that classical Mendelian genes ever behave in ways that could not even in principle be explained in purely physical terms on the assumption that they are physically realized tokens of functional types). Reductionism in the core sense, and the retentive realizationism that entails it, thus emerge unscathed once more.

Dupré's animadversions on population genetics, however, are of a different character, for, while intriguing, the main conclusion to which they lead is not antireductionism at all, but rather a thesis of local antirealism: "[E]ven if population genetics models were to show significant empirical success in modeling changes in genetic frequencies in a population, they could not be interpreted realistically" (1993, 135); and since antirealism about population genetics is consistent with realization physicalism, I need not contest it.[35] But in the course of his discussion, Dupré makes a claim that, on one interpretation at least, does pose a direct challenge to realization physicalism: he claims that gene frequencies "are, so to speak, dragged along by the selective processes that take place at the organismic level" (137). Literally expressed, the claim here is surely that *macroscopic* processes of natural selection operating on the organism *cause* those changes in *microscopic* gene frequencies that (according to population genetics) constitute evolution. On one interpretation, however, this claim poses no challenge to realization physicalism. According to this interpretation, although the claim asserts the occurrence of what is sometimes called "downward" (i.e., macro-to-micro) causation, the causal powers of the claimed macroscopic causes – the operation of natural selection on organisms – are still reducible in the core sense, that is, they are in principle completely explainable in physical terms (together with certain necessary truths).

---

34 In fact, they sound positively realizationist in spirit! Indeed, since Dupré never discusses realization physicalism, not even in the form defended in Boyd's pioneering 1980 essay, it is just about conceivable that, for all his general hostility to physicalism, he would take no exception to it.

35 I do wonder, however, whether a defender of a realistic interpretation of population genetics could reply to Dupré's argument (that so-called fitnesses are unprojectable, since they are so dependent upon the nature of the genetic environment surrounding any given gene) by treating a gene's fitness as a *function* from genetic environments to probabilities of being transmitted into the next generation; such functions presumably would be stable.

Thus interpreted, the claim is consistent with realizationism – at least it is if the account of causation presented in my Chapter 4 is correct and itself consistent with realizationism. For, on that account of causation, so long as appropriate regularities hold between the relevant macroscopic events and the relevant microscopic events, the macroscopic events will count as perfectly good causes of the microscopic events; and there is no reason why the appropriate regularities should not hold. So if Dupré's claim that gene frequencies are dragged along by selective processes is interpreted in this way, as merely asserting the occurrence of *reducible* downward causation, then it might well be literally true that (say) the macroscopic event of the contraction, by some population, of a certain viral disease caused a change in gene frequencies; but so long as the contraction of this disease had its microeffect entirely in virtue of the operation of such molecular-biological, and ultimately physical, processes as cell invasion and the hijacking of cellular machinery, it poses no threat to realization physicalism – and similarly for other macroscopic natural-selectional causes of changes in gene frequencies.

In order for Dupré's claim that gene frequencies are "dragged along by the selective processes that take place at the organismic level" to contradict and therefore to challenge realizationism, it must be interpreted as asserting the occurrence of *irreducible* downward causation – the claim must assert that the causal powers of natural-selectional causes at the organismic level *cannot* be explained, even in principle, by reference to physical conditions (plus certain necessary truths). Were such a claim true, then macroscopic natural-selectional causes would produce changes in gene frequencies that you would not have expected them to produce, on the basis of knowledge of those causes' physical realizers, of the physical realizers of the changes in gene frequencies, of the physical relations in which all these things stand to one another and to their surrounding physical conditions, of physical laws, and of all pertinent necessary truths asserting the identity of a nonphysical with some physical or suitably functional type. And there could in principle be *evidence* that macroscopic natural-selectional causes do in fact produce changes of exactly this sort in gene frequencies. But Dupré does not offer any such evidence. So when his claim about the macrocausation of changes in gene frequencies is interpreted in such a way that it does challenge realizationism, the claim turns out to be unsupported. In an earlier chapter, Dupré had claimed that "there are genuinely causal entities at many different levels of organization" and that "lower-level events may perfectly well be determined by what is happening at a higher level" (1993, 101 and 102), claims for which his later claim about gene frequencies is presumably intended to provide a concrete illustration. Of course, his earlier general claims are also ambiguous as to whether the downward causation they assert is reducible or irreducible, and the critical line just taken against the illustrative claim about gene frequencies applies also to them, mutatis mutandis.

So much, then, for Dupré's case against reductionism in biology, which has turned out to lack all force when directed against reductionism in the core sense, and hence to provide no direct evidence against realization physicalism.[36] Let us now therefore turn from philosophers of biology to actual biologists and ask whether *they* have any evidence that there are nomic and/or positive nonnomic biological facts for which there is not even *an* explanation that appeals only to physical facts and appropriate necessary truths. Since obviously I cannot undertake a comprehensive survey of biologists, I instead examine the contributions to a recent volume whose title, *The Limits of Reductionism in Biology*, and the distinction of whose contributors (they are all, with one exception, scientists, mostly life scientists, and they have unimpeachably respectable credentials) encourage the expectation that it surely mentions empirical evidence against reductionism if such evidence is in fact known to contemporary biology (Bock and Goode 1998). In confining my attention to this volume, I am assuming that it provides a representative sample of biologists' thinking about reductionism; I should also add that I selected this volume for discussion because I knew that it contained critiques of reductionism

---

36 The failure of Dupré's case against reductionism in the core sense has a noteworthy consequence for an argument he wishes to launch against the assumption of what he calls "causal completeness," the assumption that "for every event there is a complete causal story to account for its occurrence" (1993, 99); the argument is that, since reductionism is false, and since causal completeness requires reductionism, causal completeness must be false (102). Obviously Dupré's argument has an unsupported premise if he has failed to show that reductionism is false. The argument also suffers from other flaws. Causal completeness alone could not possibly require reductionism, since a Cartesian dualist world could be a deterministic one, in which case causal completeness would be true while reductionism of every kind was false. In fact, however, in his detailed exposition of the reasoning that allegedly leads from causal completeness to "reducibility at least in principle" (100–1), Dupré includes, as indeed he must include, certain additional premises (e.g., the contingent assumption that human hands are composed of microphysical particles); so he does not really mean that causal completeness alone requires reductionism. Also, and somewhat bizarrely, in the detailed reasoning the assumption of causal completeness does not actually appear as a premise! The look-alike premise doing the work evidently intended for it is the claim that every *microphysical* event has a complete *microphysical* causal explanation, which the assumption of causal completeness as officially formulated does not entail (any more than that every philosopher has a parent entails that every happy philosopher has a happy parent).

in biology, but without knowing whether those critiques had any force against reductionism in the core sense.[37]

In fact, however, no contributor to the volume either presents or cites even the tiniest shred of empirical evidence against reductionism in the core sense. Not that the contributors fail to include several scientists who are highly skeptical of reductionism. However, all the contributors whose skepticism about reductionism goes beyond pointing out the obvious fact that many biological phenomena have not yet been reduced assume definitions of "reductionism" that impose on the truth of reductionism some requirement that reductionism in the core sense does not impose; and because in every case their argument is that reductionism fails precisely because this requirement is not met, the frequently interesting things they have to say simply leave reductionism in the core sense untouched. For example, Paul Nurse expresses his opposition to reductionism by claiming that "to explain living things completely in terms of their basic components...may neither be practically possible nor even necessary to provide an adequate explanation of living phenomena" (1998, 93). But this claim implicitly assumes that reductionism is true only if (a) it *is* "practically possible" to discover complete reductive explanations, and (b) reductive explanations of living phenomena *are* necessary for providing adequate explanations of those phenomena. But reductionism in the core sense does not impose either of these requirements: it does not require the explainability in practice, only in principle, of facts to be reduced, and it leaves open the possibility that a single biological phenomenon should have more than one adequate explanation (e.g., a reductive and a nonreductive one), so that a reductive explanation of a biological phenomenon is not necessary in order for the phenomenon to have an adequate explanation.

Neither does the substance of Nurse's case against the practical possibility of completely explaining living things in terms of their basic components tell at all against reductionism in the core sense. For this case is in fact directed against one particular methodology for *discovering* reductionist explanations (viz., the combining of biological molecules in vitro and the observation of what then happens) and consists in pointing out that biological molecules in vitro differ from the same molecules in vivo in various respects which are in fact relevant to giving reductive

---

[37] A generation ago, the chemist and philosopher Michael Polanyi argued that biology is not reducible to physics and chemistry; for an effective critique, however, see Robert Causey (1969).

biochemical explanations of real cellular phenomena; for instance, biological molecules in vitro differ from the same molecules in vivo in respect of their biochemical environment, their structure, their concentrations, and their spatial separations from one another (Nurse 1998, 94–5). But to point out such things is merely to point out that laboratory experiments sometimes abstract away from, and hence ignore, significant explanatory factors that operate in the real world; Nurse makes no suggestion that there exists any barrier *in principle* to the explanation of cellular phenomena in biochemical terms, and indeed he allows that there is scope for techniques in computational modeling to overcome the practical obstacles to discovering reductive explanations that he mentions (Nurse 1998, 99; see also Brenner 1998). Nurse's putatively antireductionist position therefore closely resembles that of another contributor, molecular biologist Richard Henderson, who does *not* regard himself as an antireductionist. Henderson writes: "The reductionist approach in this field seems to be limited only by the accuracy by which it is possible to describe inter- and intra-molecular interactions in terms of hydrogen bonds, van der Waals interactions and electrostatic forces. At present, there is no fundamental limit in sight" (1998, 36).

Another contributor to the volume whose opposition to reductionism leaves reductionism in the core sense unscathed is the physical chemist R. J. P. Williams. The central tenet of the reductionism he opposes is that "a complex system can be *fully reduced* in terms of its component parts" (Williams, 1998, 15; emphasis in original). But although this formulation of reductionism may sound harmless, it imposes on reductionism a very strong requirement, namely, that a reductive explanation of a complex system may appeal *only* to the system's *component parts*. Reductionism in the core sense, however, does not impose this requirement: it allows that a reductive explanation of a complex system may appeal to factors that are *not* among the system's component parts (e.g., features of its *environment*). But it is precisely a failure to meet the very strong additional requirement that he imposes on reductionism that Williams gives as his grounds for rejecting reductionism. For he claims that while a lake can be "fully reductively described," a river cannot; and his reason is simply that the water in a river is constantly affected by factors *external* to the river itself, such as the Sun's heat and gravitational forces, which vary with the contours of the land over which the water in the river flows (22). Because reductionism in the core sense would allow the citation of external factors in a reductive explanation of a river, reductionism in the core sense is quite consistent with Williams's antireductionism.

A third example of opposition to reductionism that leaves reductionism in the core sense unscathed is provided by the distinguished physiologist Dennis Noble, who cites his own work on heartbeat to demonstrate what he terms "the limits of the reductive approach" (1998, 56). But the burden of his cry turns out to be not that the functioning (or malfunctioning) of a heart involves properties that are not even in principle explainable in biochemical terms, but that, despite our knowing so much about the biochemical *parts* of a heart, the "integrative work," as he calls it, needed to show how those parts interact with one another and with biochemical factors external to the heart so as to produce the observed working of a heart has by and large not been done (Noble, 1998, 56; similarly, see Barlow 1998, 148ff.). In effect, then, Noble identifies the reductionism he rejects with a certain research program, that of first taking biological complexes to pieces, and next investigating the properties of the pieces, but then *stopping* before any explanation of the complex has been achieved. But reductionism thus understood is a far cry indeed from reductionism in the core sense. Strictly speaking, of course, reductionism in the core sense is not a research program at all, but rather a thesis, properly evaluatable as true or false; but to the extent that it *suggests* a research program, it suggests one according to which discovering the biochemical parts of a biological complex is valuable only because, having done so, you do *not* stop, but rather go on to *explain* the biological complex. So Noble does not have reductionism in the core sense in his sights at all. Indeed, an examination of his detailed discussion confirms that, despite his emphasis on the limits of reductionism, he means to cast no doubt at all on the implication of reductionism in the core sense that all cardiac phenomena are in principle explainable in terms of their biochemical constituents, the enormously complex biochemical properties of and interrelations among those constituents, and the equally complex biochemical relations between those constituents and the biochemical phenomena that constitute their environment.

Noble does make the antireductionist-sounding remark that the oscillation of a single cell of the sinoatrial node of the heart (where natural heart rhythm is generated) is "a *global property* of the complete system of ionic transporters [in the cell]" (emphasis added). When we read on, however, we learn that apparently we can record "the opening and closing kinetics of the individual ion transporters... set up systems of differential equations accurately describing these kinetics and then incorporate them all into an integrated description of the cell," thereby enabling us "fully to reconstruct the pacemaker rhythm" (Noble 1998, 57). In fact, therefore,

Noble intended by his use of the phrase "global property" nothing that conflicts with reductionism in the core sense. He goes on to report, however, that when these sinoatrial cells are isolated from the sinoatrial node, "they all beat at different frequencies," instead of at the same frequency, as in normal heartbeat (58–9); and this remarkable fact might encourage an emergentist to hope that, contrary to reductionism in the core sense, the synchronized beating of heart cells when they form collectives in actual hearts is not explainable, even in principle, in biochemical terms, even if their beating as individuals in vitro is so explainable. But the emergentist idea is certainly not what Noble intends. For he adds that "[I]t is possible to show, using a multicellular model in which large numbers of SA [sinoatrial] node cells are connected up into a network, that these interconnections . . . ensure synchronization [of the beating of individual cells]" (59). Finally, however, Noble informs us that in these multicellular models something very strange happens: "[T]he wave of excitation propagates in towards the centre, not out towards the rest of the heart [as actually happens in real hearts]" (59). But the explanation for this result is merely that the multicellular model ignores the biochemical *environment* of the sinoatrial node: "[T]o reconstruct the whole node to account for normal rhythm, you also need to connect it up to the atrium," since "[t]he electrical interactions between the atrial cells and the sinus node are so large that they are responsible for determining the sequence of excitation within the node and for ensuring that the signal propagates outwards towards the atrium itself" (59). In short, then, although Noble's examples brilliantly illustrate the important point that in order to provide a reductive explanation of some feature of a complex biological system, it is necessary to take into account both interactions among the constituents of the system and interactions between these constituents and elements in the system's environment, they have no tendency to show (nor does Noble think otherwise) that reductive explanations of the sort reductionism in the core sense implies to be possible are not really so.

The only other contributor to *The Limits of Reductionism in Biology* who seems to have any sort of in-principle objection to reductionism is Steven Rose, but his main aim is to attack the sort of reductionism with which sociobiologists or evolutionary psychologists are charged when they offer selectionist explanations of human behavior. He does devote a short discussion to what he calls "philosophical reductionism," concluding with the remark that "Wholes, emerging, may in themselves constrain or demand the appearance of parts" (Rose 1998, 177–8). But although this remark *may* be intended to express something incompatible with reductionism in the core sense (e.g., what in my discussion of Dupré I called irreducible downward causation), Rose neither presents nor cites any evidence for thinking that the remark is true. At least as revealed by *The Limits of Reductionism in Biology*, then, the limits of reductionism in biology constitute no direct evidence against realization physicalism.

4. INDIRECT EVIDENCE AGAINST REALIZATION PHYSICALISM

Our search for direct evidence against realization physicalism in psychology and biology has yielded no evidence that there exist psychological or biological tokens, falling within the scope of (R), that are neither physical nor physically realized. But is there any *indirect* evidence against realization physicalism? One potential source of such evidence lies in the fact that realization physicalism entails the thesis that the physical is *closed*, a thesis that we could in principle discover empirically to be false. On the assumption of universal determinism, realization physicalism entails the closure thesis that for every physical token there is a preceding physical condition that is sufficient for it, given the physical laws.[38] For suppose there were a physical token that had *no* preceding sufficient condition that was physical; since, by universal determinism, this token must have *some* preceding sufficient condition, this condition would have to be in part nonphysical and nonphysically realized, which would contradict the assumption of realizationism. (This condition would have to be nonphysically realized as well as nonphysical, for if it were nonphysical but physically realized, its physical realizer, being sufficient for it, would help make up a physical condition sufficient for the physical token we were originally supposing to *lack* a preceding sufficient physical condition.) So if this closure thesis were found to be false, then, so long as the assumption of universal determinism was retained, realization physicalism would have to be rejected as false also.

However, in view of the irreducibly indeterministic character of quantum mechanics, the assumption of universal determinism should

---

[38] However, this closure thesis, though entailed by realizationism, does not entail realizationism; for it might hold true while there existed nonphysical and nonphysically realized tokens that were *causally isolated* from every physical token, or while there existed nonphysical and nonphysically realized tokens that *overdetermined* the existence/occurrence of certain physical tokens.

presumably be rejected. So what closure thesis does realizationism entail given indeterminism? On the assumption that every physical token has some determinate probability (possibly < 1) of existing given preceding conditions and laws, it entails the probabilistic closure thesis that for every physical token its probability of existing given preceding conditions and laws of *all* kinds *equals* its probability of existing given preceding *physical* conditions and laws. We now therefore have the potential for indirect evidence against realizationism, because this probabilistic closure thesis might conceivably be discovered to be false: we might discover some physical type such that, in two circumstances identical with regard to all physically relevant physical factors but different psychologically, tokens of this physical type have different determinate probabilities of occurring; or we might compute the probability that some physical type be tokened, given the totality of physically relevant physical factors in certain circumstances, but then discover empirically that the actual probability in such circumstances was, though determinate, not as predicted.[39] But has the probabilistic closure thesis actually been discovered to be false? I have been able to find no evidence against it at all. It is true that certain experiments in parapsychology have been intended to demonstrate psychokinetic influence on the probabilities of microphysical events; but these experiments are open to very grave objections (Alcock 1990, 81–110). It is also true that John Dupré has interestingly challenged the assumption that every event (whether physical or not) even *has* a determinate probability of occurring, given earlier events and laws (1993, 194–214); but he provides no reason to think that any physical events do have determinate probabilities, given earlier events and laws, but that their probabilities given earlier events and laws fail to equal their probabilities given earlier *physical* events and physical laws. I conclude, then, that realizationism's commitment to the closure of the physical yields no actual indirect evidence against it.

In the remainder of this section, however, I shall show that another potential source of indirect evidence against realization physicalism does indeed yield some actual evidence against it, but that its impact on realization physicalism is very much smaller than has sometimes been thought; and I shall show this via an examination of what some philosophers, as we

---

39 By calling a physical factor "physically relevant" to the tokening of a physical type, I mean that the laws of physics imply that the physical factor could in principle affect the probability of a tokening of the type. It follows that the physical conditions preceding the tokening of a given type could therefore include physical factors that were *not* physically relevant to it.

saw in Chapter 1, have supposed to be a knockdown argument against any formulation of physicalism that, like realizationism, defines "physical" in terms of current physics.

Here is the putatively knockdown argument, which we may call "the historical objection." Past theories in physics, when judged from the standpoint of current physics, have usually turned out to be false; it is therefore very likely (though not, of course, absolutely certain) that current physics will also turn out to be false. But if so, and if physicalism formulated in terms of current physics assumes the truth of current physics, then it is very likely (though not, of course, absolutely certain) that physicalism is false too – which requires one to cease to be a physicalist. A variant on the objection argues that since past theories in physics have usually turned out to be *incomplete*, current physical theories are very likely incomplete also. But since physicalism formulated in terms of current physics is false if current physics is incomplete, it follows again that physicalism is very likely to be false – which also requires one to cease being a physicalist.[40]

My reply to the historical objection – and equally to the variant – is to challenge its final step: the inference that one should cease to be a physicalist just because physicalism is very likely false. The objection assumes that a physicalist is someone who must assign a high (i.e., > 0.5), or even very high, probability to the thesis of physicalism, wherefore it is unreasonable for a physicalist to define "physical" in terms of current

---

40 The past history of physical theorizing is not the only evidence relevant to an assessment of the truth or falsity of current physics, since independent (i.e., nonhistorical, observational) evidence that current physics is true must also be taken into account; and when this other evidence is taken into account, it is far from obvious that current physics will emerge on balance as very unlikely (see Michael Levin 1979, 407–24, especially 420–1). Similarly, the past history of physical theorizing is not the only evidence relevant to current physics's likelihood of being *complete*. For the fact that we know of no (physical) phenomena which we have reason to think that current physics cannot *in principle* explain provides independent, nonhistorical evidence that current physics is complete.

Let me note also that it is not entirely clear what "incomplete" in the variant on the historical objection should or even could mean. The intuitive idea is that current physics is incomplete iff it fails to mention some entity or property which (a) exists and which (b) would, if discovered, unhesitatingly be classified as physical – such a thing as a new particle with mass, charge, and spin; but, put that way, the idea presupposes that we have a viable conception of "physical" in terms of which we could steer between the horns of Hempel's dilemma (see Chapter 1, Section 2), defining "physical" more broadly than in terms of current physics, but not so broadly as to evacuate "physical" of content determinable now by us.

physics if doing so implies that physicalism is improbable. But I deny this assumption, claiming that a physicalist need *not* assign a high probability to physicalism, and can therefore comfortably live with the result that physicalism has a very low probability. However, there are different ways of developing such a reply to the argument, ways that vary in their positive account of what attitude to physicalism a physicalist should take. For instance, one could say that a physicalist is someone who merely treats the thesis of physicalism as some sort of regulative ideal for science, a role it could play while being literally false (Hellman 1985, 610). Alternatively, one could say that a physicalist is someone who holds that physicalism, while literally false, is nevertheless closer to the truth, a better approximation to the truth, than its rivals. But both these suggestions have drawbacks. The first requires us to abandon the intuition that a physicalist is someone who takes some sort of attitude toward the *truth* of physicalism. The second can only be as good as the account of verisimilitude or approximation to the truth on which it relies, and these notions are notoriously hard to explicate satisfactorily. By contrast, the account I give respects the intuition that a physicalist is someone who takes some sort of attitude toward the truth of physicalism; and it has no dependence on the concepts of verisimilitude or approximation to the truth.

My development of a different basis for the claim that a physicalist need not regard physicalism as more probable than not involves giving an account not of the thesis of physicalism, which was satisfactorily formulated in Chapter 1, but of what sort of *attitude* toward that thesis is required in order to be a physicalist. Intuitively, the idea is that partisans of physicalism are no more obliged to regard physicalism as more probable than not than are partisans of *any* scientific hypothesis obliged to regard that hypothesis as more probable than not; it turns out, in both cases, that it is enough to regard the favored view merely as the best theory that we have so far. Here is my detailed argument in outline.

(P1) To be a physicalist is to take the same attitude – whatever that attitude is – toward the hypothesis of physicalism that those who have broadly scientific realist and antirelativist intuitions take toward what they regard as the best of current scientific hypotheses.

(P2) The attitude that those who have broadly scientific realist and antirelativist intuitions take toward what they regard as the best of current scientific hypotheses is identical with an attitude (to be defined later) that I shall call the *SR attitude*.

(C1) Therefore, to be a physicalist is to take the SR attitude toward physicalism.

(P3) But to take the SR attitude toward a hypothesis does not require regarding it as likely to be true (let alone very likely to be true).

(C2) Therefore, to be a physicalist does not require regarding physicalism as likely to be true (let alone very likely to be true).

The premise (P1) is very plausible, once physicalism is viewed as no more and no less than a scientific hypothesis; for what could justify holding the endorsement of physicalism to higher standards than those to which the endorsement of Darwinism or quantum mechanics is held, if physicalism is just another scientific hypothesis? And surely physicalism should be viewed as a scientific hypothesis. For, as we saw in Chapter 1, it makes a contingent claim about the world; the claim it makes about the physical realization of the world is strongly analogous in form to such obviously scientific hypotheses as that genes are made of DNA or that clouds are made of water droplets or any number of other reductionist hypotheses (though it obviously has a much broader scope); it could not with any plausibility be described as either a commonsensical or a religious claim; and, as we will see in Chapter 6, it can both in principle and in practice be supported evidentially by detailed scientific findings. What more could reasonably be required for a claim to count as a scientific hypothesis? Physicalism does not, admittedly, assert the holding of any law, nor does it have a special connection to only *one* branch of science. But plenty of scientific hypotheses do not assert the holding of laws (e.g., Darwinism does not); and having a special connection to *many* branches of science, rather than to just one, does not seem a good reason to disqualify a claim from being scientific. It is also true that physicalism has been much discussed by philosophers. But that is surely compatible with its being a scientific hypothesis, as the thesis of universal determinism illustrates. If, however, despite all these considerations, one still insists that physicalism is not a scientific hypothesis, then surely one must at least allow that it *resembles* a scientific hypothesis in every respect relevant to current purposes.

The premise (P3) will turn out to be a triviality, once the nature of the SR attitude has been made clear. The premise (P2), however, which urges the identification of attitudes not obviously identical, is far from trivial and requires both elucidation and defense. This must begin, however, with an explanation of what I mean by the "SR attitude" toward a hypothesis. Here is a *stipulative* definition:

(SR) To take the SR attitude toward a hypothesis is (i) to regard the hypothesis as true or false in virtue of the way the mind-independent world is, and (ii) to assign the hypothesis a higher probability than that of its *relevant rivals*.[41]

But what are the relevant rivals to a hypothesis? Here is another stipulative definition:

(RR) Hypothesis H1 is a relevant rival to H2 iff (a) H1 is sensibly intended to achieve a significant number of H2's theoretical goals; (b) the hypotheses, H1 and H2, fail to supervene on one another; and (c) H1 has actually been formulated.

Clauses (a) through (c) require some unpacking and motivation. Take clause (a) first. The theoretical goals of a hypothesis will include such things as the satisfactory explanation of certain phenomena and the solution of certain problems. The reference to a "significant number" of such shared goals is supposed to do (rough) justice to the fact that advocates of rival hypotheses almost never completely agree on what theoretical goals their respective hypotheses can reasonably be expected to achieve; insisting that *all* theoretical goals be shared for two hypotheses to count as rivals would therefore leave almost no pairs of hypotheses as rivals. The reference to goals that are "sensibly" intended for a hypothesis to achieve is supposed to ensure that the hypothesis that, say, the moon is made of green cheese does not qualify as a relevant rival to Darwinism just because some lunatic thinks it can account for the origin of species. Let us now turn to clause (b). It is included so that hypotheses at different levels of explanation (e.g., folk psychology and scientific psychology), whose theoretical goals arguably overlap considerably, are not mistakenly classified as rivals; presumably folk psychology does supervene upon scientific psychology. It also serves to exclude hypotheses that are merely notational variants of one another from counting as relevant rivals. Finally, clause (c). I have no full account of what it is for a hypothesis to be formulated, but two points are crucial. First, to count as formulated, a hypothesis need

---

41 Notice that although regarding a hypothesis as more likely than its relevant rivals may not *require* being able to estimate *how* likely the hypotheses in question are, it is quite consistent with being able to do so; hence (SR) neither assumes nor implies that "the testing of theories yields only a comparative warrant" (see Peter Lipton 1996, 93).

not have been formulated in any great detail, but we must have been told something about its basic principles. So, for instance, I would count creationism as having been formulated, on the grounds that (sometimes) we are told *something* about the basic mechanism it hypothesizes to account for life, even though, as I noted earlier, creationists are notoriously stingy with suggestions as to the details of God's plans for flora and fauna. Second, we must distinguish formulating a hypothesis from referring to it. The expression "the set of laws accepted by people at Harvard who call themselves 'physicists' in 2500" very probably refers to a hypothesis, but it does not formulate one; for it tells us nothing about the basic principles of the hypothesis (if any) referred to, which hypothesis therefore fails to count as a relevant rival to any current hypothesis.

One especially important consequence of (RR) is that the sheer negation of a hypothesis, unsupplemented by any other claims, does *not* count as a relevant rival to the hypothesis, since the unsupplemented negation of a hypothesis fails to meet condition (a): it cannot sensibly be intended to achieve the theoretical goals of the hypothesis. Simply denying the existence of electrons, for instance, goes no way toward accounting for the phenomena electrons are introduced to explain. Of course, the negation of a hypothesis can certainly be *part* of – one conjunct of – a relevant rival to the hypothesis; and I suspect that this is typically so when it appears that a hypothesis has a pure negation as a rival. So, for example, the denial of electrons' existence conjoined with appropriate phenomenological generalizations can perfectly well be a relevant rival to electron theory. Similarly, while (RR) implies that atheism unadorned is not a relevant rival to theism, it can allow that atheism plus the findings of contemporary science is a relevant rival to theism.

According to (RR), the relevant rivals to a hypothesis are (1) certain predecessors in the history of the branch of science to which the hypothesis belongs, (2) certain current, actually formulated hypotheses in the branch of science to which the hypothesis belongs, and (3) certain current, actually formulated hypotheses – call them fringe hypotheses – that in some sociological sense do not belong to the branch of science to which the hypothesis belongs (though they may once have done so). So, for instance, to take the SR attitude toward the hypothesis of evolution by gradualist natural selection is (i) to regard the hypothesis as true or false in virtue of the way the mind-independent world is, and (ii) to regard it as likelier to be true than (at least) Lamarckianism, evolution via genetic drift, and creationism.

In the light of the stipulative definitions (SR) and (RR), it is now tolerably clear at least what (P2) and (P3) are claiming. But are they true? Take (P3) first. Because, according to clause (ii) of (SR), taking the SR attitude toward a hypothesis requires only regarding it as more likely to be true than its relevant rivals, and because the relevant rivals to a hypothesis do not include the sheer negation of that hypothesis, it is possible to take the SR attitude toward a hypothesis without regarding it as likely, still less very likely, to be true: a hypothesis might be unlikely, and yet still more likely than its relevant rivals. (If the relevant rivals of a hypothesis did include the sheer negation of the hypothesis, then taking the SR attitude toward a hypothesis – regarding it as likelier than all its relevant rivals – would entail regarding it as likelier than its negation, and hence regarding it as likelier than not, and hence as likely.) What about (P2)? Is it true, as (P2) asserts, that the SR attitude, as stipulatively defined, can be identified with the attitude that those who have broadly scientific realist and antirelativist intuitions take toward what they regard as the best of current scientific hypotheses? I now argue that it can.

What is the deepest intuitive commitment of those who would call themselves scientific realists and antirelativists? It consists, I suggest, in the respectful way in which they regard (certain) current scientific hypotheses. By and large, they regard these current scientific hypotheses as

(I) true or false in virtue of the way the mind-independent world is;

(II) objectively superior, in some truth-connected sense, to earlier hypotheses in the field, so that science has, in this sense, progressed;

(III) objectively superior, in the same sense, to current rival scientific hypotheses;

(IV) objectively superior, in the same sense again, to current rival hypotheses advocated by people outside the scientific establishment; and

(V) such that whether the regard for a hypothesis expressed by I through IV is appropriate is generally independent of whether or not the hypothesis postulates entities and properties that cannot be observed.

Someone with these attitudes to the best of current scientific hypotheses will therefore find repugnant each of the following three ideas: (i) the possibly neo-Kantian idea that the postulates of a scientific hypothesis are somehow conjured into existence by the widespread acceptance of the hypothesis; (ii) the epistemologically egalitarian idea that all hypotheses, past or present, scientific or fringe, are more or less on a cognitive par with one another (even if their *political* influence is unequal); and (iii) the empiricist idea that the difference between being observable and being unobservable marks a distinction of great epistemological significance.

The argument for (P2) — for identifying the stipulatively defined SR attitude with the attitude that those who have broadly scientific realist and antirelativist intuitions take toward what they regard as the best of current scientific hypotheses — has two premises. The first premise is that the attitude that those who have broadly scientific realist and antirelativist intuitions take toward what they regard as the best of current scientific hypotheses is adequately characterized by I through V. (One who denies this premise has only to specify something that has been left out or wrongly included.) The second premise is that the SR attitude, as stipulatively defined, should be identified with the attitude characterized by I through V. Five observations together provide evidence for this identification. First, clause (i) of (SR) says exactly what I say. Second, to take the SR attitude toward a hypothesis is surely *one* way of taking a truth-connected attitude (as mentioned in II, III, and IV) toward it. It is not, of course, to have an all-or-nothing belief that the hypothesis is true; nor is it even to believe that the hypothesis is closer to the truth — enjoys greater verisimilitude — than other false hypotheses. But it is, in part, to assign to the hypothesis a higher probability of being *true,* true in the fullest-blooded realist sense you like, than is assigned to its relevant rivals. Third, to take the SR attitude toward a hypothesis, and in particular to assign it a higher probability than any of its relevant rivals, is surely *one* way of regarding it as objectively superior (as mentioned in II, III, and IV) to certain rivals, at least on the assumption that assignments of probability are answerable to objective constraints, such as would be supplied by a reliabilist theory of confirmation (or by a Bayesian theory, appropriately supplemented by some account of objective constraints on assigning prior probabilities). Fourth, the relevant rivals that the SR attitude concerns include just the sort of rivals that II, III, and IV concern. Finally, nothing in the SR attitude rules out that one could perfectly well take the SR attitude toward a hypothesis postulating unobservables.

(P2)'s identification of the SR attitude with the attitude that those with broadly scientific realist and antirelativist sympathies take toward the best of current hypotheses evidently assumes that nothing compels a scientific realist-antirelativist to assign a high probability to the theories he or she picks out as best. Yet it is hard, I admit, to dislodge the intuition that *something* requires the assignment of a high probability. But what? Not the need to reject the egalitarian suggestion that all theories, past or present, scientific or fringe, are really on a cognitive par with one another, since that suggestion can be rejected merely by adopting an attitude that, like the SR attitude, only assigns a higher, not a high, probability to favored hypotheses. Here is a better suggestion: "A scientific realist-antirelativist must *believe* the theories he or she picks out as best, and since to believe a theory just is to assign it a high probability, the high probability requirement swiftly follows." Indeed it does, but neither premise is very plausible. To begin with, it is not at all clear why a scientific realist-antirelativist must *believe* the theories he or she picks out as best; certainly belief is not required to explain practical reliance on the theories; for a sufficient basis for action can be the assignment of only a low probability, as when I carry a spare tire, even though I certainly do not believe that I will have a flat. And while it might plausibly be claimed that scientific realists-antirelativists must in *some* sense accept the theories they favor, argument is needed to show that this attitude of acceptance amounts to anything more than the SR attitude. More seriously, the identification of belief with the assignment of a high probability runs into the problem of the Lottery Paradox, in which, given the identification, an apparently quite rational person must be regarded as holding contradictory beliefs: a person assigns a high probability to each proposition saying, of one lottery ticket, that it will lose, and also to the proposition that some ticket will not lose; but if belief just is the assignment of high probability, then the person must *believe* of each ticket that it will lose, and also that some ticket will not lose – which commits her to a contradiction (for elaboration and defense, see Kaplan 1996, 93–8, and Maher 1993, 134–5). Nor is it true that the assignment of a high probability is even a logically necessary condition of belief: surely it is logically possible for someone who believes ten (probabilistically independent) propositions, to each of which he assigns a probability of 0.9, to believe also the conjunction of those propositions, even though the probability of the conjunction is low, being the product of the probabilities of each conjunct (for this argument as applied to acceptance, see Maher 1993, 137–9 and 152–5).

Here is a second suggestion for supporting a high-probability requirement: "Even if believing a theory does not logically require assigning it a high probability, *rationally* believing it surely does. So let us assume some analysis of belief that makes belief quite independent of probability assignments.⁴² Then, because a scientific realist-antirelativist must believe the theories he or she picks out as best, and because *rationally* believing a theory requires assigning it a high probability, a scientific realist-antirelativist must on pain of irrationality assign a high probability to his or her favored theories." But this second argument for a high probability requirement is also inconclusive. It retains the nonobvious assumption of its predecessor that a scientific realist-antirelativist must believe the theories he or she picks out as best. But the premise that rational belief requires assigning a high probability seems clearly wrong. For surely it is always rational to believe the immediate logical consequences of what one rationally believes; but then the person who rationally believes ten (probabilistically independent) propositions, to each of which he assigns a probability of 0.9, is rational in believing their conjunction, even though, as already noted, this conjunction has a low probability (Maher 1993, 137–9 and 152–5.). Let me also note that there are theories of rational *acceptance* that leave open the possibility of accepting hypotheses that are improbable, and these theories could presumably be modified to cover rational *belief*, nonprobabilistically construed (see Maher 1993, ch. 6, sec. 6; Kaplan 1996, ch. 4). Neither Kaplan's nor Maher's theory is at all reliabilist in spirit, but a reliabilist theory that also yields the same result is easy to imagine in vague outline: if one's cognitive goal is not just truths, but truths that, say, provide a basis for prediction and explanation, then a belief-forming method could be rational to adopt, and its products count as rational (even though unlikely to be true), just so long as those products made up for their improbability, as it were, by constituting a superior basis for prediction and explanation. Unformulated theories, or the sheer negations of formulated theories, might be likelier to be true, but cannot provide such a basis.⁴³

Now, a natural answer to the question what a physicalist is that a physicalist is just someone who *believes* some appropriately formulated thesis of physicalism. So it is important to notice that nothing in the previous two paragraphs commits me to claiming that a physicalist cannot be someone

---

42 For such analyses of a belieflike notion of acceptance, see, e.g., Kaplan (1996, ch. 4) and Maher (1993, ch. 6).

43 Perhaps scientific realist-antirelativist intuitions include the idea that the best of current scientific hypotheses are things we *know*. Perhaps; but it is far from clear that one knows that p only if it is likelier to be true than false that p. For it is easy to envisage reliabilist accounts of knowledge that, because they do not construe truth as the only cognitive goal, do not imply that this is so; and a staunch defender of scientific knowledge might indeed be expected to favor such an account.

who believes physicalism (notwithstanding Montero 1999, 193, commenting on my 1997b article). By my lights, what a physicalist cannot be is someone who assigns a high probability to physicalism. So a physicalist can perfectly well be someone who believes physicalism – so long as one can believe physicalism, and believe it rationally, without assigning it a high probability; and the arguments in the previous two paragraphs show that in general neither believing nor rationally believing a proposition requires assigning it a high probability. Furthermore, I am not even committed to the weaker view that one can be a physicalist without believing physicalism (Montero 1999, 189). For, because I leave unexplicated the relationship (if any) between taking the SR attitude toward a theory and believing a theory, it remains possible, for all that I have said, that believing a theory should simply *be* taking the SR attitude toward it, so that being a physicalist actually requires believing physicalism. As a result, I am not committed to the unintuitive view that saying "Everything is physical, but I don't believe it" is perfectly acceptable (Montero 1999, 189).[44]

In the absence of any compelling reason for insisting on a high-probability requirement, (P2)'s identification of the SR attitude with the attitude that those who have broadly scientific realist and antirelativist intuitions take toward what they regard as the best of current scientific hypotheses can stand. However, it may be possible to go on the offensive here. Resisting a high-probability requirement offers scientific

---

44 A different kind of objection to (P2) claims that one could take the SR attitude toward a hypothesis without also favoring it in the manner distinctive of a scientific realist-antirelativist. But naturally I doubt that this could happen, and I know of no example. Barbara Montero, responding to my article (1997b), proposes a pair of examples, but I find them unpersuasive. The main trouble is that they do not concern scientific hypotheses, whereas (P2) speaks only of scientific hypotheses. She notes that "holding that Buddhism is better than its rivals does not make one a Buddhist" (Montero 1999, 190), but so what? It is independently plausible that religious belief, in particular, involves an especially strong kind of commitment to the truth of certain propositions, a commitment so strong, indeed, that it exceeds what the available evidence warrants (which would explain why religious belief is so often called "faith"); but if so, then, given that physicalism is a scientific hypothesis, holding that physicalism is more probable than its rivals may still make you a physicalist, even if holding that Buddhism is more probable than its rivals does not make you a Buddhist. Montero also offers a philosophical example in which, by her intuitions, someone who thinks that Humean compatibilism is the best of a very bad lot would not count as a Humean compatibilist. But, so long as the person does not find Humean compatibilism contradictory (so that it has zero probability), it is not clear to me that the person is not a Humean compatibilist; in any case, as with the religious example, being an X-ist in science may require less than it does in philosophy. I doubt that any good *scientific* counterexample to (P2) exists; I conjecture that any putative example would be a case in which many relevant rivals no less likely could easily be formulated (even though ordinarily no one would bother to).

realists-antirelativists an attractive reply to the so-called pessimistic induction that claims that, because most past theories have turned out to be false, current theories are probably false too (a reply noted earlier, and independently, in Maher 1993, 137). Moreover, it is arguable that insisting on a high-probability requirement would be unreasonable, so that the SR attitude toward hypotheses (or something like it) is all we can decently hope for. For suppose a scientific realist-antirelativist insists that we should regard our best current theories as more likely to be true than false. That implies regarding them as more likely to be true than the disjunction of their rivals, and hence more likely than each disjunct taken individually. But some of those disjuncts are unborn hypotheses, hypotheses that have not yet been formulated and perhaps never will be (see Sklar 1979). And how could our current evidence make it reasonable to regard a current hypothesis as likelier than a hypothesis that has not even been formulated? So if we claim that a current hypothesis is likelier to be true than not, we may be going beyond any attitude it could possibly be reasonable to take.

My response to the historical objection, then, if the objection is supposed to be a knockdown argument against any formulation of physicalism in terms of current physics, is now complete. Let physicalism (e.g., realization physicalism) be formulated in terms of current physics. Then, given that a physicalist is simply someone who takes the SR attitude toward physicalism, the mere fact that the history of physical theorizing makes physicalism unlikely to be true provides no reason by itself to abandon being a physicalist; one can remain a physicalist, even though physicalism is unlikely, just so long as it is more likely than its relevant rivals. Nor will it do to complain that this is simply special pleading on behalf of physicalism, a lowering of the bar for physicalism alone. For the SR attitude, as I have extensively argued, is exactly the same attitude that scientific realists-antirelativists take toward *all* of their favored scientific hypotheses. A physicalist is just someone who takes a scientific realist-antirelativist attitude toward the scientific hypothesis of physicalism.

Of course, for all that I have said, it remains true that the history of physical theorizing still constitutes evidence against realization physicalism, in the sense of lowering the probability that it is true; and presumably it does not in the same way constitute evidence against realizationism's relevant rivals. So it still threatens realization physicalism. But the probability of realizationism *tout court* is the probability of realizationism on *total* evidence; so any evidence *against* it, including therefore the evidence constituted by the history of physical theorizing, must obviously be weighed against evidence *for* it, and the balance of probabilities in light of total evidence may yet leave realizationism likelier than its relevant rivals. And, as I argue in Chapter 6, there *is* strong evidence for realizationism, evidence capable in principle of giving its probability the necessary boost. Such counteracting evidence, moreover, does not have to raise its probability to 0.5 or higher; given my proposed account of what it is to be a physicalist, it need only lift it above that of its closest relevant rival, an easier requirement to fulfill.

In fact, and contrary to the presumption of the preceding paragraph, the history of physical theorizing is arguably just as damaging to realization physicalism's relevant rivals as it is to realizationism itself. Relevant rivals to realizationism are actually formulated hypotheses that are sensibly intended to address the problem that it is the central theoretical goal of physicalism to address: giving an account of the relations among the ontologies that the many sciences (including honorary sciences like folk psychology and folk physics) respectively postulate, in light of such cross-scientific regularities as have been discovered empirically. (An example of one sort of crude cross-scientific regularity might be that nothing is ever in a mental state unless it is in some simultaneous brain state; but the sciences [e.g., the neurosciences] present more refined regularities.) To identify realizationism's relevant rivals, it is helpful to view realization physicalism as the conjunctive thesis that

(i) there is some science, S, distinct from the totality of all the sciences, such that every token that falls within the scope of (R) is either a token of a type mentioned as such in the laws and theories of S or an S-ly realized token of some or other functional type,

and that

(ii) S is current physics.

Relevant rivals to realization physicalism therefore fall into two categories: (A) those that endorse (i) without endorsing (ii), by agreeing that there is a basic science, to which all the other sciences stand in a special relation, but proposing that this basic science is something other than physics; and (B) those that deny (i), maintaining that no science is basic, since all sciences are on an ontological par, linked to one another merely by various fundamental laws (see, e.g., Crane and Mellor 1990; possibly Dupré 1993). Do relevant rivals of either sort gain any advantage over physicalism from evidence constituted solely by the history of physical theorizing?

Take rivals in category (A). Suppose one such rival asserts that there is a basic science, but that it is, say, biology. Such a view is evidentially quite untouched by the history of physical theorizing. On the other hand, the track record of biological theorizing is arguably no better than that of physical theorizing, which evens things out, and obviously there is other evidence decisive against taking biology to be the basic science. However, the best-known relevant rival in category (A) is traditional dualism, which I interpret as the view that, to put it very crudely, physicalism is true of everything except the mind: there is a basic science, but it is the *conjunction* of physics and folk psychology (presumably linked to one another by fundamental psychophysical laws). The impact of the history of physical theorizing on traditional dualism, relative to that on physicalism, is trickier to assess. To the extent that the history of physical theorizing makes it likely that current physics is *false*, there is exactly the same evidence against traditional dualism as there is against physicalism, given my interpretation of traditional dualism as the view that the conjunction of physics and folk psychology constitutes the basic science. It might appear, though, that historical evidence that current physics is *incomplete* would leave traditional dualism unharmed, since traditional dualism, unlike physicalism, is not committed to regarding current physics as complete. But in fact what the history of physical theorizing makes likely is that current physics has left out something like a new kind of particle, with mass and charge, and traditional dualism *is* committed to regarding current physics as complete in respect of that sort of thing.[45]

---

[45] In a critical discussion of my article (1997b), Seth Crook and Carl Gillett present a relevant rival in category (A) that they claim is likelier to be true than realization physicalism (2001, 339–41). According to this rival, S is current physics, exactly as I understand it, *plus* the claim that there exists at least one further entity that has features and magnitudes similar to those spoken of as such in current physics. Crook and Gillett claim that since the history of research in physics in the twentieth century has been one in which new fundamental entities have regularly been discovered, this rival is likelier to be true than realization physicalism. Now this advantage over realization physicalism might be nullified by the fact that the rival is less economical, since it postulates at least one kind of fundamental entity unpostulated by current physics. However, as Crook and Gillett note, realizationism is not likelier than its relevant rivals if it is even *equally* as likely as some relevant rival. So my main point is that probably we *should* prefer the rival that Crook and Gillett present to realization physicalism as I have formulated it. (Or, better, realization physicalism should be understood as embodying the modification they suggest.) Why would that be bad? Not because it entails abandoning the idea that "physical" should be defined by appeal to current physics, since, for the most part, "physical" would still be defined by appeal to current physics, which would supply physicalism with enough content to make it possible for us to evaluate its empirical credentials. Not because the requisite notion of similarity is too vague, since Crook and Gillett themselves spell it out clearly enough for their purposes, and that seems

What about relevant rivals in category (B)? The egalitarian and pluralist view that there is no basic science, the view, in effect, that cross-scientific regularities should be treated as fundamental laws, appears initially not to be committed either to the truth or to the completeness of current physics; so on evidence constituted solely by the history of physical theorizing, physicalism appears less likely than antiphysicalist pluralism. Actually, though, on pain of simply saying nothing at all about interscientific relations (in something like the way in which creationists typically leave God's creative intentions utterly unspecified), antiphysicalist pluralism is committed to law statements connecting events *as characterized by current physics* to events as characterized by each of the special sciences; and if current physics is probably false, then so too, surely, are those law statements. Surprisingly, then, antiphysicalist pluralism may derive no advantage at all over physicalism from evidence constituted solely by the history of physical theorizing.

> good enough. And not because acceptance of their rival would force us to count all sorts of weird stuff as physical; for as proposed additions to the ontology of current physics become progressively wilder, and less connected to the ontology of current physics, the historical evidence for thinking that current physics is going to expand in *that* sort of direction becomes progressively weaker (e.g., to take an extreme case, consensus physics in the twentieth century has *no* track record of adding irreducibly *mental* phenomena to its stock of fundamental things).

6

The Evidence for Realization Physicalism

1. INTRODUCTION

The aim of this chapter is to argue that there is indeed empirical evidence in favor of realization physicalism. This evidence is evidence in the sense that it *raises the probability* of realization physicalism, although I do not attempt a precise estimate of how *high* it raises this probability. The availability of such evidence, I claim, is a consequence of certain scientific findings that are neither recondite nor especially controversial. Indeed, they may be found in standard textbooks in such fields as condensed matter physics, physical chemistry, and molecular biology. But the fact that a scientific finding is relatively uncontroversial does not imply that its evidential relevance to some particular hypothesis will likewise be uncontroversial. For the evidential relevance of an uncontested claim can be overlooked: Sherlock Holmes's stock-in-trade, after all, was not merely to notice facts that others had missed but also to expose the hitherto unnoticed evidential relevance of facts already known to everyone (e.g., the fact that the dog did not bark in the night). Accordingly, I conceive my task in this chapter as that of exposing the evidential relevance to realization physicalism of certain well-known scientific findings.

The relevance of the scientific findings I have in mind consists in their enabling the deployment of a certain complex strategy of nondeductive reasoning in favor of realization physicalism. This strategy involves the combined use of three tactics. The first tactic rests on the assumption of the *transitivity of realization* – the fact that if F-type tokens are G-ly realized, and if G-type tokens are H-ly realized, then F-type tokens are H-ly realized. (We can understand "G-ly realized" and "H-ly realized" on the model of "physically realized" as this was defined in Chapter 1.)

In line with this assumption, if we learn that all cellular phenomena are biochemically realized, and that all biochemical phenomena are physically realized, we may then conclude that all cellular phenomena are physically realized. The second tactic is the use of *inference to the best explanation* to argue for the truth of specific *identity hypotheses* – that is, particular a posteriori claims to the effect that certain special- or honorary-scientific types are identical with certain types that are either physical or functional but physically realized.[1] It is in constructing these inferences to the best explanation that the scientific findings alluded to earlier play their vital role, though not, as we shall see, exclusively or even mainly as *data* for the inferences. The third tactic is the use of *enumerative induction*, whereby the fact that realization physicalist identity hypotheses have turned out to be true of *some* special- or honorary-scientific phenomena of a given kind provides evidence that similar identity hypotheses are true of *all* special- or honorary-scientific phenomena of that same kind. How these three tactics can be combined to yield an empirical case for realization physicalism becomes clear as the chapter proceeds.

The evidential relevance to physicalism of the scientific findings I have in mind is certainly not something that I can claim to be the first to have noticed. On the contrary, I suspect that many practicing scientists noticed it long ago. For there is a strong consensus among them – a consensus often deplored by antiphysicalists – that some kind of materialism is true, and I am inclined to explain this consensus by supposing (i) that many scientists are familiar, as a result of their general science education, with the sorts of scientific findings that I claim can be used to argue for physicalism, and (ii) that these scientists are more or less clearly aware of *how* such findings can be used to argue for physicalism; and I am inclined to explain the less extensive but still considerable prophysicalist consensus among certain sorts of philosopher in similar fashion. Nevertheless, the present chapter is, to the best of my knowledge, the first-ever attempt at a full and explicit characterization of the prophysicalist reasoning that these scientific findings make possible.

Some readers may find that this chapter puts them in mind of a classic paper by Paul Oppenheim and Hilary Putnam (1958). And so it should, because this chapter also aims to show how actual scientific findings

---

1 The reader may have noticed that I here speak of *types* as physically realized, whereas according to the canonical definition of "physically realized" in Chapter 1 it is only *tokens* that, strictly speaking, can be physically realized. Please understand talk of physically realized types as simply shorthand for talk of types, *all of whose actual tokens* are physically realized.

provide evidence that science is unified in some interesting sense (though not the same sense that Oppenheim and Putnam had in mind). But a close reading of Oppenheim and Putnam's paper reveals that they never make at all clear the character of the reasoning that they take to support their version of reductionism over its emergentist rivals; and obviously they only take into account scientific knowledge prior to 1958. The present chapter aims to avoid both these weaknesses.

So I argue that there is evidence that realization physicalism is true. In Sections 2 through 5, I shall argue that there is evidence – really quite a bit of evidence – that physicalism about everything nonmental is true. In Section 6, the last of the book, I argue that there is also evidence – admittedly less evidence – that physicalism about the mental is true. I present this evidence in sufficient detail to rebut the charge that physicalists are merely hand-waving when they claim that science supports physicalism (see, e.g., Burge 1993, 117). But it should be possible for readers who desire more detail than I provide to apply the pattern of prophysicalist reasoning that I describe in this chapter to scientific findings that I do not consider here.

2. THE ROLE OF INFERENCE TO THE BEST EXPLANATION

As noted earlier, the second element of the overall strategy of nondeductive reasoning by which, I claim, realization physicalism can be empirically validated is inference to the best explanation, which can be used to support identity hypotheses asserting the identity of particular special- or honorary-scientific types with particular types that are physical or functional but physically realized. But how exactly can inference to the best explanation be used to support these identity hypotheses? And what is the precise role in such inferences of the textbook scientific findings that I claimed make such inferences possible?

In order to answer these two questions, I work with the relatively simple example of *solidity*, on the assumption (i) that the reader will happily concede that some sort of physicalism is true of solidity and (ii) that the relative simplicity of the case will throw into sharp relief the general features of the pattern of reasoning I wish to exhibit. Solids (i.e., objects that possess solidity) are standardly treated by contemporary condensed matter (or solid-state) physics as structures composed of particles bound to one another electrostatically, that is, by forces that hold in virtue of the electric charges possessed by the constituent particles (see, e.g., Guinier and Jullien 1989; Chandrasekhar 1998). The nature of this structure, the nature of the particles making it up, and the nature of the electrostatic bonding between them vary in different kinds of solids. Some solids are glassy, in which case their constituent particles are in no kind of orderly spatiotemporal arrangement at all; other solids are single crystals, in which case their constituent particles form a highly ordered lattice arrangement; yet other solids are polycrystals, which, though not single crystals, are made up of grains that are single crystals. In some solids (e.g., sodium chloride), the constituent particles are oppositely charged ions; in others (e.g., diamonds, polystyrene), they are atoms or molecules; in metals, they are ions and electrons. The particles making up solids are held together sometimes by ionic bonds (in which oppositely charged ions are attracted to one another), sometimes by covalent bonds (in which neighboring atoms share electrons), sometimes by metallic bonds (in which electrons move relatively freely around a lattice structure of positively charged ions), sometimes by hydrogen bonds (in which the exposed positive nucleus of a hydrogen atom that is bonded to another atom attracts a different atom), and sometimes by the operation of van der Waals forces (in which slight variations in the relative positions of the nucleus and electrons of an atom turn the atom into a sort of temporary magnet); in each case, the nature of the bonding is a consequence of the quantum mechanical character of the particle system in question.

Now it is important to see that the *physicist's* account of solids just sketched is not yet a *physicalist* account of solids: the physicist's account of solids does not entail that solids are physical or physically realized objects, nor does it entail that solidity is a physical or functional-but-physically-realized property. For the physicist's account of solids, in claiming that solids are composed of structured physical particles, is logically consistent with the possibility that solids should also have *other* components that are neither physical nor physically realized, in which case solids themselves would be neither physical nor physically realized. Similarly, even if the physicist's account of solids just sketched were fully fleshed out, it would still be logically consistent with the possibility that the *property* of solidity should be *emergent* relative to the structured physical components of objects that are solids, and hence neither a physical nor a functional-but-physically-realized property.

But if a physics textbook account of solids does not *entail* physicalism about solidity, what *is* its evidential bearing on physicalism? To see what it is, we should first note that a suitably fleshed out version of the account of solids sketched earlier enables us to *explain* certain facts about items that possess solidity (see, e.g., Guinier and Jullien 1989, ch. 4 ; Chandrasekhar

1998, ch. 7). Here are some of the facts that it enables us to explain: (a) the fact that items possessing solidity each have a reasonably definite size and shape; (b) the fact that solid items retain their size and shape despite the effects of gravity, and despite the application to them of (a restricted range of) mechanical forces; (c) the fact that solid items retain their shape, at least in the short term, regardless of the shape of the container they are in; and (d) the fact that solids include particular items (e.g., this table, that spoon) in their number. These facts are explained by a suitably fleshed out version of the physicist's account of solids in the sense that if we assume that solids have the structured physical constitution that this account says they have, then facts (a) through (d) describe features that we would expect solids to possess. But the availability of such explanations enables us to use inference to the best explanation to support the conclusion that solidity is either a physical or a functional-but-physically-realized property of the items that possess it and hence not an emergent property. It does so by showing that, at least as far as facts (a) through (d) are concerned, there is no theoretical need to construe solidity as anything *more* than a physical or a functional-but-physically-realized property. For since we can explain facts (a) through (d) about solids on the hypothesis that solidity just *is* a physical or a functional-but-physically-realized property (e.g., the property of having one or other of the structured physical constitutions sketched previously), and since this hypothesis is more economical, and hence more credible, than any hypothesis according to which solidity is *more* than a physical or a functional-but-physically-realized property, the hypothesis that solidity just is a physical or a functional-but-physically-realized property is the best explanation of facts (a) through (d). But if a certain hypothesis is the best explanation of certain facts, then those facts provide evidence for that hypothesis. (This is the principle of inference to the best explanation as I understand it.) So facts (a) through (d) about solids provide evidence for the hypothesis that solidity just is, and hence is no more than, a physical or a functional-but-physically-realized property.

Let us examine this reasoning at greater length. Consider, for example, fact (b): that items with solidity retain their size and shape despite the effects of gravity, and despite the application to them of (a restricted range of) mechanical forces. How is this fact to be explained? The textbooks tell us that we have independent (observational) reasons for thinking that every item with solidity in fact possesses one or another of the sorts of structured physical constitution that I began this section by sketching. They also tell us that, because of the nature of the bonds between the physical particles that constitute any item with such a physical constitution, those physical particles will be unable to move freely past one another, given merely the effects of gravity and the application to them of (a restricted range of) mechanical forces. On the basis of textbook information, then, we should *expect* that every item possessing one of the sorts of structured physical constitutions that solids have will retain its size and shape despite the effects of gravity, and despite the application to it of (a restricted range of) mechanical forces. Now suppose we hypothesize – what we have not thus far assumed – that solidity just *is* the property of possessing one or another of the sorts of structured physical constitution that I began this section by sketching. It follows from this physicalist identity hypothesis, together with what we know to expect about items with structured physical constitutions of these sorts, that items with solidity will retain their size and shape despite the effects of gravity, and despite the application to them of (a restricted range of) mechanical forces. We can therefore *explain* why items with solidity retain their size and shape despite the effects of gravity, and despite the application to them of (a restricted range of) mechanical forces; we can do so by claiming (i) that solidity just *is* the having of a certain structured physical constitution, and (ii) that anything that has such a structured physical constitution will retain its size and shape despite the effects of gravity, and despite the application to it of (a restricted range of) mechanical forces. Whereas claim (ii) is vouchsafed to us by the textbooks, claim (i) is the specific physicalist identity hypothesis that we aim to support by noting its indispensability to the best explanation of the accepted fact (b).

But is this physicalistic explanation of fact (b) the *best* explanation of it? Is it the potential explanation of fact (b) that best meets the criteria for goodness of explanations? Since "best" means better than the alternatives, let us consider the alternatives to this explanation, restricting ourselves for obvious reasons to antiphysicalist alternatives.[2] An alternative explanation

---

[2] One alternative, which will doubtless have occurred to the reader already, proposes to explain fact (b) by first identifying solidity with a certain *functional* property, namely, the property of having some or other property in virtue of which one retains one's size and shape despite the effect of gravity, and despite the application of (a restricted range of) mechanical forces, and then noting that this functionalist identity hypothesis straightforwardly *entails* the generalization to be explained. But this alternative explanation can be safely ignored in the context of the present discussion, since, though it might be true, it is not an *antiphysicalist* alternative. For if solidity is identified with the functional property suggested, it would surely be very plausible to argue that every token of this functional property is in fact physically realized – by tokens of the types of physical structure noted earlier, types that we have independent reason to think can play the right associated role for their tokens to realize tokens of the

that is genuinely antiphysicalist must treat solidity as a nonphysical and nonphysically realized property, one that, in accordance with a fundamental law of emergence, comes to be possessed by an object whenever that object possesses one or another of the structured physical constitutions sketched earlier. The explanation of why items possessing the property of solidity, thus nonphysicalistically construed, retain their size and shape despite the effects of gravity, and despite the application to them of (a restricted range of) mechanical forces, will then take one of two forms. It might be claimed (1) that items with solidity retain their size and shape in the specified ways because the very same structured physical constitution that gives rise, via a fundamental law of emergence, to their possession of (nonphysical and nonphysically realized) solidity explains *also* their retention of size and shape in the specified ways, so that a solid thing's solidity, on the one hand, and its retention of size and shape, on the other, are something like the joint effects of a common cause. (The explanation of the solidity-retention regularity will in that case closely resemble that of the rash-fever regularity discussed in Chapter 4.) Alternatively, it might be claimed (2) that items with solidity retain their size and shape in the specified ways because there is a strongly autonomous *law* to the effect that items with (nonphysical and nonphysically realized) solidity retain their shape and size in the specified ways.

These antiphysicalist explanations, however, are clearly less good than the physicalist explanation presented earlier; indeed, in view of the availability and credibility of the physicalist explanation, they may even strike us as ridiculous. Can we say what exactly is wrong with them? Because they certainly account for the data, in the sense that they each yield *an* explanation of fact (b), we must suppose that their inferiority lies elsewhere than in their empirical adequacy. The most obvious suggestion – which I accept – is that they are inferior to the physicalist explanation in point of *economy*. They are less economical than the physicalist explanation in two distinct respects. First, they are obliged to postulate more *fundamental entities* than does the physicalist explanation. For they construe tokens of solidity as tokens of a nonphysical and nonphysically realized property, and hence as logically additional to the physical property tokens that they already countenance, whereas the physicalist explanation, because it identifies solidity with a physical or a functional-but-physically-realized

(putatively) functional type, solidity, and which we have independent reason to think are such that *one* of them is tokened when and only when (and where and only where) solidity is tokened.

property, can construe tokens of solidity as (nonbrutally) necessitated in the strongest sense by those physical property tokens, and hence as *not logically additional* to them.³ Second, both of the antiphysicalist explanations are obliged to postulate more *fundamental laws of nature* than does the physicalist explanation. Both of the antiphysicalist explanations must postulate a fundamental law of emergence connecting certain physical structures with the putatively nonphysical and nonphysically realized property of solidity, a fundamental law of which the physicalist explanation obviously has no need; in addition, the second antiphysicalist explanation must postulate a fundamental (and strongly autonomous) law connecting the putatively nonphysical and nonphysically realized property of solidity with the retention of size and shape in the specified ways. When the criterion of economy is taken into consideration, therefore, the physicalist explanation of fact (b) emerges as a better explanation of that fact than either of its antiphysicalist rivals. So fact (b) constitutes evidence – some evidence – that this explanation, and hence the physicalist identity hypothesis that forms an indispensable part of it, is true.

But an obvious worry arises. Is it right to treat economy – in the senses specified – as a good-making feature of a potential explanation, and hence as relevant, other things being equal, to the probability of its being true? I can hardly settle such a vexed question here, because it is asking whether a certain principle of nondeductive inference is correct, and to answer it fully would require nothing less than solving the venerable problem of induction. What I can do, however, is, first, to make a case for the thesis that we do in fact employ economy as a guide to the truth of a hypothesis in other, relevantly similar contexts, and hence that, in consistency, we ought to do so in the present context also; and, second, to suggest how it could even be so much as *possible* for us to be correct in doing so (notwithstanding the apparently widespread feeling that economy just *could not* be an objectively correct guide to the truth).⁴

First, then, a case for thinking that we actually do invoke economy in evaluating the likely truth of competing hypotheses. Why do apples

---

3 The physicalist explanation can construe tokens of solidity not merely as necessitated in the strongest sense by physical property tokens, but as *nonbrutally* necessitated by them. Nonbrutal necessitation, it will be recalled, is necessitation solely in virtue of some combination of analyticity, syntactic derivability, and the necessity of identity.
4 In his recent defense of simplicity as a guide to the truth of hypotheses, Richard Swinburne also argues that we do in fact treat, and can hardly avoid treating, simplicity as a guide to truth (2001, 83–102). But he does not address the deeper question of how simplicity *could* be a guide to truth. I doubt that skepticism about simplicity as a guide to truth can be dispelled unless this deeper question is plausibly answered.

drop from apple trees when they do? The currently accepted scientific explanation goes, I presume, something like this: in the fall, as a result of some such factor as the shortening of the days or lower average temperatures, the stalks connecting each apple to a branch undergo biochemical changes as a result of which they weaken to the point where the gravitational force acting on each apple suffices to snap it off and pull it to the ground. Now suppose, however, that someone comes along and says, "The scientific explanation you have just given is perfectly correct, as far as it goes, but it is not the whole story. There is also a fundamental law of emergence according to which, whenever an apple grows to its full size, an unobservable *apple demon* comes into existence, one apple demon for each apple. And later, when conditions are right, apple demons cause their respective apples to drop to the ground, in accordance with a strongly autonomous law connecting apple demons to the dropping of apples. So a complete explanation of why apples drop when they do must mention apple demons as well as rotting stalks."

Now we all agree, I take it, that there is no question of adopting the compound explanation that *adds* the apple demon explanation to the scientific one. But why? Surely the reason is that the compound explanation explains no fact that the unsupplemented scientific explanation cannot already explain, and yet it postulates the existence of entities and the holding of fundamental laws of which the physicalist hypothesis has no need. The general principle operative here seems to be this: if two hypotheses explain the same data, but one of them is more economical than the other, then, other things being equal, we should prefer the more economical one. But if it is indeed this principle that guides our reaction to the admittedly fanciful apple demon example, then, on pain of inconsistency, we should apply it also to the case – and to others like it – where we must choose between hypotheses to explain why items with solidity retain their size and shape under certain specified conditions. And, as we have already seen, when we do apply it to that case, we get the result that the proposed physicalist explanation should be preferred to each of the rival antiphysicalist explanations.[5]

---

5 Elliott Sober presents a rationale, based on the work of statistician H. Akaike, for using parsimony as a guide to theory choice, but he also shows that if this rationale is the *only* rationale for using parsimony as a guide to theory choice, then there is no rationale for using parsimony as a guide to theory choice when the theories to choose from are predictively equivalent, for the Akaike-based rationale does not apply in such a case (Sober 1996). Since this kind of case is the very one in which I am claiming that we *should* use economy (or parsimony) as a guide to theory choice, I need a response to Sober's challenge. My response

It might be objected that the principle of economy operative in the apple demon case need not be applied also in the solidity case, since there is a disanalogy between the two cases. For in the apple demon case, the inferior explanation postulates something (i.e., apple demons) whose existence the superior explanation does not countenance at all, whereas in the solidity case, the putatively inferior explanations postulate something (i.e., solidity) whose existence the putatively superior explanation fully accepts. But though this disanalogy is perfectly genuine, it does not entail that the principle of economy has no application in the solidity case. The principle of economy applies in both cases, albeit slightly differently in the solidity case. It is true that, in the solidity case, the antiphysicalist explanations postulate tokens of solidity, and that the putatively superior physicalist explanation also asserts the existence of tokens of solidity. But this truth does not entail that the ontological commitments of the antiphysicalist explanations and those of the physicalist explanations are equal. For when the *antiphysicalist* explanations postulate tokens of solidity, they are construing those tokens as neither physical nor physically realized, and hence as tokens logically *additional* to those physical tokens whose existence is agreed on all hands. But when the *physicalist* explanation asserts the existence of tokens of solidity, it is insisting, precisely, that those tokens *are* physical or physically realized, and hence that they are *not* logically additional to physical tokens whose existence is already agreed on all hands.

So there can be no getting away from the fact (i) that the antiphysicalist explanations postulate *more* than does the physicalist explanation (since they postulate tokens of solidity *construed as neither physical nor physically realized*), and (ii) that the additional entities they postulate explain nothing that cannot already be explained without them. In that case, however, we can still apply our general principle of economy, namely, that if two hypotheses explain the same data, but one of them is more economical

is to deny that the Akaike-based rationale is the only rationale for using parsimony as a guide to theory choice. It would be surprising if it were, for we have strong intuitions that appealing to parsimony is appropriate even when the theories to choose from are predictively equivalent, and on Sober's view such intuitions have to be dismissed as erroneous, presumably to be explained away as the result of the thoughtless transference of a principle legitimate in one context to another context in which it is not; and in any case there is the reliabilist rationale for parsimony that I shall shortly present. In fact, it is not clear that the Akaike-based rationale accounts for *any* of our intuitions about the role of parsimony in theory choice. For according to that rationale parsimony is a relevant consideration only because, and to the extent that, there are *errors* in the data. But this alleged error dependence of the relevance of parsimony strikes no responsive chord with us.

247

than the other, then, other things being equal, we should prefer the more economical one. For if it is objectionable to postulate previously uncountenanced entities when they would explain nothing that we cannot already explain without postulating them, then how could it be any less objectionable to construe already countenanced entities as logically additional to entities that all sides acknowledge, when so construed they would explain nothing that we cannot already explain without so construing them? The antiphysicalist explanations of fact (b) that we have been considering cannot be said, in any natural sense, to *postulate* tokens of solidity, for every party to the debate already accepts that tokens of solidity exist; but they do *construe* all tokens of solidity *as* neither physical nor physically realized, and, given the availability of the alternative physicalist explanation that does not, that construal is just as explanatorily gratuitous as would be the postulation of complete novelties.

A preference, even when other things are equal, for the more economical among a set of hypotheses still treats the greater economy of a hypothesis as an objectively correct guide to its truth. But some philosophers find this idea very hard to stomach. "Granted," it may be said, "that we should prefer more economical hypotheses on *pragmatic* grounds, since more economical hypotheses will probably be more tractable computationally and hence easier to use as a basis for prediction. But how could it possibly be right to use economy as a guide to *truth*, especially since it is evidently not a priori that the world itself is economical?" Let me now answer this rhetorical question and dispel the skepticism that it expresses by sketching a way in which it could in principle be objectively right to treat economy as a guide to truth. I am not arguing that we are *in fact* right to treat economy as a guide to truth, for any such argument would inevitably be circular, itself requiring an appeal to the principle of economy. (This is just a manifestation of the general truth that, even if it is rational to use induction, there is no noninductive way, and hence no noncircular way, to *show* that it is rational.) I just want to show how there *could* be such a thing as correctly viewing economy as a guide to truth. Elliott Sober writes: "The natural philosophical goal of generality has encouraged the idea that these [methodological maxims, including Ockham's razor] are methodological maxims that apply to all scientific subject matters. If this were so, then whatever justification such maxims possess would derive from logic and mathematics" (1994, 153). In fact, we will see that Sober's conditional here is false: there is another possible source for the justification of such maxims, and that is a suitably general, but still contingent, feature of the world.

Let us assume, to begin with, that the objective rightness of treating economy as a guide to truth can be identified with the *epistemic rationality* of doing so: one is objectively right to treat economy as a guide to truth iff one is epistemically rational to do so. What, then, is epistemic rationality? Well, let us make the further assumption that one is rational *simpliciter* (in at least one important sense) to the extent that one employs the best available means to the achievement of one's ends. The best available means may still not be very good means, of course, or even good at all; in order to be best, they need only be means (and hence have a nonzero probability of producing the end in question) and better means than the available alternatives. Given this account of rationality *simpliciter*, we can then say that one is *epistemically* rational, in particular, to the extent that one employs the best available means to one's *epistemic* ends. And let us add that one's epistemic ends are those of preferring hypotheses that are not only true, but that also enable one to explain and predict phenomena that one wants explained or predicted.

If we now turn to the question of which *principles of theory preference* one is epistemically rational in using, we can answer that one is epistemically rational in using those principles whose employment constitutes the best available means to one's epistemic ends. If this answer is correct, then one would be epistemically rational in using the principle of theory preference favoring the most economical among a set of available hypotheses, other things being equal, just in case that principle was a member of a set of principles whose employment constituted the best available means to one's epistemic ends. But the principle of economy might in fact meet this condition. For, in general, whether something is or is not the best available means to a given end is a contingent matter of fact; and if the world itself were appreciably economical, which it might be, and which it would be to the extent that hypotheses about it that we judge to be economical tended to be *true*, then the principle of economy could easily be one of a set of principles of theory preference whose collective use was for us the best available means for achieving our epistemic ends. Given our epistemic ends, we would in that case be epistemically rational, and hence objectively correct, to use the principle of economy in choosing among competing hypotheses.

A few comments on this account of the objective correctness of using economy as a guide to truth will help fill it out. First, on this account, our being correct in using the principle of economy would be *contingent*, since dependent on the contingent fact that the world is economical; but being correct contingently is a perfectly good way of being correct, and only those who yearn for a scientific methodology composed of necessary principles knowable a priori will demur. Second, on this account, even if we were in fact correct in using the principle of economy, we would not necessarily *know* that we were. But I take it that this is no more troublesome than the fact that unsophisticated users of *modus ponens* do not *know* that *modus ponens* is a reliable mode of inference. As a matter of fact, it may be *possible* to know that we are correct in using the principle of economy. For if a reliably formed true belief that p counts as knowledge that p, and if the formation of beliefs via the use of the principle of economy is in fact reliable, then one could come to know, and come to know empirically, that one is correct in using the principle of economy, even if one had to rely on the principle of economy itself in doing so. What makes such knowledge possible is that, on an externalist account of knowledge, a circularity that would be fatal for an attempted public justification of a claim might present no obstacle to knowledge of that claim.[6] Third, and in consequence of the second comment, there is no point on the suggested account in calling the principle of economy a priori. For the principle is either not known at all – it is used unreflectively – or else known a posteriori. And to call it a priori, as Richard Swinburne does, makes it seem as if one holds the mysterious view that the principle of economy is some kind of sui generis methodological or epistemological truth (Swinburne 2001, 102).

Finally, on the suggested account, the set of principles of theory preference to which the principle of economy belonged would probably not be *reliable*, in the specific and commonly assumed sense of leading to the acceptance of true hypotheses more often than not; but this set of principles would not *need* to be reliable in that sense in order for us to be epistemically rational in using it. The set of principles would probably not be reliable in the specified sense, because the principles only advise us on which hypothesis to choose from among the class of *available* hypotheses, and it is arguably rather unlikely that the class of available hypotheses (i.e., those that we have thought up and formulated so far) should contain the true one. Indeed, a policy of preferring a randomly chosen hypothesis from the class of *unavailable* hypotheses might be a *more* effective means of promoting the goal of identifying truths. On the other hand, if our

---

6   Richard Swinburne seems to miss this point when he argues that the principle of economy must be a priori because any empirical justification of it would be circular (2001, 100–2). I say that we could *know* the principle, and know it a posteriori, even though any empirical justification of it would be circular.

epistemic goal is more elaborate than that of identifying truths, if, for example, our goal is that of preferring hypotheses that are not only true, but that also enable us to explain and predict phenomena that we want explained or predicted, then a policy of preferring a randomly chosen hypothesis from the class of unavailable hypotheses would be *no means at all* to our epistemic goal, since an unavailable hypothesis is in principle incapable of enabling us to explain or predict anything. By contrast, the use of a set of principles for choosing the best explanation from among some class of available hypotheses might well be our *most* effective means to that same epistemic goal, even if it is not very effective at all. In that case, it would be reliable in the rather different and weaker sense of being such that the hypotheses that the principles in the set enjoin us to rank as best turn out to be true more often than do those hypotheses which the principles enjoin us to rank lower, even though the hypotheses that the principles in the set enjoin us to rank as best may not turn out to be true very often.

By discussing the particular example of solidity, I have been aiming to make clear how it is possible in general, given appropriate scientific textbook findings, for inferences to the best explanation to support specific physicalist identity hypotheses. Schematically, the reasoning involved, at least in the simplest kind of case, can be represented like this:

(1) Target entities Ts (e.g., solids) have characteristics $C_1, C_2, \ldots C_n$ (e.g., they retain their shape, at least in the short term, regardless of the shape of the container they are in).

(2) Ts have physical systems Ps (e.g., one or another of the sorts of physical structures mentioned earlier) as physical constituents (or as physical coincidents).

(3) Ps can be expected, on the basis of physical considerations, to have characteristics $C_1, C_2, \ldots C_n$.

(4) So the hypothesis that Ts are, or are realized, by Ps provides *an* explanation of why Ts have characteristics $C_1, C_2, \ldots C_n$.

(5) The hypothesis that Ts are, or are realized, by Ps is more economical than its antiphysicalist rivals, and suffers from no theoretical vice.

(6) So the hypothesis that Ts are, or are realized, by Ps provides the best explanation of why Ts have characteristics $C_1, C_2, \ldots C_n$.

(7) So the fact that Ts have characteristics $C_1, C_2, \ldots C_n$ provides evidence for the hypothesis that Ts are, or are realized, by Ps.

This schematic account of the reasoning by which inference to the best explanation can be used to support specific physicalist identity hypotheses also illustrates the *three* different kinds of contribution that scientific textbook findings can make to such inferences. In the first place, scientific textbook findings can contribute to such inferences by supplying the *data* for the inference – the facts for which the identity hypothesis to be supported is claimed to provide the best candidate explanation – so that schematic premise (1) can be instantiated. Now in the preceding example of solidity, the data mentioned, though empirical, were commonsense truisms that did not require peculiarly scientific investigation to uncover. But the data will not be commonsense truisms in all cases, or even in many; and indeed they are not always so in the case of solidity. For example, although one fact that can contribute to the case for construing solidity as physical or physically realized is that there comes a point when the application of a mechanical force to a solid causes it to undergo either plastic deformation or fracture, when *precisely* that point is reached in the case of solids of particular types is obviously not a commonsense truism and requires sophisticated measurement for its discovery.

Second, textbook scientific findings contribute to inferences to the best explanation that support physicalist identity hypotheses by supplying information about the *physical composition* of the entities that the facts constituting the data for the inferences are about, so that schematic premise (2) can be instantiated. In the example of solidity, since the data were facts about solids, the scientific textbook contribution of this second kind was to supply information about the physical composition of solids (e.g., the information that solids are composed of physical particles bound to one another electrostatically). Now, for reasons that we noted earlier, such information does not by itself *entail* physicalism about solids or solidity; so we have not begged the question in favor of physicalism by allowing such information as a premise in the case for physicalism. But if one is still suspicious, then we can characterize this second kind of textbook information a little differently: we can say that scientific textbooks supply information about the *physical coincidents* of the entities that the data for the inferences are about, where something is a physical coincident for a nonphysical entity just in case it is a (or the) physical entity that occupies approximately the same spatiotemporal region as does the nonphysical entity.[7]

---

7 The spatiotemporal coincidence need not be very precise, but that does not matter. For example, it is not very clear what is to count as the spatiotemporal location of my current cold; but it can hardly be doubted that, whichever precise region was selected, there would be plenty that is physical going on in it.

We can thereby avoid even a trace of a suspicion of begging the question, since there is no reason why something neither physical nor physically realized should not still have a physical coincident. (Or so, at any rate, antiphysicalists must hope, since every causal or contingent token universally agreed to exist does in fact have a physical coincident.)

Finally, and perhaps most important, textbook scientific findings contribute to inferences to the best explanation that support physicalist identity hypotheses by informing us that entities with physical constitutions (or physical coincidents) of the kinds possessed by the entities that the data describe can be *expected* to exhibit just those characteristics which the data describe the entities as having. In the example of solidity, as we saw, condensed-matter physics tells us that certain of the characteristics that solids possess are precisely those that we would expect them to possess on the basis of our knowledge of their physical constitutions. In other cases, the situation will be a little more complex. In cases where the data for the explanatory inference characterize the target entities in terms that are neither physical nor quasi-logical, textbook findings in the third category will lead us to expect that entities with physical constitutions (or coincidents) of the kinds possessed by the entities the data describe will exhibit the characteristics the data describe the entities as having *only given* the assumption of certain physicalist identity hypotheses *additional* to the hypothesis that the entities the data describe are physical or physically realized; these additional physicalist identity hypotheses will assert the identity of the characteristics of the entities the data describe with certain physical or physically realized phenomena. But more complex cases of this sort present no problem of principle; they will merely be ones in which the proposed physicalist explanation for the data in question is a *package deal*, comprising *several* physicalist identity hypotheses advanced simultaneously, rather than just one.[8] Once textbook scientific

---

8   A schematic account of the reasoning involved in these more complex cases can be arrived at by modifying the schematic reasoning given earlier in the text. Schematic claim (3) must be replaced by

(3*) Ps can be expected, on the basis of physical considerations, to have *physical* characteristics $D_1, D_2, \ldots D_n$.

Then schematic claims (4) through (7) must be replaced by the following:

(4*) So the hypothesis (i) that Ts are, or are realized, by Ps and (ii) that characteristics $C_1, C_2, \ldots C_n$ are, or are realized by, physical characteristics $D_1, D_2, \ldots D_n$ provides *an* explanation of why Ts have characteristics $C_1, C_2, \ldots C_n$.

findings have made this third contribution, however, the stage is then set for advancing the argument that construing the entities that the data are about (and perhaps also the characteristics that the data attribute to these entities) as neither physical nor physically realized is a hypothesis that explains nothing left unexplained by the physicalist alternative that construes them as physical or physically realized, and which, in view of its relative diseconomy, we should therefore reject in favor of the more economical physicalist alternative.

On my account of the matter, then, and as the schematic reasoning given previously reveals, whether an inference to the best explanation can be constructed to support a particular physicalist identity hypothesis (or cluster of such hypotheses) depends upon how the contingent textbook facts stand; for only if the contingent textbook facts turn out right will true instantiations of schematic premises (1), (2), and (3) be possible. But the schematic reasoning given earlier includes no *conceptual* premises; so whether an inference to the best explanation can be constructed to support a particular physicalist identity hypothesis (or cluster of such hypotheses) in the way that I have described seems to be an *entirely* a posteriori question. In this respect, then, the pattern of reasoning for supporting identity hypotheses that I have described differs sharply from one originated by David Lewis (1983b, 99–107) and recently endorsed by Frank Jackson (1998a, 57–60):

(A) Target-entity type T = the C.

(B) Physical-entity type P = the C.

(C) So T = P.

For the first schematic premise in the Lewisian schema is explicitly intended to be the result of a priori conceptual analysis. (Obviously there are two further important differences too: (i) in the Lewisian schema, the

(5*) The hypothesis (i) that Ts are, or are realized, by Ps and (ii) that characteristics $C_1, C_2, \ldots C_n$ are, or are realized by, physical characteristics $D_1, D_2, \ldots D_n$ is more economical than its antiphysicalist rivals and suffers from no theoretical vice.

(6*) So the hypothesis (i) that Ts are, or are realized, by Ps and (ii) that characteristics $C_1, C_2, \ldots C_n$ are, or are realized by, physical characteristics $D_1, D_2, \ldots D_n$ provides the best explanation of why Ts have characteristics $C_1, C_2, \ldots C_n$.

(7*) So the fact that Ts have characteristics $C_1, C_2, \ldots C_n$ provides evidence for the hypothesis (i) that Ts are, or are realized, by Ps and (ii) that characteristics $C_1, C_2, \ldots C_n$ are, or are realized by, physical characteristics $D_1, D_2, \ldots D_n$.

identity hypothesis follows validly, by the transitivity of identity, from the premises, whereas in mine the identity hypothesis is only inductively supported; (ii) in the Lewisian schema, the first premise purports to identify the target type as *the* satisfier of a certain description, whereas in mine the first premise merely claims that the target type is *a* satisfier of a certain description.)[9]

But, one might object, whether an inference to the best explanation can be constructed to support physicalist identity hypotheses in the way that I have described is not an entirely a posteriori question. For inference to the best explanation can support a hypothesis only if it is *possible* that the hypothesis be true. But since we might have good *a priori* grounds for holding that a particular physicalist identity hypothesis could not possibly be true, the constructibility of an explanatory inference that supports a particular physicalist identity hypothesis cannot be an entirely a posteriori affair. However, this objection is weak. It is doubtful, to begin with, that the falsity of *any* identity hypothesis can be established a priori; certainly we cannot do so in any way that requires moving from the mere *conceivability* of its falsity to the *genuine possibility* of its falsity, for the reason given in Chapter 1: the reference of a term is not in general known a priori; neither, therefore, is the coreferentiality of a pair of terms, and hence the conceivability that something be F but not G is consistent with the absence of any genuine possibility that something be F but not G.[10] But even if it *could* be shown a priori that some nonphysical property, F-ness, could not be identical with any physical property, the *credibility of physicalism* would still remain an entirely a posteriori affair. For it would still be open to the physicalist to defend a *nonretentive* physicalist hypothesis, which denied the existence of F-ness, and the defensibility of *this* hypothesis would be an entirely a posteriori matter. So, to continue our earlier example, even if solidity were shown a priori to be neither a physical nor a physically realized property, the physicalist could still hypothesize that nothing really has the property of solidity and that all the evidence apparently

---

9 It is worth noting that the account I have provided of how inference to the best explanation can be used, *without appeal to a priori conceptual analyses of any kind*, to support physicalist identity hypotheses refutes Frank Jackson's important metaphilosophical claim that a priori conceptual analysis is indispensable for supporting such hypotheses and hence for solving what he calls the location problem (1998a, ch. 2).

10 If the conceivability of an F that is not G is taken only to provide *empirical evidence* against the identity of F-ness and G-ness, then such evidence as it provides must be weighed against the evidence *for* the identity of F-ness and G-ness provided by inferences to the best explanation of the sort considered in the text; accordingly, the conceivability of an F which is not G does not automatically make such inferences nonstarters.

to the contrary can be explained, and indeed more economically and hence better explained, by treating so-called solids as *merely* physical objects with certain structured physical constitutions. Since the credibility of this hypothesis turns upon whether tokens of solidity, construed as *neither* physical *nor* physically realized, actually exist, and since, *pace* Anselm, it is an entirely a posteriori matter what exists and what does not, and hence whether such tokens exist, the credibility of this nonretentive physicalist hypothesis is itself an entirely a posteriori matter.

Before ending this section, let me note how its main conclusion can easily be extended in a way that will be important for the sequel. If it is true that textbook findings can enable us to construct inferences to the best explanation that support specific hypotheses identifying nonphysical items with physical or physically realized items, then, by parity of reasoning, appropriately different textbook findings – if they are available – ought to be capable of enabling the construction of inferences to the best explanation that support specific hypotheses identifying, say, cell-biological items with biochemical items. All the points made in this section surely apply to explanatory inferences supporting identity hypotheses of these different sorts, mutatis mutandis.

3. THE ROLE OF ENUMERATIVE INDUCTION

But let us return to solids. The application to a solid of a mechanical force that apparently leaves the shape of the solid unaffected in fact produces in the solid a tiny and experimentally detectable deformation; in producing this deformation, the application of the force thereby changes the distribution of charges within the solid in such a way that the force is resisted. And when such a force is withdrawn, the solid bounces back to resume its original shape. But in the case of some solids (e.g., most metals), a larger mechanical force can be applied that has the result of producing in the solid a deformation that is permanent, in the sense that the change in shape persists for some time even after the removal of the mechanical force that caused it; a simple example would be a spoon that has been bent out of shape. Now this fact – that certain solids undergo *plastic deformation* when a sufficiently large mechanical force is applied to them – provides evidence that the undergoing of plastic deformation is a physically realized process; it also provides further evidence for construing solids as physical or physically realized. It provides evidence of both kinds, of course, in the way that has just been discussed, by constituting the data for an inference to the best explanation.

Let us briefly consider how. The physics textbooks tell us that the physical constitutions of the solids (e.g., metals) that, under certain conditions, undergo plastic deformation have a three-dimensional lattice structure and that, thanks to the presence within these structures of imperfections called *dislocations* (which have been observed experimentally), it is possible for one part of such a structure to *slide across* a contiguous part of the same structure if a sufficient lateral force is applied to it. Were these structures perfect, such sliding movements would require much larger forces than we observe experimentally to be sufficient for them, just because so many interparticular bonds would need to be broken simultaneously; but the presence of the dislocations allows bonds to be broken and re-formed in a piecemeal fashion that requires only much smaller forces (see Guinier and Jullien 1989, 190–220; Chandrasekhar 1998, 136–41). Now, with this textbook information in mind, let us advance two specific physicalist hypotheses: first, that the solids that undergo plastic deformation in response to a suitable force are, or are realized by, the three-dimensional lattice structures of physical particles, with dislocations, that we have just been talking about; and, second, that the undergoing by a solid of a plastic deformation is, or is always realized by, a certain sequence of many movements, each movement being a sliding by some part of the three-dimensional lattice structure that is or realizes the solid across some contiguous part of that structure. These identity-realization hypotheses enter into an explanation of why certain solids, when subjected to forces beyond a certain magnitude, undergo certain plastic deformations: given the first physicalist hypothesis, the solids in question are or are realized by certain physical structures; given the textbook information, such physical structures should be *expected*, when subjected to forces of the magnitudes envisaged, to undergo certain complex sequences of movements whereby some of their parts slide across others of their parts; and given the second physicalist hypothesis, undergoing such sequences of movements is or realizes, and hence necessitates, undergoing plastic deformations of the kinds in question. So the assumption of the two identity-realization hypotheses, plus the textbook information, would provide an explanation of the fact that certain solids, when subjected to forces beyond a certain magnitude, undergo certain plastic deformations. And surely this physicalistic explanation is the best of the available explanations, since any antiphysicalist rival would be less economical and, hence, inferior. The fact that it explains – that certain solids undergo plastic deformation – therefore provides evidence for thinking that the physicalist identity-realization hypotheses that it incorporates are true.

Thus far, we have seen that an empirical case can be made for regarding two of the so-called *mechanical* properties of solids – solidity and plastic deformation – as physical or physically realized. But exactly analogous empirical cases, similarly based on information readily available in physics textbooks, can also be made for regarding certain *other* mechanical properties of solids as physical or physically realized. Examples of such properties are the fact that metals undergo work hardening (i.e., can be hardened as a result of being deformed), and that this hardening can be reversed by annealing; the fact that the elastic limits of homogeneous alloys are higher than those of pure metals; the fact that solids such as glass rods or crystals of rock salt undergo brittle fracture when subjected to certain forces; the fact that other solids undergo ductile fracture when subjected to certain forces; the fact that, in the case of some solids, which kind of fracture they undergo varies with such conditions as temperature; and the fact that metals are subject to metal fatigue (for details, see Guinier and Jullien 1989, ch. 4).

But now let us ask whether textbooks of condensed matter physics contain information on the basis of which an empirical case can be made, via inference to the best explanation, for holding that *all* the mechanical properties of solids are physical or physically realized. The answer is that they do not. What, then, of the universal hypothesis that *every* mechanical property of solids is physical or physically realized? Well, it *might* be that some of the mechanical properties of solids are physical or physically realized whereas others are not; that is a logical possibility that our current evidence does not contradict. On the other hand, those mechanical properties which are, we have reason to think, physical or physically realized do constitute confirming *positive instances* (in Hempel's sense) of the universal hypothesis that every mechanical property of solids is physical or physically realized; they constitute positive instances of apparently diverse types; nothing in our background knowledge gives us reason to expect that it might be especially hazardous to extrapolate from them; and we have no evidence whatsoever *against* the universal hypothesis. We may therefore conclude that those mechanical properties of solids which are, we have reason to think, physical or physically realized provide evidence – some evidence – for the universal hypothesis that *all* mechanical properties of solids are physical or physically realized. We are certainly in no position today to establish this universal hypothesis by exhaustion, constructing a distinct inference to the best explanation for the truth of each and every instance of it, and we probably never will be, though we can confidently expect to discover more positive instances of it in the future; but it would be a kind of epistemic hypercaution to assume that *only* through such a method of exhaustion could the universal hypothesis be supported. Successful reductions to date of *some* mechanical properties of solids provide inductive, admittedly nonconclusive, but still perfectly genuine evidence for expecting the reducibility of *all* such properties.

Similar universal conclusions can be reached in a similar way for other properties of solids than mechanical properties. We have some evidence for thinking that every *thermal* property of solids is physical or physically realized, because textbook information enables us to argue via inference to the best explanation that such particular thermal properties as thermal conductivity (including differing thermal conductivities) and the possession of specific heats (including the possession by different substances of different specific heats) are physical or physically realized (see, e.g., Guinier and Jullien 1989, ch. 1; Chandrasekhar 1998, ch. 8). We have some evidence for thinking that every *optical* property of solids is physical or physically realized, because textbook information enables us to argue via inference to the best explanation that such particular optical properties as transparency, opacity, color, and the ability to refract and to disperse light are physical or physically realized (see, e.g., Chandrasekhar 1998, ch. 9). We have some evidence for thinking that every *electrical* property of solids is physical or physically realized, because textbook information enables us to argue via inference to the best explanation that such particular electrical properties as electrical resistance (including the different resistances of different materials, and the effects on resistance of alloying and changes in temperature) and conductivity are physical or physically realized (see, e.g., Guinier and Jullien 1989, ch. 2; Chandrasekhar 1998, ch. 10). We also have evidence for thinking that all the "mixed" properties of solids are physical or physically realized, because textbook information enables us to argue via inference to the best explanation that certain "mixed" properties of solids are physical or physically realized – such properties as the fact that heating solids can produce light, the fact that the application of mechanical stresses to solids can produce electricity, the fact that heating solids can make them expand, the fact that the motions of certain solids can produce electricity (as in a dynamo), and the fact that electrical changes in solids can produce both heat and light.

Furthermore, the existence of particular properties of solids (i.e., particular mechanical, thermal, and so on properties) that can be argued by appeal to textbook information to be physical or physically realized confers some (albeit lesser) inductive support on other universal hypotheses than the ones just considered. One such further hypothesis is that all the mechanical, thermal, optical, and electrical properties *of liquids and of gases* are physical or physically realized. This hypothesis gains support, in part, because all samples of liquids and gases, like all solids, have physical coincidents. But it also gains support because sometimes apparently the *same* properties characterize both solids and liquids or gases. So, for example, if the electrical conductivity of electrically conductive *solids* is physical or physically realized, then surely the electrical conductivity of electrically conductive *liquids* is a bit likelier to turn out to be physical or physically realized; if the transparency of a transparent *solid* is physical or physically realized, then surely the transparency of a transparent *gas* is a bit likelier to turn out to be physical or physically realized. However, the hypothesis that all the mechanical, thermal, optical, and electrical properties of liquids and gases are physical or physically realized does not rest only on indirect support of this kind; it can be supported directly too. For textbooks on the physics of liquids and gases provide information on the basis of which one can argue via inference to the best explanation that *particular* properties of liquids and gases are physical or physically realized, and these particular properties constitute positive instances of the universal hypothesis about the properties of liquids and gases, just as particular properties of solids found to be physical or physically realized constitute positive instances of the corresponding universal hypothesis about the properties of solids (see, e.g., Walton 1983, chs. 5, 6, and 7, on gases, and 12 and 13, on liquids).

The evidence we have considered so far might even be regarded as providing a *very* little support for the view that absolutely *all* the properties of solids, liquids, and gases are physical or physically realized. But there are certainly grounds for considerable inductive caution here, because "*all* the properties" would obviously include all the chemical and biological properties (to speak of no others) of solids, liquids, and gases, and these properties seem, pretheoretically, to fall into a different class from that to which the kinds of properties mentioned thus far belong, thus making it quite reasonable to take seriously the possibility that whereas mechanical, thermal, and so on properties of solids, liquids, and gases *are* physical or physically realized, many of their other properties are not. So further evidence is needed before we can conclude that *all* the properties of solids, liquids, and gases are physical or physically realized. Fortunately, further evidence is available. Let me begin with the case for holding that *chemical* phenomena are physical or physically realized.

4. THE PHYSICAL REALIZATION OF CHEMICAL PHENOMENA

Chemistry begins, historically and conceptually, with the observation that everyday substances can apparently be transformed, as a result of mixing and heating, into other substances with strikingly different properties. Thus a shiny, liquid metal, mercury, can be heated in air to yield a reddish, solid powder; a corrosive liquid, sulfuric acid, can be poured onto a gray metal to yield a flammable gas and a noncorrosive liquid. A major development in chemistry was the identification of everyday substances as either elements or compounds produced (or at least producible) from elements, and the formulation of generalizations describing regularities in the production of elements and compounds from other elements and compounds. A further step, of course, was the construal of elements as kinds of *atoms*, that is, discrete, indivisible "packets" of stuff of different types. Now chemistry could have stopped at this point, content to explain transformations of everyday substances in terms of regularities of combination and dissociation holding among the elemental atoms that constitute them, but leaving those regularities themselves unexplained. In fact, of course, chemistry in the twentieth century went on to identify the atoms it had postulated with certain *physical* systems.

Accordingly, as everybody knows, chemistry today treats each type of atom as a type of quantum-mechanically describable system composed of a nucleus of protons and (usually) neutrons surrounded by one or more electrons, which occupy so-called shells, including the shell most directly relevant to chemical phenomena, the outermost or *valence* shell. Such systems are distinguished from one another by the number of protons in their nuclei, a different number for each element. The internal structure of each kind of system is modeled on Bohr's description of the hydrogen atom, and conforms to the requirements of (among other principles) Bohr's building-up principle and the Pauli exclusion principle (see, e.g., Atkins 1994, ch. 13). So although each kind of element is identified with a different kind of physical system, both the physical constituents of the systems and their principles of organization are shared.

The claim that the chemist's atoms contain physical *parts* (or have physical *coincidents*, as I put it earlier) is supported by abundant evidence, including the pioneering experimental work of J. J. Thomson, of Ernest Rutherford, and of James Chadwick. But the claim that the chemist's atoms are *identical* with physical systems of certain kinds is a stronger claim: first, it precludes what the weaker claim does not, that the chemist's atoms should contain nonphysical as well as physical parts; and, second, it entails something the weaker claim does not entail, that all the *properties* of the chemist's atoms are physical (or functional but physically realized). What supports the stronger claim? This identity hypothesis is supported by the fact that it is an indispensable part of the best explanation of a wide variety of facts about the chemist's atoms. So it is supported by reasoning of the same general kind as that by which the mechanical, thermal, electrical, and optical properties of solids, liquids, and gases were argued earlier to be physical or physically realized.

To start with a very simple example: the chemist's atoms in fact have certain *masses*, different masses for the different types of atom. Now on the independently testable assumption that electrons, neutrons, and protons have certain masses, together with the identity hypothesis that the chemist's atoms of different kinds just *are* physical systems of different kinds, as indicated earlier, all composed entirely of electrons, neutrons, and protons, we would *expect* the chemist's atoms to have certain masses; and these expected masses turn out to be the very masses that they do in fact have (see Atkins 1995, 125–6). So the assumption about the masses of electrons, neutrons, and protons, together with the hypothesis about what the chemist's atoms *are*, constitutes at least a candidate explanation of the observed masses of the chemist's atoms. And surely this candidate explanation is the best explanation. Other candidate explanations are certainly *conceivable* – for example, the hypothesis that the mass of an atom of, say, gold is a property independent of the masses of its constituent particles, a property that arises in accordance with a brute law of emergence that operates whenever a certain arrangement (the gold-type arrangement) of electrons, neutrons, and protons is formed. But such alternative candidate explanations are inferior to the explanation of which the identity hypothesis is a part when judged by the principle of economy discussed in Section 2. The candidate explanation that includes the identity hypothesis is therefore the best available candidate explanation of the observed masses of the chemist's atoms. So those observed masses should be taken as evidence that the identity hypothesis is true. Likewise, the observed diameters and densities of the chemist's atoms can also be explained, and best explained, on the identity hypothesis that the chemist's atoms just are physical systems of the relevant kind (see Atkins 1995, 126–9); and so these diameters and densities should also be taken as evidence for the hypothesis.

A logically more complex case concerns the *ionization energies* of the chemist's atoms, that is, the energy needed to turn each kind of (electrically neutral) atom into a positively charged particle. These energies, which can be determined spectroscopically, exhibit interesting variations from atom to atom (see Atkins 1994, 445). However, if, in the spirit of the hypothesis that atoms just are physical systems of the kind already indicated, the ionization energy of an atom is identified with the energy needed to remove an electron from the valence shell of the physical system alleged to be identical with the atom, it then becomes possible to give a qualitative explanation of the variations in ionization energy among atoms.[11] Ionization energies tend to rise as the number of protons in the nucleus and hence the strength of the nuclear charge increases; they tend to fall if orbitals (i.e., quantum-mechanically permissible regions) are occupied by two electrons, so that there is electron-electron repulsion, and also to the extent that the valence shell electrons are *shielded* from the nuclear charge by electrons in shells closer to the nucleus; ionization energies are also affected by the *shape* of the orbital occupied by the electron in question, since some though not all orbitals allow the electron to penetrate right to the nucleus (445–6). Not only do elements vary in their ionization energies, however; they also have systematic tendencies to form positively charged ions with different charges (e.g., sodium forms singly charged cations, magnesium doubly charged ones), but these tendencies too can be given a qualitative explanation by identifying elements with certain physical systems, and ionization with the loss of one or more electrons from the valence shell (129–34). Now, these candidate explanations for facts about ionization energies and for tendencies to form ions are the best available candidate explanations for those facts, since alternatives that treated these facts about elements as emergent would fare very poorly by the principle of economy. But because these candidate explanations include the hypothesis that the chemist's atoms are merely physical systems of a certain kind, the facts about ionization energies and the tendencies to form ions provide further evidence that this identity hypothesis is true. The only logical difference between these cases and the earlier cases of atoms' masses, diameters, and densities is that in these cases the best explanation of the evidence-constituting facts does not leave those facts alone; by identifying ionization with a certain physically characterizable process (i.e., electron loss), it redescribes the facts and then explains them only as redescribed. Such redescription of the facts to be explained will always be necessary when the proprietary vocabulary

---

11 Approximate quantitative predictions are made possible by the Hartree-Fock procedure, which can be used when analytic solutions for the relevant Schrödinger equations cannot be found (see Atkins 1994, 446–7).

used to characterize the facts to be explained is not included within the proprietary vocabulary in terms of which the explanation is cast.

So far, the facts about the chemist's atoms that we have seen to be explainable on the physicalist hypothesis that atoms are one and the same as certain physical systems have concerned atoms in isolation. But obviously the chemist's atoms interact with one another, combining to form compounds, and they do so in certain systematic ways: an element will not form a compound with just any old element, and even when elements do combine, they do so in definite proportions. Can facts about the tendencies of the chemist's atoms to form compounds also be explained on the assumption that atoms are nothing more than certain physical systems operating in accordance with fundamental physical laws? They can; indeed, atoms' tendencies to form compounds are a consequence of their quantum mechanical descriptions.

Here, in a very few strokes, is a sketch of the explanation. Once the chemist's atoms have been identified with physical systems of the appropriate kinds, the next step is to identify the formation of compounds from elements with the formation of chemical bonds between the relevant physical systems, where a chemical bond is construed as a distribution of electrons in the valence shells of the ingredient physical systems, which results in the physical systems' being attracted electrostatically to one another. With these identifications in place, the task of explaining why elements form compounds as they do becomes the task of explaining why chemical bonds arise as they do – why the valence electrons of the ingredient physical systems redistribute themselves in a way that results in the mutual attraction of the physical systems. This redistribution occurs because, first, according to the quantum mechanical description of the physical systems hypothesized to constitute the compound, the lowest-energy configuration of the valence electrons in those systems is one in which some of those electrons have a higher probability of lying *between* the physical systems in such a way that they interact with the positively charged nuclei of both systems; and because, second, according to the second law of thermodynamics, physical systems tend toward their lowest-energy configurations.

Determining the exact energies of molecular systems would require finding exact solutions to the Schrödinger equation for those systems, something that we cannot do (Atkins 1994, 462). Approximate methods, however, can be used. In the molecular orbital theory, for example, the valence electrons of all the constituent atoms in a molecule are treated as spread throughout the whole molecule in so-called molecular orbitals. Molecular orbitals can then be calculated approximately by treating them as the linear combination of the atomic orbitals of their constituent atoms. The molecular orbital theory can explain why neither helium nor neon forms diatomic molecules, why oxygen and fluorine do form diatomic molecules, and why the nitrogen molecule, N_2, has a triple bond, with three pairs of shared electrons (474–93). It can also explain the occurrence of the biologically very important *hydrogen bond*, an attractive interaction between molecules that involves a hydrogen atom and two so-called electronegative elements (770–1). The theory can also be extended to polyatomic systems. For instance, because the energies of some orbitals vary with the bond angle, it can explain the *shapes* of molecules (493–505).

Much else can be explained by using the quantum mechanical treatment of the chemist's atoms that modern physical chemistry provides. Phenomena in which chemical conditions interact with physical conditions provide several striking examples: the need for heat in order to get some chemical reactions to occur (Atkins 1991, 107); the generation of electricity by chemical batteries (91–2); electrolysis, in which electricity causes chemical reactions (115); chemical reactions triggered by light (197); and chemical reactions producing light (205ff.). An account of these phenomena that treats chemical phenomena as basic (rather than as physical) must regard these chemicophysical interactions, and others like them, as brute and inexplicable. Chemical phenomena that can *only* be accounted for on a quantum mechanical approach are also noteworthy: the fact that isotopes of the same element, despite the exact similarity in their valence shells, react at different rates, thanks to quantum tunneling (116–7); and the Diels-Alder reaction, in which a ring of six carbon atoms is formed, thanks in part to the sign of an electron's wave function (184ff.). Here are chemical phenomena that cannot be explained at all unless chemical elements are construed as physical systems.

The upshot of my discussion of chemical phenomena can be summarized as follows. In many cases, the chemist's atoms behave in exactly the ways in which one would expect them to behave on the assumption that they are no more (though certainly no less) than physical systems of certain kinds. Rival hypotheses that treat these behavioral tendencies of chemical elements as emergent relative to their physical constitutions are inferior because they are less economical while meeting no unmet explanatory need. These behavioral tendencies should therefore be regarded as physical; nothing is gained by treating them as anything more. Of course, it is conceivable that even though some of the behavioral tendencies of the chemist's atoms are physical, some are not. But the many and varied behavioral tendencies of the chemist's atoms that *do* seem to be purely physical surely constitute positive instances of, and hence enumerative-inductive evidence for, the universal hypothesis that *all* the behavioral tendencies of the chemist's atoms are purely physical.

Although I have been sketching the evidence for holding that the chemist's atoms are one and the same as certain physical systems, I regard it as an open question, as far as my discussion is concerned, whether *all* chemical types should be treated as physical types, or whether some or all of them should instead be treated as (physically realized) *functional* types. Indeed, in view of the existence of chemically very similar isotopes of the same element, it is tempting to treat even atoms as functional types whose associated conditions are specified in purely physical terms, but which are multiply realized by physical systems that differ from one another only in the number of neutrons their nuclei include (and hence in mass). It is even more tempting to treat, say, acidity as a functional type (or perhaps, since chemistry seems to use more than one notion of an acid, as several functional types), because a so-called Brønsted acid, for example, is standardly defined as a proton donor, which sounds like a splendidly functional definition. But these questions need not be settled here, for even if some chemical types are functional, their physical realization is in no serious doubt. So let us now turn to the case for holding that biological phenomena are physical or physically realized, beginning with *cells*.

5. THE PHYSICAL REALIZATION OF BIOLOGICAL PHENOMENA

Biology has made the remarkable discovery that all living things either are or are made of cells of various kinds (plus the chemicals produced by cells). This discovery is remarkable because things need not have turned out that way. We could have found that tigers are made of a distinctive kind of tiger stuff, whose nature it is to behave in characteristically tigerish ways when organized into a tigerish shape; that oak trees are made of an entirely different kind of stuff, oak stuff, whose (different) nature it is to behave in characteristically oaken ways when organized into an oaken shape; and so on. Or we could have found that animals and plants are indeed made of parts, but that all the parts of a tiger are quite different from all those of an oak, which are quite different from all those of a sponge, and so on. In fact, of course, we have found that all living things exhibit the remarkable commonality of either being or being made of cells. Nor is this commonality trivial. For all cells have substantial things in common; for example, they share membranes made largely of lipid bilayers and the same basic genetic processes (e.g., DNA transcription) leading to protein synthesis.

More recently, molecular biology has made the further discovery that all cells are made of chemicals, which is to say that among their parts are chemicals: for example, small organic molecules such as sugars, fatty acids, amino acids, and nucleotides, together with the larger organic molecules – polysaccharides, phospholipids, proteins, and polynucleotides – that they form. Molecular biology has therefore discovered not only that all cells possess an internal structure but also that all cells, though they fall into different types, possess a similar kind of internal structure (since composed of the same kinds of chemical constituents). And this discovery is no less remarkable than the first, for it might have turned out that cells possess no internal structure at all, or that the internal structure of each type of cell was entirely different in character from that of every other type of cell.

Now the claim that cells have atoms, molecules, and ions as parts is uncontroversial and widely known. But it is, we should note, logically weaker than the physicalistic claim that cells are *chemically realized*, and for two reasons of a now familiar sort. First, the claim that cells have chemical parts is compatible with the possibility that cells possess, in addition to their chemical parts, certain nonchemical parts that make a difference to the cells' properties. For example, the claim that cells have chemical parts is compatible with the possibility that cells possess vital forces that, either by themselves or through interacting with cells' chemical parts, endow cells with behavioral properties that their chemical parts alone could not have produced. Second, the claim that cells have chemical parts is also compatible with the different possibility that, though cells possess no nonchemical parts, they still possess behavioral properties that are *emergent* relative to their chemical constitutions. For example, a cell that had no nonchemical parts might still possess an ability to make a copy of itself which was reductively inexplicable in terms of its chemical constitution and chemical laws alone, so that the best one could do to explain this ability would be to appeal to a brute law of emergence according to which certain complexes of biological molecules under certain chemically specifiable conditions *just do* acquire the ability to make copies of themselves. However, even though the uncontroversial claim that cells have chemical parts does not *entail* the physicalistic claim that cells are chemically realized, there is still abundant evidence that the physicalistic claim is true, evidence uncovered by molecular biology.[12]

Cells, it has been discovered, *do* things. For example, they make copies of themselves, in undergoing cell division; they manufacture various molecules, both those common to all cells (e.g., the energy-store ATP) and those specific to certain cell types (e.g., the hemoglobin in red blood cells); they move from place to place (e.g., in embryonic development, in the metastasis of cancer cells, and, amazingly, even in vitro), and certain of their *parts* move from place to place *within* cells (e.g., vesicles containing molecules move around cells along microtubules); they extract energy from their surroundings (e.g., from ambient light, as in plants); they communicate with one another (e.g., by secreting hormones).

But *how* do cells do these things, and other things besides? The answer uncontroversially given by molecular biology is that cells do what they do solely in virtue of the behavior of their chemical parts, which operate in accordance with perfectly standard chemical principles. This answer is arrived at in two stages. First of all, molecular biologists identify the (relatively) large-scale *cellular* activity in question (e.g., cell division, the manufacture of molecules) with a *sequence* of smaller-scale activities involving the cell's *chemical parts* (e.g., the action of an enzyme in prizing a complex molecule apart). Consider, for example, the cellular activity of manufacturing a specific protein. To a first approximation, manufacturing a specific protein might be identified with the following sequence of smaller-scale activities: transcription (whereby a messenger-RNA copy of the appropriate segment of the cell's DNA is made in the cell nucleus), RNA splicing (in which those triplets of nucleotide bases in the messenger-RNA strand that do not code for amino acids are edited out), and then translation (in which first the order of the nucleotide bases in the messenger-RNA strand is read, and then a protein is strung together out of amino acids in accordance with the order of nucleotide bases in the messenger-RNA strand). But the specification of this sequence of processes must be made much more detailed before we can say that manufacturing a protein has been identified with a sequence of activities of *chemical* entities. And it can be. Consider the following description from

12 Although I do not refer to them later, two very readable primers on molecular biology are Rensberger (1996) and Goodsell (1998).

a standard textbook of the third process, translation:

The codon [i.e., triplet of nucleotide bases] recognition process by which genetic information is transferred from mRNA [i.e., messenger-RNA] via tRNA [i.e., transfer-RNA, a complex molecule with a triplet of nucleotide bases on one end and an amino acid molecule on the other] depends on the same type of base-pair interactions that mediate the transfer of genetic information.... from DNA to RNA [i.e., the interactions in which, during transcription, triplets of nucleotide bases on a strand of DNA bond with triplets of nucleotide bases on molecules of RNA]. But the mechanics of ordering the tRNA molecules on the mRNA are complicated and require a *ribosome*, a complex of more than 50 different proteins associated with several structural RNA molecules... Each ribosome is a large protein-synthesizing machine on which tRNA molecules position themselves so as to read the genetic message encoded in an mRNA molecule. The ribosome first finds a specific start site on the mRNA that sets the reading frame and determines the amino-terminal end of the protein. Then, as the ribosome moves along the mRNA molecule, it translates the nucleotide sequence into an amino acid sequence one codon at a time, using tRNA molecules to add amino acids to the growing end of the polypeptide [i.e., protein] chain. When a ribosome reaches the end of the message, both it and the freshly made carboxyl end of the protein are released from the 3' end of the mRNA molecule into the cytoplasm. (Alberts et al. 1994, 107)

The description of translation in this passage evidently speaks of the activities of *chemical* entities – RNA molecules, ribosomes, amino acids, polypeptides – that are parts of the cell.

Having identified the cellular activity in question with a sequence of activities involving the cell's chemical parts, molecular biologists proceed, second, to explain *how* the cell's chemical parts are able to do what they have been described as doing, and to do so in terms of perfectly standard chemical phenomena, such as the breaking and forming of covalent bonds (in which shared electrons bind atoms together) and the breaking and forming of much weaker hydrogen bonds (in which a hydrogen atom that is covalently bonded to an atom like oxygen that tends to hog shared electrons is left with its positively charged nucleus exposed and is therefore attracted to atoms of certain kinds in other molecules). Remarkably, such simple phenomena are capable of accounting for the apparently much more sophisticated behavior that the chemical parts of cells are described by molecular biologists as engaging in. For example, macromolecules are often described as *recognizing* one another, and countless cellular processes depend on the possibility of such recognition. And even if we explicitly disavow any mentalistic connotations that the word "recognize" may have, molecular recognition is still a striking achievement. How is it done? In the aqueous environment of a cell's interior, where the temperature is about 37° centigrade, macromolecules are in constant motion, diffusing randomly through the cell. Because noncovalent bonds are very weak when compared with covalent bonds, if two macromolecules should happen to collide but form only a single noncovalent bond, they will promptly be torn apart by their thermal motions. But if the three-dimensional structure of the two macromolecules permits them to fit together snugly, then several noncovalent bonds may form between them, and these may indeed be strong enough to withstand the thermal shaking they receive, at least for long enough to allow a chemical reaction to proceed. Because not just any old pair of macromolecules will fit snugly together in this way, macromolecules will interact selectively with one another – which is all that molecular recognition comes to (Alberts et al. 1994, 89–98).

This example illustrates one of the ways in which the *conformation* of a protein – the three-dimensional arrangement of its constituent atoms – crucially affects its chemical behavior, and one might wonder how the conformation itself arises. The answer is that a chain of amino acids adopts the conformation it does because certain (covalent) peptide bonds between the amino acids form hydrogen bonds with one another, so that the chain sticks to itself at various points, and also because hydrophobic regions of the chain, unable to form hydrogen bonds with water, arrange themselves as best they can to avoid the water with which they are surrounded. Noncovalent bonding also accounts for the formation from proteins of larger structures such as ribosomes (as mentioned earlier), the membranes of cells and organelles (which tend to keep molecules where they need to be for reactions to occur), and multienzyme complexes (whose effect is to keep all the enzymes required for a given reaction pathway together, so that limitations imposed on reactions by low concentrations of reagents and low rates of diffusion can be overcome). Similarly, noncovalent bonding can produce polymers of proteins that form helices, sheets, tubes, and spheres. Larger protein structures of these sorts will often self-assemble from their constituents in vitro, including both bacterial ribosomes that can engage in protein synthesis and fully infective viruses (Alberts et al. 1994, 111–28)!

The most important chemical activity that the conformation of a protein affects is its functioning as an enzyme, that is, as a protein *catalyst* of chemical reactions. In part, the conformation of an enzyme matters because the enzyme must bind to its substrate before the reaction can occur and, as we have already noted, whether such binding occurs depends on the conformation of the molecules concerned; whether a given reaction occurs at all will therefore depend on the presence or absence of the right enzyme in the cell. The catalysis then works, in part, because the enzyme holds atoms in the right orientations for reactions to occur, again a matter of conformation. Enzymes also catalyze reactions by preferentially binding to, and hence stabilizing, certain intermediate states in the reactions, thus reducing the reactions' activation energies. A further catalytic effect results because enzymes can promote the making and unmaking of covalent bonds through simultaneous acid and base catalysis (in which electrons are subtly redistributed by proton donation and proton removal, respectively); but these two forms of catalysis can occur simultaneously only because the appropriate atoms on the enzyme's surface are spatially separated, yet again a matter of conformation (Alberts et al. 1994, 128–5).

Not only do macromolecules *have* a shape, but this shape can be *altered* by the binding to them of other molecules. For example, the shape of the enzyme hexokinase is such that when glucose noncovalently binds to it, the glucose forms attachments at two different sites and therefore pulls those sites toward one another, thus changing the enzyme's shape. Such shape changes can make enormous differences to what molecules can do. When glucose binds to hexokinase, for instance, the resulting shape change means that the energy-store molecule ATP can more easily bind to neighboring sites on hexokinase, which helps hexokinase to catalyze a reaction between ATP and glucose. Other shape-changes that are caused to occur in an enzyme by molecular binding can increase (or decrease) the chances of some *other* molecule's binding to a site on that enzyme far away from the first binding site; thus whether one molecule undergoes or catalyzes a given reaction may depend on the shape-changing effects of a second molecule with which it does not interact chemically at all. Chemical feedback mechanisms can therefore arise: the final product of a metabolic pathway may bind to a *regulatory site* on the enzyme that initiates the pathway, thus putting the enzyme into an *inactive conformation*, and therefore inhibiting the activity of the enzyme.

The ability of molecules to change shape in response to molecular binding has even more dramatic consequences, for different changes in shape can be coordinated spatially and temporally so as to give rise to *molecular machines*. So-called motor proteins can actually move along by undergoing an appropriate series of conformational changes (though one step in the process must be irreversible, and hence powered by an energy source, or else the motion will not be unidirectional); DNA helicase enzymes, which assist in unwinding DNA during transcription, travel along strands of DNA in this fashion. Similarly, certain enzymes embedded in cell membranes can function as *ion pumps*, again as a result of appropriate sequences of conformational changes produced by molecular binding. For example, one membrane enzyme pumps sodium ions out of, and potassium ions into, the cell; the resulting sodium ion gradient across the cell membrane drags valuable glucose and amino acid molecules into the cell (Alberts et al. 1994, 195–212).

The past few paragraphs have shown how relatively simple chemical phenomena, suitably selected and arranged, can give rise to remarkable and unexpected effects; they therefore also suggest how, in principle, molecular biologists can claim to be able to explain, in purely chemical terms, those activities of cells' chemical components which, in proper sequence, they identify with such distinctively cellular activities as the manufacture of a specific protein. For a fuller illustration, however, let us return to the case of DNA translation. This process was described earlier in the long quotation, but although it was construed there as a sequence of events *involving* chemical entities, no purely *chemical* explanation was given of how those chemical entities could behave in the ways described – how they could "position themselves" on a molecule, "find" sites, "move along" molecules, or "translate" one sequence of chemicals into another. So let me sketch such a chemical explanation.

The set-up in the cytoplasm prior to DNA translation is as follows. There is a single-stranded mRNA molecule (earlier copied, of course, from a segment of DNA in the nucleus); there are tRNA molecules, folded up (thanks both to bonding between complementary nucleotide bases *within* the single strand of RNA and to other hydrogen bonds) into a distinctive conformation with an anticodon exposed at one end and the ability to form a bond with an amino acid at the other; there are amino acid molecules of the twenty various kinds; and there are both the large and the small subunits that make up ribosomes. Now before translation proper begins, each tRNA molecule bonds to its "correct" amino acid ("correct," of course, given the genetic code and the sequence of nucleotide bases in each tRNA's anticodon), thus forming an aminoacyl-tRNA molecule; this is accomplished by a set of twenty specialized enzymes, each one of which binds preferentially to just one particular kind of tRNA, catalyzes the formation of a covalent bond between that kind of tRNA and the right amino acid, and also activates it, so that it will be able to form a peptide bond with the neighboring amino acid in the growing chain of amino acids. A further preliminary concerns the ribosome. Its small subunit has three binding sites for RNA: one for a segment of mRNA, one (the P-site) for molecules of peptidyl-tRNA (tRNA molecules whose attached amino acid has formed a bond with the growing chain of amino acids), and one (the A-site) for molecules of aminoacyl-tRNA (the newly arrived tRNA molecules loaded up with their correct amino acids); the P-site and the A-site are next to one another. Before translation can start, an initiator tRNA molecule, with the amino acid methionine, must bind to the P-site of a small ribosome subunit, this subunit must bind to a molecular "cap" structure at one end of the mRNA molecule, and then the subunit must move along the mRNA molecule until it reaches the first AUG codon (the start codon), whereupon a large ribosome subunit must bind to it.

The ribosome is now assembled on the mRNA molecule, ready to string together a protein from its amino acid constituents. The first step in the actual stringing together of the protein is the binding of a new aminoacyl-tRNA molecule to the A-site of the ribosome's small subunit; it will be a tRNA molecule with the "correct" amino acid on it because only such a molecule will have an anticodon whose nucleotide bases are complementary to − and hence bind preferentially to − those of the codon next to the AUG start codon on the mRNA. The next step in the process is the formation of a peptide bond between the amino acid carried by the new aminoacyl-tRNA and the methionine that was carried by the initiator tRNA molecule, and the breaking of the bond between the methionine and the initiator tRNA that carried it; this reaction is catalyzed by peptidyl transferase, a region of the ribosome's large subunit. Finally, using energy from the hydrolysis of an energy-storing compound to power a series of conformational changes, the ribosome moves three nucleotide bases along the mRNA strand, relocating the tRNA molecule formerly bound to the A-site to the P-site, and allowing the tRNA molecule formerly in the P-site to diffuse away. This three-step procedure is then repeated with different aminoacyl tRNA molecules until all the amino acids needed to make the protein coded for by the mRNA strand have been added to the growing chain. The ribosome knows when to stop, because there are stop codons on the mRNA to which certain release factors preferentially bind when the ribosome reaches them, thus causing peptidyl transferase to attach a molecule of water, rather than an amino acid, to the now complete chain of amino acids, and hence allowing the chain to diffuse away into the cytoplasm (Alberts et al. 1994, 227–36).

According to molecular biology, then, the distinctively cellular behavior of cells can in principle be completely accounted for in terms of the standard chemical behavior of their chemical parts. Not that molecular biologists have actually produced biochemical explanations of every aspect of every cellular behavior, for they certainly have not. But over the past twenty-five years they have produced biochemical explanations of so large and so diverse a sample of aspects of cellular behavior – not only of basic genetic processes, but also of such phenomena as membrane transport, the transportation of molecules within cells, the harnessing of energy from molecules, intercell signaling, cell division, and cell differentiation – that they are well within their rights to conclude, inductively, that every aspect of every cellular behavior is explainable in the same sort of way.

But this finding in molecular biology clearly provides strong evidence for a physicalistic conclusion that is presumably no part of molecular biology proper, namely, that cells and distinctively cellular phenomena are *chemically realized*. For if all the doings of cells can be completely explained by reference to the chemical doings of their undisputed chemical parts, then it would be quite gratuitous to suppose either that cells have nonphysical parts in addition to their chemical parts or that cells possess behavioral powers that are emergent relative to their chemical parts; to make either supposition would be to reduce the economy of one's world view without thereby securing any compensating gain in explanatory power. Or, to put the reasoning a little differently, the findings of molecular biology tell us that cells have just those features which we would expect them to have on the hypothesis that they and their distinctive features are chemically realized; so the hypothesis that cells and their distinctive features are chemically realized, when conjoined with biochemistry, is at least a candidate to explain why cells have the features they do. But because this physicalistic hypothesis is a more economical candidate than any of its emergentist rivals, it deserves to be rated the best explanation, with the result that the distinctive features that cells have been discovered to possess must be treated as evidence that cells and their distinctive features are chemically realized. A further step shows, moreover, why we can now claim to have evidence that cells and their distinctive features are *physical* or *physically realized*. For if cells and their distinctive features are chemically realized, then, since chemical phenomena, as there is much evidence to think, are physical or physically realized, it follows by the transitivity of realization (and identity) that cells and their distinctive features are themselves physical or physically realized.

What about the organs into which cells and their chemical products are organized? A parallel line of reasoning reveals that there is evidence to treat organs too as physically realized. Let me illustrate with the example of the human heart. The human heart is a four-chambered structure made chiefly of muscle. Obviously it has a certain physical appearance, but it is what it does – its behavior as a whole – that is of most interest. Because the walls of its constituent chambers contract rhythmically, it can function as a pump, squeezing blood through itself. The upper chambers, or atria, contract first, forcing blood from the vessels that lead into them through a one-way valve into the lower chambers, or ventricles, which contract next, the contractions starting at their bottoms, so that the blood now in the ventricles is forced out of them into the blood vessels that lead from them. Moreover, this regular pattern of contractions is generated by the heart itself. Innervations to the heart from the autonomic nervous system affect the *rate* of the heart's beat but do not initiate it; left to itself, the heart would still beat – at a rate of about one hundred beats per minute.

How can the distinctively cardiac behavior of the human heart, as just described, be explained? One possible explanation is a reductive explanation, on the following lines. First, the heart itself is claimed to be identical with (or realized by) a certain organized collection of cells of certain types (e.g., cardiac muscle cells) and of chemical products of cells (e.g., the proteins forming connective tissue in the heart wall); this organized collection of cells is the cell-biological coincident (analogous to a physical coincident) of the heart. On this identity (or realization) hypothesis, then, much of the heart consists of individual cardiac muscle cells, roughly rectangular in shape, joined together at their short ends, not unlike bricks in a wall, by so-called intercalated disks. Second, the complex contractile behavior of the heart is claimed to be identical with (or realized by) the suitably organized and coordinated sequence of behaviors of the individual muscle cells that compose it. With these identity (or realization) hypotheses in place, the task of explaining the contractile behavior of the heart then becomes the task of, first, identifying the relevant behavior of individual cardiac cells and, second, explaining how such behavior on the part of many cells comes to be suitably organized and coordinated.

Contemporary physiology undertakes this twofold task. The starting point is that regular cardiac muscle cells, even in culture, contract – become shorter and fatter – when their membranes are depolarized. (As it happens, molecular biology has uncovered in exquisite detail exactly how and why they do this, but for the present purpose of reductively explaining the distinctively cardiac behavior of the whole heart, we can simply take the behavior of individual cardiac muscle cells as given.)

Because the individual muscles cells that make up the chambers of the heart become shorter and fatter when suitably simulated, and because they are arranged like bricks in a wall, it is easy to see that, if they all contract in a coordinated way, the chambers themselves must contract, so that the internal volumes of the chambers are reduced. But how are these individual muscle cells stimulated to contract? The answer is that certain specialized cardiac cells in a small region near the top of the heart called the sinoatrial node undergo rhythmic depolarizations of their membranes, even in culture, that are *spontaneous*, that is, not triggered by any external cause; and this ability to undergo spontaneous depolarization explains how heartbeat can originate within the heart itself. (As in the previous case, the internal cause of these spontaneous depolarizations is known – changes in the permeability of the cell membrane to ions – but may be ignored for present purposes.) Moreover, because the intercalated disks that connect adjacent cardiac muscle cells contain so-called gap junctions, waves of depolarization can spread from individual cell to individual cell. So spontaneous depolarizations originate in the cells of the sinoatrial node and then spread throughout the atria, causing the contractile cells in the atria to contract and, because of the rapidity of signal transmission, to contract together.

The wave of depolarization then reaches the atrioventricular node, at the top of the ventricles, which is composed of specialized cardiac cells through which waves of depolarization spread relatively *slowly*; because it is only via the atrioventricular node that the spreading wave of depolarization gets from the atria to the ventricles at all, this relative slowness of the atrioventricular cells explains why, when the heart beats, it is the atria that contract first, and the ventricles second. From the atrioventricular node, the wave of depolarization travels through the cells, specialized for conduction, that make up the atrioventricular bundle, which branches repeatedly till its finest fibers make contact with regular cardiac muscle cells at the base of the ventricles, causing those ventricular cells to contract, and thus generating a wave of contraction that spreads upward throughout the whole of the ventricles; this structural arrangement obviously accounts for why ventricular contraction starts at the bottom (Vander, Sherman, and Luciano 1990, 362–81; Ross, Romrell, and Kaye 1995, 316–19).

This sketch omits complications; for example, individual sinoatrial cells, when isolated, spontaneously beat at *different* rates and, as computer modeling of many interconnected cells reveals, they beat in the heart at the same rate only because of the intercell communication permitted by the gap junctions between adjacent cells (Noble 1998, 59). But the general moral is clear: by construing the human heart as identical with, or realized by, its cell-biological coincident, and by construing the distinctively cardiac behavior of the whole heart as identical with, or realized by, a suitably organized and coordinated sequence of behaviors of individual cells, we can draw upon contemporary physiology to explain the distinctively cardiac behavior of the whole heart. Moreover, this explanation is superior to its antiphysicalist rivals. For while it is logically possible that human hearts should contain non-cell-biological parts, and that the presence of these parts should change the overall behavior of hearts from what it would otherwise have been, there are no facts about the overall behavior of hearts for the explanation of which the hypothesis of such non-cell-biological parts is necessary. Likewise for the logically possible hypothesis that human hearts, while they contain no non-cell-biological parts, nevertheless possess certain emergent behavioral tendencies above and beyond those they possess solely in virtue of their cell-biological constitutions. So the antiphysicalist rivals to our reductive explanation of the distinctively cardiac behavior of hearts are less economical than it is, but without any compensating explanatory gain. The distinctively cardiac behavior of human hearts therefore provides evidence that the reductive explanation is true, and thus that human hearts and their behaviors are cell-biological or cell-biologically realized.

But contemporary physiology can tell a similar story to the one about the distinctively cardiac behavior of hearts about many other behaviors of many other organs: the behaviors in question are just what you would expect the organs in question to exhibit if they and their behaviors were cell-biological or cell-biologically realized (Vander et al. 1990; Ross et al. 1995). So, by reasoning parallel to that of the previous paragraph, we must treat these behaviors as evidence that these other organs, with their behaviors, are cell-biological or cell-biologically realized. But then, because these behaviors of these organs constitute numerous and varied positive instances of the universal hypothesis that *all* behaviors of *all* organs are cell-biological or cell-biologically realized, these behaviors also constitute enumerative-inductive evidence that the universal hypothesis is true. Finally, by appealing to the transitivity of realization (and of identity) and to the claim, for which we have already provided evidence, that cell-biological phenomena are physical or physically realized, we can see that there is evidence that all organs and their behaviors are physical or physically realized.

6. THE EXTENSION OF THE ARGUMENT TO OTHER SCIENTIFIC PHENOMENA

Thus far, I have presented evidence that all macrophysical phenomena, all chemical phenomena, and all biological phenomena are physical or physically realized. But essentially the same line of reasoning could also be applied to the proprietary phenomena that other sciences investigate. Consider, for example, astronomy. No contemporary astronomer doubts that the objects of astronomical study – stars, planets, nebulae – have a physical composition (or, if you prefer, have a physical coincident). Moreover, in accounting for the behavior of these physically composed objects, it is physics (and physics alone) to which appeal is made. According to astrophysicist Martin Harwit, "Nowadays *astrophysics* and *astronomy* have come to mean almost the same thing. In earlier days it was not clear at all that the study of stars had anything in common with physics. But physical explanations for the observations not only of stars, but of interstellar matter and of phenomena on the scale of galaxies, have been so successful that we confidently assume all astronomical processes to be subject to physical reasoning" (1998, 9). Admittedly, immediately after this passage Harwit proceeds to emphasize astronomical phenomena that have *not* been explained – by physics or by anything else. But the existence of such unexplained phenomena does not undermine the main point of his quoted remarks: the recently discovered physical explainability of *many* astronomical phenomena provides some evidence to expect the physical explainability of *all* astronomical phenomena.

Next, consider geology. Geologists standardly view rocks as aggregates of minerals, where minerals are understood to be naturally occurring, solid, inorganic chemical compounds, and they construe geological phenomena as sequences of chemical and physical changes in rocks, often precipitated by interaction with such physical phenomena as air and water. Furthermore, in accounting for geological phenomena construed in this way, geologists appeal to (and only to) causal influences that are physical or physically realized. For example, they appeal to gravity in order to account for the separation of the Earth's materials into core, mantle, and crust; the deposition of sediment; glacial ice flow; lava flow; and the phenomenon of isostasy, whereby the loading of the crust with sediment causes subsidence and the removal of a load because of erosion causes uplift. They regard convection currents in the material of the Earth's mantle as the source of the movement of tectonic plates. In order to explain the weathering of rocks, they appeal to mechanical physical processes such as ice-wedging (in which the expansion of freezing water prizes rocks apart) and to chemical processes such as oxidation, dissolution, and hydrolysis. They understand the formation of metamorphic rocks from igneous, sedimentary, or previously metamorphosed rocks as involving the formation of new minerals on account both of physical changes in temperature and pressure undergone by the old rocks and of chemical changes occurring within them (Hamblin 1992). The application of physics to geological phenomena is elaborated, of course, in geophysics (see, e.g., Lowrie 1997).

For a final example of a science whose proprietary phenomena could easily be argued to be physical or physically realized by means of essentially the same reasoning as that used in the preceding sections, let us look briefly at meteorology. Meteorologists aim to understand changes in the state of the atmosphere – changes in the temperature, humidity, and pressure of the air, in the speed and direction of the wind, and in the type and amount of cloudiness and of precipitation. Unsurprisingly, contemporary meteorologists unanimously assume that the atmosphere is entirely physically composed, consisting of various gases, such as nitrogen, oxygen, and carbon dioxide, together with water vapor and minute solid and liquid particles. And, as in geology, it is to physics and chemistry that they appeal in their attempts to understand meteorological phenomena; for example, to the physics of gases in order to account for the formation of winds, to the physics of heat in order to understand the absorption of the Sun's heat by water vapor and the relative coolness of the air over water, and to chemistry in order to understand the Sun-caused formation of ozone from oxygen and the absorption of heat by carbon dioxide (Lutgens and Tarbuck 2001).

Before proceeding, let me pause to take stock of where realization physicalism now stands, evidentially, given what has been accomplished in this chapter thus far. It will be recalled from Chapter 5 that, in order to be a reasonable physicalist, it is necessary only that, in light of available evidence, physicalism be more probable than its relevant rivals. It will also be recalled, from the Introduction and elsewhere, that just two main forms of antiphysicalism constitute serious rivals to physicalism. The first form of antiphysicalism corresponds most closely to the intentions of traditional mind-body dualists and claims, in effect, that physicalism is false but *very nearly* true: what physicalism says about the relation between the nonphysical sciences and physics is true of every nonphysical science *except* folk psychology, which must instead be treated as describing real phenomena that are every bit as basic, and that warrant just as much privilege, as those described by fundamental physics. The second form of antiphysicalism claims that physicalism is *entirely false*, alleging instead that a kind of pluralistic egalitarianism prevails among the various sciences and honorary sciences, so that the proprietary phenomena of every science are on an ontological par with those of every other, and the world turns out not to be stratified at all. Although temperamentally opposed to traditional mind-body dualism, an advocate of this second form of antiphysicalism will join with the traditional mind-body dualist in denying that the mental is physical, but will add that the geological and the biological are not physical either; today's most influential antiphysicalists seem to favor this second form of antiphysicalism (Goodman 1978, Putnam 1987, Crane and Mellor 1990, Dupré 1993, and Daly 1997).

The evidence for physicalism presented so far in this chapter counts strongly against this second form of antiphysicalism. For this evidence is precisely evidence that macrophysical phenomena, chemical phenomena, cell-biological phenomena, physiological phenomena, astronomical phenomena, geological phenomena, and meteorological phenomena are all either physical or physically realized; hence it is evidence that all the many sciences, including physics, are *not* on an ontological par with one another, and thus that pluralistic egalitarianism about the many sciences is false. Of course, pluralistic egalitarians who set their epistemic standards high enough can still maintain that their view has not been *conclusively* ruled out, on the grounds that it is still logically consistent with the evidence I have presented; similarly, they can, if they like, insist on the propriety of suspending judgment on the question of physicalism until such time as some higher threshold of probability in light of the evidence has been reached. But what they cannot reasonably do, I claim, is deny that the evidence made available by the findings of contemporary science favors — indeed strongly favors — realization physicalism over pluralistic egalitarianism. By the same token, anyone who supposes that scientists are merely in the grip of an ideological prejudice when they assume, as they almost invariably do, that there is an underlying physical mechanism for every apparently nonphysical phenomenon that they study should consider an alternative hypothesis to account for this widespread assumption: that the scientists who make it are responding quite rationally to the sort of antipluralist evidence that this chapter presents.

However, the evidence presented so far in this chapter, because it does not address the question of mental phenomena, does not count in any direct way against the first form of antiphysicalism distinguished earlier, the traditionally dualistic form. To the question of mental phenomena, therefore, we must now turn.

7. THE PHYSICAL REALIZATION OF MENTAL PHENOMENA

It is best to admit candidly that the evidence for regarding mental phenomena as physical or physically realized is much weaker than the evidence for regarding chemical, biological, geological, and similar phenomena as physical or physically realized. Nevertheless, there *is* evidence that mental phenomena are physical or physically realized, and in this section I indicate what it is.

But why, you might ask, is the empirical case for treating mental phenomena as physical or physically realized so much weaker than the empirical case for treating the other phenomena we have considered as physical or physically realized? Because, I suggest, in contrast with (say) biochemistry, the neurosciences have not yet enabled us to construct *detailed* instantiations of the kind of best-explanation reasoning that I used in earlier sections to argue for the physicality or physical realization of various phenomena. To be sure, the neurosciences have enabled us to construct very *general* instantiations of that kind of reasoning. So, for example, we can argue as follows:

The mind of an organism receives information about its environment from its sense organs, stores and modifies this information, and then causes movement in the organism's bodily parts. Now dualist and physicalist alike can agree that this is an accurate characterization of the mind,[13] but what *explains* why the mind is thus characterizable? Well, according to the neurosciences, a normally functioning and embodied *brain* would be expected to receive information via sense organs about the containing organism's environment, to store and modify that information, and then to cause movement in the containing organism's bodily parts; for obviously the neurosciences have discovered such familiar facts as that neuronal signals travel from the sense organs to the brain and from the brain to the muscles that cause bodily movement. Given these neuroscientific findings, then, the physicalist hypothesis that the mind is, or is realized by, a normally functioning and embodied brain would lead us to expect, and hence would *explain*, the fact that the mind of an organism receives information about its environment from its sense organs, stores and modifies this information, and then causes movement in the organism's bodily parts. Since this explanatory hypothesis is more economical than its rivals, it counts as the best explanation of the fact it would explain. So the fact that the mind of an organism receives information about its environment from its sense organs, stores and modifies this information, and then causes movement

---

13 In calling this characterization accurate, I do not mean to suggest either that it is *complete* or that it expresses the *essence* of the mind or that it is *knowable a priori*; it is merely a fact about the mind.

in the organism's bodily parts provides evidence – some evidence – that the mind is, or is realized by, a normally functioning and embodied brain.

And I do not deny that this line of reasoning genuinely succeeds in displaying one piece of evidence for the physicalistic view that the mind is, or is realized by, the brain; I suspect, indeed, that this line of reasoning, even if not in exactly this explicit form, has been highly influential among both philosophers and scientists. But clearly it is far less impressive than, say, the very detailed case for treating DNA translation as biochemically realized that I sketched in the preceding section.

It would be really impressive if we could take a relatively specific and detailed fact about the (human) mind, such as that most people are much better at figuring out what follows from premises of the form "All Fs are Gs, and all Gs are Hs" than they are at figuring out what follows from premises of the form "All Fs are Gs, and no Hs are Fs" (Johnson-Laird 1983, 67–9), and then show that exactly this pattern of response to presented premise pairs was to be *expected*, given our knowledge of neuronal behavior, and of the human brain's neuronal composition and arrangement. If we could achieve this feat, and others like it, we would then be in a position, with regard to the mind, analogous to the position that, as we saw earlier, we are actually in with regard to the heart: with the brain demonstrably capable (solely in virtue of its cellular constitution) of doing mindlike things, we could then argue that construing the mind as *more* than physical or physically realized was a hypothesis of which we have no need. Alas, we are not yet able – as far as I am aware – to achieve such feats as this.[14] So my diagnosis of why the empirical case for treating mental phenomena as physical or physically realized is so much weaker than the empirical case for treating other phenomena as physical or physically realized is this: even though individual brain cells (including neurons) are very well understood, and there is much evidence that they are biochemically (and hence physically) realized, we have at present only a rather general understanding of how the activities of ensembles of brain cells give rise to distinctively mindlike activities (or to activities identifiable with such activities).[15]

---

14 For example, the irrepressibly optimistic Paul Churchland describes some fascinating reductive strategies for cognitive neurobiology, but even he does not claim that these strategies have as yet yielded actual reductions (1989, 77–110).

15 An intriguing exception to my claim here is provided by Clyde Hardin. Very crudely, according to the neurologically confirmed opponent process theory of color vision, complementary colors (e.g., red and green) are coded on a *single* channel, with neuronal

At any rate, I cannot make an empirical case for treating mental phenomena as physical or physically realized simply by reemploying the reasoning strategy of the preceding sections. Instead, what I can do is to present four lines of argument that, given the assumption that both the brain and the neural events occurring within it are physical or physically realized, will provide empirical support for the view that mental phenomena are physical or physically realized.

The first line of argument may be found in the following remarks taken from a classic paper by Smart: "[S]cience is increasingly giving us a viewpoint whereby organisms are able to be seen as physico-chemical mechanisms.... There does seem to be, so far as science is concerned, nothing in the world but increasingly complex arrangements of physical constituents. All except for one place: in consciousness.... That everything should be explicable in terms of physics... except the occurrence of sensations seems to me to be frankly unbelievable" (1959, 142). Although in the next paragraph Smart disparages his own remarks as "largely a confession of faith" (143), it is clear to me that they nevertheless express a sound line of reasoning in favor of physicalism about the mind. This reasoning has the form of an *enumerative induction*. The premise describes a sample of a population and claims that concrete phenomena of many different kinds – for instance, chemical, cell-biological, histological, physiological, geological, meteorological, and astronomical phenomena – are physical or physically realized. Evidence for the truth of this premise is obviously provided by the preceding sections of this chapter. The conclusion generalizes to the whole of the population and claims that concrete

excitation *above* a certain base rate coding for one hue and excitation *below* that base rate coding for the other. If having a green sensation is regarded as identical with (or as realized by) above-base-rate excitation on a single channel, and having a red sensation is regarded as identical with (or as realized by) below-base-rate excitation on the same channel, then, because excitation on a single channel cannot be both above and below the base rate at the same time, it will be impossible under ordinary circumstances, as Hardin points out (1987, 295), to have a reddish green sensation – which is true. Similarly, it seems true, phenomenally, that orange sensations somehow combine red and yellow sensations, although red sensations themselves are "pure." Now, on the opponent process view, red is coded by non-base-rate firing in the red-green channel, with merely base-rate firing in the yellow-blue channel; orange, however, is coded by non-base-rate firing in the red-green channel, as for red, with non-base-rate firing in the yellow-blue channel too, as for yellow. Given appropriate identity-realization hypotheses, the opponent process theory can therefore explain the binary character of orange sensations and the unary character of red sensations (Hardin 1987, 286–8). Hardin's suggested explanations provide concrete examples of Paul Churchland's idea that "humdrum facts about the manifold(s) of subjective sensory qualia" can be "reconstruct[ed] ..., in some revealingly systematic way, in neurobiological terms" (1989, 103).

phenomena of *all* kinds, including therefore all *mental* phenomena, are physical or physically realized. So the fact that many and varied things have turned out to be physical or physically realized is evidence – some evidence – that everything, including everything mental, is physical or physically realized.

This line of argument is often underestimated. One reaction is to point out that the premise could be true while the conclusion is false – correct, of course, but entirely irrelevant to the evaluation of reasoning that is intended only to be inductive, not deductive. A less naive reaction is to protest that the premise fails to prove the intended conclusion even in an inductive sense of "prove." But this reaction, too, rests on a misunderstanding. The physicalist's claim is not that physicalism about mental phenomena is *probable* (i.e., more probable than not) in light of the evidence of the premise; the claim is that physicalism about mental phenomena is *more probable* in light of the evidence of the premise than it was before – that its probability is *raised* by the evidence, even though it may not be raised very high. Alternatively: if your life depended on correctly stating whether mental phenomena were physical or physically realized, and if the only available consideration was that chemical, cell-biological, histological, physiological, geological, meteorological, and astronomical phenomena are all physical or physically realized, then you should judge that mental phenomena are physical or physically realized too. A third reaction is to answer that the premise cannot support the conclusion because the conclusion itself is so implausible. But this reaction rests on a non sequitur. As I argued in Chapter 5, there is in fact no evidence at all against the conclusion that mental phenomena are physical or physically realized; but even if there were, and even if it were very strong, it would not follow that there could not also be evidence for it: if my fingerprints are found on the pistol that fired the fatal shot, then that is evidence (i.e., some evidence) that I am guilty, and it is *still* evidence that I am guilty even if there exists conclusive evidence that I could not possibly have committed the crime.

The final reaction I discuss tries to play down the evidential significance of the kinds of phenomena mentioned in the premise by alleging, in effect, that they are not *typical* of the population as a whole; the idea is that since it is hardly surprising that chemical, cell-biological, histological, and similar phenomena should all be physical or physically realized (who indeed would have expected otherwise?), the fact that they are provides no evidence that mental phenomena are too. But it *is* surprising that chemical, cell-biological, histological and similar phenomena should all have turned out to be physical or physically realized, as I hinted in my earlier discussions by noting logically possible but nonactual alternatives to this outcome; and as a matter of historical fact it was not expected. We forget too easily that until the Copernican Revolution even astronomical (i.e., celestial) phenomena were assumed to be entirely different in their composition from nonastronomical (i.e., terrestrial) phenomena; that Friedrich Wöhler's synthesis in 1828 of the organic compound urea from inorganic ingredients was found deeply shocking precisely because it contradicted the then popular view that animate and inanimate entities possessed fundamentally different constitutions; that vitalism was not the province of crackpots but rather a respectable scientific hypothesis; and that as recently as 1925 so shrewd and scientifically minded a philosopher as C. D. Broad could doubt that *chemical* phenomena – surely the most "obviously" physical of "obviously" physical phenomena – were physically realized, since he held that chemistry "seems to offer the most plausible example of emergent behavior" (1925, 65). Of course, the suggestion that mental phenomena might be physical or physically realized strikes many people (though certainly not all) as outlandish *today*, but parallel suggestions in the past about astronomical, chemical, and biological phenomena no doubt struck many people (though certainly not all) as outlandish *then*.

Let me turn now to a second line of argument that provides empirical support for the view that mental phenomena are physical or physically realized (see, e.g., Peacocke 1979, 134–43).[16] The argument can conveniently be cast into the form of a reductio ad absurdum of the antiphysicalist assumption that a particular mental state – your decision to clench your fist – is neither physical nor physically realized. It requires three premises in addition to the assumption that is to be reduced to absurdity. Since two of these premises are supported by empirical considerations, the argument can still be regarded as showing that there is empirical evidence for physicalism about the mind.

If you clench and unclench your fist a few times, you will notice that, on each occasion, your decision to clench your fist *caused* certain muscles in your forearm to contract, muscles whose contraction partially constitutes your clenching of your fist; no doubt your decision was not

---

16 Independently of Peacocke, I presented a version of this argument in Melnyk (1994). The version that follows is intended to bolster the argument against various challenges that it faces (see, e.g., Mills 1996 and Sturgeon 1998; see also Witmer 2000 for an excellent discussion of Sturgeon).

sufficient *all by itself* for the contraction of those muscles, but that is no problem since causes do not in general have to be sufficient all by themselves for their effects. Also, although you might – conceivably – be mistaken in claiming that your decisions caused your muscles to contract, you nonetheless have exactly the sort of evidence for this claim that in everyday life we regard as entirely adequate to establish causal claims. Now, as a matter of fact, what goes on when skeletal muscles contract is very well understood biochemically (Alberts et al. 1994, 847–58). In particular, whenever skeletal muscles contract, individual muscle cells that make up the muscles contract. Moreover, the contraction of individual muscle cells consists in the sliding, within each cell, of protein filaments of one kind over protein filaments of another kind; and the immediate cause of this sliding is always the *release of calcium ions* from flattened vesicles that form a structure inside the cell called the sarcoplasmic reticulum. Because, whenever your forearm muscles contract, releases of calcium ions occur in the muscle cells of your forearm, and indeed must occur in order for your muscles to contract, it is hard to deny that, on each occasion of fist clenching, your decision to clench your fist caused releases of calcium ions. Suppose you could somehow magically see inside the cells of your forearm muscles as you clenched a fist, and therefore inspect the intracellular releases of calcium ions directly; surely as you did so you would feel every bit as certain that your decisions to clench a fist caused releases of ions as you felt just now that your decisions to clench a fist caused contractions of the muscles in your forearm – and rightly so, since the evidence to support the causal claim in each case would be of exactly the same type and strength. But calcium ions are physical things, even in the strict sense of "physical" with which I am operating; and releases of calcium ions are physical events in the same strict sense. It is therefore very plausible to claim, contrary to epiphenomenalists of all sorts, including epiphenomenalist dualists, that, with regard to some particular fist-clenching episode,

(P1) Your decision to clench your fist caused (i.e., was an indispensable part of a sufficient cause of) certain *physical* events, viz., certain particular releases of calcium ions.

It is worth noticing that the case just made for P1 appeals only to certain scientific discoveries plus the intuitive and everyday idea that an observed correlation provides good prima facie grounds for judging that one thing caused another. In particular, the case just made for P1 does *not* assume any principle, of the sort criticized by Scott Sturgeon in his

1998 article, to the effect that if an event causes a certain macroevent, then it also causes all the microevents that make up the macroevent; accordingly, P1 can sidestep Sturgeon's objections.[17] However, I think that it is still possible to make a convincing case for P1 – or at least for some claim that would serve a physicalist just as well – in the indirect way that Sturgeon envisages. The first premise of this subargument for P1 – supported by commonsense observation – is that my decision to clench a fist caused the contraction of muscles in my forearm. The second premise of this subargument, supported by the earlier arguments of this chapter, is that the contraction of muscles in my forearm is realized by a certain physical event. The third premise of the subargument is a general principle distinct from any that Sturgeon discusses: if a mental event causes some physically realized macroevent, M, then the mental event causes at least some physical event that is part of M's physical realizer. From these three premises it follows that my decision to clench a fist caused some physical event (though the argument does not tell us which). The only question is whether premise three is true. It certainly seems so, for it is hard to see how a mental event could cause a physically realized macroevent, M, without *something's* causing some physical event that is part of M's physical realizer (Witmer 2000). But it might be asked whether the something that is doing the causing has to be the mental event; perhaps it is some event that realizes, or partly realizes, the mental event, so that the mental event *itself* is no cause of the physical event. Perhaps; but this is not a possibility that *dualists* can allow to be actual, since they must certainly hold that the mental event is neither physical nor physically realized, and they will probably hold that it is not realized by anything at all.[18] So *dualists* must endorse premise three, and that commits them to something like P1.

---

17 In an earlier presentation of the current argument, I illustrated the idea of a mental event's causing a (narrowly) physical effect with the example of an electron gun, a device that emits a stream of electrons when triggered to do so by the deliberate pressing of a button by a human operator (Melnyk 1994, 228). Such devices, as well as other items of experimental equipment designed to enable human decisions to cause physical effects, exist; and, just as with the biological example in the text, reflection on their operation makes it enormously plausible to judge that mental events can and do cause physical effects.
18 It will not help them to hold that the mental event is nonbasic but still not physically realized. They might indeed suggest that (a) the mental event is realized, but by something itself neither physical nor physically realized, and that (b) it is part of this realizer (rather than the mental event itself) that is causing some physical event that is part of M's physical realizer. But it will then be possible to show, by an argument exactly parallel to the prophysicalist argument now being expounded, that such a suggestion leads to incredible consequences of just the same sort as does a dualist treatment of the mental event.

So much, then, for P1. It is also very plausible to claim, with regard to the same particular fist-clenching episode, that

(P2) There were sufficient *physical* causes for the particular releases of calcium ions mentioned in P1.

Because P2 is clearly contingent, it is appropriate to seek empirical support for it. And two lines of evidence provide such support, of which the first is as follows. The releases of calcium ions that occur in muscle cells whenever skeletal muscles contract are phenomena whose biochemical causal antecedents can be traced in some detail, first to activities in the motor neurons that innervate the muscle, and then to activities in other neurons that interact with motor neurons, and so on back into the brain as far as you care to go; the reason for thinking this to be possible is that neuroanatomists have traced the pathways of bundles of neurons into and out of the brain, and the molecular biology of individual neurons is well understood. Given, then, that the biochemical causal ancestry of releases of calcium ions can be traced back into the brain as far as you like, and given the physical realization of biochemistry, one could in principle (though not in practice) trace the *physical* causal ancestry of releases of calcium ions back into the brain as far as you like. Would the physical causes revealed in this way be *sufficient* physical causes, as P2 claims? Only to the extent that the biochemical causal story is complete (i.e., leaves no biochemical event without a sufficient explanation). But although the biochemical story is certainly *not* complete, because we are far from a biochemical understanding of every single intra- and intercellular process, the enormous successes of molecular biology to date provide evidence that it is completeable. We may not *know* – with heavy emphasis on the word "know" – that the physical causal ancestry of the releases of calcium ions that occur when muscles contract can be traced back into the brain as far as you like; but we surely have substantial evidence that it can be.

The second line of evidence that provides empirical support for P2 is that the particular releases of calcium ions mentioned in P1 are physical events, and there is much evidence that the physical is *causally closed* – that *all* physical events have sufficient physical causes.[19] The evidence

---

19 The formulation of the closure principle in the text is not quite right, since it speaks of "sufficient" physical causes of physical effects, whereas, given the indeterminism of quantum mechanics, *no* physical events have sufficient physical causes. To avoid this difficulty, we should instead express the closure principle as the claim that the *chances* of all physical events are determined by earlier physical events plus physical laws, including the irreducibly statistical laws of quantum mechanics. I ignore this refinement in the ensuing discussion.

for thinking that all physical events have sufficient physical causes may be found by reading physics textbooks. Not that the causal closure of the physical itself is explicitly stated in physics textbooks; but it can be inferred from things that are explicitly stated in physics textbooks. Reading such textbooks reveals that contemporary physics has found sufficient physical causes for very many kinds of physical effects and has found no physical effects at all for which it is necessary (or even likely to turn out to be necessary) to invoke nonphysical causes. The success to date of current physics in finding sufficient physical causes for physical effects therefore provides inductive evidence that *all* physical events, including *both* unexamined physical events *and* examined-but-as-yet-unexplained physical events, have sufficient physical causes. One might conceivably feel reluctant to extrapolate conclusions reached about the physical events studied in physics laboratories to those physical events that occur in the limbs and brains of humans; but there are no grounds for such reluctance. Current physics shows no sign at all that contemporary physicists expect to find any physically anomalous phenomena whatever inside human brains, which seem indeed, from the physical point of view, to be quite unexceptional (Lycan 1987, 2–3). Unsurprisingly; for although brain cells are highly specialized types of cells, their biochemistry is apparently no different from that of cells of other types; likewise, presumably, for their physics, given the physical realization of biochemistry.

It is occasionally suggested that advocacy of physicalism on the basis of the causal closure of the physical involves some sort of circularity; but it is hard to find any foundation for this charge. The causal closure of the physical does not itself beg the question in favor of physicalism, since it is logically consistent with physicalism's falsity.[20] For the physical might be causally closed while there exist phenomena that are neither physical nor physically realized but that never causally influence physical events; alternatively, the physical might be causally closed while there exist phenomena that are neither physical nor physically realized but that causally overdetermine physical events. Either way, the causal closure of the physical might coexist with the falsity of physicalism. Nor is it true that in order

---

20 The authentic causal closure principle states that all physical events have sufficient physical causes. It should not be confused with the claim that all physical events have *only* physical causes. Unlike the former claim, the latter claim rules out the existence of all nonphysical and nonphysically realized phenomena that causally influence physical events, even those that would overdetermine physical events. However, even the latter claim is consistent with the existence of nonphysical and nonphysically realized phenomena that never causally influence physical events in any way at all.

to be persuaded of the causal closure of the physical one must already be persuaded of physicalism. To see this, it is necessary only to review how the closure principle is evidenced. First we become persuaded, on the basis of observational evidence and ordinary canons of scientific reasoning, that various physical effects have sufficient physical causes, since the best available explanations of those effects posit physical and only physical causes; surely no assumption of physicalism is needed to take this first step. Then, employing enumerative induction, we treat these well-supported explanations as evidence that *all* physical effects have sufficient physical causes; obviously some antiphysicalists may not *like* to take this second step, for they know where it will ultimately lead, but that psychological fact does nothing to impugn the reasoning involved.

We are now in a position to state the *reductio*. Assume, contrary to physicalism, that your decision to clench your fist was neither identical with nor realized by any physical state token; assume, that is, that your decision was in no sense at all physical. It then follows, from P1 and P2, that the particular releases of calcium ions mentioned in P1 were *causally overdetermined* in the following sense: two simultaneous states, each numerically distinct from the other and neither realized by the other, were *both* causally sufficient by themselves for the particular releases of calcium ions mentioned in P1. The first causally sufficient state was a physical state of your brain; the second causally sufficient state was a complex state consisting of your decision to clench your fist, together with whatever physical states your decision "tops up" to sufficiency; and the two causally sufficient states, though they might share some physical parts, are still numerically distinct from one another, with neither realizing the other, just because of the assumption that your decision to clench your fist was neither physical nor physically realized. However, because, and to the extent that,

(P3) It is implausible that the particular releases of calcium ions mentioned in P1 were causally overdetermined in the relevant sense,

we should reject the assumption that led to it, holding instead, with realization physicalism, that your decision to clench your fist was either physical or physically realized.

Obviously the same kind of reasoning could be used to make a case for regarding many other mental states as either physical or physically realized. And, by enumerative induction, the physical or physically realized character of these mental states could be treated as evidence that all mental states are physical or physically realized.

But why accept P3? What exactly is the implausibility in the idea that the particular releases of calcium ions mentioned in P1 were causally overdetermined in the relevant sense? In fact, there are two implausibilities in the idea, of which the first is *metaphysical* and the second is *epistemological*. Let us begin with the metaphysical implausibility. Suppose that the particular releases of calcium ions mentioned in P1 *were* causally overdetermined in the relevant sense; then there must be a causal law subsuming the sequence from physical cause to ion releases *and* a causal law subsuming the sequence from mental cause to ion releases – that is, there must be *two* causal laws mandating the occurrence of the very *same* kind of effect. It is, to repeat an earlier analogy, as if a platoon received separate orders from both the captain and the colonel, and yet the orders were always to do exactly the same thing. We would not be content to treat such a case as mere coincidence; we would insist on an explanation, if one could possibly be got. Likewise, I suggest, in the case of the two causal laws mandating the occurrence of the very same kind of effect: unless explained, it is an intolerable coincidence. But there is no explanation for this agreement in kind of effect, given the assumption that your decision to clench your fist was neither physical nor physically realized. The point can be made by noting that it is precisely here that my military analogy breaks down. For the agreement in content of the officers' orders *could* be explained – in one of two ways. One way would be to suppose that whenever the colonel issues orders to the platoon he sends a copy of them to the craven captain, who always reissues the orders to the platoon, and who always fears issuing any independent orders of his own. Another way would be to suppose that, because they received identical training at Staff College and receive exactly the same information about their strategic and tactical circumstances, the colonel and the captain independently arrive at the same conclusions as to what the platoon should do. However, neither of these explanations can be adapted to the case of the two causal laws mandating the occurrence of the very same kind of effect. There is no way in which the causal law subsuming the sequence from physical cause to ion releases could *bring about* the causal law subsuming the sequence from mental cause to ion releases; nor are causal laws the sort of things that can have undergone identical training regimes.

It might be pointed out that two causal laws could hardly *conflict* in their outcomes, else contradictory states of affairs would ensue, so that their harmonious operation is no surprise. But this entirely correct observation misses the point. What needs explaining is not why two causal laws, whose holding is just being assumed, fail to conflict; given that such laws hold, they certainly *could not* conflict, and precisely for the reason suggested. Rather, what needs explaining is why two causal laws that agree in kind of effect hold in the first place, rather than just one. Why didn't we have the actual physical cause we have, lawfully connected to the actual ion releases, and also the actual mental event we have, but *not* lawfully connected to the ion releases, and so not a cause of them? Logical consistency cannot explain why we have two causal laws that agree in kind of effect, rather than just one, since this is not the only logically possible state of affairs. Nor will it do to suggest that the *physical* cause of the ion releases might *lawfully suffice* for the *mental* cause of the ion releases (i.e., your decision). True, if this were so, it would certainly ensure that, as a matter of law, your decision to clench your fist was lawfully followed by ion releases, since the physical cause of the ion releases would lawfully suffice first for your decision and then for the ion releases. But it would not ensure *that* there was, and hence would not explain *why* there was, a *causal* law connecting the mental cause to the ion releases, a causal law *additional* to the causal law connecting the *physical* cause to the ion releases.

A possible objection is that in the preceding two paragraphs I have been assuming an excessively robust conception of causation and causal laws, one according to which causes make their effects happen, so that *causal* sufficiency can be distinguished from lawful but noncausal sufficiency. What if the antiphysicalist were permitted a more modest conception of causation and causal laws? However, I have not been assuming the robust conception out of conviction, for it conflicts, of course, with my official account of causation in Chapter 4; I have been assuming it because I expect my opponents to assume it. They are welcome to drop it in favor of a more Humean account if they wish. But if they do so, they face a difficulty perhaps graver than that of commitment to intolerable coincidence: they are committed to the view that your decision to clench your fist is *no cause at all* of ion releases – or indeed of any other effect for which there is a sufficient physical cause! For even if the physical cause of the ion releases is construed as sufficient first for your decision to clench your fist and then for the ion releases, with the result that your decision is indeed sufficient for the ion releases, all that we have achieved is the description of an *epi-world* (in the sense introduced in Chapter 4). Precisely because, on the antiphysicalist assumption that we are reducing to absurdity, your decision is neither identical with nor realized by any physical state token, your decision has no physical parts; and precisely because it has no physical parts, your decision is exactly analogous to the rash in the rash-fever case, where a viral infection produces first a rash and then a fever. But intuitively, in this case, the rash is no cause of the fever, and surely this intuition is one that any acceptable Humean account of causation must somehow contrive to respect. But now, because in this case the rash is no cause of the fever, your analogous decision is no cause of the ion releases either.[21] So the metaphysical implausibility in the idea that the particular releases of calcium ions mentioned in P1 were causally overdetermined in the relevant sense is disjunctive: either an intolerable coincidence (for those who favor a robustly non-Humean notion of causation) or epiphenomenalism about mental states that appear to have physical effects (for the rest).

Let us turn now to the second – epistemological – implausibility. In view of the fact that the particular releases of calcium ions mentioned in P1 already have a sufficient cause (namely, a sufficient *physical* cause), the question arises as to what reason we have, if any, to construe your decision to clench your fist as neither physical nor physically realized. (The sheer existence of your decision is not in question, of course; so the question is not why we should posit it, but how we should construe it.) For when construed as neither physical nor physically realized, your decision to clench your fist would appear to be surplus to explanatory requirements. Certainly a decision construed as neither physical nor physically realized is not required in order to explain the particular releases of calcium ions mentioned in P1. But if there is no explanatory purpose at all for which construing your decision as neither physical nor physically realized is required, then, because it would obviously be less economical to construe it as neither physical nor physically realized than to construe it as either physical or physically realized, we should not construe it as neither physical nor physically realized.

So *is* there any explanatory purpose for which construing your decision as neither physical nor physically realized is required? Clearly it is not required for explaining any *physical* event, since the causal closure of the physical ensures that every physical event, like the ion releases mentioned in P1, has a sufficient physical cause. Might construing your decision as neither physical nor physically realized be required for the explanation of some nonphysical but still physically realized event (e.g., your hand's forming a fist)? It seems not. For it is very obscure how, given that an event

---

21 By contrast, of course, if your decision is treated as physical or physically realized, then it does have a physical part, and so is *not* analogous to the rash in the rash-fever case. Moreover, given the theory of causation in Chapter 4, it can still be a cause of the ion releases, even though the ion releases have sufficient physical causes.

is physically realized and that there is a sufficient physical cause for each physical constituent of the event, there could possibly be anything left for the explanation of which a neither-physical-nor-physically-realized cause is required.[22] The only remaining possibility is to claim that construing your decision as neither physical nor physically realized is required for the explanation of some nonphysical *and nonphysically realized* event (e.g., some other mental event, *construed as neither physical nor physically realized*). But although such a claim might conceivably be true, it already *assumes* the existence of events that are neither physical nor physically realized, and hence begs the question against the physicalist. So we are left without a nontendentious explanatory need for the fulfillment of which your decision to clench your fist, when construed as neither physical nor physically realized, is required. Hence we are also left without a nontendentious reason for construing your decision to clench your fist as other than physical or physically realized. The *reductio* of the assumption that your decision to clench your fist was neither identical with nor realized by any physical state token is secure.

Let me now consider two important objections to this second line of argument exhibiting empirical support for the view that certain mental phenomena are physical or physically realized. The first objection challenges the inference *from* P1, P2, and the assumption that your decision to clench a fist was neither physical nor physically realized *to* the conclusion that the ion releases were causally overdetermined. Specifically, it describes a possible state of affairs in which there is no causal overdetermination, even though P1 and P2 are true, and your decision to clench a fist was neither physical nor physically realized. The idea is that a mental event that is neither physical nor physically realized might still constitute a link in an otherwise entirely physical causal chain: a physical state of your brain that is causally sufficient for the ion releases might be so precisely *because* it is itself a sufficient cause for your decision to clench a fist (construed as neither physical nor physically realized), which decision in turn is causally sufficient for the ion releases. Were this situation to obtain, (i) your decision to clench a fist, despite its being neither physical nor physically realized, would still be causally sufficient in the circumstances for the ion releases (as P1 claims), (ii) there would still be a sufficient

---

22 So I claim that there is no explanatory work for nonphysical and *nonphysically realized* events to do. And that is consistent with claiming, as I claimed in Chapter 4, that there are explanatory roles for nonphysical but *physically realized* events to play, notwithstanding the causal closure of the physical (because of the unobjectionability of multiple explanation of the same event in a *realizationist* world).

physical cause for the ion releases (as P2 claims), and yet (iii) there would intuitively be no causal overdetermination.[23]

The trouble with this first objection is that the situation it describes, while logically possible, is one that it would nonetheless be very implausible to regard as actual; and surely the dualist must hold out for more than the logical possibility of some form of dualism, which physicalists will concede as willingly as they concede the logical possibility of pretty much every false theory that the history of human inquiry has thrown up. So although the position outlined in the previous paragraph technically avoids overdetermination, it is still, I say, a very implausible one for a dualist to adopt. The implausibities of adopting it, like those of adopting the overdeterminationist dualist scenario discussed earlier, are two: one metaphysical and one epistemological.

1. The metaphysical implausibility is that it requires a remarkable coincidence in the kinds of effect that events of two entirely different kinds are lawfully sufficient for. For the (nonphysical and nonphysically realized) mental event of your decision to clench a fist has to be sufficient for a physical effect of exactly the same kind as we would independently expect the physical event that caused your decision to be sufficient for. That is, the nonoverdeterminationist dualist scenario has to be that physical event p_1 caused mental event m, which in turn caused physical event p_2; but p_2 has to be just what we would have *expected* p_1 to produce on the basis of our knowledge of p_1's nature plus the laws of physics – else we would have a counterexample to the claim that the physical is causally closed. In that case, however, the nonoverdeterminationist dualist scenario, though admittedly free of overdetermination, still requires an inexplicable coincidence of the very sort that, as we saw earlier, makes overdetermination unappealing: it requires that your decision to clench a fist be causally sufficient for a physical effect of exactly the same kind as a quite distinct type of physical event would be expected to be sufficient for, given standard physical principles. (Obviously it would be possible to postulate a nonphysical and nonphysically realized mental event whose occurrence helped produce physical outcomes *different* from those that would have arisen had that mental event not occurred; but although such a postulation would be internally consistent, it would be inconsistent with the causal closure of the physical, and so it cannot be part of the nonoverdeterminationist dualist scenario that we are now considering.)

---

23 Thanks for this objection to a percipient reader for the Press.

2. The epistemological implausibility of adopting the nonoverdeterminationist dualist scenario is simply that its construal of your decision to clench a fist as neither physical nor physically realized is less economical, but can explain no more, than the rival view that construes your decision as physical or physically realized. Why should we think that there is *really* a nonphysical and nonphysically realized link in the otherwise entirely physical or physically realized causal chain that culminates in the ion releases in question? Not because we *must* postulate such a link in order to explain the ion releases. And not because we must do so in order to explain any *other* physical occurrence, for we have all the physical bases covered already. Because we must do so to explain some nonphysical and nonphysically realized occurrence? But, as we have already seen, to assume that there are such occurrences would beg the question against physicalism. Some philosophers might think there is an explanatory need to adopt the nonoverdeterminationist dualist scenario outlined earlier *given* that mental events have already been shown a priori to be neither physical nor physically realized. But I am assuming that it cannot be shown a priori that we must construe mental events as neither physical nor physically realized.

Let me turn, finally, to the second important objection to the current line of prophysicalist argument. The objection claims that abandoning the dualist assumption that your decision was neither physical nor physically realized, as the current line of argument urges, merely dumps us from the frying pan into the fire, since physicalism about decisions is no better than dualism about them. One possible form of this objection holds that if mental states were physically realized functional states, as abandoning the dualist assumption might require us to claim, then problems of overdetermination would arise that are parallel to, and as serious as, those to which the dualist assumption leads: ion releases would be overdetermined by physical and by *functional* causes. A second possible form of this objection alleges that if your decision were physical or physically realized, then it would not really be a cause, or causally relevant as such, at all – a consequence distinct from but arguably even worse than the problems of overdetermination to which the dualist assumption leads.

My reply to the first form of this objection is that construing mental states as physically realized functional states simply does not generate the problems of overdetermination to which dualism leads (see Chapter 4, Section 4, for the full story). The reason, in a nutshell, is that if mental states are physically realized functional states, then, given the physical way the world is, the existence of the mental states that actually exist is a logically necessary consequence. As a result, neither the metaphysical nor the epistemological implausibility of overdetermination arises. The metaphysical implausibility does not arise because, given the *physical* states and laws that exist, the *mental* states that exist are logically inevitable – could not logically have failed to exist – and hence there is no contingent coincidence in need of explanation. The epistemological implausibility does not arise because one cannot be convicted of being uneconomical in postulating certain entities – of postulating them beyond necessity – if those entities are the logically inevitable consequence of phenomena to which one is *already* committed; and this condition is met if mental states are physically realized functional states, because in that case the former *are* the logically inevitable consequence of the latter.

My reply to the second form of the objection is that, given the account of causation and causal relevance given in Chapter 4, and as argued there at length, it is just not true that the physical or physically realized character of a decision automatically robs it of causal power. Discovering that a decision is physically realized certainly *seems* to rob it of its causal power, since the decision then seems analogous to the rash in the rash-fever case. But a decision that is physically realized, as I understand realization, is *not* analogous to the rash in the rash-fever case, since rashes are *caused* but not *realized* by viral infections. And the fact that decisions are physically realized, I hold, makes all the difference. The discovery that one's rash is caused by a viral infection which in turn causes one's fever *does* undermine the claim that one's rash caused one's fever; but the discovery that coffee is realized (in part) by caffeine, and that caffeine is coffee's only stimulant, does *not* undermine the claim that one's consumption of *coffee* made one lightheaded.

There are dualist scenarios that, like the physicalist hypothesis that your decision to clench your fist is physical or physically realized, are logically *consistent* with P1 and P2; and we have now seen two such scenarios. But they are not as *plausible* in light of P1 and P2 as the physicalist hypothesis is. That is why P1 and P2, taken together, are empirical evidence for a physicalist view of mental phenomena.[24]

---

24 This point is apparently missed by Tyler Burge (1993). The culmination of his critique of an argument for physicalism that at least resembles mine is the claim that "we have no ground for assuming that the failure of mental causes to interfere in the physical chain of events must be explained in terms of mental causes' consisting in physical events" (Burge 1993, 116). But we certainly have such a ground, and it consists in the fact that no *alternative* explanation consistent with dualism is as plausible as the physicalist explanation. In the same

Let us turn now to a third line of reasoning that provides empirical support for the view that mental phenomena are physical or physically realized. It is what Paul Churchland has called the argument "from the neural dependence of all known mental phenomena" (1988, 20, 28). This argument is presented by Churchland as an argument in support of type-type identity physicalism; but as appropriated by me, it is intended only to support the weaker view that mental states are physical or physically realized. It is best viewed, I suggest, as having the form of an inference to the best explanation. The datum for the inference is the claim that, for any person you like, and for any mental state or mental process that person might be in or might undergo, in order for that person to be in that mental state or to undergo that mental process, there is something neurophysiological that has to be going on – simultaneously – in that person's brain. This claim is consistent with the multiple realizability of mental states and processes; so, for example, what has to be going on in a person's brain, in order for that person to feel a pain in the foot, need not be of the same neurophysiological type as what has to be going on in the brain of a second person in order for the second person to feel an exactly similar pain in the foot, even though, according to the claim, *something* neurophysiological in the second person's brain has to be going on simultaneously with the pain. Similarly, it is consistent with the spirit of this claim that a single type of mental state or process should be multiply realizable, over time, in the *same* individual, so that what has to be going on in a person's brain right now, in order for that person to feel a pain in the foot right now, need not be the same as what has to be going on in his or her brain next week in order for that person to feel a pain in the foot next week.

The claim describing the data for the inference is strongly supported by a wide array of empirical evidence. For example, cerebral blood flow studies have revealed distinctive regions of the cortex that are active, or especially active, when subjects open their eyes and look at something; when they are stimulated with loud, meaningless noise; when they hear simple spoken words; when they hear more complex verbal stimuli; when they have to judge which of two objects placed successively in the palm of a hand is larger; when they clinch a fist rhythmically; when they initiate

essay, Burge himself provides no clue whatsoever as to how he thinks that robust mental causation might plausibly be reconciled with the causal closure of the physical on the assumption that physicalism is false. In particular, his frequent invocation of an unexplicated notion of "explanatory practice" provides no such clue.

voluntary movements of other bodily parts; when they mentally rehearse the initiation of voluntary movements; when they are reading aloud; and when they are reading silently (Lassen, Ingvar, and Skinhøj 1978). And to these results we should add those cited by Sir John Eccles concerning the brain activity correlated with various forms of silent thought (1994, 74–80). Even more impressive is evidence derived from the use of positron emission tomography (PET) scans, which have shown the existence of distinctive regions of the brain (not necessarily in the cortex) that are activated above control levels when subjects perform certain cognitive tasks, when they perform certain memory tasks, when they perform certain sequential motor tasks, and even when they use different strategies for the single task of determining whether two sequences of musical notes are the same or different (Phelps and Mazziotta 1985, 805–6).

Now the neural dependence claim – the claim that, for any person you like, and for any mental state or mental process that person might be in or might undergo, in order for that person to be in that mental state or to undergo that mental process, there is something neurophysiological that has to be going on simultaneously in that person's brain – is logically consistent with dualist antiphysicalism, and therefore does not *conclusively* rule it out. (The claim is logically consistent with dualist antiphysicalism because it is open to a dualist to account for the neural dependence of all mental phenomena by saying that every kind of entirely nonphysical mental phenomenon is merely *causally* or *nomologically* dependent on some or other kind of brain activity.) But because this is so, how can the neural dependence claim support physicalism over dualist antiphysicalism? In fact, there is no more difficulty in this idea than there is in the analogous idea that the presence of my fingerprints on the murder weapon should support the conclusion that I am guilty over the conclusion that I am innocent, even though the presence of my fingerprints is logically consistent with my innocence as well as with my guilt. In both cases, the evidence, though logically consistent with a pair of hypotheses, can still support one hypothesis over the other; and it can do so because it is *better explained* by one hypothesis than it is by the other. So the neural dependence claim supports physicalism over dualist antiphysicalism if its holding is better explained by physicalism than it is by dualist antiphysicalism.

Realization physicalism can certainly explain the holding of the neural dependence claim. For if realization physicalism is true, then mental states and processes are either identical with or realized (perhaps narrowly) by certain neurophysiological states and processes. But if mental states and processes are identical with certain neurophysiological states and processes, then of course a person must be in some or other neurophysiological state or undergo some or other neurophysiological process in order to be in any mental state or to undergo any mental process at all. Alternatively, if mental states and processes are invariably realized (perhaps narrowly) by certain neurophysiological states and processes, then it will also follow that a person must be in some or other neurophysiological state or undergo some or other neurophysiological process – the realizing state or process – in order to be in any mental state or to undergo any mental process at all.

But does realization physicalism provide a *better* explanation of the holding of the neural dependence claim than dualist antiphysicalism? It does, and for two reasons. The first reason is that the explanation provided by realization physicalism is more economical than any dualistic explanation. As ever, there are two dimensions to this greater economy. The realization physicalist explanation requires the existence only of neurophysiological states and processes whose existence is acknowledged by all, plus whatever other states and processes are (nonbrutally) necessitated by the existence of these states and processes;[25] the dualist explanation, by contrast, in construing mental states and processes as neither identical with nor realized by neurophysiological states and processes, requires the existence of entities that are logically additional to those required by the realization physicalist explanation – and not just a few entities, either, since every single kind of mental state or process will be such an entity, and even on a very conservative estimate there must be many thousands of kinds of mental states and processes. Furthermore, in order to account for the systematic and apparently nonaccidental relationship between mental states and processes and the neurophysiological states and processes on which they depend, the dualist explanation must postulate the holding of a system of natural laws that connect mental phenomena with neurophysiological phenomena. But because, if these laws were reductively explainable, mental states and processes could no longer be construed as entirely nonphysical, the dualist explanation must instead treat these laws as reductively unexplainable and hence as basic.[26] So it requires the holding of more basic laws than does the realization physicalist

---

25 On nonbrutal necessitation, see note 3.
26 The dualist explanation might treat these laws as explainable, though not reductively so – if, for instance, their holding were explained as resulting from the decisions of an omnipotent God. But the laws would still count as basic; for their holding would still not be *constituted* by facts about God.

explanation – and not just a few more, either, for presumably there must be a basic law for every kind of mental state or process that there is and, as we just noted, there are very many kinds of mental state and process.

The second reason why realization physicalism provides a better explanation of the holding of the neural dependence claim than does dualism is less familiar. I remarked earlier that a dualist can account for the neural dependence of all mental phenomena by saying that every kind of mental phenomenon, though neither physical nor physically realized, is nevertheless causally or nomologically dependent on some or other kind of neurophysiological phenomenon. But saying this comes periously close to merely restating the neural dependence claim that we wanted to have explained in the first place; or perhaps it amounts to declaring the neural dependence of the mental basic and hence unexplainable. Either way, dualism has not supplied much of an explanation for neural dependence.

In order to achieve greater explanatory power, the dualist must provide some account of *why* all mental phenomena – conceived dualistically, as neither physical nor physically realized – are dependent on particular neurophysiological phenomena. It is, after all, rather puzzling why every single mental phenomenon should be so unenterprising as to be quite incapable of activity without assistance from a neurophysiological helper. Indeed, it is rather puzzling why an entirely nonphysical mind, or why entirely nonphysical mental states or processes, should require any brain at all; all the more so since minds and mental states are credited by the dualist with virtually miraculous powers to do what no merely physical thing can do. On the input side, for instance, why is the optic nerve running from the eye not by itself all that we need by way of neural hardware for vision, with no further brain areas required? Surely the nonphysical mind *could* be sensitive to the outputs of the optic nerve, which certainly carries very rich information; so why isn't it? And if it could not, then *why* could it not? On the output side, why are the motor neurons running from the brain to the body's muscles not by themselves all that we need by way of neural hardware for action? Surely the nonphysical mind *could* directly activate the appropriate motor neurons; so why doesn't it? And if it could not, then *why* could it not?

No principled answers can be given to questions of this sort, however, unless and until some account is provided of what sort of system the nonphysical mind is supposed to be, and of how it is supposed to work; for only then will dualists be able to say what it is that the brain *does* for the nonphysical mind, and why therefore the nonphysical mind *needs* the brain. Presumably the reason why the nonphysical mind needs the brain is that there is some sort of division of labor between the nonphysical mind and the physical brain; and an account of the mind's nature and of its workings would be necessary to specify what this division of labor is. No such account, however, has ever been provided, the produalist literature having been devoted overwhelmingly to the negative tasks of (a) discrediting physicalism and (b) defending dualism against various objections; nor, as far as I know, is any such account in prospect.[27] Dualists have no doubt been tempted to think that so long as they have proof that physicalism must be false and can rebut all potentially knockdown objections to dualism, it simply does not matter what *positive* account of the mind they give – or even whether they give a positive account of the mind at all. And this line of thought would certainly be reasonable if physicalism could be refuted a priori, since in that case the epistemic status of dualism would not turn on its explanatory power (i.e., on how well it would, if true, explain nontendentious data). But if physicalism cannot be refuted a priori, as nearly all physicalists maintain that it cannot, then the epistemic status of dualism does turn, in part, upon its explanatory power; and the explanatory power of a hypothesis can be evaluated only to the extent that the hypothesis has actually received a detailed formulation. At any rate, because dualism – as it currently stands – has no positive account of the mind's nature and of its workings, it simply has no account of why all mental phenomena are dependent on particular neurophysiological phenomena. It can certainly explain the experimental findings mentioned earlier – as manifestations of our having bumped into certain basic laws of nature that make mental phenomena dependent upon neural phenomena; but it has no explanation to offer of *why* mental phenomena are dependent upon neural phenomena in accordance with these basic laws. Because realization physicalism does have such an explanation to offer, we therefore have a second reason to regard it as providing a better explanation of the neural dependence of all mental phenomena than does the dualistic hypothesis.

It might be objected that my demand for a dualistic account of the nonphysical mind's nature and workings is unfair, since it assumes something that certain dualists explicitly deny, namely, that the mind is the sort

---

27 I recall having read the suggestion that a dualist could just take on board cognitive science's information-processing account of the mind. But how exactly would this work, in view of the fact that cognitive science currently sees no need at all for any nonphysical supplement to the physical activities of the brain? The suggestion neither provides nor points us toward any explanation of why the nonphysical mind needs the brain in any of the ways, general or particular, in which it apparently does.

of thing that is susceptible in principle to scientific description; for if the mind simply lies beyond the reach of any conceivable scientific inquiry, then it is unreasonable to expect dualists to provide a positive account of the mind and its workings. But, to begin with, it is not very plausible to suppose that the mind does lie beyond the reach of any conceivable scientific inquiry. The supposition that it does, we should notice, is far stronger than the claim that the mind cannot be reductively explained in terms of *current* science (or even in terms of any imaginable development of current science); the supposition that the mind lies beyond the reach of any conceivable scientific inquiry must be the claim that the mind's nature is such as to elude in principle the possibility of *any* kind of systematic analysis or description, in whatever terms you like. But how *could* the mind have such a nature? Is it meant to be because mental facts are essentially *subjective*, whereas any systematic description worthy of the name "scientific" would have to be *objective*, and hence inadequate to describe the mental? But it is doubtful that the notion of essentially subjective facts even makes any sense (see Lycan 1987, 78–9, and 1996, 50–1; also perhaps Wittgenstein's polemic against private language, which I suspect is best interpreted as an attack on the idea of a private reality). Or is it meant to be because the realm of the mental is insufficiently *regular* for systematic description of any kind whatever? But we know that the mind is full of regularity: for example, it exhibits the regularities that Fodor and Pylyshyn summarize as "systematicity" (Fodor and Pylyshyn 1988); it exhibits regularity in the kinds of reasoning found easy or difficult, and in the fallacies to which it is prone (e.g., Johnson-Laird 1983, 67–9; Kahneman, Slovic, and Tversky 1982); it exhibits regularities galore in its linguistic capacities (e.g., Pinker 1999); and, as perhaps Hume first pointed out, it exhibits enough regularity in general to enable us to predict one another's thoughts, feelings, and behavior pretty well, and certainly well enough for the success of our everyday dealings with others (Hume 1975, 83–8). These regularities are not exceptionless, of course; but they are as robust as the regularities characterizing phenomena (e.g., geological phenomena) whose systematic describability by science lies in no serious doubt.

More important, though, even if, because the mind exceeds the reach of any conceivable kind of scientific inquiry, dualists *cannot* provide a positive account of the mind and its workings, it does not follow that dualists thereby escape the main *drawback* of not having a positive account of the mind and its workings; for no matter how excusable and explicable their lack of such an account might be, the inconvenient fact nevertheless remains that, without such an account, no case can be made for dualism (or rebuttal provided to any case for physicalism) on the basis of dualism's explanatory power.[28] Mysterian dualists are in an analogous position to that of theists who insist that the will of God is so inscrutable that we simply cannot say whether the world's natural evils constitute evidence against God's existence, but who, by reason of the very same inscrutability, cannot say that any feature of the world is to be expected on theism, and hence cannot say that any feature of the world is evidence *for* God's existence. Whatever the reason, mysterian dualists still have no explanation to offer of why mental phenomena are dependent upon neural phenomena.

I turn, finally, to a fourth line of argument that provides empirical support for the view that mental phenomena – in particular, phenomenally conscious states – are physical or physically realized (Hill 1991, 19–26). Like the immediately preceding line of argument, this one also has the form of an inference to the best explanation. Unlike it, however, the data for this inference are not the *necessity* of certain neural occurrences for certain mental states, but rather the *sufficiency* of certain neural occurrences for certain mental states: certain regions of the occipital cortex in the human brain are such that activity in them *suffices* for the simultaneous occurrence in the brain's owner of certain visual sensations.

This claim of sufficiency is supported by a number of experiments (Brindley 1973; Dobelle and Mladejovsky 1974). In most of the experiments, points on the surface of a fully conscious neurosurgical patient's occipital cortex were electrically stimulated with a single small electrode (or with a few such electrodes); in some cases, the stimulation was effected by an implanted prosthesis composed of many electrodes. The patient was then asked to describe the sensations (if any) that he or she enjoyed. The

---

28   Not quite no case: a sufficiently long and varied history of failed attempts at a scientific understanding of the mind might be held to be best explained by the hypothesis that the mind is in principle resistant to scientific analysis and description and hence neither physical nor physically realized. But (a) scientific attempts to understand the mind hitherto, even if they be judged failures, are surely not numerous and extensive enough to support the premise this argument needs; and (b) other hypotheses might be invoked to account for even a very long history of failure (e.g., the hypothesis that the mind, though physical or physically realized, is in principle scientifically accessible by cognitive agents of some kind, but not by *humans*). In any case, even if the hypothesis that the mind is in principle resistant to scientific analysis and description, and hence neither physical nor physically realized, could be supported by appeal to its explanatory power in this way, that would not undermine my main contention in the text, namely, that, for whatever reason, dualism has in fact no explanation to offer of why mental phenomena are dependent on neural phenomena.

kinds of results achieved are as follows. Stimulation of a patient's occipital cortex by a single electrode reliably results in the patient's "seeing" a patch of light at some point in his or her visual field; as far as can be determined, with due allowance made for the patient's motor response time, the light is seen simultaneously with the stimulation. The size of the patch of light varies from that of a star as viewed in the night sky to that of a quarter as viewed at arm's length. The shape of the patch is also variable and includes stars, wheels, and spots, but is usually round. The light seen is often white or yellow, but also sometimes red, blue, or green. The phenomenal location of the light seen varies systematically with the physical location of the electrode causing the stimulation. The use of several electrodes simultaneously can produce patches of light that form recognizable shapes, such as a square, a question mark, a capital L, and a capital V.

How are we to explain the fact that activity in certain regions of the human occipital cortex suffices for the simultaneous occurrence of certain visual sensations? One possibility, obviously, is the realizationist hypothesis that the visual sensations in question are either physical or functional but physically realized. For if they are physical, and if they are, in particular, one and the same as the physical processes that have been found to suffice for the occurrence of the sensations, then it could hardly fail to be true that the occurrence of those physical processes sufficed for the simultaneous occurrence of those sensations – on the general principle that if $X = Y$, then the occurrence of X must suffice for the simultaneous occurrence of Y. Similarly, if the visual sensations are functional but physically realized in humans, and if they are (narrowly) realized, in particular, by the neural activities in the human occipital cortex that have been found to suffice for the sensations, then their sufficiency is also no surprise – on the general principle that narrow realizers (in the right conditions) are sufficient for the occurrences that they realize. So realization physicalism can explain the empirically discovered sufficiency that wants explaining. But dualism can obviously explain it too. For the dualist can suppose that the neural activities in the human occipital cortex that have been found to suffice for the sensations in question are the (simultaneous) causes of, or at least nomologically sufficient conditions for, certain entirely distinct occurrences that are neither physical nor physically realized, namely, the sensations in question.

As usual, however, considerations of economy favor the physicalistic hypothesis over its dualistic rival. The physicalistic hypothesis, in construing sensations as physical or physically realized, is committed to postulating the existence of fewer entities than is the dualistic hypothesis, which construes sensations as neither physical nor physically realized; the physicalistic hypothesis is also committed to postulating fewer basic laws of nature than is the dualistic hypothesis, because it has no need to treat the empirically discovered sufficiency of certain neural occurrences for certain sensations as reflecting the holding of a fundamental law of nature. So the physicalistic hypothesis provides a better explanation of this empirically discovered sufficiency than does the dualistic hypothesis. Here is an analogy: we can reliably produce water by forming a certain compound of hydrogen and oxygen (i.e., H_2O), so that the presence of the compound is sufficient for the simultaneous presence of water; but we would not take seriously the hypothesis that the compound was merely the simultaneous cause of, or merely a nomologically sufficient condition for, the water, even though this hypothesis is certainly a conceivable rival to the usual hypothesis that the compound and the water are one and the same stuff. Likewise, we should not take seriously the dualistic hypothesis that the neural activities in the human occipital cortex that have been found to suffice for the sensations in question are merely the simultaneous causes of, or merely nomologically sufficient conditions for, the sensations; the better explanation is the physicalistic identity hypothesis. Consequently, the empirically discovered sufficiency of certain neural occurrences for certain sensations constitutes evidence for the physicalistic hypothesis that the sensations in question are either physical or functional but physically realized. And the same discovery surely also provides evidence, albeit weaker evidence, that *all* sensations are either physical or physically realized, for it would be somewhat surprising if only some, but not all, sensations were physical or physically realized.

Against this fourth line of reasoning, however, and perhaps also against its three predecessors, some readers will want to protest that there just *cannot* be empirical evidence for the hypothesis that mental states are physical or physically realized; so it is pointless even to look for it. Because we know *a priori* that mental state-types are neither physical nor functional types, the putative "hypothesis" that mental states are physical or physically realized is not even a *candidate* to be supported by empirical evidence.

But such a protest leaves me unmoved. First of all, I reject its assumption that a putative hypothesis cannot even be considered a candidate to be supported by empirical evidence until it has first been subjected to, and has cleared, an a priori "background check." Closely related to this assumption is the metaphilosophical view that although the proper role of philosophy does not include deciding the truth of scientific hypotheses, it can and does include the filtering out of hypotheses that are unacceptable a priori. The assumption is defective, for even if there were good a priori reasons not to accept a particular hypothesis, it would not follow that the hypothesis is thereby disqualified as a candidate to be supported by a posteriori reasons. It would not follow because the a prioricity of an argument does not entail the indubitability of its conclusion.[29] To call an argument a priori is to say something about the *kind* of epistemic access we have to its premises and to the reasoning it employs; it is not to say anything about the *reliability* of that access. A premise may be, *if true*, known a priori (because arrived at independently of experience), but still conceivably false (because arrived at in a fallible way). For example, the premise that I can conceive myself in pain while no physical object exists will be, if true, known by me a priori, because in coming to believe it I make no appeal to sensory experience; but it may still be possible to be *deluded* as to what one can conceive, so that really I *cannot* conceive myself in pain in the absence of any physical object, even though I think that I can. So an a priori argument against a hypothesis provides *at best* a merely *defeasible* reason to judge the hypothesis false, so that the reason to judge the hypothesis false may yet be *outweighed* by a reason to judge the hypothesis true. Because this outweighing reason might take the form of empirical evidence, it is still permissible to try to gather empirical evidence for a hypothesis even when there is a plausible a priori objection to the hypothesis. Consequently, even if there were such a thing as a good a priori reason to disbelieve a physicalist identity hypothesis, that reason would still have to go into the hopper along with any good a posteriori reasons there might be to believe the hypothesis; and the outcome of a weighing up of the reasons for and against the hypothesis would not be a foregone conclusion.

By way of illustration, consider a concession that David Chalmers makes in his recent conceivability argument for holding that phenomenal properties are neither physical nor functional. He allows that judgments of conceivability may err; they will err if we are insufficiently reflective (Chalmers 1996a, 67 and 98–9). In that case, however, his argument, which relies on a judgment of conceivability, can at most provide a

---

29 My claim here is meant to be in the spirit of Hume's point that a lengthy train of pure reasoning, especially if it reaches implausible conclusions from plausible premises, may well contain an undetected error.

defeasible reason for accepting its conclusion, even if the argument is in every other respect flawless. But reason for *rejecting* its conclusion is provided by evidence – such as I have been presenting – for holding that phenomenal properties *are* physical or functional; given Chalmers's concession, such evidence would in effect also be evidence that we had *in fact* been insufficiently reflective in the way he envisages.

The protest also leaves me unmoved because – of course – I deny that we do know a priori that mental state types are neither physical nor functional. Not only do I continue to insist that whether a given mental state type is identical to some or other physical or functional type is a question that can in principle only be settled a posteriori, but I regard all particular extant a priori objections to identifying mental states with physical or functional states as open to specific, and powerful, objections (see, e.g., Lycan 1987; Hill 1991, ch. 4; Tye 1999; on Chalmers's objection in particular, see Melnyk 2001).

At the end of the preceding section, I distinguished between two forms of antiphysicalism and claimed that the evidence for physicalism presented in the first six sections of this chapter counts strongly against the first form of antiphysicalism I distinguished, the pluralistic egalitarian form. In the current section, I have presented four lines of argument for holding that mental phenomena are physical or physically realized, lines of argument that therefore count against the second form of antiphysicalism I distinguished, the form of antiphysicalism that corresponds most closely to the intentions of traditional mind-body dualists. Now an antiphysicalist of this second kind might be tempted to react to the first of these lines of argument by thinking, "Well, that doesn't prove physicalism about the mind," to react to the second by thinking, "That doesn't prove it, either," and similarly for the two remaining lines of argument. But a reaction of that sort would be a mistake. None of the four lines of argument even aims to provide proof – in the sense of a sufficient or a conclusive reason for thinking – that mental phenomena are physical or physically realized; so pointing out that they do not succeed in doing so achieves nothing. Their more modest aim is to provide *some* reason for thinking that mental phenomena are physical or physically realized, by adducing facts that *raise the probability* that mental phenomena are physical or physically realized; and this they can succeed in doing even though they fail to provide a sufficient or a conclusive reason for accepting their conclusion. Moreover, even if none of these four lines of argument *when taken individually* accomplishes any more than to give a small boost to the probability that mental phenomena are physical or physically realized, when taken together they may give it a large boost – perhaps even enough to raise it above 0.5 (Swinburne 1979, 13–15).[30]

I shall not even try, however, to estimate *how* probable it is that mental phenomena are physical or physically realized in light of the evidence I have presented. But if the conclusion in Section 2 of Chapter 5 is right that there is no evidence whatever *against* the hypothesis that all mental phenomena are physical or physically realized, then it is clear where the balance of probabilities lies: realization physicalism has a higher probability in light of the currently available evidence than does its traditionally dualistic antiphysicalist rival. This is not to say that the probability of realization physicalism in light of the evidence is high, or that it reaches some putative threshold for rational acceptance; so someone whose doxastic policy it is to suspend judgment on a hypothesis until its probability in light of the evidence reaches a certain threshold remains at liberty, for all that I have said, to suspend judgment on physicalism about the mind. But what such a person is not at liberty to do is to pretend that physicalism about the mind is an open question in the sense that physicalism about the mind and its dualistic rival are *equally probable* in light of the currently available evidence. They are not equally probable; and the mind-body problem is simply not open in that sense.

The empirical case for physicalism can be summarized briefly. There are, right now, many phenomena of many kinds that can be explained on the assumption that they are physical or physically realized. At the same time, there are no nontendentious phenomena (i.e., phenomena not already *assumed* to be neither physical nor physically realized) for the explanation of which it is required *either* to postulate the existence of hitherto unacknowledged items that are neither physical nor physically realized *or* to *construe as* neither physical nor physically realized any items whose existence is already universally acknowledged. With regard to any suggestion that there is more to contingent or causal reality than realization physicalism allows, we must therefore conclude, perhaps sadly, that we have no need of that hypothesis.

---

30 Not that I regard P > 0.5 as any kind of threshold for rational belief.

References

Adams, Fred, and Ken Aizawa. 1994. "Fodorian Semantics." In Stich and Warfield 1994: 223–42.
Alberts, B., D. Bray, J. Lewis, M. Raff, K. Roberts, and James D. Watson. 1994. *Molecular Biology of the Cell*. 3d ed. New York: Garland.
Alcock, James E. 1990. *Science and Supernature: A Critical Appraisal of Parapsychology*. Buffalo, N.Y.: Prometheus Books.
Antony, Louise. 1991. "The Causal Relevance of the Mental: More on the Mattering of Minds." *Mind and Language* 6: 295–327.
Antony, Louise, and Joseph Levine. 1997. "Reduction with Autonomy." In *Philosophical Perspectives*, vol. 11, *Mind, Causation, and World*, ed. James E. Tomberlin, 83–105. Cambridge, Mass.: Blackwell.
Atkins, P. W. 1991. *Atoms, Electrons, and Change*. New York: Scientific American Library.
  1994. *Physical Chemistry*. 5th ed. New York: W. H. Freeman.
  1995. *The Periodic Kingdom: A Journey into the Land of the Chemical Elements*. New York: Basic Books.
Baker, Lynne R. 1997. "Why Constitution Is Not Identity." *Journal of Philosophy* 94: 599–621.
  1999. "Unity without Identity: A New Look at Material Constitution." In *Midwest Studies in Philosophy*, vol. 23, ed. Peter French, Theodore Uehling Jr., and Howard Wettstein, 144–65. Minneapolis: University of Minnesota Press.
Barlow, Horace. 1998. "The Nested Networks of Brains and Minds." In Bock and Goode 1998: 142–55.
Bealer, George. 1993. "Materialism and the Logical Structure of Intentionality." In Robinson 1993a: 101–26.
Bedau, Mark A. 1992. "Where's the Good in Teleology?" *Philosophy and Phenomenological Research* 52: 781–806.
  1993. "Naturalism and Teleology." In *Naturalism: A Critical Appraisal*, ed. Steven J. Wagner and Richard Warner, 23–51. Notre Dame, Ind.: University of Notre Dame Press.
  1996. "The Nature of Life." In Boden 1996: 332–57.

1997. "Weak Emergence." In *Philosophical Perspectives,* vol. 11, *Mind, Causation, and World,* ed. James E. Tomberlin, 375–99. Cambridge, Mass.: Blackwell.
Beloff, John. 1989. "Dualism: A Parapsychological Perspective." In *The Case for Dualism,* ed. John R. Smythies and John Beloff, 167–85. Charlottesville: University Press of Virginia.
Bickle, John. 1998. *Psychoneural Reduction: The New Wave.* Cambridge, Mass.: MIT Press.
Blackmore, Susan. 1996. *In Search of the Light: The Adventures of a Parapsychologist.* Amherst, N.Y.: Prometheus Books.
Block, Ned. 1997. "Anti-Reductionism Slaps Back." In *Philosophical Perspectives,* vol. 11, *Mind, Causation, and World,* ed. James E. Tomberlin, 107–32. Cambridge, Mass.: Blackwell.
Block, Ned, and Robert Stalnaker. 1999. "Conceptual Analysis, Dualism, and the Explanatory Gap." *Philosophical Review* 108.1: 1–46.
Bock, Gregory R., and Jamie A. Goode, eds. 1998. *The Limits of Reductionism in Biology.* New York: J. Wiley.
Boden, Margaret. 1990. *The Philosophy of Artificial Intelligence.* New York: Oxford University Press.
 ed. 1996. *The Philosophy of Artificial Life.* New York: Oxford University Press.
Boyd, Richard. 1980. "Materialism without Reductionism: What Physicalism Does Not Entail." In *Readings in the Philosophy of Psychology,* vol. 1, ed. Ned Block, 268–305. London: Methuen.
Brenner, Sydney. 1998. "Biological Computation." In Bock and Goode 1998: 106–11.
Brindley, Giles S. 1973. "Sensory Effects of Electrical Stimulation of the Visual and Paravisual Cortex in Man." In *Central Processing of Visual Information,* ed. Richard Jung, 583–94. New York: Springer-Verlag.
Broad, C. D. 1925. *The Mind and Its Place in Nature.* London: Routledge and Kegan Paul.
Brooks, D. H. M. 1994. "How to Perform a Reduction." *Philosophy and Phenomenological Research* 54: 803–14.
Burge, Tyler. 1993. "Mind-Body Causation and Explanatory Practice." In *Mental Causation,* ed. John Heil and Alfred Mele, 97–120. New York: Oxford University Press.
Byrne, Alex. 1999. "Cosmic Hermeneutics." In *Philosophical Perspectives,* vol. 13, *Epistemology,* ed. James E. Tomberlin, 347–83. Cambridge, Mass.: Blackwell.
Causey, Robert L. 1969. "Polanyi on Structure and Reduction." *Synthèse* 20: 230–37.
Chalmers, David. 1996a. *The Conscious Mind: In Search of a Fundamental Theory.* New York: Oxford University Press.
 1996b. "Does a Rock Implement Every Finite-State Automaton?" *Synthèse* 108: 309–33.
Chandrasekhar, B. S. 1998. *Why Things Are the Way They Are.* Cambridge: Cambridge University Press.
Charles, David. 1992. "Supervenience, Composition, and Physicalism." In Charles and Lennon 1992: 265–96.

Charles, David, and Kathleen Lennon, eds. 1992. *Reduction, Explanation, and Realism.* New York: Oxford University Press.
Child, William. 1997. "Crane on Mental Causation." *Proceedings of the Aristotelian Society* 97: 97–102.
Chomsky, Noam. 1972. *Language and Mind.* New York: Harcourt Brace Jovanovich.
Churchland, Patricia. 1981a. "On the Alleged Backwards Referral of Experiences and Its Relevance to the Mind-Body Problem." *Philosophy of Science* 48: 165–81.
1981b. "The Timing of Sensations: Reply to Libet." *Philosophy of Science* 48: 492–97.
Churchland, Paul. 1981. "Eliminative Materialism and the Propositional Attitudes." *Journal of Philosophy* 78: 67–90.
1988. *Matter and Consciousness: A Contemporary Introduction to the Philosophy of Mind.* Cambridge, Mass.: MIT Press.
1989. *A Neurocomputational Perspective: The Nature of Mind and the Structure of Science.* Cambridge, Mass.: MIT Press.
Copeland, B. Jack. 1996. "What Is Computation?" *Synthèse* 108: 335–59.
Crane, Tim. 1991. "Why Indeed? Papineau on Supervenience." *Analysis* 51: 32–7.
1995. "The Mental Causation Debate." *Proceedings of the Aristotelian Society, Supplementary Volume* 69: 211–36.
1997. "Reply to Child." *Proceedings of the Aristotelian Society* 97: 103–8.
Crane, Tim, and D. H. Mellor. 1990. "There Is No Question of Physicalism." *Mind* 90: 185–206.
Crick, Francis. 1994. *The Astonishing Hypothesis: The Scientific Search for the Soul.* New York: Maxwell Macmillan International.
Crook, Seth, and Carl Gillett. 2001. "Why Physics Alone Cannot Define the 'Physical': Materialism, Metaphysics, and the Formulation of Physicalism." *Canadian Journal of Philosophy* 31: 333–60.
Daly, Chris. 1995. "Does Physicalism Need Fixing?" *Analysis* 55.3: 135–41.
1997. "Pluralist Metaphysics." *Philosophical Studies* 87: 185–206.
1998. "What Are Physical Properties?" *Pacific Philosophical Quarterly* 79: 196–217.
Davidson, Donald. 1980. *Essays on Actions and Events.* New York: Oxford University Press.
Dennett, Daniel. 1987. *The Intentional Stance.* Cambridge, Mass.: MIT Press.
1991. *Consciousness Explained.* Boston: Little, Brown.
Descartes, René. 1985. *The Philosophical Writings of Descartes.* Vol. 1. Trans. John Cottingham, Robert Stoothoff, and Dugald Murdoch. Cambridge: Cambridge University Press.
Dobelle, W. H., and M. G. Mladejovsky. 1974. "Phosphenes Produced by Electrical Stimulation of Human Occipital Cortex, and Their Application to the Development of a Prosthesis for the Blind." *Journal of Physiology* 243: 553–76.
Dretske, Fred. 1995. *Naturalizing the Mind.* Cambridge, Mass.: MIT Press.
Dupré, John. 1993. *The Disorder of Things: Metaphysical Foundations of the Disunity of Science.* Cambridge, Mass.: Harvard University Press.
Eccles, John C. 1994. *How the Self Controls Its Brain.* New York: Springer-Verlag.
Endicott, Ronald. 1998. "Collapse of the New Wave." *Journal of Philosophy* 95: 53–72.

Fales, Evan. 1996. "Plantinga's Case against Naturalistic Epistemology." *Philosophy of Science* 63: 432–51.
Field, Hartry. 1975. "Conventionalism and Instrumentalism in Semantics." *Nous* 9: 375–405.
———. 1986. "The Deflationary Conception of Truth." In Macdonald and Wright 1986: 55–117.
———. 1992. "Physicalism." In *Inference, Explanation, and Other Frustrations: Essays in the Philosophy of Science*, ed. John Earman, 271–91. Berkeley: University of California Press.
Fitelson, Branden, and Elliott Sober. 1998. "Plantinga's Probability Arguments against Evolutionary Naturalism." *Pacific Philosophical Quarterly* 79: 115–29.
Fodor, Jerry A. 1974. "Special Sciences, or the Disunity of Science as a Working Hypothesis." *Synthèse* 28: 97–115.
———. 1986. *Psychosemantics: The Problem of Meaning in the Philosophy of Mind*. Cambridge, Mass.: MIT Press.
———. 1990. *A Theory of Content and Other Essays*. Cambridge, Mass.: MIT Press.
———. 1997. "Special Sciences: Still Autonomous after All These Years." In *Philosophical Perspectives*, vol. 11, *Mind, Causation, and World*, ed. James E. Tomberlin, 149–63. Cambridge, Mass.: Blackwell.
Fodor, Jerry, and Zenon Pylyshyn. 1988. "Connectionism and Cognitive Architecture: A Critical Analysis." *Cognition* 28: 3–71.
Forrest, Peter. 1988. "Supervenience: The Grand-Property Hypothesis." *Australasian Journal of Philosophy* 66: 1–12.
Foster, John. 1991. *The Immaterial Self: A Defence of the Cartesian Dualist Conception of the Mind*. New York: Routledge.
Futuyma, Douglas J. 1995. *Science on Trial: The Case for Evolution*. Sunderland, Mass.: Sinauer Associates.
Gell-Mann, Murray. 1994. *The Quark and the Jaguar: Adventures in the Simple and the Complex*. New York: W. H. Freeman.
Gillett, Carl, and Barry Loewer. 2001. *Physicalism and Its Discontents*. Cambridge: Cambridge University Press.
Gillett, Grant. 1993. "Actions, Causes, and Mental Ascriptions." In Robinson 1993a: 81–100.
Godfrey-Smith, Peter. 1994. "A Modern History Theory of Functions." *Nous* 28: 344–62.
Goldman, Alvin I. 1986. *Epistemology and Cognition*. Cambridge, Mass.: Harvard University Press.
Goodman, Nelson. 1978. *Ways of Worldmaking*. Indianapolis, Ind.: Hackett.
Goodsell, David S. 1998. *The Machinery of Life*. New York: Copernicus, Springer-Verlag.
Gould, Stephen J. 1980. *The Panda's Thumb: More Reflections in Natural History*. New York: Norton.
Guinier, André, and Rémi Jullien. 1989. *The Solid State: From Superconductors to Superalloys*. New York: Oxford University Press.
Hamblin, W. Kenneth. 1992. *Earth's Dynamic Systems*. 6th ed. New York: Macmillan.
Hansel, C. E. M. 1989. *The Search for Psychic Power: ESP and Parapsychology Revisited*. Buffalo, N.Y.: Prometheus Books.

Hardin, Clyde L. 1987. "Qualia and Materialism: Closing the Explanatory Gap." *Philosophy and Phenomenological Research* 48: 281–98.
Harwit, Martin. 1998. *Astrophysical Concepts*. 3d ed. New York: Springer-Verlag.
Haugeland, John. 1982. "Weak Supervenience." *American Philosophical Quarterly* 19: 93–103.
Hellman, Geoffrey. 1985. "Determination and Logical Truth." *Journal of Philosophy* 82: 607–16.
Hellman, Geoffrey, and Frank Thompson. 1975. "Physicalism: Ontology, Determination, and Reduction." *Journal of Philosophy* 72: 551–64.
Hempel, Carl G. 1969. "Reduction: Ontological and Linguistic Facets." In *Philosophy, Science, and Method: Essays in Honor of Ernest Nagel*, ed. Sidney Morgenbesser, Patrick Suppes, and Morton White, 179–99. New York: St. Martin's.
    1980. "Comments on Goodman's *Ways of Worldmaking*." *Synthèse* 45: 193–9.
Henderson, David K. 1994. "Accounting for Macro-Level Causation." *Synthèse* 101: 129–56.
Henderson, Richard. 1998. "Macromolecular Structure and Self-Assembly." In Bock and Goode 1998: 36–52.
Hill, Christopher S. 1991. *Sensations: A Defense of Type Materialism*. Cambridge: Cambridge University Press.
Horgan, Terry. 1987. "Supervenient Qualia." *Philosophical Review* 96: 491–520.
    1989. "Mental Quausation." In *Philosophical Perspectives*, vol. 3, *Philosophy of Mind and Action Theory*, ed. James E. Tomberlin, 47–76. Atascadero, Calif.: Ridgeview.
    1991. "Actions, Reasons, and the Explanatory Role of Content." In *Dretske and His Critics*, ed. Brian P. McLaughlin, 73–101. Cambridge, Mass.: Blackwell.
    1993. "From Supervenience to Superdupervenience: Meeting the Demands of a Material World." *Mind* 102: 555–86.
Horgan, Terry, and James Woodward. 1985. "Folk Psychology Is Here to Stay." *Philosophical Review* 94: 197–226.
Hume, David. 1975. *Enquiries concerning Human Understanding and concerning the Principles of Morals*. 3d ed. New York: Clarendon Press.
Humphrey, Nicholas. 1996. *Leaps of Faith: Science, Miracles, and the Search for Supernatural Consolation*. New York: Basic Books.
Humphreys, Paul. 1996. "Aspects of Emergence." *Philosophical Topics* 24: 53–70.
    1997a. "How Properties Emerge." *Philosophy of Science* 64: 1–17.
    1997b. "Emergence, Not Supervenience." In *PSA 1996, Proceedings of the 1996 Biennial Meetings of the Philosophy of Science Association, Part II, Symposia Papers*, ed. Lindley Darden, S337–S345. Supplement to *Philosophy of Science* 64.4.
Hyman, Ray. 1989. *The Elusive Quarry: A Scientific Appraisal of Psychical Research*. Buffalo, N.Y.: Prometheus Books.
Jack, Andrew. 1994. "Materialism and Supervenience." *Australasian Journal of Philosophy* 72: 426–44.
Jackson, Frank. 1982. "Epiphenomenal Qualia." *Philosophical Quarterly* 32: 127–36.
    1998a. *From Metaphysics to Ethics: A Defence of Conceptual Analysis*. New York: Oxford University Press.

1998b. "Reference and Description Revisited." In *Philosophical Perspectives*, vol. 12, *Language, Mind, and Ontology*, ed. James E. Tomberlin, 201–18. Cambridge: Blackwell.
Johnson-Laird, Philip. 1983. *Mental Models*. Cambridge, Mass.: Harvard University Press.
Kahneman, Daniel, Paul Slovic, and Amos Tversky. 1982. *Judgement under Uncertainty: Heuristics and Biases*. Cambridge: Cambridge University Press.
Kaplan, Mark. 1996. *Decision Theory as Philosophy*. Cambridge: Cambridge University Press.
Kazez, Jean. 1995. "Can Counterfactuals Save Mental Causation?" *Australasian Journal of Philosophy* 73: 71–90.
Kim, Jaegwon. 1993. *Supervenience and Mind: Selected Philosophical Essays*. Cambridge: Cambridge University Press.
1998. *Mind in a Physical World: An Essay on the Mind-Body Problem and Mental Causation*. Cambridge, Mass.: MIT Press.
Kincaid, Harold. 1997. *Individualism and the Unity of Science: Essays on Explanation, Reduction, and the Special Sciences*. Lanham, Md.: Rowman and Littlefield.
Kirk, Robert. 1996a. "How Physicalists Can Avoid Reduction." *Synthèse* 108: 157–70.
1996b. "Strict Implication, Supervenience, and Physicalism." *Australasian Journal of Philosophy* 74: 244–57.
Kitcher, Philip. 1984. "1953 and All That. A Tale of Two Sciences." *Philosophical Review* 93: 335–73.
1993. *The Advancement of Science*. New York: Oxford University Press.
Klagge, James C. 1995. "Supervenience: Model Theory or Metaphysics?" In Savellos and Yalçin 1995: 60–72.
Kornblith, Hilary. 1993. *Inductive Inference and Its Natural Ground: An Essay in Naturalistic Epistemology*. Cambridge, Mass.: MIT Press.
Kripke, Saul. 1980. *Naming and Necessity*. Oxford: Blackwell.
Kvanvig, Jonathan L., ed. 1996. *Warrant in Contemporary Epistemology: Essays in Honor of Plantinga's Theory of Knowledge*. Lanham, Md.: Rowman and Littlefield.
Langton, Christopher G. 1996. "Artificial Life." In Boden 1996: 39–94.
Lassen, Niels A., David H. Ingvar, and Erik Skinhøj. 1978. "Brain Function and Blood Flow." *Scientific American* 239: 62–71.
Laudan, Larry. 1996. *Beyond Positivism and Relativism: Theory, Method, and Evidence*. Boulder, Colo: Westview Press.
LePore, Ernest, and Barry Loewer. 1987. "Mind Matters." *Journal of Philosophy* 84: 630–42.
1989. "More on Making Mind Matter." *Philosophical Topics* 17: 175–91.
Levin, Michael E. 1979. "On Theory-Change and Meaning-Change." *Philosophy of Science* 46: 407–24.
1987. "Rigid Designators: Two Applications." *Philosophy of Science* 54: 283–94.
1997a. "Plantinga on Functions and the Theory of Evolution." *Australasian Journal of Philosophy* 75: 83–98.
1997b. *Why Race Matters: Race Differences and What They Mean*. Westport, Conn.: Praeger Publishers.

Lewis, David. 1983a. "New Work for a Theory of Universals." *Australasian Journal of Philosophy* 61: 343–77.
   1983b. *Philosophical Papers: Volume I.* New York: Oxford University Press.
   1986. *Philosophical Papers: Volume II.* New York: Oxford University Press.
   1993. "Many, but Almost One." In *Ontology, Causality and Mind: Essays on the Philosophy of D. M. Armstrong*, ed. John Bacon, Keith Campbell, and Lloyd Reinhardt, 23–38. Cambridge: Cambridge University Press.
Libet, Benjamin. 1973. "Electrical Stimulation of Cortex in Human Subjects, and Conscious Memory Aspects." In *Handbook of Sensory Physiology*, vol. 2, ed. A. Iggo, 743–90. New York: Springer-Verlag.
   1978. "Neuronal vs. Subjective Timing, for a Conscious Sensory Experience." In *Cerebral Correlates of Conscious Experience*, ed. P. Buser and A. Rougeul-Buser, 69–82. Amsterdam: Elsevier.
   1981. "The Experimental Evidence for Subjective Referral of a Sensory Experience Backwards in Time: Reply to P. S. Churchland." *Philosophy of Science* 48: 182–97.
Lipton, Peter. 1996. "Is the Best Good Enough?" In *The Philosophy of Science*, ed. David Papineau, 93–106. New York: Oxford University Press.
Loar, Brian. 1992. "Elimination versus Non-Reductive Physicalism." In Charles and Lennon 1992: 239–63.
Lockwood, Michael. 1993. "The Grain Problem." In Robinson 1993a: 271–91.
Lowrie, William. 1997. *Fundamentals of Geophysics*. Cambridge: Cambridge University Press.
Lutgens, Frederick K., and Edward J. Tarbuck. 2001. *The Atmosphere: An Introduction to Meteorology*. 8th ed. Upper Saddle River, N.J.: Prentice-Hall.
Lycan, William G. 1987. *Consciousness*. Cambridge, Mass.: MIT Press.
   1988. *Judgement and Justification*. Cambridge: Cambridge University Press.
   1996. *Consciousness and Experience*. Cambridge, Mass.: MIT Press.
Macdonald, Cynthia. 1989. *Mind-Body Identity Theories*. New York: Routledge.
Macdonald, Graham, and Crispin Wright, eds. 1986. *Fact, Science, and Morality: Essays on A. J. Ayer's Language, Truth and Logic*. Cambridge, Mass.: Blackwell.
Mackie, John L. 1965. "Causes and Conditions." *American Philosophical Quarterly* 2: 245–64.
Madell, Geoffrey. 1988. *Mind and Materialism*. Edinburgh: Edinburgh University Press.
Maher, Patrick. 1993. *Betting on Theories*. Cambridge: Cambridge University Press.
Martin, Michael. 1990. *Atheism: A Philosophical Justification*. Philadelphia: Temple University Press.
May, Robert. 1998. "Levels of Organization in Ecological Systems." In Bock and Goode 1998: 193–8.
McLaughlin, Brian P. 1989. "Type Epiphenomenalism, Type Dualism, and the Causal Priority of the Physical." In *Philosophical Perspectives*, vol. 3, *Philosophy of Mind and Action Theory*, ed. James E. Tomberlin, 109–35. Atascadero, Calif.: Ridgeview.
   1995. "Varieties of Supervenience." In Savellos and Yalçin 1995: 16–59.
Melnyk, Andrew. 1991. "Physicalism: From Supervenience to Elimination." *Philosophy and Phenomenological Research* 51: 573–87.
   1994. "Being a Physicalist: How and (More Importantly) Why." *Philosophical Studies* 74: 221–41.

1995a. "Physicalism, Ordinary Objects, and Identity." *Journal of Philosophical Research* 20: 221–35.

1995b. "Two Cheers for Reductionism; or, The Dim Prospects for Non-Reductive Materialism." *Philosophy of Science* 62: 370–88.

1996a. "Formulating Physicalism: Two Suggestions." *Synthèse* 105: 381–407.

1996b. "Searle's Abstract Argument against Strong AI." *Synthèse* 108: 391–419.

1997a. "On the Metaphysical Utility of Claims of Global Supervenience." *Philosophical Studies* 87: 277–308.

1997b. "How to Keep the 'Physical' in Physicalism." *Journal of Philosophy* 94: 622–37.

1998. "The Prospects for Kirk's Non-Reductive Physicalism." *Australasian Journal of Philosophy* 76: 323–32.

2001. "Physicalism Unfalsified: Chalmers' Inconclusive Conceivability Argument." In Gillett and Loewer 2001: 329–47.

Merricks, Trenton. 1998. "Against the Doctrine of Microphysical Supervenience." *Mind* 107: 59–71.

Millikan, Ruth G. 1984. *Language, Thought, and Other Biological Categories: New Foundations for Realism*. Cambridge, Mass.: MIT Press.

1993. *White Queen Psychology and Other Essays for Alice*. Cambridge, Mass.: MIT Press.

Mills, Eugene. 1996. "Interactionism and Overdetermination." *American Philosophical Quarterly* 33: 105–17.

Montero, Barbara. 1999. "The Body Problem." *Noûs* 33: 183–200.

Mortensen, Chris. 1980. "Neurophysiology and Experiences." *Australasian Journal of Philosophy* 58: 250–64.

Moser, Paul K. 1996. "Physicalism and Mental Causes: Contra Papineau." *Analysis* 56: 263–7.

Nagel, Ernest. 1979. *The Structure of Science: Problems in the Logic of Scientific Explanation*. Indianapolis, Ind.: Hackett.

Nagel, Thomas. 1971. "Brain Bisection and the Unity of Consciousness." *Synthèse* 22: 396–413.

Noble, Dennis. 1998. "Reduction and Integration in Understanding the Heart." In Bock and Goode 1998: 56–68.

Nurse, Paul. 1998. "Reductionism and Explanation in Cell Biology." In Bock and Goode 1998: 93–101.

Oppenheim, Paul, and Hilary Putnam. 1958. "Unity of Science as a Working Hypothesis." In *Minnesota Studies in the Philosophy of Science*, vol. 2, ed. H. Feigl, M. Scriven, and G. Maxwell, 3–36. Minneapolis: University of Minnesota Press.

Papineau, David. 1986. "Laws and Accidents." In Macdonald and Wright 1986: 189–218.

1993. *Philosophical Naturalism*. Cambridge, Mass.: Blackwell.

Parfit, Derek. 1984. *Reasons and Persons*. New York: Oxford University Press.

1997. "Reasons and Motivation." *Proceedings of the Aristotelian Society, Supplementary Volume* 71: 99–130.

Peacocke, Christopher. 1979. *Holistic Explanation: Action, Space, Interpretation*. New York: Oxford University Press.

Pennock, Robert T. 1999. *Tower of Babel: The Evidence against the New Creationism*. Cambridge, Mass: MIT Press.

Phelps, Michael E., and John C. Mazziotta. 1985. "Positron Emission Tomography: Human Brain Function and Biochemistry." *Science* 228: 799–809.

Pinker, Steven. 1997. *How the Mind Works*. New York: Norton.

——— 1999. *Words and Rules: The Ingredients of Language*. New York: Basic Books.

Plantinga, Alvin. 1993. *Warrant and Proper Function*. New York: Oxford University Press.

Poland, Jeffrey. 1994. *Physicalism: The Philosophical Foundations*. New York: Oxford University Press.

Popper, Karl R. 1972. *Objective Knowledge: An Evolutionary Approach*. New York: Oxford University Press.

Popper, Karl R., and John C. Eccles. 1977. *The Self and Its Brain: An Argument for Interactionism*. New York: Springer-Verlag.

Post, John F. 1987. *The Faces of Existence: An Essay in Nonreductive Metaphysics*. Ithaca, N.Y.: Cornell University Press.

Putnam, Hilary. 1975. *Mind, Language, and Reality: Philosophical Papers*. Vol. 2. Cambridge: Cambridge University Press.

——— 1987. *The Many Faces of Realism*. LaSalle, Ill.: Open Court.

Pylyshyn, Zenon. 1984. *Computation and Cognition: Toward a Foundation for Cognitive Science*. Cambridge, Mass.: MIT Press.

Ravenscroft, Ian. 1997. "Physical Properties." *Southern Journal of Philosophy* 35: 419–31.

Rea, Michael C. 1998. "In Defense of Mereological Essentialism." *Philosophy and Phenomenological Research* 58: 347–60.

Rensberger, Boyce. 1996. *Life Itself: Exploring the Realm of the Living Cell*. New York: Oxford University Press.

Robb, David. 1997. "The Properties of Mental Causation." *Philosophical Quarterly* 47: 178–94.

Robinson, Howard, ed. 1993a. *Objections to Physicalism*. New York: Oxford University Press.

——— 1993b. "The Anti-Materialist Strategy and the 'Knowledge Argument.'" In Robinson 1993a: 159–83.

Roland, P. E. 1981. "Somatotopical Tuning of Postcentral Gyrus during Focal Attention in Man: A Regional Cerebral Blood Flow Study." *Journal of Neurophysiology* 46: 744–54.

Roland, P. E., and L. Friberg. 1985. "Localization of Cortical Areas Activated by Thinking." *Journal of Neurophysiology* 53: 1219–43.

Roland, P. E., B. Larsen, N. A. Lassen, and E. Skinhøj. 1980. "Supplementary Motor Area and Other Cortical Areas in Organization of Voluntary Movements in Man." *Journal of Neurophysiology* 43: 118–36.

Rose, Steven. 1998. "What Is Wrong with Reductionist Explanations of Behaviour?" In Bock and Goode 1998: 176–86.

Ross, Michael H., Lynn J. Romrell, and Gordon I. Kaye. 1995. *Histology: A Text and Atlas*. 3d ed. Baltimore: Williams and Wilkins.

Ruben, David-Hillel. 1994. "A Counterfactual Theory of Causal Explanation." *Nous* 28: 465–81.

Ryle, Gilbert. 1954. *Dilemmas*. Cambridge: Cambridge University Press.
Salmon, Wesley C. 1990. *Four Decades of Scientific Explanation*. Minneapolis: University of Minnesota Press.
Savellos, Elias E., and Ümit D. Yalçin, eds. 1995. *Supervenience: New Essays*. Cambridge: Cambridge University Press.
Schiffer, Stephen. 1987. *Remnants of Meaning*. Cambridge, Mass.: MIT Press.
Segal, Gabriel, and Elliott Sober. 1991. "The Causal Efficacy of Content." *Philosophical Studies* 63: 1–30.
Sellars, Wilfrid. 1963. *Science, Perception, and Reality*. New York: Humanities Press.
Shaffner, Kenneth. 1967. "Approaches to Reduction." *Philosophy of Science* 34: 137–57.
Shepherd, Gordon M. 1994. *Neurobiology*. New York: Oxford University Press.
Shoemaker, Sydney. 1984. *Identity, Cause, and Mind: Philosophical Essays*. Cambridge: Cambridge University Press.
Sidelle, Alan. 1989. *Necessity, Essence, and Individuation: A Defense of Conventionalism*. Ithaca, N.Y.: Cornell University Press.
Sklar, Larry. 1979. "Do Unborn Hypotheses Have Rights?" *Pacific Philosophical Quarterly* 62: 17–29.
Smart, J. J. C. 1959. "Sensations and Brain Processes." *Philosophical Review* 68: 141–56.
1978. "The Content of Physicalism." *Philosophical Quarterly* 28: 339–41.
Smith, A. D. 1993. "Non-Reductive Physicalism?" In Robinson 1993a: 225–50.
Smith, Peter. 1992. "Modest Reductions and the Unity of Science." In Charles and Lennon 1992: 19–43.
Snowdon, Paul F. 1989. "On Formulating Materialism and Dualism." In *Cause, Mind, and Reality: Essays Honoring C. B. Martin*, ed. John Heil, 137–58. Dordrecht: Kluwer.
Sober, Elliott. 1994. *From a Biological Point of View*. Cambridge: Cambridge University Press.
1996. "Parsimony and Predictive Equivalence." *Erkenntnis* 44: 167–97.
Staple, Julie, and Stefan Catsicas. 1997. "Molecular Biology of Neurotransmitter Release." In *Molecular Biology of the Neuron*, ed. R. Wayne Davies and Brian J. Morris, 123–43. Herndon, Va.: BIOS Scientific Publishers.
Stich, Stephen P., and Ted A. Warfield, eds. 1994. *Mental Representation: A Reader*. Cambridge, Mass: Blackwell.
Sturgeon, Scott. 1988. "Physicalism and Overdetermination." *Mind* 107: 411–32.
Swinburne, Richard. 1979. *The Existence of God*. New York: Oxford University Press.
1987. "The Structure of the Soul." In *Persons and Personality: A Contemporary Inquiry*, ed. A. R. Peacocke and G. Gillett, 33–55. New York: Blackwell.
1996. *Is There a God?* New York: Oxford University Press.
2001. *Epistemic Justification*. New York: Oxford University Press.
Teller, Paul. 1986. "Relational Holism and Quantum Mechanics." *British Journal for the Philosophy of Science* 37: 71–81.
Thagard, Paul. 1988. *Computational Philosophy of Science*. Cambridge, Mass.: MIT Press.
Thomson, Judith J. 1998. "The Statue and the Clay." *Nous* 32.2: 149–73.
Tye, Michael. 1995. *Ten Problems of Consciousness: A Representational Theory of the Phenomenal Mind*. Cambridge, Mass.: MIT Press.

1999. "Phenomenal Consciousness: The Explanatory Gap as a Cognitive Illusion." *Mind* 108: 705–25.
Unger, Peter. 1980. "The Problem of the Many." In *Midwest Studies in Philosophy*, vol. 5, *Studies in Epistemology*, ed. Peter French, Theodore Uehling Jr., and Howard Wettstein, 411–68. Minneapolis: University of Minnesota Press.
Van Fraassen, Bas C. 1996. "Science, Materialism, and False Consciousness." In Kvanvig 1996: 149–81.
Van Gulick, Robert. 1993. "Who's in Charge Here? And Who's Doing All the Work?" In *Mental Causation*, ed. John Heil and Alfred Mele, 233–56. New York: Oxford University Press.
Van Inwagen, Peter. 1990. *Material Beings*. Ithaca, N.Y.: Cornell University Press.
Vander, Arthur J., James, H. Sherman, and Dorothy S. Luciano. 1990. *Human Physiology: The Mechanisms of Body Function*. 5th ed. New York: McGraw-Hill.
Walker, Ralph. 1993. "Transcendental Arguments against Physicalism." In Robinson 1993a: 61–80.
Walton, Alan J. 1983. *Three Phases of Matter*. 2d ed. New York: Oxford University Press.
Waters, C. Kenneth. 1990. "Why the Anti-Reductionist Consensus Won't Survive: The Case of Classical Mendelian Genetics." In *PSA 1990*, ed. A. Fine, M. Forbes, and L. Wessels. East Lansing, Mich.: Philosophy of Science Association.
Weinberg, Steven. 1994. *Dreams of a Final Theory: The Scientist's Search for the Ultimate Laws of Nature*. New York: Vintage Books.
Wiggins, David. 1980. *Sameness and Substance*. Oxford: Blackwell.
Williams, R. J. P. 1998. "Reductionism in Physical Sciences." In Bock and Goode 1998: 15–24.
Wilson, Jessica. 1999. "How Superduper Does a Physicalist Supervenience Need to Be?" *Philosophical Quarterly* 49: 33–52.
Witmer, D. Gene. 2000. "Locating the Overdetermination Problem." *British Journal for the Philosophy of Science* 51: 273–86.
Worley, Sara. 1993. "Mental Causation and Explanatory Exclusion." *Erkenntnis* 39: 333–58.
Wright, Larry. 1973. "Functions." *Philosophical Review* 82: 139–68.
Yablo, Stephen. 1992. "Mental Causation." *Philosophical Review* 101: 245–80.
Zangwill, Nick. 1993. "Supervenience and Anomalous Monism: Blackburn on Davidson." *Philosophical Studies* 71: 59–79.
     1997. "Explaining Supervenience: Moral and Mental." *Journal of Philosophical Research* 22: 509–18.

Index

a posteriori, 3–4, 7–8, 33, 35–7, 50, 54–5, 72–3, 77, 86, 110, 175–6, 178–80, 202–3, 239, 250, 254–6, 307–8
 status of physicalism, 27–8, 175–6
a priori, 8, 27, 33, 35–7, 54–5, 66, 71, 73, 77, 110, 115, 140–1, 171, 177–80, 210–11, 248, 250, 254–5, 281, 296, 302, 306–8
abstract objects, 11, 39–40
accidental generalizations, 147, 155–9
Adams, F., 41
Aizawa, K., 41
Alberts, B., 269–73, 286
Alcock, J. E., 190, 223
anomalous monism, 125
antiphysicalism, 4–5, 26, 37, 78, 169, 176–7, 188, 195, 213, 237, 239, 243–8, 251, 253, 257, 277, 279–80, 290, 292, 299–300, 308–9
antireductionism
 among scientists, 83, 199, 217–22
 among nonphilosophers, 72–6
 among philosophers, 85, 105–6, 199, 110–22, 200–17
Antony, L., 79, 118, 149
astronomy, 278
Atkins, P. W., 261–5
autonomy, special- or honorary-scientific, 3, 72, 107–9, 117–22, 171–4, 244–6

Baker, L. R., 20, 50
Barlow, H., 186, 220
Bealer, G., 178
Bedau, M. A., 42, 190–2
Beloff, J., 189
Bickle, J., 82
biological phenomena, 39, 190–222, 266–77, 284–5, 285–6

biology, 1, 4, 85, 236, 238
Blackmore, S., 190
Block, N., 55, 79, 111, 118
Bock, G. R., 217
Boden, M., 40, 118, 190
Boyd, R., 6, 50, 71, 215
brain, 117, 178–80, 182–8, 235, 281–3, 288–90, 294, 298–304, 304–6
Brenner, S., 219
bridge laws/principles, 32, 52–4, 66, 77–8, 82, 86–8, 95–6, 110–12, 112–17, 202, 209, 212
Brindley, G. S., 304
Broad, C. D., 285
Brooks, D. H. M., 81
brute facts, 53, 57, 63, 65–6, 265
brute laws, 46, 52, 119, 134, 139, 197, 262, 267
brute necessitation, 58–61, 63–64, 69, 88, 245, 300
Burge, T., 50, 240, 297–8
Byrne, A., 55

Cartesian dualism, 4, 180, 217
Catsicas, S., 181
causal laws, 143–5, 147–55, 291–3
causal powers, 19–20, 64, 120, 189, 215–17, 297
causal relevance, 3, 21, 91, 125–9, 131, 133, 136, 139–46, 150, 160–3, 296–7
causal role, 21, 38, 163
causal tokens, 10–11
causation, 91, 104, 123–5, 128–31, 139–50, 152–6, 159–63, 187, 292–3, 297
 downward, 215–17, 222
 mental, 3, 124, 161–2, 187–8, 285–7, 292, 297
Causey, R. L., 218

323

cells, 22, 24, 29–30, 181, 186, 191, 200–2, 220, 221, 266–77, 282, 284, 286, 288–9
Chadwick, J., 261
Chalmers, D., 27–8, 37, 39, 54–5, 66, 77, 99, 177, 307–8
Chandrasekhar, B. S., 16, 240–1, 257, 259
Charles, D., 57, 60
chemical phenomena, 8, 29, 85, 260–6, 268–74, 280, 285
chemistry, 4, 35, 85, 218, 238, 261, 265–6, 279, 285
Child, W., 160
Chomsky, N., 12
Churchland, P. M., 166, 171, 190, 282–3, 298
Churchland, P. S., 182
closure, 184, 187–8, 222–3, 288–90, 293–5, 297
coincidences, 106–7, 118, 149, 155, 167–9, 291–3, 295, 297
commissurotomy, 178–9
common causes, 104–5, 107, 132, 244
conceivability arguments, 35–7, 73, 175, 177–8, 255, 306–8
consciousness, 5, 16, 73, 178–9, 181, 283
constitution, 20, 49, 60, 66, 206–7, 242–4, 267, 282
Constitution Intuition, 60–1
contingency (of realization physicalism), 27–8, 64, 95–6
Copeland, B. J., 39
counterfactuals, 39, 54, 108, 124, 126–7, 133, 138–9, 158–9
Crane, T., 5, 12, 17, 160, 169, 235, 280
Crick, F., 82
Crook, S., 15, 236

Daly, C., 5, 12, 15, 34, 280
Darwinism, 17, 39, 182, 193, 198–9, 215–17, 226–8
Davidson, D., 112–17
Dennett, D., 182, 194
Descartes, R., 187
design argument, 195–9
determination, 52, 62–3
determinism, 38, 217, 222, 226, 288
disjunctive types, 18, 78–80, 111–12, 155, 207
Dobelle, W. H., 304
Dretske, F., 177
dualism, 4, 96, 177, 178–82, 184–9, 217, 236, 279–81, 286–7, 295–7, 299–306, 308–9
Dupré, J., 5, 30, 188, 202–17, 222–3, 235, 280

Eccles, J. C., 180–6, 299
economy, 82, 170, 196–9, 236, 242, 244–51, 253–4, 257, 262–3, 265, 274, 277, 281, 293, 296, 300–1, 305
eliminativism, 2, 42–4, 59, 73, 192, 194–5
emergence, 32, 46, 119, 190, 197, 244–6, 262, 267
emergent phenomena, 16–19, 23, 29–30, 32, 190–1, 201, 241–2, 263, 265, 267, 274, 277, 285
emergentism, 75, 221, 240, 274
Endicott, R., 82
enumerative induction, 239, 256–60, 283–5, 290
epiphenomenalism, 124, 129–30, 139, 293
epiphenomenalization, 123–5, 128–30, 132, 138–9, 159–60, 182
exclusion principles, 136, 171
explanation, 3, 8, 21, 26, 35–6, 43, 49, 52–4, 57, 63–5, 67, 69, 72, 81–7, 98–109, 112, 118–19, 121–4, 126–9, 144–5, 148–60, 162–74, 178–81, 190, 192–4, 196–8, 200–2, 212, 217–21, 227, 232, 239–40, 242–8, 251–60, 262–4, 272, 274–5, 277–8, 281–2, 288, 290–1, 293–4, 297–8, 300–2, 304, 306, 309
externalism, 250

Fales, E., 194, 199
Field, H., 6
fine-tuning, 195–6
Fitelson, B., 199
Fodor, J., 41, 71, 111–12, 118, 120, 140, 145, 177, 303
Forrest, P., 66
Foster, J., 177
Friberg, L., 184
function, biological, 39, 190–5, 199
functional event, 8, 22
functional object, 8, 21–2
functional property, 8, 10, 21–2, 26, 28, 39, 41–3, 47, 54, 60, 67–8, 206, 243
functional type, 20–3, 25, 27–8, 31, 32–5, 37–40, 42, 47–8, 52–6, 58, 67, 69, 73, 76–80, 86, 90, 92–3, 95–5, 110–11, 134–5, 161–3, 171, 173, 175, 179, 202–8, 210–11, 213, 215–16, 235, 243, 266, 306, 308
functionalism, 41, 163, 171, 243
Futuyma, D., 199

Gell-Mann, M., 82, 85–6
genes, 41–2, 200, 214–17, 226
geological phenomena, 278–81, 283–4, 303
Gillett, C., 15, 236
Gillett, G., 178
Godfrey-Smith, P., 192–3

Goldman, A., 177
Goode, J. A., 217
Goodman, N., 5, 280
Goodsell, D. S., 268
Gould, S. J., 198
Guinier, A., 240–1, 257–9

Hamblin, W. K., 279
Hansel, C. E. M., 190
Hardin, C. L., 282–3
Harwit, M., 278
Haugeland, J., 49
Hellman, G., 12, 49, 225
Hempel, C. G., 12–14, 224, 258
Henderson, D. K., 136, 140
Henderson, R., 219
higher-order types, 8, 10, 20, 38–42, 76
Hill, C. S., 35, 39, 177, 304, 308
honorary sciences, 1, 25, 32, 53, 66, 72, 77–8, 83–4, 117–20, 170, 174, 235, 280
honorary scientific phenomena, 32–4, 37–40, 42–4, 47–8, 52–5, 57, 59–61, 64, 73–80, 83–92, 94–5, 97–100, 102–3, 105–11, 117–20, 123–6, 128–32, 135, 138–40, 143, 147, 150, 159–61, 163–73, 200–1, 214, 239–40
Horgan, T., 44, 49, 59, 62, 67, 133, 136, 145
Hume, D., 303, 307
Humphrey, N., 189
Humphreys, P., 16, 30
Hyman, R., 190

identity hypotheses, 32, 34–5, 37, 73, 163, 239–40, 243, 245, 251–6, 262–3, 306–7
inductive reasoning, 17, 99, 103, 154, 178, 234, 239, 245, 248, 256, 259–60, 266, 277, 283–4, 289–90
inference to the best explanation, 35, 170, 239–40, 242, 252–6, 258–60, 298, 304
Ingvar, D. H., 299
intentionality, 5, 177
intentions, 6, 21, 181–2, 191–3, 195–8, 237, 279, 308

Jack, A., 61
Jackson, F., 13, 27, 35–7, 49, 54–5, 60, 62, 77, 179, 254–5
Johnson-Laird, P., 282
Jullien, R., 240–1, 257–9

Kahneman, D., 303
Kaplan, M., 231–2
Kazez, J., 127, 140

Kim, J., 20–1, 27, 30, 38, 50, 57, 63, 68, 78–80, 112–13, 115, 120, 127, 130–1, 163, 166, 171
Kincaid, H., 85, 102, 173, 200–2
Kirk, R., 51, 59
Kitcher, P., 102, 171
Klagge, J. C., 18
Kornblith, H., 209
Kvanvig, J. L., 194

Langton, C. G., 190
Lassen, N. A., 299
Laudan, L., 177
lawlikeness, 83–4, 147, 155–9
laws, 12, 16, 19–20, 22–4, 27–9, 31–4, 37–8, 41, 46, 50–2, 59, 61, 65–6, 77, 79–82, 84, 86, 89–96, 99, 103, 108, 111–20, 123, 129–31, 133–5, 137–40, 144, 149, 155, 158–9, 167–70, 172–3, 181, 185, 188, 197–9, 202–3, 208–9, 211–12, 216, 222–3, 226, 228, 235–7, 244–6, 262, 264, 267, 288, 291–2, 295, 297, 300–2, 306
  ceteris paribus, 38, 41, 84, 97, 118, 143–8, 150–1, 159, 161–2, 164
  physical, 16, 19–20, 24, 27–9, 31, 33, 50–2, 59, 61, 65, 79, 84, 86, 89–96, 99, 103, 108, 111, 123, 130, 134–5, 144, 158, 167–9, 172–3, 188, 216, 222–3, 264, 288
LePore, E., 21, 127, 144
levels, 5, 30–1, 82, 109–10, 121, 129, 150, 152, 167, 173, 186, 210–12, 215–16, 227, 299
Levin, M. E., 41, 54, 192, 224
Levine, J., 79, 118
Lewis, D., 46–7, 49, 62, 100, 133, 254
Libet, B., 182
Lipton, P., 227
Loar, B., 66, 74
Lockwood, M., 178
Loewer, B., 21, 127, 144
Lowrie, W., 279
Lutgens, F. K., 279
Lycan, W. G., 6, 112, 177, 289, 303, 308

Macdonald, C., 112–13, 115
Mackie, J. L., 132, 145
Madell, G., 177
Maher, P., 231–2, 234
Martin, M., 195
mathematics, 11, 32, 39, 175, 199, 248
May, R., 211
Mazziotta, J. C., 299
McLaughlin, B. P., 56, 126, 144
mechanisms, 110, 148–9, 152, 185–7, 200, 228, 271, 280, 283

325

Mellor, D. H., 5, 12, 17, 235, 280
Melnyk, A., 37, 50–1, 55, 66, 177, 211, 285, 287, 308
mental phenomena, 2–4, 8, 27, 41, 59–60, 68–9, 73, 75, 112–17, 123–4, 128–32, 160–1, 169, 177, 180–4, 186–7, 191, 235–6, 240, 280–5, 287, 290–304, 306, 308–9
Merricks, T., 44, 46
metaphysics, 9–10, 35, 47–8, 50, 76, 82, 213
meteorology, 1, 279
methodology, 120–1, 166, 170–4, 218, 232, 248–51
Millikan, R. G., 177, 192–5
Mills, E., 285
minds, 37, 48, 73–4, 110, 115, 142, 176–177, 180–1, 185–6, 188–90, 236, 281–3, 285, 301–4, 308–9
Mladejovsky, M. G., 304
Montero, B., 18, 146, 233
Mortensen, C., 182
Moser, P. K., 124
multiple explanations of the same thing, 8, 101–2, 128, 164–74, 294
multiple realizability, 79, 105, 110–12, 118, 200–1, 214, 298

Nagel, E., 77, 81, 86
Nagel, T., 178
necessitation, 31–3, 45, 49–52, 54, 58, 60–1, 63, 69, 88–9, 91–2, 99, 103, 133, 135, 137–9, 163, 169–70, 245, 257, 300
necessity, 45, 48, 52–4, 57, 65–9, 90, 94, 107–8, 116, 142–3, 155, 166, 169–71, 203, 245, 297, 304
neurophysiological phenomena, 178, 187–8, 298–302
neurophysiology, 1
Noble, D., 220–1, 277
Nurse, P., 218–19

Oppenheim, P., 239–40
overdetermination, 101, 128–9, 154–5, 165–9, 188, 222, 290–1, 293–7

pain, 68, 80, 125, 143, 163, 191, 232, 237, 246, 298, 307
Papineau, D., 124, 140
parapsychology, 189–90, 223
Parfit, D., 37–8, 74
Peacocke, C., 285
Pennock, R., 195
Phelps, M. E., 299
phenomenal properties, 5, 10–11, 177, 283, 304–5, 307–8

"physical facts," 84
"physical laws," 23–4
"physical types," 11–20, 223–37
physicalism, 2–22, 24–35, 37, 42–4, 46–52, 54–5, 57–72, 74–8, 81, 88, 97, 105, 107–9, 119–20, 122–5, 129–30, 132, 139, 142, 150, 160, 163, 170, 175–81, 184–5, 188–90, 195, 199–200, 202, 206, 209, 211, 213, 215–17, 222–6, 232–41, 243–8, 251–7, 264, 279–81, 283–5, 287, 289–90, 294–302, 304–5, 307–9
  eliminative, see eliminativism
  retentive, 37, 74–5, 123–4, 129–30, 132
  retentive realizationist, 32–5, 37–8, 42–7, 49–50, 53–4, 59, 73–5, 77–8, 81–3, 88–94, 96–8, 103, 108–12, 123–5, 128–30, 132, 134–5, 137–40, 144, 149, 159–61, 163–71, 173–4, 199, 208, 215
  supervenience, 2, 44, 61, 63–5, 69–70, 139
  token, 67–9, 125
physics, 1–5, 7–18, 22–5, 27, 32, 34, 44, 51–2, 59, 66, 77–9, 84–6, 89–96, 99–101, 108, 111, 121–2, 124, 129, 135, 138, 149, 158, 167, 170, 181, 189, 202, 204, 218, 223–5, 234–8, 240–1, 253, 257–8, 260, 278–80, 283, 289, 295
Pinker, S., 199, 303
Plantinga, A., 191–5, 199
Poland, J., 6, 12–13, 17–18, 22, 34, 82
Popper, K. R., 180–2
Post, J. F., 18, 49, 62, 71
probability, 14, 140, 181, 195, 215, 223–5, 227, 230–5, 238, 245, 249, 264, 280, 284, 308–9
psychological phenomena, 61, 112–17, 135, 176–90, 281–309
psychology, 1, 63, 159, 212, 221–2, 227, 235–6, 279
Putnam, H., 5, 36, 100, 102, 239–40, 280
Pylyshyn, Z., 119, 303

quantum mechanics, 16, 159, 181, 222, 226, 241, 264–5, 288

Ravenscroft, I., 13
Rea, M. C., 19
realism, 206, 225, 229–34,
realization, 20–4
  realization-independence, see autonomy,
  special- or honorary-scientific
reduction, 81, 83–8, 111–12, 202, 212
reductionism, 2–3, 21, 46, 50, 64, 66–7, 71–5, 77–83, 86, 88, 97–8, 103, 105–7, 109–12, 117–22, 199–204, 208–12, 214–15, 217–22, 226, 240
reliabilism, 177, 230, 232, 246, 249–51

Rensberger, B., 268
Robb, D., 131
Robinson, H., 177–8
Roland, P. E., 183–4
roles, 8–10, 16, 20–2, 26, 37–8, 44, 49, 53, 61–2, 69, 79, 99, 101, 121, 127, 129, 132, 136, 138, 140, 143–4, 147, 149, 153, 162, 201, 213, 225, 239–40, 243, 246, 256, 294, 306
Rose, S., 221–2
Ross, M. H., 276–7
Ruben, D.-H., 127, 160
Rutherford, E., 261
Ryle, G., 1

Salmon, W. C., 158
Schiffer, S., 59
Segal, G., 131, 136, 139, 161
Sellars, W., 1
Shaffner, K., 83
Shepherd, G. M., 187
Shoemaker, S., 28
Sidelle, A., 54
simplicity of concepts or things, 18–19, 23, 30, 141, 204
Skinhøj, E., 299
Sklar, L., 234
Slovic, P., 303
Smart, J. J. C., 12, 283
Smith, A. D., 37, 178
Smith, P., 81
Snowdon, P. F., 57
Sober, E., 131, 136, 139, 161, 199, 246, 248
souls, 12, 189
special sciences, 17, 28, 32, 120–2, 143, 174, 237
special scientific phenomena, 32–5, 37–40, 42–4, 47–8, 52–5, 59–61, 64, 73–80, 83–92, 94–5, 98–100, 102–3, 105–11, 117–26, 128–32, 135, 138–40, 143, 147, 150, 159–61, 163–73, 200–1, 239–40
Stalnaker, R., 55
Staple, J., 181
Stich, S. P., 177

Sturgeon, S., 285–7
superdupervenience, 67
supervenience, 2–4, 20, 39, 44, 49–51, 55–8, 61–70, 88, 139, 227
Swinburne, R. G., 178–80, 199, 245, 250, 309

Tarbuck, E. J., 279
Teller, P., 19
Thagard, P., 177
Thompson, F., 49
Thomson, Joseph J., 261
Thomson, Judith J., 20
truth, 229–30
Truthmaker Intuition, 33, 59–60, 68
Tversky, A., 303
Tye, M., 163, 177, 308

Unger, P., 44
universals, 9, 47, 76, 84

van der Waals forces, 219, 241
Van Fraassen, B. C., 12, 15
Van Gulick, R., 118
Van Inwagen, P., 18–19
Vander, A. J., 276–7

Walker, R., 178
Walton, A. J., 260
Warfield, T. A., 177
Waters, C. K., 81, 200
Weinberg, S., 82, 86
Weirich, P., 116
Wiggins, D., 20
Williams, R. J. P., 219
Wilson, J., 64, 67
Witmer, D. G., 285, 287
Wöhler, F., 285
Woodward, J., 136
Worley, S., 127, 137
Wright, L., 192

Yablo, S., 136

Zangwill, N., 58, 63

RECENT TITLES *(continued from page iii)*

DERK PEREBOOM *Living without Free Will*
BRIAN ELLIS *Scientific Essentialism*
JULIA DRIVER *Uneasy Virtue*
ALAN H. GOLDMAN *Practical Rules: When We Need Them and When We Don't*
ISHTIYAQUE HAJI *Deontic Morality and Control*
ANDREW NEWMAN *The Correspondence Theory of Truth*
JANE HEAL *Mind, Reason and Imagination*
PETER RAILTON *Facts, Values, and Norms*
CHRISTOPHER S. HILL *Thought and World*
WAYNE DAVIS *Meaning, Expression and Thought*
JONATHAN L. KVANVIG *The Value of Knowledge and the Pursuit of Understanding*

For EU product safety concerns, contact us at Calle de José Abascal, 56–1°, 28003 Madrid, Spain or eugpsr@cambridge.org.

www.ingramcontent.com/pod-product-compliance
Ingram Content Group UK Ltd.
Pitfield, Milton Keynes, MK11 3LW, UK
UKHW040159230326
469255UK00012B/195